COMMUNICATION UNDER LAW

Volume II:
Journalistic Freedom

JOSEPH J. HEMMER, JR.

The Scarecrow Press, Inc.
Metuchen, N.J., & London 1980

Library of Congress Cataloging in Publication Data

Hemmer, Joseph J
 Journalistic freedom.

 (His Communication under law ; v. 2)
 Bibliography: p.
 Includes index.
  1. Press law--United States--Cases. I. Title.
KF2750.A73H46 vol. 2 [KF2750] 343.73'099s 80-7960
ISBN 0-8108-1315-7   [343.73'0998]

Dedicated to

JOY, JOEY, and ANDY

Without whose understanding
this work would have been impossible

PREFACE

The purpose of Volume 2 is to analyze the primary issues related to journalism law. This book focuses on libel, invasion of privacy, copyright, free press and fair trial, broadcast regulation, and regulation of advertising. The methodology, as with Volume 1, is a case-by-case examination of the various issues.

Again, I am indebted to Bob Beitz. His work in researching, writing, editing, and proofreading is deeply appreciated. I also want to thank my family--Joy, Joey, and Andy--for their enthusiastic assurance and warm understanding.

J. J. H., Jr.

Carroll College
Waukesha, Wisconsin
May 7, 1979

TABLE OF CONTENTS

CHAPTER I

INTRODUCTION

In their ongoing effort to satisfy the public's need to know, print and broadcast journalists strive to gather and publish vital "news" information free from interference and restraint by private or governmental elements. When journalistic efforts clash with the goals of other societal groups, the resulting conflict of interests must ultimately be adjudicated in the courts. Naturally, in such instances, members of the news media hope for a broad interpretation of First Amendment freedoms.

Throughout the history of communication case law, the U. S. Supreme Court has applied a variety of tests while interpreting the freedoms of speech, press, petition, and assembly. The specific tests have varied with the issue facing the Court, the historical setting of the period, and the characteristics of the individual justices. A fairly narrow view of the First Amendment, the "bad tendency" test, was offered by Justice Edward Sanford in Gitlow v. New York. He claimed "that a State ... may punish those utterances inimical to the public welfare, tending to corrupt public morals, incite to crime, or disturb the public peace, is not open to question." Generally, however, the tests have favored free speech and press. According to Justice Oliver Wendell Holmes, who introduced the "clear and present danger" test in Schenck v. United States, the question was whether the statements were "in such a nature as to create a clear and present danger that they will bring about the substantive evils that Congress has the right to prevent." In American Communications Association, CIO v. Douds, Justice Fred Vinson described the "balancing" test.

> When particular conduct is regulated in the interest of public order, and the regulation results in an indirect, conditional, partial abridgement of speech, the duty of the Courts is to determine which of these two conflicting interests demands the greater

1

protection under the particular circumstances presented.

In <u>Thomas v. Collins</u>, Justice Wiley Rutledge, citing the "preferred position" test, acknowledged "the preferred place given in our scheme to the great, the indispensable democratic freedoms secured in the First Amendment." The most liberal interpretation was that of Justices William Douglas and Hugo Black. They supported the "absolutist" test. In his dissent in <u>Konigsberg v. State Bar of California</u>, Black upheld "the First Amendment's unequivocal command that there shall be no abridgement of the rights of free speech and assembly." Throughout history, the Court has clearly applied a variety of tests in reconciling the conflict between freedom of expression and other of society's freedoms.

While the First Amendment has been awarded a "high" position by the Court, the rights of communicators are not absolute. Journalists have been subjected to several specific restrictions.

<u>Libel</u>--Under libel law, the press cannot publish knowing or reckless falsehoods that damage an individual's reputation.

<u>Privacy</u>--The press must respect privacy. Even when the press publishes a matter of public interest, it cannot intrude upon a person's privacy. And, using a person's name for commercial purposes is actionable when prior consent has not been obtained.

<u>Copyright</u>--Borrowing material from another source may constitute a copyright infringement unless such borrowing is protected under the generally undefined doctrine of "fair use."

<u>Fair Trial</u>--A publisher or reporter assigned to cover a court trial may be punished for contempt under certain circumstances and subjected to a "gag order" under others.

<u>Access to Information</u>--In terms of publishing news, prior restraint of the press is permissible under certain conditions, although the government faces a heavy burden for justifying such restraint. Generally, the press does not enjoy a constitutional right of access to information that is not accessible to the general public. The Freedom of Information Act exempts nine categories of federal government data from

disclosure. And, except where protected by state shield laws, news reporters enjoy no special privilege to protect sources of information from legal investigative bodies.

Broadcasting--The broadcasting media are more subject to governmental regulation than the print media. Specifically, broadcasters are responsible for providing the listening and viewing audiences with access to a balanced presentation on issues of public importance.

Advertising--Generally, commercial speech has a weaker claim to First Amendment protection than other forms of expression.

This brief list outlines only a part of the restrictions that regulate the communication behavior of the news journalist.

In this volume, relevant court cases are examined in terms of their impact on the formation of communication case law--especially as it relates to the purposes and methods of the journalist. The current status of the law is identified, and where possible, speculation is offered regarding its future.

Bibliography

(Sources that were helpful in the preparation of Chapter I)

Books

Francois, William E. Mass Media Law and Regulation. 2nd ed. Columbus, Ohio: Grid, 1978.

Franklin, Marc A. The First Amendment and the Fourth Estate: Communications Law for the Undergraduate. Mineola, N. Y.: Foundation Press, 1977.

Pember, Don R. Mass Media Law. Dubuque, Iowa: Wm. C. Brown, 1977.

Cases

American Communications Association, CIO v. Douds 339 U. S. 382 (1950)

CHAPTER II

LIBEL

Freedom of expression is perhaps the single most important liberty protected by the courts. With it, society may engage in the healthy and unimpaired discussion of ideas. Yet, its practice is not absolute. Certain forms of expression have never found refuge in the law. Among these are slander and libel. Clearly, the courts have controlled the dissemination of malicious or false statements that harm another's character or reputation.

THE LIBEL ACTION

Defamatory statements, either through speech or writing, have a crippling effect on an individual's ability to relate to his or her fellows. Appropriate legal relief must be made available to anyone so harmed. This section will focus on the nature of the libel action.

Definition

Libel consists of defamatory words that are either written or broadcast. Slander, by contrast, is a defamatory statement that is spoken to a smaller audience. By its very nature, slander is less harmful than libel. It has a comparatively fleeting impact. It is not permanently recorded and cannot be effectively transmitted to a larger audience after its utterance. Consequently, it is more difficult to prove slander than libel.

Two types of libel have been recognized by the courts. Libel per se is a statement judged defamatory on its face. The harm accruing from the statement is immediately apparent. Words that have been held libelous on their face include "liar, " "fool, " "hog, " "drunkard, " and "criminal. " A 1964 case provides an example.

Hornby v. Hunter 385 S. W. 2d 473 (1964)

Curtis H. Hunter instituted a suit against Harry Hornby, Jr. , and the Uvalde Leader-News, alleging that he had
been libeled by the publication. On October 13, 1963, an
article reported that it appeared that a specific car had been
stolen and that a warrant for C. H. "Curly" Hunter of Corpus
Christi, Texas, had been issued in connection with the theft.
The report continued:

> Hunter and another man, Al Smith, had previously
> leased the pasture where the car was found. The
> seven room house on the lease was well stocked,
> according to Deputy Large, with food, ammunition,
> a radio, and TV set.

In court, Hunter maintained that the 1959 Cadillac
automobile referred to in the article had been in the posses-
ion of Hunter and his wife for almost a year preceding the
publication, that Hunter did not steal the automobile, and
that no warrant had been issued for his arrest. The court
concluded that the article was not true and was defamatory.
The article did "impute to Hunter the commission of a crime
for which punishment by imprisonment in jail or the penitentiary may be imposed and is therefore, libelous per se. "

Libel per quod is not immediately apparent. The words
themselves are not defamatory, but become so when other
relevant facts or extrinsic circumstances are associated so
as to cause special damages. With libel per quod, defamation is indirect and dependent on the particular context in
which the words are written. The plaintiff has the burden
of proving the defamatory sense of the publication. A 1957
Kansas case is illustrative.

Karrigan v. Valentine 184 Kansas 783 (1957)

On November 3, 1956, the Clay Center (Kansas) Dispatch carried the following item:

> Stork-O-Grams. Ellen Marie is the name Mr. and
> Mrs. Phillip Karrigan of Clay Center gave to their
> daughter, who was born Thursday, Nov. 1, at the
> Clay Center Hospital. The little girl weighed nine
> pounds, three ounces.

Philip Karrigan sued because the announcement, innocent on its face, was scandalous because he was a bachelor, the only person in the vicinity with his name, and because the article made readers think that he "was married to one Betty Ellen Carpenter, a woman of ill repute and who has given birth to four children out of wedlock." Karrigan complained that he had been deprived of public convenience and social intercourse. The Kansas Supreme Court ruled for Karrigan.

> Pecuniary loss to one's trade, profession or business should not be the sole test in a case of this kind. The article in question being nondefamatory on its face, plaintiff, in order to state a cause of action for libel per quod, was required to allege explanatory extrinsic facts in connection with the subject of the article and the resulting special damage and injury to him.

The Kansas court was satisfied that Karrigan met his burden of proof. The damage done or injury suffered was substantial and real, not fictitious or imaginary. It was sufficient to justify a cause of action for libel per quod.

Necessary Elements

A successful libel action must include three elements: publication, identification, and defamation. Without a preponderance of evidence proving each of these elements, the plaintiff cannot hope to recover damages.

Publication--Of the three, publication is easiest to prove. The plaintiff need only demonstrate that a third person read or viewed the libel, and interpreted it in a defamatory sense. In the age of mass media and mass audiences, a statement printed in a newspaper or broadcast over the radio or television constitutes publication. With instances involving limited audiences, the courts usually give the benefit of the doubt to the plaintiff.

Arvey Corporation v. Peterson 178 F. Supp. 132 (1959)

On September 18, 1958, Robert Shapiro, Executive Vice President of the Transo Envelope Company, answered a letter he had received from an attorney, Wesley Caldwell. In his letter, Shapiro provided information requested by Caldwell concerning a client, William Peterson. Shapiro claimed that Caldwell was misinformed. Peterson was not due any back wages. On the contrary, Peterson was indebted to the company for the sum of $1,329 for "overdraw of advances." Shapiro then wrote,

> A demand for repayment of the above has been de-
> layed, pending completion of the investigation which
> is still incomplete. This involves areas of possible
> serious liability concerning your client. We are
> still awaiting the opinion of the Federal District
> Attorney.

Peterson initiated an action claiming that Shapiro's letter charged him "with fraud, fraudulent acts, conversion and criminal liability." The court determined that the letter was reasonably susceptible of the meaning that Peterson ascribed to it. The fact that the words were susceptible to an innocuous interpretation did not defeat an action for libel.

When the case reached a Pennsylvania district court, the justices considered the question of publication. The only possible instances of publication were the dictation of the letter to a stenographer, and the receipt of the letter by the attorney. Shapiro argued that the stenographer was not a third person because the company was merely performing a single act through two instrumentalities--the executive and the secretary. Thus, publication did not occur. The court, however, ruled that a secretary was indeed a third party and dictation by an officer of a corporation to his secretary was a publication. Shapiro also argued that the attorney was not a third party because the letter was an answer to the request of the attorney that the corporation pay Peterson some wages allegedly due to him. The court ruled that sending a communication to an agent of a defamed party was a publication. In this case, publication had occurred in both instances--to the secretary and to the attorney.

Di Giorgio Corporation v. Valley Labor Citizen
67 Cal. Rptr. 82 (1968)

A 1968 case affirmed that every repetition of a defamation is a separate publication, and thus a separate cause of action. On April 17, 1964, an article written by Jeff Boehm was published in the Union Gazette and was circulated in Santa Clara County, California. The article contained

information, supplied by Ernesto Galarza, that accused the
Di Giorgio Corporation and a congressman of faking a congressional hearing report and using the false report as a
tool against union organization of farm workers. Galarza
was not employed by the newspaper or by Boehm; he was a
labor union representative who frequently supplied information to labor newspapers for dissemination to union members.
After Boehm's article was published in the Gazette, Galarza
mailed a clipping of it to George Ballis, editor of the Valley
Labor Citizen, an independently owned and operated newspaper published and circulated in the San Joaquin Valley.
Ballis republished the article, discussing it with no one. When
Di Giorgio demanded a retraction, Ballis went to San Jose
and discussed the article with Boehm and Galarza. After-
wards, Ballis refused to publish a retraction in the Citizen.
Di Giorgio brought a libel suit against both Boehm and Ballis.
After a trial, the jury returned a verdict holding the defen
dants jointly liable for $5,000 general damages and $25,000
punitive damages. Boehm appealed.

The court noted that every repetition of a defamation
is a separate publication and hence a new and separate cause
of action even though the repeater states the source. The
originator of the defamatory matter is also liable for each
repetition if he or she could reasonably have foreseen the
repetition. In this case, however, there was no substantial
evidence to prove that Boehm authorized, consented to, or
participated in the republication of his article in the Citizen.
Furthermore, there was no evidence to implicate Boehm on
the theory of a foreseeable republication. The verdict against
Boehm was reversed.

Identification--With the element of identification, plaintiffs must prove that the defamatory meaning applies to them.
Someone must understand that the reference is to the plaintiff, whether by nickname, pseudonym, or circumstance. In
most cases, identification is straightforward. Sometimes,
though, a typographical error, wrong initials, an incorrect
address, or identical names may link an innocent person to
a criminal or other undesirable action. In such cases, the
courts usually side with the plaintiff. A person might also
be identified because of unique circumstances.

Hope v. Hearst Consolidated Publications, Inc.
294 F. 2d 681 (1961)

Frederick Hope, Palm Beach attorney who formerly

served as a special agent for the Federal Bureau of Investigation, filed a complaint alleging that Hearst Consolidated
Publications defamed Hope in a Cholly Knickerbocker column
that appeared in the April 21, 1958, New York Journal-Amer-
ican, the Palm Beach Times of a few days later, and numerous other newspapers. The item claimed: "Palm Beach is
buzzing with the story that one of the resort's richest men
caught his blonde wife in a compromising spot the other day
with a former FBI agent. " Hope claimed that he and many
others easily recognized the item as referring to himself and
to Mrs. Gregg Sherwood Dodge. Hope testified that he, unlike other former agents in Palm Beach, was known primarily
as an ex-agent; further, that he was the only former FBI man
who traveled in high-society circles. In addition to his own
testimony, Hope offered the live and written testimony of
other citizens of Palm Beach. This evidence, along with
responses to questions put to area residents, clearly supported
Hope's claim that identification had occurred. A New York
district court awarded Hope $58, 500. The court of appeals
upheld the verdict.

Defamation--The final element, defamation, is most
difficult to prove. The plaintiff must demonstrate that the
words in question do indeed belong to one of the four classes
of words the courts have recognized as actionable: 1) words
that damage the esteem or social standing in which one is
held; 2) words that expose one to public ridicule, scorn, or
derisiveness; 3) words that cause one to be avoided by a respectable segment of the community; and 4) words that damage one in occupation, profession, or trade. The various
types are exemplified by the following court cases.

Roth v. Greensboro News Company 6 S. E. 2d 882 (1940)

Of the various ways in which a person may be lowered
in public esteem, probably none has brought more libel suits
than a false charge of criminality. During the Depression,
the Greensboro (North Carolina) Daily News published an
Associated Press story from New Jersey in which the Federal
Bureau of Investigation was quoted as planning to question
Harry Roth, who was thought to be linked to the Charles
"Lucky" Luciano gang. The next day, a Greensboro FBI
agent told a Daily News reporter of his participation in recent New Jersey raids. He said he thought that Roth, now
under arrest in New York, had previously lived in Greensboro.
He added that Roth had been tried on a white slavery charge
in Greensboro a few years earlier. The reporter mentioned

that some of Roth's brothers had purchased the Palace Theatre in Greensboro about ten years earlier; the agent replied that Roth "had been in the entertainment business." The reporter examined various issues of the Greensboro City Directory. In the 1928 directory he found: "Harry Roth, Palace Theatre, residence Y. M. C. A." In the 1929 and 1930 directories he found: "Harry Roth (Palace Theatre), Ashville, N. C. ," but no listing in the next two directories. He then checked the clerk's office in the U. S. District Court, where he learned that a Harry Roth was convicted of violating the Mann Act in 1935, and sentenced to three years' imprisonment. The reporter, without checking at the Palace Theatre or the YMCA, wrote the following story, which was published in the September 1, 1937, Greensboro Record.

VICE RING MAN
IS KNOWN HERE

The recent raid of the federal investigators in Atlantic City, N. J. , and other cities that resulted in the arrest of Harry Roth on Monday night, is of local interest as Roth formerly resided in Greensboro. He is now under $25,000 bond, being charged with complicity in gigantic vice operations in violation of the Mann White Slave Law. Between 125 and 150 men were taken into custody as a result of the drive, headed by J. Edgar Hoover. Roth is regarded as one of the higher-ups in the conspiracy.

Roth, 42, listed as a resident of New York, was for a time connected with the Palace Theater in Greensboro, it is understood. In June, 1935, he was tried in United States Court for violation of the Mann White Slave Act and given two years in Atlanta on each of four counts, the sentences to run concurrently. It will be recalled that he was arrested in San Francisco, Calif. , after federal officers had traced him to various parts of the country. He was specifically charged with inducing young women to go from Greensboro to New York, promising employment. Arriving in the metropolis, it was brought out during the trial, the true motive of the journey was revealed and several girls testified to their experiences after making the trip to New York on the promise of employment.

After Roth was arrested in San Francisco it was necessary to have one of the prosecuting witnesses taken to the Pacific coast city for purpose of identification, the prisoner resisting removal.

R. L. Morgan, of the Greensboro office of the
FBI, was among the number summoned to New York
and Atlantic City to assist in the vice gang round-
up. He returned home Tuesday.

Shortly after publication, the reporter realized that an error
in identification had been made. The next day, the Greensboro Record carried a correction:

Another Harry Roth Figures in Affair

The Greensboro Record was informed Wednesday afternoon that the Harry Roth, arrested in the
vice raids in Atlantic City and other northern cities
Monday night, was not the Harry Roth who some
years ago was connected with the Palace Theatre,
as we stated in the article in Wednesday's Record.
The Harry Roth who was engaged in business here
was a much younger man, it was said, and he was
a young man of exemplary habits and character,
according to citizens who were personally acquainted
with him.
The statement in Wednesday's paper was based
on information that the prisoner, following arrest
in New Jersey, had indicated to officers he was at
one time in the movie business in Greensboro.

On September 11, the Harry Roth who owned the Palace Theatre wrote to the Greensboro Record and demanded a
retraction. The Record's managing editor wrote to Roth, enclosing the September 2 article, and requested that if the
article did not meet with Roth's approval, he should inform
the Record. The newspaper firm received no reply. Roth
brought a libel suit in lower court, and won. The Record
appealed to the Supreme Court of North Carolina, which held
that there was no error in the lower court and that Roth was
entitled to damages, the amount to be determined by the jury.
The Roth case confirms the importance of checking all sources
of information before writing a story. The possibility of a
mistake in names and addresses is ever-present, and the
courts view it as libelous to publish a story incorrectly reporting that one has been charged with a crime, or is guilty
of a crime.

Zbyszko v. New York American, Inc. 228 App. Div. 277 (1930)

A second class of libelous words includes those that

expose a person to public ridicule, scorn, or derisiveness. Zbyszko v. New York American provides an example. The New York American published an article entitled "How Science Proves Its Theory of Evolution. " It outlined a series of stages in the physical development of the human being. The body of the article did not mention Zbyszko in any way, but stated:

> Science does not believe that gorillas or other apes are the great-grandfathers of man. They are set down as remote cousins of mankind rather than direct ancestors. Gorilla evolution and human evolution split apart from a common ape-man parent millions of years ago. The gorilla is probably closer to man, both in body and mind, than any other species of ape now alive. The general physique of the gorilla is closely similar to an athletic man of today, and the mind of a young gorilla is much like the mind of a human body.

Accompanying the article were two illustrations entitled "Stanislaus Zbyszko, the Wrestler, Not Fundamentally Different from the Ape in Physique, " and "A Mounted Specimen of the Great Kivu Gorilla in Lord Rothchild's private museum at Tring, Hertfordshire, England. "

Zbyszko sued, complaining that an impression was created in the minds of readers that he and the gorilla were fundamentally alike. He asserted that as a wrestler and businessman, he was brought into public contempt and disgrace, and was shunned by relatives, neighbors, and friends. Although the lower court dismissed the complaint, the appeals court held that the tendency of the publication was to "bring him into ridicule and contempt. " It ruled against the dismissal and held the publication libelous.

Powers v. Durgin-Snow Publishing Company, Inc.
Powers v. Olesen 144 A. 2d 294 (1958)

Another example is Powers v. Durgin-Snow Publishing. The libel action arose from the publication of an article that appeared in the Westbrook (Maine) American. The article, written by Clifford "Sunny" Olesen, appeared under the heading, "Milling Around. "

> George Powers, Coating Department, is a fellow who believes in looking ahead. He's also a classic

example of typical Yankee thrift. Take his idea on
caskets now--George says, "Why spend a lot of
money for a casket when, for $15 or $20 you can
build one, yourself. After all, your family can
always use the money you've saved in that one item,
alone. "

Suiting the action to the word, George is now
busily sawing and hammering away on his own tai-
lored-to-fit coffin. And, as a sort of package deal,
he's making plans to dig the space for it next.

From all outward appearances, this thrifty, if
slightly ghoulish gent can take his time on his project, because ... he turned (approximately) 35 on
his last birthday.

Powers sued, claiming that the article injured him in his good
name and reputation, deprived him of public confidence, and
exposed him and his family to public hatred, contempt, and
ridicule.

In the opinion of the Supreme Judicial Court of Maine,
the article tended to expose Powers to laughter tinged with
contempt, or in other words--to ridicule. The reader was
given the impression that Powers was at best an odd or unusual character. The reader might well laugh with the writer
at the victim with a laughter mixed with contempt. According to the court, Olesen could not justify his assault on Powers
upon the ground that it was a mere jest, unless it was per-
fectly clear from the language used "that it could in no respect be regarded as an attack upon the reputation or business
of the person to whom it related. " In this case, the article
had a natural tendency to expose Powers to ridicule that was
more than trivial. The article was libelous.

Sally v. Brown 295 S.W. 890 (1927)

A third category includes words that cause a person to
be avoided by a respectable segment of the community. Most
notable in this category are words that falsely attribute ve-
nereal disease, mental illness, alcoholism, and other diseases.
Such unfair attribution of physical or mental illness has been
held as libelous. In 1926, Shilo Sally and Corbett Brown were
rivals for nomination for political office in Perry County, Kentucky. After being defeated, Sally allegedly claimed, in a
conversation with Ed Griffith, a brother-in-law of Brown, that
"Oh, yes, your brother-in-law is eat up with the clap. " Brown
sued for damages and was awarded $500. Sally appealed.

The court of appeals noted that if Brown was in the condition that Sally claimed, it would partially, if not wholly, exclude Brown from society. It would "certainly exclude him from all good society." Hence, the words were actionable per se. The judgment of the lower court was upheld.

Cowper v. Vannier ₁56 N. E. 2d 761 (1959)

In 1959, an Illinois court held that the imputation of mental illness was libelous per se. The case involved an alleged libel against Paul Vannier, the editor and publisher of the Bluffs Times. The July 25, 1956, issue of the paper published the following as part of an account of a meeting of the Scott County Board of School Trustees.

> One board member, Cowper of Glasgow, was absent. If he is permitted to vote, (Mr. Cowper is recovering from a mental illness) we understand the voting will be delayed until all the testimony can be transcribed and digested.

George Cowper sued. After a trial, he was awarded $6,000. Vannier appealed.

The Appellate Court of Illinois indicated that a publication imputing insanity or impairment of mental faculties was libelous per se. The ridicule or contempt involved in such a charge may tend to deprive the person of his or her right of social intercourse. According to the court, persons reputed to be of unsound mind were denied "the confidence and respect which all right thinking men normally accord their fellow members of society." The claim that a person was recovering from a mental illness clearly and unequivocally carried the imputation that such a person was not mentally sound. The judgment of the lower court was affirmed.

Fort v. Holt 508 P. 2d 792 (1973)

In 1973, however, a Colorado court ruled that merely stating that an individual had, at one time, been mentally ill was not libelous. John Miller Fort and James Anthony Fort claimed that Daisy Holt composed and published a letter that stated: "I have heard that the oldest Fort brother was released from an insane asylum shortly before they moved out here and that their father gave them $100,000 to 'get lost.'"

The letter was addressed to and received by Randy Sullivan of the Boulder, Colorado, Sheriff's Office. Sullivan read the letter and allowed others to see it. The Fort brothers alleged that as a result of the letter they suffered humiliation, embarrassment, mental anguish, loss of reputation, and diminution of credit rating. John Fort, the oldest brother, claimed general damages of $20, 000. Each brother requested punitive damages of $100, 000. The lower court dismissed the complaint. The Fort brothers appealed.

The court of appeals noted that "the allegation that at one time a person had been mentally ill does not constitute an imputation that one has a loathsome disease." The court, finding no libel, affirmed the decision of the lower court.

Blende v. Hearst Publications 93 P. 2d 733 (1939)

The fourth category of libelous words includes those that damage one in one's occupation or profession. Mistakenly attributing a "single instance" of clumsiness or error to a professional person is not enough to damage that person. There must be a suggestion of more general incompetency, and the plaintiff must prove a tangible and durable harm. In 1939, the courts had an opportunity to clarify the law of libel regarding occupation and profession.

The Seattle Post-Intelligencer printed this story about a physician:

BROKEN NECK KILLS CITY PRISONER
INJURY DISCOVERED AFTER MAN
SPENT DAY IN CELL

Charles Adolph Dettz, a middle-aged machinist, who lay all day in a padded cell at the city jail with a broken neck before attendants discovered his condition to be serious, died yesterday at King County Hospital.
Dettz was found in the street at Westlake Ave. N. and Prospect St. at 5:30 a.m. Thursday, the coroner's preliminary report showed. He was taken to police headquarters and examined by Dr. Sol Levinson of City Hospital, who said he talked and walked normally, and who diagnosed his case as plain drunkenness.
In the afternoon, Dr. O. J. Blende, another

city Hospital physician, examined Dettz and diagnosed his condition as "Alcoholic paralysis" and
ordered him removed to King County Hospital.
Dettz lived at 1526 Belmont Ave.
County Autopsy Surgeon Gale E. Wilson, after
a post-mortem examination, said that Dettz' neck
had been fractured several hours before he was
taken to jail.

Blende sued. While the trial court found for the physician, the appeals court reversed, and dismissed the action.
It said:

> To charge a professional man with negligence or
> unskilfulness in the management or treatment of
> an individual case, is not more than to impute to
> him the mistakes and errors incident to fallible hu-
> man nature. The most eminent and skillful phy-
> sician or surgeon may mistake the symptoms of a
> particular skill or learning. To say of him, there-
> fore, that he was mistaken in that case would not
> be calculated to impair the confidence of the com-
> munity in his general professional competency.

Nichols v. Bristow Publishing Company
330 P. 2d 1044 (1957)

The "single instance" rule, however, does not protect
words that assign questionable ethics or business practices
to an individual. The Bristow Record carried a front-page
article that stated that L. M. Nichols had sold a building.
The story went on to claim that while he owned the building,

> Nichols used the building for the purpose of attempt-
> ing to destroy the value of the Record-Citizen pub-
> lishing plant after he had sold that plant and col-
> lected the money from the sale.
> However, he later discovered that there was
> a large percentage of business firms in the city
> that did not enjoy doing business with organizations
> that openly operate with shady ethics. In recent
> years his publishing activities have been maintained
> on a sneak basis.

Nichols sued for libel. He lost the case in the lower
court, but won on appeal. The Oklahoma Supreme Court decided that an article accusing one of "shady ethics" and of operating on a "sneak basis" tends to injure him in his occupation.

Damages

If the three elements are adequately proven by the plaintiff, the court may assess monetary damages against the offender. Depending on the nature of the case and the circumstances surrounding publication of the libel, one or more classes of damages may be awarded: 1) compensatory, 2) punitive, 3) special, and 4) nominal.

Dalton v. Meister 52 Wis. 2d 173 (1971)

Compensatory (general) damages are intended to compensate for injury to reputation. Such damages are based on offended feelings, shame, insult, mental anguish, physical injury, and harm to business or occupation. In such cases, the court has the power to review a jury's award of damages. If it is found to be excessive, the award may be lowered. The 1971 case of Dalton v. Meister involved compensatory damages of $75,000. Howard Meister, a banker-businessman, was accused of criminal bribery and unlawful lobbying as a result of a grand jury investigation conducted by Wisconsin Assistant Attorney General LeRoy Dalton. On May 5, 1967, the criminal bribery charges were dismissed because the state's witness, Dorothy Effinger, was too sick to testify. Meister was later acquitted of the charge of unlawful lobbying. Immediately following the dismissal of the bribery charges, Meister held a meeting in the courtroom with the members of the news media at which he distributed typewritten copies of a statement that included the following paragraphs:

> Eleven months ago, I was indicted by a Grand Jury, illegally constituted, and immoral in every sense of modern day terminology conceived by gestapo leader, LeRoy Dalton, who is now slithering under his rock.
> Today, everyone knows that any and all charges made against me were groundless and conceived in the evil minds of those who thought that through illegal means they could successfully smear me.
> It is now my duty to inform the public that the gestapo, the cancer in the Attorney General's office must be cut out. I for one shall lead the fight, and good men shall join me.

Meister's statement went on to charge Dalton with purchasing, by the offer of immunity, the "perjured testimony" of "extortionist" Dorothy Effinger, who "is no sicker today than she was seven days ago when she whistled and danced in the halls of the Dane County District Attorney's office. " Meister then claimed that the only reason for dropping the charges was lack of any credible evidence. Dalton initiated a libel action. A Milwaukee circuit court jury rendered a judgment against Meister and awarded compensatory and punitive damages of $75, 000 to Dalton. Meister appealed.

The Wisconsin Supreme Court found that the libelous statements caused Dalton's transfer from his position, disfavor with the Attorney General, loss of reputation as a criminal investigator, abuse of his character as a lawyer, and public contempt, ridicule, disgrace, and humiliation. The court concluded that since Meister's wealth by his own admission exceeded $2 million, the jury award of $75, 000 in compensatory and punitive damages was not excessive.

United Press International, Inc. v. Mohs
381 S. W. 2d 104 (1964)

Punitive (exemplary) damages are intended to punish past libelous behavior and to discourage similar conduct in the future. Such damages are a direct punishment for actual malice, which the plaintiff must prove. A high degree of fault is necessary to sustain an award for punitive damages. The jury is empowered to decide whether punitive damages will be awarded, and the courts can reduce outrageously high awards of such damages. In 1964, the Court of Civil Appeals of Texas heard an appeal of an award of punitive damages. On August 10, 1961, Bruce Mohs, a licensed commercial pilot who operated an air service, flew a seaplane to Dallas, Texas. Unable to land at Love Field, Mohs ultimately set the plane down on White Rock Lake, where the operator of a marina helped him get ashore. A policeman who saw the plane land asked Mohs to accompany him to headquarters to determine whether Mohs had violated any city ordinance in landing his plane on White Rock Lake. After extensive inquiry, it was determined that Mohs could land there, so he was driven back to his aircraft.

That same evening, Brice Miller, night editor of United Press International in Dallas, sent the following story over its wires for publication throughout the world:

Dallas, Tex., Aug. 11 (UPI)--Bruce Mohs of Madison, Wis., is the kind of guy who figures any port in a pinch. And he was ... pinched. He flew his plane to Dallas yesterday and by the time he got here he was low on fuel. His plane has pontoons and no wheels, so he landed smack in the middle of White Rock Lake, a residential area and park inside the city limits.

"Hey, get that thing out of here, " a park patrolman yelled.

"Sorry, " Mohs replied, "no gas left. "

The patrolman crawled inside the plane and turned on the ignition. There was a quarter of a tank left. "You have plenty of gas to get to Lake Dallas (about 15 miles away), " he said. Mohs disagreed and about this time L. M. Cook, park superintendent, arrived and ordered Mohs arrested and handcuffed. He began thumbing through a thick book of city ordinances to find one that fit.

He did, and had Mohs charged with flying under 2, 000 feet over Dallas and landing on a publicly owned lake. "I guess I could have looked a little longer, " Mohs admitted. "I saw plenty of airports, but no water for a pontoon plane and I just set it down on the first thing that looked bigger than a puddle. "

The story was published in several newspapers, including some in Madison, Wisconsin, where Mohs lived and operated his aircraft business. Shortly thereafter, UPI was informed by Mohs's attorney that statements in the story were false and libelous. UPI sent out the following correction:

Editors:
On Aug. 11, United Press International carried a dispatch from Dallas that a private plane pilot was arrested when he landed his pontoon plane on a city lake. The story was in error. If you printed it, we request that you print the following:

Dallas, Tex., Aug. 26 (UPI)--United Press International erroneously reported on Aug. 11 that Bruce Mohs of Madison, Wis., was arrested and charged with violation of a city ordinance for landing his pontoon-equipped plane on a city lake. Mohs, who is a licensed commercial pilot, landed at the lake on a flight from Madison to Dallas on Aug. 10. A

UPI dispatch said he was ordered arrested and handcuffed. He was not arrested, nor was he handcuffed. Park Superintendent L. M. Cook, who super-
vises activities at the lake, was quoted as saying
Mohs would be charged under a city ordinance forbidding flights in Dallas under 2,000 feet and landing on a publicly owned lake. Actually, Mohs was
not charged. No summons was issued by police.

Mohs said that as he approached Dallas, he
contacted Dallas Love Field, the main city airport,
and was told to proceed to Mountain Creek Lake,
since his plane had no wheels. He said the naval
air station at the lake could not provide mooring
for his aircraft, so he contacted a former boat dock
operator at White Rock Lake who told him he could
land and moor his plane there. The UPI dispatch
of Aug. 11 quoted Mohs as telling a park patrolman
he was "out of gas. " The patrolman said later Mohs
did not say this, nor did the patrolman climb into
the plane to check on the amount of gas left in the
tanks.

UPI regrets any inconvenience or embarrassment the original story may have caused Mohs.

Mohs sued United Press International for special and punitive
damages.

The court found the UPI story was libelous and that
Mohs was harmed by the publishing of statements in the story.
He was awarded $2,500 in special damages. In addition, the
jury found that publication of the story involved malice and
awarded punitive damages of $5,000. UPI appealed, but only
complained against the punitive damages. The court of appeals noted that Miller had accepted the word of a string correspondent as the basis of the story. Though Miller was
aware of possible inaccuracies in his story, neither he nor
anyone else for UPI attempted to verify the story by inquir-
ing at the police station, or by contacting the patrolman, the
park superintendent, or anyone else. With such lack of verification, UPI sent out the story. Even though the need for
more investigation was suggested, Miller "was so pleased
with a funny story holding Mohs up to ridicule that he forth-
with sent it out for all to read and be amused at Mohs' expense. " The court concluded that "fabrication of this libelous story was a willful and wanton act sufficient to support
a finding of malice. " The lower court's judgment was affirmed.

MacLeod v. Tribune Publishing Company, Inc.
343 P. 2d 36 (1959)

Special (actual) damages represent the real, tangible
monetary loss suffered by the plaintiff as a result of a false
statement. Such damages cannot include projected future
losses. The plaintiff must prove special damages in a precise, concrete way. Malice is not an issue. MacLeod v.
Tribune Publishing Company involved a claim of special damages. On April 19, 1955, an article appeared on the front
page of the Oakland Tribune that contained the following:

Red Paper Issues Election Extra

The San Francisco People's World, recognized
throughout the state as the mouthpiece of the Communist party, distributed a last-minute extra edition
in Oakland yesterday, on the eve of the city election .... The Communist-line paper defended the
proposal to revive ward politics in Oakland and
printed a list of recommendations which included
the names of council candidates John F. Quinn,
John W. Holmdahl, and Dr. Grover H. MacLeod.

MacLeod sent a letter to the Tribune Company informing them
that the article contained false information. He demanded a
correction or retraction but none was made. He then initiated
a libel suit, claiming that he had enjoyed a good name and
reputation in his profession as a dental surgeon, and that the
publication was understood by the general public as imputing
that he was a Communist sympathizer and that he had received the recommendation of the People's World. MacLeod
claimed that in fact People's World had not endorsed him and
all imputations in the article were false and malicious, and
were intended to expose MacLeod to contempt and ridicule--
causing him to be shunned and avoided. MacLeod claimed
that he had sustained continuing nervous strain, severe mental anguish, and substantial humiliation. He also alleged to
have suffered pecuniary loss in his profession. MacLeod
sued for $5,000 in special damages, $200,000 in compensatory damages, and $200,000 in punitive damages. The trial
court dismissed MacLeod's suit. He appealed.

When the case reached the California Supreme Court,
a majority of the justices agreed that a charge of communist
affiliation or sympathy was libelous on its face. The court
acknowledged that a publication should be measured by the
probable impact upon the mind of the average reader. A

publisher was liable for what was insinuated, as well as for what was stated explicitly. In this case, readers might reasonably infer that the Tribune Company intended to charge that MacLeod was unworthy of public office because he was a communist sympathizer. The court also noted that the publisher could have checked the accuracy of the article. A copy of the People's World election extra was readily available. The defendant should have had no difficulty in accurately reporting the extra's recommendations. Failure to do so suggested intentional falsehood on the defendant's part.

Having established the act as libelous, the court then turned to the issue of special damages. MacLeod alleged that he suffered monetary loss in his profession as a dentist because a large percentage of established patients canceled appointments and there had been a sharp decline in the number of new patients. MacLeod did not know the exact amount of monetary loss, but he contended that the loss was a continuing one and would amount to $5,000 or more. MacLeod claimed that he could specify the exact amount of loss when it became known. The Tribune Company claimed that the demand for special damages was not valid because the nature of the loss or injury was not particularly set forth. The court, however, ruled that the loss, as described by MacLeod, was done so with "sufficient particularity to enable defendant to prepare its defense." Under the circumstances of this case, it was acceptable for MacLeod to estimate the amount of loss. The court concluded that MacLeod did indeed have a cause for complaint and reversed the finding of the trial court.

Goldwater v. Ginzburg 414 F. 2d 324 (1969)

Nominal damages are token damages awarded in libel actions where there has been a violation but no serious harm to the plaintiff's reputation or financial position. Nominal damages were awarded in Goldwater v. Ginzburg. In this case, the specific details of which are presented later in this chapter, Senator Barry Goldwater brought suit against a publication that outlined a psychobiography on Goldwater that claimed to alert the American people about the potential dangers of Goldwater's Presidency. The court ruled that the publisher knowingly published defamatory statements and that he was motivated by actual malice. The court punished the publisher by awarding $75,000 in punitive damages. In addition, since Goldwater had neither pleaded nor proved any special damages, the jury granted $1 in nominal compensation.

Defenses

A publisher of an alleged libel is not helpless in the face of a lawsuit. There are no less than four complete and six partial defenses against a libel action. Of course, laws in each state vary, as does the degree of immunity for reporters. In most states, the following are complete defenses: 1) truth, 2) absolute privilege, 3) qualified privilege, and 4) fair comment. Partial defenses include: 1) retraction and apology, 2) right of reply, 3) settlement out of court, 4) bad reputation of plaintiff, 5) use of reliable sources, and 6) provocation.

Truth--Truth of a libelous statement is a complete defense in several states. In others, it is unclear whether truth alone can shield a publisher from successful legal action. In some states, truth is a defense only if it is published with good motives; malice destroys the defense. In all cases, the defendant must prove the truth of his or her general imputation by a preponderance of evidence. Not every detail must be proved accurately; but substantial proof is required in order to exonerate the defendant. In 1957, the Empire Printing Company attempted to establish a defense of truth.

Empire Printing Company v. Roden 247 F. 2d 8 (1957)

Prior to May, 1951, a ferry, the "chilkoot, " had been operated by private ownership between Haines and Juneau, Alaska. The ferry closed a sixty-five-mile gap in the highway. In 1951, the owners announced that because of increased operating costs they would not continue to operate the ferry. The Territorial Board of Road Commissioners, which consisted of Henry Roden, Ernest Gruening, and Frank Metcalf, purchased the ferry in order to operate it as part of the road system. During 1951, the operating expenses of the ferry were paid out of the Territorial treasury from the funds set aside for roads and harbors. Receipts from the operation of the ferry went into the general fund of the Territority. This method of operation proved unsatisfactory. First, the processing of Territorial vouchers took considerable time and many of the bills were payable immediately. Second, the system tended to deplete the road and harbor fund. So, in 1952, the Board devised a plan for the operation of the ferry by which revenue from it could be expended to defray operating expenses.

The September 25, 1952, issue of the Daily Alaska Empire mentioned the details of the ferry operation. Almost the entire front page was devoted to the "special ferry fund." The headline, in black type an inch and a quarter high, and extending across the entire eight columns of the front page, read "Bare 'Special' Ferry Fund." Beneath that headline was another smaller headline claiming "Reeve Raps Graft, Corruption." This heading dealt with a story regarding a speech made by political candidate Robert Reeve and it had nothing to do with the ferry fund. Next to the story and directly under the headline "Reeve Raps Graft, Corruption" was a photograph of a check drawn on the "special ferry fund." Beneath the photograph of the check was an editorial entitled "Start Talking Boys" which dealt with the special ferry fund. To the right of the page was a statement "Gruening, Metcalf, Roden Divert 'Chilkoot' Cash to Private Bank Account." In the story that appeared under this headline was the statement, "The Case closely parallels that of Oscar Olson, former Territorial Treasurer who is now serving a prison term at McNeil Island Penitentiary for violating the law in the receipt and disbursement of public funds." In the editorial headed "Start Talking Boys" there was an additional reference to Olson: "Oscar Olson sits today in his prison cell, dreaming of the days when he thought Territorial laws were only for the underlings." Roden, Gruening, and Metcalf initiated a libel suit claiming that the headlines and portions of the publication constituted libel. The trial jury awarded the plaintiffs $1 in compensatory damages, and $5,000 punitive damages. The case was appealed.

The court of appeals determined that defamation can be accomplished in many ways and the manner in which the front page of the Daily Alaska Empire was set up could be regarded as a deliberate defamation by insinuation and associations, even if a direct charge was lacking. Readers of the newspaper could easily understand by what they read that the members of the Board of Road Commissioners had been guilty of embezzlement. According to the court, "Whatever a newspaper article actually says or carries to its readers must be judged by the publication as a whole. The headlines alone may be enough to make libelous per se an otherwise innocuous article." In addition, "An article may become libelous by juxtaposition with other articles or photographs." In this case, the defense argued truth as a defense. The jury found, and the court of appeals affirmed, that the establishment of truth must be as broad as the defamatory accusation. The proof of truth of only part of a charge cannot amount to a complete defense. Even though the defense demonstrated the truth of the words in the article, the truth of what the reader understood was not established. It was not shown that the Board members, with respect to the special fund, were guilty of any personal dishonesty or made any individual profit or received anything for their own use. In light of the defense's failure to establish truth as a defense, the court affirmed the jury verdicts in this case.

Absolute Privilege--A second defense that provides unconditional immunity from a libel action applies to the news media. Recognizing the importance of an unfettered press, the courts have extended the defense of absolute privilege to a number of situations that, because of their unique nature, require the interests of society to prevail over the interests of an individual. In 1923, the Supreme Court of Illinois acknowledged the absolute privilege of newspapers to report the news without fear of recrimination.

City of Chicago v. Tribune Company 139 N. E. 86 (1923)

During the 1920 Chicago political campaigns, the Tribune published numerous articles that charged that the city of Chicago was "broke"; that it "owes millions of 1921 funds"; that "bankruptcy is just around the corner from the city of Chicago"; that its "credit is shot to pieces"; that "the city's financial affairs are in a serious way"; that the city administration "having busted the city, and having reduced it to such insolvency that it is issuing Villa script to pay its bills, is reaching out for the state"; that "the city government had run on the rocks"; that "the city cannot pay its debts; it is bankrupt; the bankers have refused it credit"--along with several other similar statements. Chicago initiated a libel suit, charging that all of the publications were false, were published maliciously and in reckless disregard of the rights of the city. The city also claimed that the statements were published to promote the political and financial interests of the Tribune Company and its political friends. The city stated that competitive bidding on materials used by the city was stifled and that the sale of municipal bonds was hurt. The city sought damages of $10 million.

The court noted that the articles were published during the campaign between rival candidates for the Republican nomination for Governor of Illinois. One of the two leading candidates was supported by the Tribune Company and the other by the administration of the city of Chicago. Many of the publications were quotations from addresses of the candidate supported by the newspaper, and of his political associates. The court ruled that when a person seeks to persuade others to violate existing law or to overthrow by force or other unlawful means the exisiting government, he may be punished. However, all other utterances or publications against the government must be considered absolutely privileged.

Through the years, the courts have recognized three types of communications that are absolutely immune from libel action: 1) privileged communications, 2) communications involving prior consent of the plaintiff, and 3) political broadcasts. The following cases illustrate the various types of absolute privilege.

Barr v. Matteo 360 U. S. 564 (1959)

Privileged communications generally extend to all oral and written communication between husband and wife, attorney and client, doctor and patient, and priest and parishioner. Judges, jurors, witnesses, counsel, and the parties in both civil and criminal actions are absolutely protected. In addition, executive and legislative officials are also unconditionally immune from libel or slander when communicated in the course of their official duties. In Barr v. Matteo, the Supreme Court extended immunity to executive press releases. In 1950, the statutory existence of the Office of Housing Expediter was about to expire. John Madigan and Linda Matteo, employees of this agency, devised a plan to utilize some $2,600,000 of funds earmarked for terminal leave payments. In essence, employees were discharged, paid accrued actual leave out of the $2,600,000, rehired immediately as temporary employees, and then restored to permanent status when the agency's life was extended by law. This plan came under heavy criticism from members of Congress, as well as the press. On February 5, 1953, William Barr gave notice to Madigan and Matteo that he intended to suspend them from duty because of their conduct. At the same time, Barr issued a press release explaining his intention to suspend the pair of employees. Matteo and Madigan sued, charging that the press release, alone and coupled with the news reports of congressional reaction to their plan, defamed them and had been caused by malice on Barr's part. The jury ruled for Matteo and Madigan. Barr appealed.

When the case reached the U. S. Supreme Court, the justices upheld (5-4) Barr's claim of absolute privilege. The majority agreed that it was important that officials

... should be free to exercise their duties unembarrassed by the fear of damage suits ... which would consume time and energies which would otherwise be devoted to governmental service and the threat of which might appreciably inhibit the fearless, vigorous, and effective administration of policies of government.

The Court concluded that the action Barr took was within his line of duty. That was enough to render the privilege applicable. In a dissenting opinion, Justices Earl Warren and William Douglas expressed concern about the advantage that government officials had with the absolute privilege while critics of government were protected by only a qualified privilege. In fact, this case did provide the unscrupulous public official an opportunity to attack a defenseless individual with impunity. In the opinion of the majority, the government interests at issue overrode individual concerns.

Langford v. Vanderbilt University 318 S. W. 2d 568 (1958)

Persons who consent to acts that subsequently harm them in some way cannot collect for their suffering. Consent can be granted directly through a written release indicating prior consent. The release must be as broadly and accurately fashioned as the planned publication. Such a statement voids any libel action. Consent can also be implied. In Langford v. Vanderbilt University, the court recognized that in situations where consent is implied through words or actions, the plaintiff is unable to collect in a libel suit. On May 17, 1954, a section poking fun at Mother's Day appeared in The Chase, a student humor magazine published at Vanderbilt University. The layout included four pictures with an overall headline that read "Everyone Loves Mother." The upper left frame was a black space with the caption "Father Loves Mother" under it. The upper right frame pictured a young child with the caption "Daughter Loves Mother (And wants to be one too)." The lower left frame showed a boy, his arm tatooed with a heart enclosing the "Mother" and the caption "Sailor Boy Loves Mother." The lower right frame pictured a smiling face, partly covered by a hood, captioned "Midwife Loves Mother." None of the persons pictured were identified. Actually, the young child was Pamela Langford. The picture had been placed in the layout because of a mistake at the printing company. When the editors of the school magazine learned of the mistake, all but a few copies of the issue were seized and destroyed. In addition, the Student Publications Board banned further publication of The Chase.

Soon thereafter, Robert Langford, Pamela's father, indicated his intention to sue. Ormond Plater and Joe Puryear, student-reporters for another student publication, the Hustler, called Mr. Langford and asked for an interview. He granted the interview, stated that he was going to sue, let the student-journalists take some pictures, and showed them some photos of his daughter. He also said that he wanted publicity and recommended that the students contact his lawyers for legal details. The students talked with the lawyers and then went to the courthouse and read the papers filed in the suits. Langford had charged that the Mother's Day layout, through innuendo, implied that Pamela was amenable to acts of illicit sexual intercourse, that Mrs. Langford was sleeping in a darkened bedroom with a sailor, and that Mr. Langford was having sexual relations in a darkened bedroom with someone unknown. Plater and Puryear wrote an article for the Hustler under this headline:

$180,000.00 SUIT FILED BY LOCAL
MINISTER OVER CHASE PHOTO

Claims Issue "Lewd, Bawd, Vulgar;"
"Spread Sex, Filth, Slime and Smut"

The article accurately summarized the suits. To help illustrate the story, the page from the Mother's Day issue was reproduced and Langford's objections to the pictures were cited. Langford, his wife, and his daughter then filed suit-- this time against the Hustler. When the case reached the Tennessee Court of Appeals, the judge stressed that Langford had wanted publicity. He had referred the students to his lawyers for legal details. The students made fair and accurate statements of the pleadings by providing the alleged defamatory parts in Langford's own words. In this case, the newspaper publication was absolutely privileged.

Farmers Educational and Cooperative Union of America v.
WDAY, Inc. 360 U.S. 525 (1959)

Another type of communication that affords the defense

of absolute privilege is political broadcast. Prior to 1959, radio and television stations that granted equal time to political candidates under Section 315 of the Federal Communications Act of 1934, were liable for all defamation in those broadcasts. At the same time, stations were prohibited from endorsing any political viewpoint or sanctioning any political talk.

> If any licensee shall permit any person who is a legally qualified candidate for any public office to use a broadcasting station, he shall afford equal opportunities to all other such candidates for office in the use of the broadcasting station: provided, that such licensee shall have no power of censorship over the material broadcast under the provision of this section. No obligation is imposed upon any licensee to allow the use of its station by any candidate [47 U. S. C. Sec. 315 (a)].

Stations subsequently argued that if they were to carry libelous speeches, and were prevented from editing, they could not be held responsible for damages. In 1959, the U. S. Supreme Court agreed. On October 29, 1956, A. C. Townley, a colorful remnant of the Progressive Movement, demanded equal time as an independent candidate for the U. S. Senate. Equal time was provided by station WDAY-TV in Fargo. In the telecast, Townley charged that the North Dakota Farmer's Union was Communist-controlled. WDAY had warned Townley that this charge was probably libelous. The Farmer's Union brought a $100,000 damage suit against Townley and the station. A district court dismissed the complaint against WDAY on the ground that Section 315 rendered the station immune from liability. The Farmer's Union carried an appeal to the North Dakota Supreme Court, which ruled that radio and television stations were not liable for false or libelous statements made over their facilities by political candidates. Noting that WDAY had advised Townley that his remarks were potentially libelous, the court argued: "We cannot believe that it was the intent of Congress to compel a station to broadcast libelous statements and at the same time subject it to the task of defending actions for damages." The majority felt that the attack on Farmer's Union was "in context" with a candidate's criticism of his opponent since "communism" was a campaign issue. The majority added that the union should have brought action against Townley alone. Townley's income was, however, a mere $98.50 per month--a promise of little satisfaction to an aggrieved party. The union appealed the case to the U. S. Supreme Court.

The Court ruled (5-4) that Section 315 relieves radio and television stations from liability for broadcasting libelous remarks by candidates. The Court agreed with the state courts of North Dakota that Section 315 grants a licensee an immunity from liability for libelous material it broadcasts. Since stations cannot control what candidates say over the air, they should not be held responsible for the statements. The candidate, however, can still be sued.

Qualified Privilege--The courts have also recognized the doctrine of qualified, partial, or conditional privilege. A news medium may publish with impunity a fair and impartial report of judicial, quasijudicial, legislative, executive, or other public and official proceedings. Reports related to official documents such as formal complaints, interrogations, affidavits, depositions, and judicial opinions are likewise protected. Fairness and impartiality is measured in terms of accuracy, good faith, and the absence of malice.

Stice v. Beacon Newspaper Corporation, Inc.
340 P. 2d 396 (1959)

In Stice v. Beacon Newspaper Corporation, the court ruled that newspapers have a qualified privilege to publish matters connected with inquiries regarding the commission of crime. During January and February, 1957, the Wichita Beacon had printed stories concerning charges of corruption against a judge. Articles based largely on police statements named the judge as a leader of a gang of burglars. The judge sued for libel, seeking $1 million in damages.

The Kansas Supreme Court noted that the articles to which Stice objected were news stories based upon interviews with police officers and reports of the police department concerning the operation of a burglary ring. Whether Stice was involved in the crime was immaterial. Even though the articles concerned Stice's behavior, they were based upon information obtained from the police department and other investigative agencies that had a legitimate concern with the investigations. In fact, excerpts from the specific statements contained in the Beacon articles were directly attributed to members of law enforcement agencies--for instance, "police say, " "detective said, " "Briggs [a detective] said, " "police investigation had revealed, " "implicated by police investigations, " "detectives disclosed, " "investigations are continuing, " "according to the police evidence, " and "under investigation by law enforcement officials. " Noting the accuracy of the reports and the absence of malice, the court held for the newspaper. The publications were qualifiedly privileged.

Fair Comment--Emerging from the theory of defense of privilege is a complementary defense--fair comment. Public officials and figures, and private persons involved in matters of public interest, cannot recover for libel unless they can prove actual malice on the part of the publisher. In brief, reporters, critics, and observers may fairly comment on people who, or institutions that, offer their work for public approval or public interest.

Oswalt v. State-Record Company 158 S. E. 2d 204 (1967)

This principle was applied in Oswalt v. State-Record Company. A South Carolina newspaper had criticized police officer David Oswalt, who pursued a car at high speed. The fleeing driver crashed broadside into another car, killing the two young occupants. The State-Record printed an editorial that claimed that there was "no rime or reason, sense or justification" for police to engage in racing with offenders on public highways to the danger of citizens' lives. The editorial concluded by calling for local, county, and state officials to seek out and hire qualified men to be law enforcement officers. Oswalt brought suit. He was awarded $5,000 in actual damages by the lower court, but the case was reversed on appeal.

The Supreme Court of South Carolina held that without a showing of malice, fair and honest comment is indeed privileged. According to the court, a citizen or newspaper may criticize acts, fitness, and qualifications of a public official without being liable for damages so long as the criticism is fair and honest, and made without malice. In a sense, fair comment is a variation of qualified privilege. Yet, in practice, its scope is broader. Both of these complete defenses undoubtedly give wide protection to newspapers.

Retraction and Apology--In addition to the complete defenses available to defendants in a libel action, there are also partial defenses. Though no one of these can exonerate the defendant fully, each provides some degree of mitigation that lowers the amount of damages obtainable by the plaintiff.

A full and prompt apology following publication of a libel will usually serve to mitigate the amount of damages awarded. The retraction must be made without reservation and without an attempt to justify the libel. Such a good faith effort on behalf of the publisher indicates that publication was not made with malice. Many states have retraction statutes that limit punitive and sometimes compensatory damages when a retraction is requested and published. Yet, retraction can never be a complete defense. Many people who saw the original story may not see the retraction. There is no guarantee that the retraction, given the same prominence in space or time as the original publication, will somehow defeat the harm already suffered. Nonetheless, retraction and apology can usually save money for a publisher guilty of libel.

Brush-Moore Newspapers, Inc. v. Pollitt
151 A. 2d 530 (1959)

The Salisbury (Maryland) Times carried an article on November 14, 1956, reporting on an audit of county offices. It erroneously reported that Sheriff Jesse Pollitt kept "incomplete" records for booking prisoners, when it should have said "complete. " The effect was to charge Pollitt with breaking the law. Publication had scarcely started when the error was spotted. The press was stopped and the article corrected. The circulation manager succeeded in finding most of the incorrect papers. A correction was printed on the following day. Nonetheless, Pollitt sued and the court held that he had been libeled because the keeping of incomplete records by a sheriff was a crime. The court ruled that the libel had been published since not all of the copies had been retrieved. The jury awarded the sheriff $12,000. The newspaper appealed.

When the case reached the Maryland Court of Appeals, the newspaper fared much better. The court agreed that the sheriff had been defamed and that the libel had been published, but it argued that the newspaper's action in stopping the press and trying to retrieve the copies containing the error tended to mitigate damages. A new trial was ordered but the two parties settled out of court for approximately $7,500. The Times might have even done better in a new trial.

Right of Reply--The second partial defense, the right of reply, extends to legitimate spokespeople for one who has been defamed--such as someone in public relations, an attorney, the secretary of an organization, or a family member. A victim of slander or libel may her-or himself respond with a defamatory reply provided that 1) the reply is in direct response to a defamatory attack, and 2) the reply is related to the charges and does not exceed the scope of the original defamation. In addition, a newspaper has the right to transmit libelous remarks not only when it supports a person replying to an attack, but also when it is in a neutral position of news-gatherer.

Dickins v. International Brotherhood of Teamsters
171 F. 2d 21 (1948)

The United States Court of Appeals for the District of Columbia recognized the right of reply in 1948. In September, 1944, two naval officers went to a dance at the Statler Hotel in Washington. In another part of the hotel, a Teamster Union meeting was scheduled to hear an address by President Franklin Delano Roosevelt. One of the officers, Lietenant Randolph Dickins, Jr., and members of the Union got into an argument in the corridor. Dickins claimed that he was slugged but the Teamsters replied that he was drunk. A week later, Dickins issued a statement to the press, which subsequently received wide publicity. Dan Tobin, the Teamster president, soon published the Union's side in the International Teamster. Dickins sued for libel. The Union argued that it had a conditional privilege to reply to the earlier attacks. The jurors agreed and ruled for the Teamsters. Dickins appealed but the court of appeals rejected his claim, explaining:

> When the author of a libel writes under the compulsion of a legal or moral duty, or for the protection of his own rights or interest, that which he writes is a privileged communication, unless the writer be actuated by malice. The appellant testified that, before the publication of which he here complains, he himself released to the press his own charges that members of the union assaulted him and his companion. His act in so doing cast upon the union the moral duty and consequently conferred upon it the legal right to publish a reply which, even if it were false, was privileged unless the plaintiff proved the defendant knew it to be false or otherwise proved actual malice in the publication.

The opinion, in addition to establishing the right of reply as a judicial principle, laid the foundation for the future

definition of "actual malice." Contained within the opinion are
the prototypes of "reckless disregard for the truth" and
"knowledge of falsity"--two elements that must be established
before actual malice is presumed.

Settlement Out of Court--A third way a defendant may
reduce the amount of damages obtainable by an injured party
is to settle out of court. Even though the defendant does not
avail her- or himself of the formal judicial machinery, the
advantages to out of court settlement are many. Obviously,
court costs are eliminated. Moreover, harmful publicity is
avoided and the matter is resolved quickly and painlessly.
And, the amount of monetary damages sought by the plaintiff
can be significantly reduced through negotiation. A settlement necessarily entails a written or verbal agreement between the parties, in the presence of a witness, indicating
satisfaction of the injured party. The defendant usually
agrees to publish an apology or allows the plaintiff an opportunity to reply. A successful monetary settlement is beneficial to both parties. The plaintiff recovers at least a portion of the damages that could have been collected in court.
The defendant is able, however, to avoid paying a significant
percentage of damages originally sought, and does not have
to provide court costs.

November v. Time Inc. 13 N. Y. 2d 175 (1963)
Dempsey v. Time Inc. 43 Misc. 2d 754 (1964)

Instead of facing certain defeat in two libel cases in
the 1960s, Time agreed to settle out of court. In one case
involving the February 20, 1961, issue of Sports Illustrated,
attorney Julius November was accused of deliberately giving
erroneous advice to Floyd Patterson's manager, Cus D'Amato.
The article implied that November intended to cause Patterson
to fire D'Amato and replace him with November. While the
case was being argued in the courts, Time decided not to
risk a trial and settled out of court.

Another case involved the January 13, 1964, cover
story in Sports Illustrated, which claimed "Dempsey's Gloves
Were Loaded." The story accused Jack Dempsey of using
"loaded" gloves in his 1919 title fight with Jess Willard. Relying on Jack "Doc" Kearns, a source of questionable veracity, Sports Illustrated went ahead and published the story.
The article also indicated Dempsey did not know about the
gloves. Claiming the article was not libelous, Time was

rebuffed by the court, which noted "reckless disregard for truth" on the part of the magazine. Time settled for an undisclosed sum, supposedly equal to the cost it would have incurred if it had rejected the first cover and printed a new one. Sports Illustrated also printed Dempsey's denial that the gloves were loaded. As a result, Time undoubtedly saved face and finances.

Bad Reputation of Plaintiff--A fourth partial defense is proof of previous bad reputation of the plaintiff. A clear and unambiguous showing that the plaintiff's reputation is so bad that a fresh libel cannot harm it will mitigate damages.

Nichols v. Philadelphia Tribune Company, Inc.
22 F. R. D. 89 (1958)

In Nichols v. Philadelphia Tribune, the U. S. District Court argued that on the issue of general damages, the reputation of the plainitff is a definite issue and the defendant may show the plaintiff's bad reputation in order to mitigate such damages. The court stressed that the relationship of the demonstrably bad reputation and the libel must be close. The defendant cannot, for example, establish the bad reputation of a plaintiff by showing misconduct at a time and place far removed from the setting of the original injury. Though the defense of bad reputation may in certain cases mitigate damages, it cannot fully exonerate the defendant.

Use of Reliable Source--A fifth partial defense, recognized by some courts, is reliance on a usually trustworthy source. When a publisher can show that a story was accurately reprinted from a major news source such as AP or UPI, the court may be influenced to reduce damages. Yet, it is clear that such communication is not privileged.

Wood v. Constitution Publishing Company 194 S. E. 760 (1937)

On August 15, 1934, the Atlanta Constitution published an article that mentioned that Mr. Otis Wood "and his wife" were arrested in Mississippi and charged with violating the tariff act by having in their possession alcohol upon which no tax had been paid. Mrs. Colline Wood brought suit for libel against the Constitution Publishing Company, claiming that the article was a false and malicious defamation that injured her reputation and exposed her to public hatred, contempt, and ridicule. She also contended that the article contained false statements because she was not in Mississippi at the time stated, she had no connection whatever with the incidents stated in the article, she was not arrested at any time, she was not transporting grain alcohol from New Orleans to Atlanta, and she was not arraigned or charged with the violation of the Tariff Act. In fact, at the time of the alleged crime, Mrs. Wood was separated from her husband because he was involved in the bootlegging business. The woman arrested with Wood was not Mrs. Wood. Wood did, however, refer to her as his wife before law enforcement officials, who, in turn, reported this information to newspaper reporters. Mrs. Wood sought $50,000 in damages.

The Constitution Publishing Company in effect admitted that it published the article, but claimed that it received the news story from the Associated Press, a reliable and trustworthy news association. The paper also claimed that it was impossible to check with absolute certainty articles received from AP. The paper argued that any error in the article was the error of AP and not the error of the paper. Publication, therefore, was privileged and not malicious; the paper was not liable for damages. In court, the jury rendered a verdict for the paper. Mrs. Wood appealed.

The Georgia Court of Appeals ruled that the law did not acknowledge as privileged "the repitition of an untruthful and libelous statement on the ground that it was communicated to the person making the statement by an authority having a reputation for truth and accuracy." The court noted, however, that evidence as to the character of the Associated Press as being a reliable and trustworthy organization tended to show the lack of malice on the part of the defendant newspaper. Yet, in light of errors on the part of the lower court, the court of appeals ordered a new trial for Mrs. Wood.

A year later, in Szalay v. New York American, a case involving allegations of "marital misconduct" on the part of a physician's wife, an appellate court ruled that no punitive damages could be awarded if the jury believed that the "defendant based its publication on a communication from a reliable news service and published the same in good faith in the ordinary course of business believing it to be true." The court noted that the defense of reliable source does not apply to compensatory damages. Overall, the courts maintain that there is no substitute for scrupulous reporting and thorough follow-up investigation. Using stories from a generally trustworthy wire service may, in some cases, mitigate

or even eliminate punitive damages--but it has no effect on
special or compensatory damages. The courts, while sympathetic to the defendant's claim, must grant judicial relief
to an injured party.

Provocation--A final partial defense available to a
defendant involves the demonstration of provocation on the
part of the plaintiff. Statements uttered in the heat and passion of the moment or provoked by actions of the plaintiff
may aid in this defense.

Farrell v. Kramer 193 A. 2d 560 (1963)

In 1953, registered nurse Bernadette Farrell joined
the staff of the Cary Memorial Hospital in Caribou, Maine,
and eventually became the night supervisor of nurses. In
April, 1959, Harry Kramer, a physician and surgeon, performed an operation upon a patient at the hospital. Farrell
criticized the postoperative treatment given to the patient and
lodged a series of complaints with hospital officials. In effect, these complaints charged Kramer with neglect of the
patient. The complaints touched off a personal feud between
Farrell and Kramer that continued for more than a year.
In July, 1959, Farrell was dismissed from her employment
at the hospital, but the following August she was rehired
upon the condition that she would not discuss hospital business outside of the hospital. When Kramer learned that
Farrell had returned to staff duty, he immediately called a
hospital administrator and said, "I wanted to ask you if you
would stoop so low as to hire that creep, that malignant son
of a bitch, back to work for you in the hospital." He added
that "she was unfit for the care of patients" and that "he
could prove ... and intended to make an issue of it." This
conversation was reported at the next meeting of the hospital
directors. When Farrell learned of the statements, she
initiated a libel action. At trial, the jury awarded Farrell
$17, 500. Kramer appealed.

The Supreme Judicial Court of Maine decided that the
damages awarded in this case were grossly excessive. The
court noted that Farrell began the feud between the parties
by launching an attack upon Kramer's professional compe-
tence. A nurse should know that criticism of this type will
almost certainly induce irritation, annoyance, and anger on
the part of a medical practitioner. This attack was followed
by a direct complaint that forced Kramer to defend himself

before a grievance committee of the medical association, where the complaint was dismissed. The court found it no surprise that Kramer felt tormented and persecuted by Farrell. The court concluded:

> Although the slander is not thereby excused, such provocation will substantially diminish both the public interest in the punishment of the defendant and the plaintiff's right to have severe punishment inflicted. Under these circumstances a verdict of $17,500 is patently and grossly excessive.

The court was satisfied that an award of $5,000 would fully compensate Farrell for any injuries attributable to these defamatory remarks and would afford an adequate deterrent to the defendant.

The courts, recognizing the need for flexibility, have attempted to weigh each case on its own merits. Partial defenses, though non-uniform in their application and questionable in their effect, are undoubtedly valuable to the defendant's overall case. Owing to each case's unique nature, a combination of complete and partial defenses is usually required. Though broad guidelines are occasionally provided by statute, it is the business of the courts and juries to decide the extent of harm caused by a statement. They must weigh the conflicting claims of public versus private interests.

LIBEL DOCTRINES

During the past half-century, the courts have formulated several doctrines relating to the law of libel. While most court cases deal with the damaging effect of libel on individuals, the courts have recognized that corporations can also be damaged by unfair and malicious statements.

Corporate Libel

Each company has an integrity--a reputation to protect. A case that formally acknowledged the rights of a corporation to sue for libel was heard in 1952.

Neiman-Marcus Company v. Lait 107 F. Supp. 96 (1952)

In this case, Neiman-Marcus Company brought suit

against the authors and publishers of a book on the ground
that statements made about company-employed models and
sales personnel were libelous. The publication in question
contained the following paragraphs:

> He (Stanley Marcus, president of Neiman-Mar-
> cus Company) may not know that some Neiman mod-
> els are call girls--the top babes in town. The guy
> who escorts one feels in the same league with the
> playboys who took out Ziegfeld's glorified. Price,
> a hundred bucks a night.
> The sales girls are good, too--pretty, and of-
> ten much cheaper--twenty bucks on the average.
> They're more fun, too, not as snooty as the models.
> We got this confidential, from a Dallas wolf....
> Neiman's was a women's specialty shop until
> the old biddies who patronized it decided their hus-
> bands should get class, too. So Neiman's put in
> a men's store. Well, you should see what happen-
> ed. You wonder how all the faggots got to the
> wild and wooly. You thought those with talent ended
> up in New York and Hollywood and the plodders got
> government jobs in Washington. Then you learn the
> nucleus of the Dallas fairy colony is composed of
> many Neiman dress and millinery designers, im-
> ported from New York and Paris, who sent for
> their boy friends when the men's store expanded.
> Now most of the sales staff are fairies, too.
> Houston is faced with a serious homosexual
> problem. It is not as evident as Dallas' because
> there are no expensive imported faggots in town
> like those in the Neiman-Marcus set.

The corporation sought $2 million in compensatory and puni-
tive damages.

When the case reached the district court, the justices
determined that while a corporation has no reputation in a
personal sense, it does have prestige and position, which are
capable of being damaged by aspersive language. Furthermore, a corporation could be defamed by words directed at
its employees if they tend to discredit the method by which
its business was conducted. It was possible that a corporation could be "damaged in a business way by a publication
that it employs seriously undesirable personnel."

Cosgrove Studio and Camera Shop, Inc. v. Pane
182 A. 2d 751 (1962)

The concept of corporate libel was also affirmed a decade after Neiman-Marcus. Cosgrove Studio and Camera Shop advertised in two community newspapers that it would offer a free roll of film for every roll brought to it for developing and printing. The next day its business competitor, Cal R. Pane, placed an advertisement in one of the same newspapers. It read in part:

USE COMMON SENSE * * *
You Get Nothing for Nothing!
WE WILL NOT

1. Inflate the prices of your developing to give you a new roll free!
2. Print the blurred negatives to inflate the price of your snapshots!

Cosgrove initiated a suit for libel, alleging that Pane's advertisement suggested that Cosgrove was dishonest in business practices. The trial court said that Pane's advertisement was not libelous in itself and found for Pane. Cosgrove appealed.

The appeals court reversed the judgment, saying that Cosgrove did indeed have a cause for action. The words, it was argued, were libelous on their face. Any language that "unequivocally, maliciously, and falsely imputes to an individual or corporation want of integrity in the conduct of his or its business is actionable." In arriving at this decision, the court made a point that has been important in many subsequent cases--identification of the defamed individual or corporation need not be by name. In this case, the fact that Cosgrove was not specifically named in the advertisement was not controlling. According to the court, a party need not be specifically named if pointed to by description or circumstances tending to identify him.

Group Libel

Another major doctrine that has been applied by the courts in libel cases was enunciated in the 1917 case of Crane v. State.

Crane v. State 166 P. 1110 (1917)

In 1915, a book was circulated throughout Canadian County, Oklahoma, that was entitled Barbarous Catholicism and Moral Theology of St. Liquori, by Professor Roy Crane. In its introduction, the book claimed to reveal truths about "the murderous, treasonable, dago philosophy called Catholicism." In Chapter One, the author cited what he alleged to be the oath of the Fourth Degree Knights of Columbus--an oath that Crane claimed pledges in part to extirpate from the face of the earth any heretics, protestants, and liberals. Specifically, the oath cited by Crane pledged that: "I will spare neither age, sex or condition, and that I will hand, burn, waste, boil, flay, strangle and bury alive" these undesirable elements. A trial court convicted Crane of libel.

An Oklahoma appeals court noted that all people have the right to associate with any religious group and no person has the right to interfere with or publish false statements against the individual or the organization. The court acknowledged that the oath purported to be that of the Knights of Columbus was erroneous in total. The claim that members of an honorable organization subscribe to such an oath is not tolerable and is not permitted by law. The court said that in order to find a party guilty of circulating libelous material, it is not necessary that such matter name the individuals or any one of them composing the class against whom the material is libelous. The court concluded that "the law of libel forbids the writing, publication, or circulation of libelous matter against a class as much so as against individuals. "

The doctrine of group libel was further clarified in the 1925 case of People v. Spielman. In this case, Arthur Lorenz and Sidney Spielman were convicted of libel because of statements they wrote and published about the American Legion--"this instrument bought with British money to suppress the truth, to gag freedom of conscience, to beat down every free expression of opinion, to betray organized American labor.... " At trial, the jury returned a verdict of guilty and sentenced the defendants to six months' imprisonment in the house of correction and a fine of $1 and costs. On appeal, Illinois Supreme Court upheld the conviction, noting:

> A libel upon a class or group has as great a tendency to provoke a breach of the peace or to disturb society as has a libel on an individual, and such a libel is punishable, even though its application to individual members of the class or group cannot be proved.

Beauharnais v. Illinois 343 U. S. 250 (1952)

The concept that not only individuals but groups or classes of people could be libeled was applied in a 1952 case that was decided by the U. S. Supreme Court.   Joseph Beauharnais was president of the White Circle League, a racist "neighborhood improvement" group.   At a meeting on January 6, 1950, he passed out bundles of lithographs along with other literature to volunteers who distributed the materials on the next day in downtown Chicago.   The leaflets called on the Mayor and City Council "to halt the further enforcement, harassment and invasion of white people, their property, neighborhoods and persons, by the Negro.... "   Included was a call for "one million self-respecting white people" in Chicago to unite.   The leaflets warned:

> If persuasion and the need to prevent the white race from becoming mongrelized by the negro will not unite us, then the aggression ... rapes, robberies, knives, guns and marijuana of the negro, surely will.

The leaflets also included an application for membership in the White Circle League.   Beauharnais was convicted of violating an Illinois law by exhibiting in public places publications that portray depravity, criminality, unchastity, or lack of virtue of black citizens and which subjected the Negro race to contempt, derision, or obloquy.   Beauharnais appealed.

The U. S. Supreme Court supported (5-4) the Illinois code.   The Court examined the issue historically, noting that Illinois had been the scene of exacerbated tension between races, which had often flared into violence and destruction.   In light of this history, it seemed clear that the Illinois legislature acted within reason in making an effort "to curb false or malicious defamation of racial and religious groups, made in public places and by means calculated to have a powerful emotional impact on those to whom it was presented. "   For the minority, Justices Hugo Black and William Douglas opposed the law as a form of censorship.   They maintained that "this act sets up a system of state censorship which is at war with the kind of free government envisioned by those who forced adoption of our Bill of Rights. "   The majority of the Court upheld Beauharnais's conviction on the grounds of group libel.   Though the doctrine of group libel has not been invoked frequently, it stands as a powerful reminder to publishers that groups may well suffer the same libel long associated with individuals.

"Actual Malice" Defined

During the past two decades, the U. S. Supreme Court has refined and reformulated the law of libel by fashioning several doctrines that make it difficult for a public official or celebrity to win a libel suit. The public has the right to be informed about the activities of its elected officials. The Court has argued that information about topics of immediate public interest cannot be suppressed, regardless of the effect on the "involuntary newsmaker."

New York Times Company v. Sullivan 376 U. S. 255 (1964)

One of the most notable cases that weighed the competing claims of the public's right to know and the individual's right to a good reputation was New York Times v. Sullivan. In this case, the doctrine of "actual malice" was first enunciated. On March 29, 1960, the Times published an advertisement entitled "Heed Their Rising Voices." The ad began by stating:

> As the world knows by now, thousands of Southern Negro students are engaged in widespread nonviolent demonstrations in positive affirmation of the right to live in human dignity as guaranteed by the U. S. Constitution and the Bill of Rights.

It went on to charge that in their efforts to uphold these guarantees, the students "are being met by an unprecedented wave of terror by those who would deny and negate that document which the whole world looks upon as setting the pattern for modern freedom...." The article illustrated the "wave of terror" by describing certain events. It concluded with an appeal for funds to aid the student movement, the struggle for the right-to-vote, and the legal defense of Dr. Martin Luther King, Jr., who at the time was charged with perjury in Montgomery, Alabama. The advertisement was signed by some one hundred people, many widely known for their activities in public affairs, religion, labor, and the performing arts.

L. B. Sullivan, Commissioner of Public Affairs for Montgomery, had the duties of supervising the Police Department, Fire Department, Department of Cemetery, and Department of Scales. He brought suit against four black ministers and the New York Times. The basis of the suit rested on the third and sixth paragraphs of the ten-paragraph advertisement. The relevant paragraphs read:

In Montgomery, Alabama, after students sang
"My Country, Tis of Thee" on the State Capitol
steps, their leaders were expelled from school,
and truckloads of police armed with shotguns and
tear-gas ringed the Alabama State College Campus.
When the entire student body protested to state
authorities by refusing to re-register, their dining
hall was padlocked in an attempt to starve them
into submission....

Again and again the Southern violators have
answered Dr. King's peaceful protests with intimidation and violence. They have bombed his home
almost killing his wife and child. They have as-
saulted his person. They have arrested him seven
times--for "speeding, " "loitering" and similar "of-
fenses. " And now they have charged him with
"perjury"--a felony under which they would impri-
son him for ten years. Obviously, their real purpose is to remove him physically as the leader to
whom the students and millions of others--look for
guidance and support, and thereby to intimidate all
leaders who may rise in the South.... The defense of Martin Luther King, spiritual leader of
the student sit-in movement, clearly, therefore, is
an integral part of the total struggle for freedom
in the South.

Although neither of these paragraphs mentioned Sullivan by
name, he contended that the word "police" referred to him.
He also claimed that the word "they" referred to the police
and that "they" who did the arresting would be associated
with "they" who committed the other acts. Sullivan felt that
the paragraph would be read as accusing the Montgomery police of answering Dr. King's protests with "intimidation and
violence, " bombing his home, assaulting him, and charging
him with perjury.

Some of the statements that occur in the two paragraphs were not accurate. For example, even though black
students did stage a protest on the State Capitol steps, they
sang the National Anthem and not "My Country, Tis of Thee. "
Even though nine students were expelled by the State Board
of Education, it was not for leading the protest at the Capitol, but for demanding service at the Montgomery County
Courthouse lunch counter. Not the entire student body, but
most of it, protested the expulsion--not by refusing to register, as the article claimed, but by boycotting classes on a

single day; virtually all the students did register for the next
semester. The campus dining room had not been padlocked
on any occasion and the only students barred from eating
there were a few who had not obtained a meal ticket. Even
though the police were deployed near the campus in large
numbers on three occasions, they never did "ring" the campus. Dr. King had been arrested only four times, not seven.
Although Dr. King's home had been bombed twice when his
wife and child were there, the police were not only acquitted of the bombings, but had made every effort to apprehend
the guilty parties. Although King had been arrested four
times, three of the arrests took place before Sullivan became
Commissioner.

Alabama law prohibits a public officer from recovering
punitive damages in a libel suit brought on account of a publication concerning his official conduct unless he first makes
a written demand for a public retraction and the party re-
fuses to comply. Sullivan requested the Times to publish
such a retraction but the company responded, "We ... are
somewhat puzzled as to how you think the statements in any
way reflect on you, " and "You might, if you desire, let us
know in what respect you claim that the statements in the
advertisement reflect on you. " Sullivan brought suit a few
days later without answering the letter. Sullivan also demanded that several of the persons listed on the advertisement retract their statements, but none consented. Some
responded that they had not authorized the use of their names
in the first place. The Times subsequently published a retraction of the advertisement upon the demand of Governor
John Patterson, who asserted that the publication charged
him with "grave misconduct and ... improper actions and
omissions as Governor of Alabama and Ex-Officio Chairman
of the State Board of Education of Alabama. " The trial judge
submitted the case to the jury with instructions that the statements were libelous per se and were not privileged. Alabama law held a publication libelous per se if the words
"tend to injure a person ... in his reputation" or to "bring
(him) into public contempt. " The trial court in this case
determined that a violation occurred if the words were such
as to "injure him in his public office, or impute misconduct
to him in his office, or want of official integrity, or want
of fidelity to a public trust. " The jury must find that the
words were published "of and concerning" the plaintiff and
that he was a public official. His position in the governmental hierarchy constituted sufficient evidence to support a
finding that his reputation had been affected by statements

that reflect upon the agency of which he was in charge.   Once libel per se had been established, the defendant had no defense regarding stated facts unless he could persuade the jury that they were true.   His privilege of "fair comment" for expressions of opinion depended on the truth of the facts upon which the comment was based.   Unless he could prove the truth of the statement, general damages were presumed and could be awarded without proof of monetary injury.   Apparently, good motives and belief in truth did not negate an inference of malice.   The Times and the four ministers were held liable; the jury awarded Sullivan damages of $500,000-- the full amount claimed.   The Supreme Court of Alabama affirmed the decision.   The Times took the case to the U.S. Supreme Court.

The Court disagreed unanimously.   It held that the constitutional guarantees of free speech and press prohibited a public official from recovering damages for a defamatory falsehood relating to his official conduct unless he proved that the statement was made with "actual malice"--that is, with knowledge that it was false or made with "reckless disregard" of the truth.   In this case, the Court did not find "actual malice."   First, there was no evidence that the individuals charged, even if they authorized the use of their names, were aware of any erroneous statements or were reckless in that regard.   Second, whether the statements were "substantially correct" was not relevant in deciding whether the Times had acted in good faith.   Third, in response to Sullivan's request for retraction, the Times letter reflected reasonable doubt that the advertisement referred to Sullivan at all.   It was not a final refusal since it asked for an explanation from Sullivan, a request that Sullivan chose to ignore.   Finally, negligence in failing to discover misstatements is constitutionally insufficient to show the recklessness that is required for a finding of actual malice.   In New York Times, the Court overturned the finding of the lower courts.

Garrison v. State of Louisiana 379 U.S. 64 (1964)

In a case heard that same year, the Court further developed its "actual malice" doctrine and made it clear that the Times standard was more than a temporary phenomenon. A dispute arose between James Garrison, the District Attorney of Orleans Parish, Louisiana, and eight justices of the Criminal District Court.   The disagreement was over disbursements from the Fines and Fees Fund that was used to defray expenses of the District Attorney's office. Disbursements could be made only on motion of the District Attorney and approval by a judge of the Criminal District Court. After Garrison took office, one of the incumbent judges refused to approve a disbursement for Garrison's office. When the judge went on vacation prior to his retirement, Garrison obtained the approval of another judge, allegedly by falsely claiming that the first judge had withdrawn his objection. Shortly thereafter, the eight judges adopted a rule that no further disbursements for the District Attorney's office would be approved except with the concurrence of five of the eight judges. Later that month, the judges denied Garrison the use of the fund for conducting investigations of commercial vice in the Bourbon and Canal Street districts and expressed doubt as to the legality of such a use of the fund under the Louisiana Constitution. A few days later, the now-retired judge issued a public statement criticizing Garrison's conduct as District Attorney. The next day, Garrison held his own press conference at which he harshly criticized the conduct of the eight judges. Specifically, Garrison attributed the large backlog of criminal cases to the inefficiency, laziness, and excessive vacations of the judges, and that, by refusing to authorize disbursements to cover the expenses of undercover investigations of vice in New Orleans, the judges had hampered his efforts to enforce the vice laws. In impugning their motives, Garrison claimed:

> The judges have now made it eloquently clear where their sympathies lie in regard to aggressive vice investigations by refusing to authorize use of the DA's funds to pay for the cost of closing down the Canal Street clip joints.... This raises interesting questions about the racketeer influences on our eight vacation-minded judges.

As a result of this press conference, the judges brought suit and Garrison was tried without a jury before a judge from another parish. He was subsequently convicted of criminal defamation under the Louisiana Criminal Defamation Statute. He appealed.

The U. S. Supreme Court unanimously reversed, referring to the *Times* doctrine:

> The *New York Times* standard forbids the punishment of false statements, unless made with knowledge of their falsity or in reckless disregard of

whether they are true or false. But the Louisiana
statute punishes false statements without regard to
that test if made with ill-will; even if ill-will is
not established, a false statement concerning public officials can be punished if not made in the
reasonable belief of its truth.... The reasonable-
belief standard applied by the trial judge is not the
same as the reckless-disregard-of-truth standard.

The Court attempted to define more precisely the Louisiana
"reasonable belief" standard and clarify its own earlier interpretation of "reckless disregard." The Court noted that
according to the trial court's opinion,

... a reasonable belief is one which an ordinary
prudent man might be able to assign a just and
fair reason for; the suggestion is that under this
test the immunity from criminal responsibility in
the absence of ill-will disappears on proof that the
exercise of ordinary care would have revealed that
the statement was false.

However, the Court noted that the test it laid down in New
York Times was "not keyed to ordinary care; defeasance of
the privilege is conditioned, not on mere negligence, but on
reckless disregard for the truth." Garrison in effect rejected the concept of "reasonable belief" and made it even more
difficult for public officials (in this case judges) to win libel
suits. The plaintiff's burden of proof was thereby significantly increased.

"Actual Malice" Refined

During the past decade, the courts have clarified the
meaning of actual malice. In the process of refining this
standard, several related doctrines have emerged.

Reckless Disregard--In a series of cases during the
late 1960s, the Court attempted to pinpoint the precise limits
of "reckless disregard."

Curtis Publishing Company v. Butts
Associated Press v. Walker 388 U.S. 130 (1967)

In 1967, two companion cases not only established the

presently-held interpretation of "reckless disregard, " but also introduced the concept of "hot news. " An article entitled "The Story of a College Football Fix" was published in the March 23, 1963, issue of the Saturday Evening Post. The article reported a telephone conversation between Wally Butts, Athletic Director of the University of Georgia, and Paul "Bear" Bryant, head football coach at the University of Alabama, in which they allegedly conspired to "fix" a football game between the two schools. Due to an electronic quirk, George Burnett, an insurance salesman of questionable character, had cut into the conversation when he picked up a telephone receiver at a pay station. Burnett took notes of the conversation, some of which appeared in the article. The Post story compared this "fix" to the Chicago "Black Sox" scandal of 1919, and went on to describe the frame, the presentation of Burnett's notes to Georgia head coach Johnny Griffith, and Butts's subsequent resignation. The article's conclusion made clear its expected impact:

> The chances are that Wally Butts will never help any football team again.... The investigation by university and Southeastern Conference officials is continuing; motion pictures of other games are being scrutinized; where it will end no one so far can say. But careers will be ruined, that is sure.

There was nothing subtle about the Post's charges against Butts.

Butts sued for $5 million in compensatory and $5 million in punitive damages. The Post tried to use truth as its defense, but the evidence contradicted its version of what had happened. Evidence showed that Burnett had indeed overheard a conversation between Butts and Bryant, but the content of the conversation was hotly disputed. Butts contended that the conversation had been general football talk and that Burnett had overheard nothing of any particular value to an opposing coach. Expert witnesses supported Butts's position after analyzing Burnett's notes and the films of the game itself. The jury awarded $60,000 in general damages and $3 million in punitive damages. Soon after the trial, the New York Times case was decided, and the Post sought a new trial. The trial judge rejected the motion, holding the Times case inapplicable because Butts was not a "public official" and there was ample evidence of "reckless disregard" of truth in the researching of the Post article.

On appeal, the U. S. Supreme Court argued that "the evidence showed that the Butts story was in no sense 'hot' news and the editors of the magazine recognized the need for a thorough investigation of the serious charges." Elementary precautions were, nonetheless, ignored. The Post knew that Burnett was on probation in connection with bad check charges but proceeded to publish his story without additional support. Burnett's notes were not even viewed by any of the magazine's personnel. John Carmichael, who was supposed to have been with Burnett when the phone call was overheard, was not interviewed. No attempt was made to screen the films of the game to see if Burnett's information was accurate. No effort was made to determine whether Alabama had changed its game-plan after the alleged divulgence of information. In short, the evidence supported a finding of "highly" unreasonable conduct constituting an extreme departure from the standards of investigation and reporting ordinarily adhered to be responsible publishers." The Court affirmed (5-4) the trial court's finding. The Curtis case defined reckless disregard for truth in terms more precise than in any case decided before.

The Walker case, heard on the same day, further developed the concept of hot news. General Edwin Walker was involved in the events surrounding the entry of James Meredith into the University of Mississippi, in September, 1962. An Associated Press report stated that Walker, who was present on the campus, had taken command of the violent crowd and had personally led a charge against federal marshals. It also reported that Walker encouraged rioters to use violence, and provided them with technical advice on how to avoid the harmful effects of tear gas. Walker was a private citizen at the time of the riot, but since his resignation from the army he had become a political activist. There was little evidence regarding the preparation of the news dispatch. Van Savell, the reporter, was present during the events he described and had communicated them almost immediately to the Associated Press Office in Atlanta. There was no evidence of personal prejudice or incompetency on the part of Savell or the AP. Walker sought to collect substantial damages in a chain suit against newspapers and broadcasting stations that had carried the AP reports. A Texas trial court awarded Walker $500,000 in general damages and $300,000 in exemplary damages. The trial judge, finding no actual malice to support the punitive damages, entered a final judgment of $500,000. The case went to the U. S. Supreme Court.

The Court said that Walker was most assuredly a public figure, for he had thrust his personality into the whirlpool of an important public controversy. Moreover, in contrast to the Butts article, the Walker dispatch was news that required immediate dissemination. The Associated Press received the information from a correspondent who was present at the scene of the events and who gave every indication of being trustworthy and competent. His account was internally consistent and seemed reasonable to anyone familiar with Walker's prior publicized statements on the controversy. The Court determined (9-0) that "considering the necessity for rapid dissemination, nothing in this series of events gives the slightest hint of a severe departure from accepted publishing standards." The Court concluded that Walker should not be entitled to damages from the Associated Press.

St. Amant v. Thompson 390 U.S. 727 (1968)

In a 1968 case, the Court admitted that the outer limits of "reckless disregard" had not yet been drawn. Such limits could only be determined on a case-by-case basis. The case itself involved a televised political libel. On June 27, 1962, Phil St. Amant, a candidate for public office, made a televised speech in Baton Rouge, Louisiana, in which he read a series of questions he had asked J. D. Albin, a member of a Teamsters Union local, and Albin's answers. The exchange concerned the allegedly illicit activities of E. G. Partin, the president of the local, and the relationship between Partin and St. Amant's political opponent. One of Albin's answers concerned his effort to prevent Partin from hiding union records. Albin referred to Herman A. Thompson, an East Baton Rouge Parish deputy sheriff:

> Now we know that this safe was gonna be moved that night, but imagine our predicament, knowing of Ed's connections with the Sheriff's office through Herman Thompson, who made recent visits to the Hall to see Ed. We also know of money that had passed hands between Ed and Herman Thompson.... We also know of his connections with State Trooper Lieutenant Joe Green. We know we couldn't get any help from there and we didn't know how far that he was involved in the Sheriff's office or the State Police office through that, and it was out of the jurisdiction of the City Police.

Thompson promptly brought suit for defamation, claiming that the publication had "imputed ... gross misconduct" and "inferred conduct of the most nefarious nature. " The Louisiana Supreme Court ruled that St. Amant had recklessly broadcast false information about Thompson, though not knowingly. The court pointed to St. Amant's reliance on Albin's affidavit even though the record was silent as to Albin's reputation for veracity. The court also noted that St. Amant failed to verify the facts. He gave no consideration to whether or not the statements defamed Thompson, and went ahead, heedless of the consequences. Most importantly, he mistakenly believed that he had no responsibility for the broadcast because he was merely quoting Albin's words.

The U. S. Supreme Court reversed (8-1) the decision.

> ... reckless conduct is not measured by whether a reasonably prudent man would have published, or would have investigated before publishing. There must be sufficient evidence to permit the conclusion that the defendant in fact entertained serious doubts as to the truth of his publication. Publishing with such doubts shows reckless disregard for truth or falsity and demonstrates actual malice.

The decision added, however, that a defendant may not count on a favorable verdict merely by testifying that he published with a belief that the statements were true.

> The finder of fact must determine whether the publication was indeed made in good faith. Professions of good faith will be unlikely to prove persuasive, for example, where a story is fabricated by the defendant, is the product of his imagination, or is based wholly on an unverified anonymous telephone call. Nor will they be likely to prevail when the publisher's allegations are so inherently improbable that only a reckless man would have put them in circulation. Likewise, recklessness may be found where there are obvious reasons to doubt the veracity of the informant or the accuracy of his reports.

In this case, the Supreme Court found no evidence that St. Amant was aware of the probable falsity of Albin's statement about Thompson. Albin had sworn to his statements and St. Amant had verified some of them. Thompson's evidence had failed to demonstrate "a low community assessment of Albin's trusthworthiness." The Court felt that the reasons cited by the Louisiana court fell far short of proving St. Amant's reckless disregard for the accuracy of the statements. Nothing referred to by the Louisiana courts indicated an awareness by St. Amant of the probable falsity of Albin's statements. Failure to investigate does not, in itself, establish bad faith. In effect, the Court gave St. Amant the benefit of the doubt. Negligence, though undesirable, does not constitute reckless disregard.

Goldwater v. Ginzburg 414 F. 2d 324 (1969)

A year later, the doctrine of "reckless disregard" was evoked in a federal case involving a public official. The district court ruled that the defendant had indeed acted in "reckless disregard of the truth" and agreed with Senator Barry Goldwater that the publication was motivated by actual malice. The suit by Goldwater was based upon the publication of the September-October, 1964, issue of Fact magazine, an issue entitled "The Unconscious of a Conservative: A Special Issue on the Mind of Barry Goldwater." The magazine had sought to put together a psycho-biography of the Arizona Senator so as to alert the American people of the potential dangers of his Presidency. A selected bibliography of sources was assembled but complimentary references to Goldwater were carefully screened out. On the basis of some preliminary research, Editor Ralph Ginzburg concluded that Goldwater was suffering from paranoia, and was, therefore, mentally ill. An early draft of the magazine article also suggested that Goldwater was suffering from "repressed homosexuality." The editor conducted what was purported to be a survey of psychiatrists of the United States. A sample of 12, 356 psychiatrists was drawn from a rented mailing list-- 2, 417 responded, and of these 1, 189 agreed with some aspect of Ginzburg's thesis. A letter written by Ginzburg was attached to the questionnaire. It stated in part:

> A recent survey by Medical Tribune showed that psychiatrists--in sharp contrast to all other MDs-- hold Goldwater in low esteem.... We would appreciate, first, your indicating whether you think Goldwater is stable enough to serve as President.... We would also appreciate any remarks you might care to make concerning Goldwater's general mental stability, insofar as you are able to draw inferences, his political viewpoints, and whatever

knowledge you may have of his personality and
background.   Does he seem prone to aggressive
behavior and destructiveness?   Does he seem callous
to the downtrodden and needy?   Can you offer any
explanation of his public temper-tantrums and his
occasional outbursts of profanity?   Finally, do you
think that his having had two nervous breakdowns
has any bearing on his fitness to govern this country?

At the trial, the poll was impugned by Burns Roper, appearing as an expert witness.   Returned questionnaires favorable
to Goldwater were ignored.   Many of those critical of Goldwater were anonymous.   Responses were edited or rewritten
to fit the magazine's editorial predispositions.   The published
article contained repeated references to Goldwater's supposed
mental illness, his "infantile fantasies of revenge and dreams
of total annihilation of his adversaries, " his "paralyzing, deep-
seated irrational fear, " and his "fantasy of a final conflagra-
tion" which Ginzburg compared with the "death-fantasy of
another paranoiac woven in Berchtesgarden and realized in
a Berlin Bunker. "   Ginzburg also claimed that many people
around Goldwater "think he needs a psychiatrist--probably not
because they realize how sick he is--but because of the daily
symptoms of hostility he manifests.... "   At trial, Ginzburg
was unable to identify a single source of his statement.   Nor
could he document in any medical sense his reports that Goldwater had suffered two nervous breakdowns.   The courts
awarded Goldwater $75, 000.   Ginzburg appealed.

    The circuit court saw many parallels between this evi-
dence tending to prove actual malice and the proof in Butts.
The Goldwater article did not contain "hot news. "   Ginzburg
was very much aware of the possible resulting harm.   The
seriousness of the charges called for a thorough investigation,
but the evidence revealed only the careless utilization of slip-
shod and sketchy investigative techniques.   The publisher per-
sisted in his polling project despite warnings by reputable
professional organizations that the techniques lacked validity.
Most importantly, there was evidence of a preconceived plan
to attack Goldwater, regardless of the facts.   This evidence,
together with the other facts brought out at trial, established
that Ginzburg not only knowingly published defamatory statements but also established with convincing clarity that he was
motivated by actual malice.   The U. S. Supreme Court denied
certiorari.   Though the Court did not directly affirm the specific
reasoning of the lower court, it did uphold the original conviction.

Indeed, there are limits beyond which publishers cannot transgress. Even public officials can expect some degree of protection from maliciously motivated defamation.

Time, Inc. v. Pape 401 U. S. 279 (1971)

In 1971, the Court dealt directly with the reportorial standards of a news magazine. The Court had to determine to what extent non-malicious, but harmful, statements could be permitted. The issue was whether the failure of Time magazine to use the word "alleged" constituted actual malice. In 1961, the magazine carried a report of the findings of the U. S. Commission on Civil Rights in which charges of brutality were made against the Chicago Police. At one point, the report claimed that thirteen police officers, led by Detective Frank Pape, broke through the doors of a family's apartment, woke the parents with flashlights, and forced them at gunpoint to stand naked in the center of the living room. The report claimed that Pape struck the father with a flashlight and called him "nigger" and "blackboy" while his six children stood by, watching. After police ransacked the apartment, the report continued, the man was taken to the police station, where he was neither advised of his rights nor permitted to call an attorney. He was subsequently released without criminal charges being filed against him. The allegations in the Commissioner's report had not been proven and the Time article failed to make clear it was reporting mere allegations. Pape sued. The case ultimately reached the U. S. Supreme Court.

The Court said (8-1) that the article, at worst, reflected an error in judgment. Media that maintain professional standards, the Court reasoned, should not be subject to financial liability for non-malicious errors in judgment. The Court felt that if freedom of expression was to have "the breathing space that they need to survive, misstatements of this kind must have the protection of the First and Fourteenth Amendments. " The Court stressed, however, that nothing in this decision rendered the word "alleged" a superfluity in published reports of information damaging to reputation. The decision in Pape was based only on the specific facts of that case.

From the discussion of Curtis, Walker, St. Amant, Goldwater, and Pape, it is apparent that the Court has tried to balance the relative public and private interests at stake in each case. Freedom of expression and the right of the public to be informed on issues of immediate vital concern have consistently held a preferred position. Individuals and groups have generally free reign to publish statements about public officials, figures, or issues as long as that publication is not made with a reckless disregard for the truth. No publication motivated by actual malice, however, is protected. To prove such malice, public officials and figures must establish more than mere negligence--they must demonstrate a knowing, uncaring, and malicious disregard on the part of the publisher.

Robust Debate--Consistent with its concern for protecting freedom of expression, the Court in a 1970 decision enunciated the doctrine of "robust debate."

Greenbelt Publishing Association v. Bresler 398 U.S. 6 (1970)

In the autumn of 1965, Charles S. Bresler, a prominent local real estate developer and member of the Maryland House of Delegates, was engaged in negotiations with the Greenbelt City Council to obtain certain zoning variances that would allow the construction of high-density housing on land that he owned. At the same time, the city was attempting to acquire another tract of land owned by Bresler for the construction of a new high school. Extensive litigation concerning compensation for the school site seemed imminent unless there would be an agreement on its price; the concurrent negotiations obviously provided both parties considerable bargaining leverage. These joint negotiations produced substantial local controversy and several stormy city council meetings were held at which numerous members of the community freely expressed their views. The meetings were reported at length in the news columns of the Greenbelt News Review. Two news articles in consecutive weekly editions of the paper, stated that at the public meetings some citizens had described Bresler's negotiating position as "blackmail." Bresler brought suit, seeking both compensatory and punitive damages. The primary thrust of his complaint was that the articles, individually, and along with other items published in the newspaper, imputed that he had committed blackmail. The case went to trial. The jury awarded Bresler $5,000 in compensatory damages and $12,500 in punitive damages. The Maryland Court of Appeals affirmed the judgment.

The U.S. Supreme Court reversed (8-0) the decision on the ground that the news stories were accurate accounts of the public debates. According to the Court, there was "no question that the public debates at the sessions of the city council regarding Bresler's negotiations with the city were a subject of substantial concern to all who lived in the community. " The debates themselves were heated; Bresler's opponents characterized his position as "blackmail. " The Court noted that by publishing the story the Greenbelt News Review was performing its wholly legitimate function as a community newspaper. Indeed, any editing of the full and accurate account of the debates would constitute distortion of an unacceptable kind. The newspaper's headlines made it clear to all readers that the paper was reporting the public debates on the pending land negotiations. Bresler's proposal was accurately and fully described. The Court concluded:

> It is simply impossible to believe that a reader who reached the word "blackmail" in either article would not have understood exactly what was meant: it was Bresler's public and wholly legal negotiating proposals that were being criticized. No reader could have thought that either the speakers at the meetings or the newspaper articles reporting their words were charging Bresler with the commission of a criminal offense. On the contrary, even the most careless reader must have perceived that the word was no more than rhetorical hyperbole, a vigorous epithet used by those who considered Bresler's negotiating position extremely unreasonable. Indeed, the record is completely devoid of evidence that anyone in the city of Greenbelt or anywhere else thought Bresler had been charged with a crime.

In brief, the Court made it clear that the societal interests in providing for "robust debate" and the discussion of subjects of substantial concern took precedence over an individual's interest in maintaining his good name.

Public Official--The actual malice doctrine received clarification in 1966, when the Court considered the matter of libelous statements made about public officials.

Rosenblatt v. Baer 383 U.S. 75 (1966)

Alfred Rosenblatt, a columnist for the Laconia (New Hampshire) Evening Citizen, frequently commented on political matters in his column. As an outspoken proponent for

change in operations at the Belkamp Recreation Area, Rosenblatt often sharply stated his views and indicated his disagreement with the actions taken by Frank Baer, Supervisor of the
Recreation Area, as well as those taken by other County Commissioners. In January, 1960, some six months after Baer
was discharged, Rosenblatt published the following:

> Been doing a little listening and checking at
> Belkamp Recreation Area and am thunderstruck by
> what am learning.
> This year, a year without snow till very late,
> a year with actually few very major changes in
> procedure; the difference in cash income simply
> fantastic, almost unbelievable.
> On any sort of comparative basis, the Area
> this year is doing literally hundreds of per cent
> BETTER than last year.
> When consider that last year was excellent
> snow year, that season started because of more
> snow, months earlier last year, one can only pon-
> der following question:
> What happened to all the money last year? and
> every other year? What magic has Dana Beane
> (Chairman of the new commission) and rest of the
> commission, and Mr. Warner (Baer's replacement
> as Supervisor) wrought to make such tremendous
> difference in net cash results?

Baer sued for libel on the ground that the column charged
mismanagement. A jury awarded him $31,500; Rosenblatt
appealed. The case reached the U.S. Supreme Court.

The Court noted that the column on its face contained
no clearly actionable statement. Indeed, the statements might
be interpreted as praise for the administration. No references were made to Baer. Persons familiar with the controversy might read it as complimenting the luck or skill of
the new management in attracting increased patronage. In
overturning the lower court decision, the Court gave meaning
(8-1) and comparative precision to the concept of "public
official." The Court noted that in the New York Times case,
they did not determine how far down into the lower ranks of
government employees the "public official" designation would
extend, nor did the Court specify categories of persons who
would or would not be included. In this case, the Court decided that it was clear that the public-official designation applied "at the very least to those among the hierarchy of government employees who have, or appear to the public to have,

substantial responsibility for or control over the conduct of governmental affairs. " Implied in the <u>Rosenblatt</u> decision was the idea that either Baer was not important enough as a public person to warrant large damages for injury to his reputation, or that he was important enough to be subject to the limitations of the <u>New York Times</u> doctrine. For the journalist the guideline is this: the lower the person in the official hierarchy--the greater the risk of libel.

<u>Monitor Patriot Company v. Roy 401 U. S. 265 (1971)</u>

The Court continued to apply the rigid <u>Times</u> standard of actual malice to cases involving public officials as plaintiffs. In two companion cases heard on February 24, 1971, the Court again emphasized that libel actions dealing with public figures must be accompanied by evidence of actual malice. In <u>Monitor Patriot Company v. Roy</u>, Alphonse Roy, a former New Hampshire Congressman who was running for the U. S. Senate, objected to a column written by Drew Pearson. The article, which appeared in the <u>Concord</u> (New Hampshire) <u>Monitor,</u> described Roy as a "former small-time bootlegger. " Roy lost his bid for the Senate in the Democratic primary. Since the alleged criminal conduct had occurred in the 1920s, Roy argued, and had involved the candidate's private life rather than his performance as a public servant, the newspaper was vulnerable to a possible libel judgment. A court jury agreed and awarded damages of $10, 000. The newspaper appealed.

The Supreme Court unanimously disagreed. According to the Court, the principal task of candidates in our political system consists of putting before the electorate every conceivable aspect of their public and private lives that they think might lead the voters to gain a favorable impression of them. Candidates, however, who vaunt their spotless records and sterling integrity before the electorate cannot convincingly cry "Foul!" when opponents or industrious reporters attempt to demonstrate the contrary. Subsequently, the Court ruled that a charge of criminal conduct, no matter how remote in time or place, is relevant to a candidate's or official's fitness for office for purposes of application of the actual malice doctrine. The judgment was reversed and the case remanded.

Ocala Star-Banner Company v. Damron 401 U. S. 295 (1971)

In the second case, a newspaper, the Ocala (Florida) Star-Banner, reported that the mayor of Crystal River, Leonard Damron, who was then a candidate for county tax assessor, had been charged in Federal Court with perjury in a civil rights case. It was, in fact, Damron's brother who had been accused of perjury. An editor who was unfamiliar with the background of the story had changed the first name in the story to the mayor's. Damron lost the election, which was held two weeks after the story appeared. At trial, the judge had instructed the jury that the New York Times rule did not apply since the error did not involve Damron's official conduct, that the story amounted to libel per se, and that the mayor could be awarded damages. The jury awarded Damron $22,000 in compensatory damages.

The U. S. Supreme Court unanimously reversed the decision. As the mayor of Crystal River, Leonard Damron was without question a "public official" within the meaning given the term in New York Times. Also, as a candidate for the office of county tax assessor, he fell within the Times rule. That rule clearly prohibits a public official from recovering damages for a defamatory falsehood relating to his official conduct unless he proved that the statement was made with "actual malice." It was clear that the Times rule had not been applied at the trial. The Court was unimpressed with Damron's claim that the Times rule applied only to "official conduct." Citing the Monitor decision, the Court reiterated that a charge of criminal conduct against an official or candidate, no matter how remote in time or place, was always "relevant to his fitness for office" for purposes of applying the Times rule. The case was remanded.

It is clear from the Rosenblatt, Monitor, and Ocala decisions that those who have, or appear to the public to have, significant responsibility for or control over the conduct of governmental affairs are not substantially protected from libelous statements made against them.

Private Citizen--The Court has recently attempted to clarify the law of libel as it concerns private citizens. One of these attempts occurred in 1971.

Rosenbloom v. Metromedia 403 U. S. 29 (1971)

George Rosenbloom was a distributor of nudist magazines in the Philadelphia metropolitan area. During fall, 1963, in response to citizen complaints, the Special Investigations Squad of the Philadelphia Police Department enforced sections of local obscenity laws. The police, under the command of Captain Ferguson, purchased magazines from more than twenty newsstands throughout the city. Based upon Ferguson's determination that the magazines were obscene, police arrested newsstand operators on charges of selling obscene material. While the police were making an arrest at a newsstand, Rosenbloom delivered some of his nudist magazines. He was immediately arrested. Three days later, the police obtained a warrant to search Rosenbloom's home and subsequently seized the inventory of books and magazines they found. Ferguson then telephoned a wire service, a local newspaper, and local radio station WIP to inform them of the raid on Rosenbloom's home and of his arrest. WIP's 6:00 p. m. broadcast on October 4, 1963, included the following item:

> The Special Investigations Squad raided the home of George Rosenbloom in the 1800 block of Vesta Street this afternoon. Police confiscated 1, 000 allegedly obscene books at Rosenbloom's home and arrested him on charges of possession of obscene literature. The Special Investigations Squad also raided a barn in the 20 hundred block of Welsh Road near Bustleton Avenue and confiscated 3, 000 obscene books. Captain Ferguson says he believes they have hit the supply of a main distributor of obscene material in Philadelphia.

The report was rebroadcast in substantially the same form at 6:30 p. m. , but at 8:00 p. m. , when the item was broadcast for the third time, WIP changed the third sentence to read "reportedly obscene." News of Rosenbloom's arrest was broadcast five more times in the following twelve hours but each report described the seized books as "allegedly" or "reportedly" obscene. Rosenbloom brought suit against police officials and against several local news media. The suit claimed that the magazines were not obscene; Rosenbloom sought injunctive relief prohibiting further police interference with his business as well as further publicity of the incident.

A second series of allegedly defamatory broadcasts related to WIP's news reports of the lawsuit itself. There were ten broadcasts on October 21, two on October 25, and one on November 1. None mentioned Rosenbloom by name. Most of the broadcasts were like the first one on October 21:

Federal District Judge Lord will hear arguments
today from two publishers and a distributor all seeking an injunction against Philadelphia Police Commissioner Howard Leary ... District Attorney James
C. Crumlish ... a local television station and a
newspaper ... ordering them to lay off the smut
literature racket.

The girlie-book peddlers say the police crackdown and continued reference to their borderline
literature as smut or filth is hurting their business.
Judge Lord refused to issue a temporary injunction
when he was first approached. Today he'll decide
the issue. It will set a precedent ... and if the
injunction is not granted ... it could signal an even
more intense effort to rid the city of pornography.

On October 27, Rosenbloom called WIP's studios and inquired
about the stories WIP had broadcast about him. Rosenbloom
told the newscaster that his magazines were "found to be
completely legal and legitimate by the United States Supreme
Court. " When the newscaster replied that the district attorney had stated the magazines were obscene, Rosenbloom responded that he has a public statement of the district attorney declaring the magazines legal. At this point the conversation terminated. Rosenbloom apparently made no request
for retraction, and none was forthcoming.

In May, a jury acquitted Rosenbloom in state court of
the criminal obscenity charges. The judge stated that, as a
matter of law, the nudist magazines distributed by Rosenbloom
were not obscene. Following his acquittal, Rosenbloom sought
damages under Pennsylvania's libel law. He argued that WIP's
unqualified characterization of the books seized as "obscene"
in the October 4, 6:00 p.m. and 6:30 p.m. broadcasts constituted libel per se and was proved false by Rosenbloom's
subsequent acquittal. He charged that the broadcasts describing his court suit for injunctive relief were also false and defamatory in that WIP characterized Rosenbloom and his business associates as "smut distributors" and "girlie book peddlers. " He further claimed that the broadcasts falsely characterized the suit as an attempt to force the media "to lay
off the smut literature racket. " The jury awarded $25,000
in general damages and $725,000 in punitive damages. The
district court, however, reduced the punitive damages to
$250,000. In reversing the lower court decision, the court
of appeals emphasized that the broadcasts concerned matters
of public interest and that they involved "hot news" prepared

under deadline pressure. The court of appeals concluded that "the fact that plaintiff was not a public figure cannot be accorded decisive significance if the recognized important guarantees of the First Amendment are to be adequately implemented. " Rosenbloom took the case to the U. S. Supreme Court.

The narrow question he raised was whether, because he was not a public official or a public figure, he had to establish actual malice on the part of Metromedia, the owner of station WIP. The Court ruled (5-3) against Rosenbloom.

> If a matter is a subject of public or general interest, it cannot suddenly become less so merely because a private individual is involved, or because in some sense the individual did not "voluntarily" choose to become involved. The public's primary interest is in the event; the public focus is on the conduct of the participant and the content, effect, and significance of the conduct, not the participant's prior anonymity or notoriety.
> In that circumstance we think the time has come forthrightly to announce that the determinant whether the First Amendment applies to state libel actions is whether the utterance involved concerns an issue of public or general concern, albeit leaving the delineation of the reach of that term to future cases.... Drawing a distinction between "public" and "private" figures makes no sense in terms of the First Amendment guarantees.

In effect, the decision held that no persons--public or private--involved in an event of public interest could collect libel damages unless they could prove actual malice. Rosenbloom was, without question, a significant victory for the press. It seemed to indicate a renewed interest by the Court in liberal interpretation of the First Amendment.

Gertz v. Robert Welch, Inc. 418 U. S. 323 (1974)

Three years later, the Court overturned the Rosenbloom rule. After reevaluating its earlier decision, the Court ruled that private citizens do indeed have greater protection against libelous statements than do public officials or figures. In 1968, Richard Nuccio, a Chicago police officer, shot and killed a young man named Nelson. The state authorities prosecuted Nuccio for homicide and ultimately obtained a conviction for second degree murder. The Nelson family retained Elmer Gertz, a reputable attorney, to represent them in civil litigation against Nuccio. At that time, Robert Welch published American Opinion, a monthly outlet for the opinions of the John Birch Society. Early in the 1960s, the magazine warned of a nationwide conspiracy to discredit local law enforcement agencies and create instead a national police force capable of supporting a communist dictatorship. As part of the continuing effort to alert the public to this alleged danger, American Opinion published an article on Nuccio's trial entitled "FRAME-UP: Richard Nuccio and the War on Police." The article purported to demonstrate that the testimony against Nuccio was false and that his prosecution was part of the communist campaign against the police. The article contained serious falsehoods. The implication that Gertz had a criminal record was false. Gertz had been a member and officer of the National Lawyer's Guild some fifteen years earlier but there was no evidence that he or the Guild had taken any part in planning the 1968 demonstrations in Chicago. There was also no basis for the charge that Gertz was a "Leninist" or a "Communist-fronter." Further, Gertz had never been a member of the "Marxist League for Industrial Democracy" or the "Intercollegiate Socialist Society." The editor of American Opinion made no effort to verify the charges against Gertz. Instead, he appended an editorial introduction claiming that the author had "concluded extensive research into the Richard Nuccio case." He included in the article a photograph of Gertz and wrote the caption that appeared under it: "Elmer Gertz of the Red Guild harasses Nuccio." Welch placed the issue on sale throughtout the country and distributed reprints of the article on the streets of Chicago.

Gertz filed suit claiming that the falsehoods injured his reputation as a lawyer and citizen. The jury awarded him $50,000. The court of appeals, referring to Rosenbloom, ruled that the case required the application of the New York Times standard to any publication or broadcast about an issue of significant public interest--without regard to the position, fame, or anonymity of the person defamed. It concluded that Welch's statements were of such public concern. The court of appeals decided that Gertz failed to show that Welch had acted with "actual malice." There was no evidence that the editor of American Opinion knew of the falsity of the accusations made in the article. In fact, he knew nothing about Gertz except what he learned from the article. The court concluded that mere proof of failure to investigate, without more, cannot establish reckless disregard for the truth.

When the case reached the U. S. Supreme Court, however, the main issue was whether a newspaper or broadcaster that publishes defamatory falsehoods about a private citizen may claim a constitutional privilege against liability for the injury inflicted by those statements. According to the Court:

> ... we conclude that the state interest in compensating injury to the reputation of private individuals requires that a different rule should obtain with respect to them.... The first remedy of any victim of defamation is self help--using available opportunities to contradict the lie or correct the error and thereby minimize its adverse impact on reputation. Public officials and public figures usually enjoy significantly greater access to the channels of effective communication and hence have a more realistic opportunity to counteract false statements than private individuals normally enjoy. Private individuals are therefore more vulnerable to injury, and the state interest in protecting them is correspondingly greater.

The Court, in effect, conditioned a libel action by a private person on a showing of negligence as contrasted with a showing of willful or reckless disregard.

The issue of whether Gertz was a public figure was secondary. The Court noted that although Gertz was "well-known in some circles, he had achieved no general fame or notoriety in the community...." The Court acknowledged that the public figure question should be considered by looking to the extent of an individual's participation in the particular controversy giving rise to the defamation. In this light, Gertz was not a public figure. He played a minimal role at the coroner's inquest. His participation related only to his representation of a private client. He took no part in the criminal prosecution. He never discussed the litigation with the press and was never quoted as having done so. He plainly did not thrust himself into the center of this public issue, nor did he engage the public's attention in an effort to influence its outcome. The Court concluded that the Times standard was inapplicable to cases involving private citizens, regardless of the degree of public concern in the matter.

Time, Inc. v. Firestone 424 U. S. 448 (1976)

Two years later, the Court again seemed unsympathetic

to the news media's claim of First Amendment protection.
In 1964, Mary Alice and Russell Firestone were separated.
Mrs. Firestone subsequently filed a complaint against her
husband in a Florida circuit court for separate maintenance;
he counterclaimed for divorce on grounds of cruelty and adultery. Charges of infidelity abounded on both sides. The
circuit court judge finally granted the husband a divorce,
finding "that the equities in this cause" were with him and
concluding that "in the present case, it is abundantly clear
... that neither of the parties has shown the least suscep-
tibility to domestication, and that the marriage should be
dissolved. " Time magazine printed a note in the "Milestones"
section that read:

> DIVORCED. By Russell A. Firestone Jr. , 41,
> heir to the tire fortune: Mary Alice Sullivan Fire-
> stone, 32, his third wife; a one-time Palm Beach
> schoolteacher; on grounds of extreme cruelty and
> adultery; after six years of marriage, one son; in
> West Palm Beach, Fla. The 17-month intermittent
> trial produced enough testimony of extramarital ad-
> ventures on both sides, said the judge, "to make
> Dr. Freud's hair curl. "

Mary Alice Firestone brought suit against Time, Inc. , claiming that the squib was "false, malicious, and defamatory. "
The Supreme Court of Florida affirmed a $100,000 award of
damages against the publisher. Time, Inc. , appealed, alleging that the magazine could not be liable for publishing any
falsehood unless it was established that the publication was
made with actual malice as defined in New York Times.
Time, Inc. , argued that Mrs. Firestone was a "public figure" and that the Time item constituted a report of a judicial
proceeding, a class of subject matter that deserves the protection of the actual malice standard even if the story was
proven to be defamatorily false.

The U. S. Supreme Court disagreed (5-3) with Time,
Inc. 's arguments and held that the New York Times standard was inapplicable in this case. Mrs. Firestone was not
a public figure. In applying the Gertz rule, the Court noted
that Mrs. Firestone had not assumed a role of "especial
prominence in the affairs of society" and had not been "thrust
to the forefront of particular public controversies in order
to influence the resolution of the issues involved. " The Court
also found no reason why a litigant should forfeit protection
afforded against defamation simply by being drawn into court.

As the divorce court did not find Mrs. Firestone guilty of adultery, as reported by Time, and although Time, Inc., contended that it reported the precise meaning of the divorce judgment, the lower courts had properly found the claim of accurate reporting to be invalid. Yet, since liability for defamation cannot be established without a finding of fault--a question that was not determined in this case--the judgment for Mrs. Firestone was vacated and the case remanded. In essence though, the Firestone ruling indicates that the period of relative freedom of the press was short-lived indeed.

Criminal Libel

Though the vast majority of libel cases are civil actions, some important instances of criminal libel should be noted. The courts have reasoned that an individual who has been libeled has reasonable remedy in a civil suit for damages. No public interest is at issue. However, in cases where the wrong is of so flagrant a character as reasonably to jeopardize the public peace, criminal prosecution may be necessary on public grounds. Many states, particularly those in the South, have criminal libel statutes, most of which hinge on whether the defamation causes or could cause a breach of peace. In 1966, the U. S. Supreme Court overturned a Kentucky "breach of the peace" statute.

Ashton v. Kentucky 384 U. S. 195 (1966)

In 1963, Steve Ashton went to Hazard, Kentucky, where a bitter labor conflict was raging, to appeal for food, clothing, and aid for the unemployed miners. His pamphlet, which had a limited circulation, attacked the Chief of Police, the Sheriff, and Mrs. W. P. Nolan, co-owner of the Herald Citizen. He accused these people of highly unethical antilabor activity at best and patent criminality at worst. The trial court convicted Ashton of criminal libel, arguing that "criminal libel is defined as any writing calculated to create disturbances of the peace, corrupt the public morals, or lead to any act, which, when done, is indictable." The court of appeals affirmed the decision.

The U. S. Supreme Court unanimously overturned the lower court's decision. The Court emphasized that

since the English Common law of criminal libel is

inconsistent with constitutional provisions, and since
no Kentucky case has redefined the crime in under-
standable terms, and since the law must be made
on a case to case basis, the elements of the crime
are so indefinite and uncertain that it should not
be enforced as a penal offense in Kentucky.

According to the Court, the Kentucky law suffered from vagueness and overbreadth. And, where First Amendment rights
were involved, the Court had to "look even more closely lest,
under the guise of regulating conduct that is reachable by the
police power, freedom of speech or of the press suffer. Because of the indefinite nature of the law's target, the Court
overturned the Kentucky "breach of peace" statute--thereby
spelling the end of similar laws.

The Beauharnais and Garrison decisions, already discussed in this chapter, also involved state criminal libel
laws. In Beauharnais, a case that involved the criminal libel of a group, a divided court determined that libel of a
class of people was not protected by the First Amendment.
The Court upheld a conviction that was based on words that
were "unquestionably libelous" against blacks. This was,
however, the only case since 1952 to deal with the issue of
group libel. And, in Beauharnais, the application of the criminal statute was only secondary. It is difficult to predict
how the Court would rule on a similar case today. In Garrison, a case in which a criminal libel action was brought for
criticism of public officials, the U. S. Supreme Court vigorously moved to apply the same standards to criminal libel
cases as to civil libel cases. Criticism of public officials
was given the same extent of First Amendment protection
that such criticism was afforded in civil actions--an action
could be maintained only if actual malice could be demonstrated.

It seems obvious that, while statutes remain on the
books, criminal libel is a passing phenomenon. The few
cases in recent years to reach the Supreme Court have resulted in the overturning or weakening of the respective state
laws. Generally, the public injury resulting from a criminal
defamation is minor or non-existent. Libel, in short, is a
private matter.

Bibliography

Books

Ashley, Paul P. Say It Safely: Legal Limits in Publishing, Radio, and Television. 5th ed. Seattle: University of Washington Press, 1976.

Phelps, Robert H., and E. Douglas Hamilton. Libel: Rights, Risks, Responsibilities. New York: Macmillan, 1966.

Articles

Boisseau, Merribeth. "Time, Inc. vs. Firestone: The Supreme Court's Restrictive New Libel Ruling, " San Diego Law Review 14 (March, 1977), 435-57.

Kalven, Harry, Jr. "The Reasonable Man and the First Amendment: Hill, Butts, and Walker, " Supreme Court Review (1967), 267-309.

McKey, Arthur Duncan. "Defamation Law After Time, Inc. vs. Firestone, " Idaho Law Review 13 (Winter, 1976), 53-65.

Cases

Arvey Corporation v. Peterson 178 F. Supp 132 (1959)

Ashton v. Kentucky 384 U. S. 195 (1966)

Barr v. Matteo 360 U. S. 564 (1959)

Beauharnais v. Illinois 343 U. S. 250 (1952)

Blende v. Hearst Publications 93 P. 2d 733 (1939)

Brush-Moore Newspapers, Inc. v. Pollitt 151 A. 2d 530 (1959)

City of Chicago v. Tribune Company 139 N. E. 86 (1923)

Cosgrove Studio and Camera Shop, Inc. v. Pane 182 A. 2d 751 (1962)

Cowper v. Vannier 156 N. E. 2d 761 (1959)

Crane v. State 166 P. 1110 (1917)

Curtis Publishing Company v. Butts; Associated Press v. Walker 388 U. S. 130 (1967)

Dalton v. Meister 52 Wis. 2d 173 (1971)

Dempsey v. Time Incorporated 43 Misc. 2d 754 (1964)

Dickins v. International Brotherhood of Teamsters 171 F. 2d 21 (1948)

DiGiorgio Corporation v. Valley Labor Citizen 67 Cal. Rptr. 82 (1968)

Empire Printing Company v. Roden 247 F. 2d 8 (1957)

Farmers Educational and Cooperative Union of America v. WDAY, Inc. 360 U. S. 525 (1959)

Farrell v. Kramer 193 A. 2d 560 (1963)

Fort v. Holt 508 P. 2d 792 (1973)

Garrison v. State of Louisiana 379 U. S. 64 (1964)

Gertz v. Robert Welch, Inc. 418 U. S. 323 (1974)

Goldwater v. Ginzburg 414 F. 2d 324 (1969)

Greenbelt Publishing Association v. Bresler 398 U. S. 6 (1970)

Hope v. Hearst Consolidated Publications, Inc. 294 F. 2d 681 (1961)

Hornby v. Hunter 385 S. W. 2d 473 (1964)

Karrigan v. Valentine 184 Kansas 783 (1957)

Langford v. Vanderbilt University 318 S. W. 2d 568 (1958)

MacLeod v. Tribune Publishing Company, Inc. 343 P. 2d 36 (1959)

Monitor Patriot Company v. Roy 401 U. S. 265 (1971)

Neiman-Marcus Company v. Lait 107 F. Supp. 96 (1952)

New York Times Company v. Sullivan 376 U. S. 255 (1964)

Nichols v. Bristow Publishing Company 330 P. 2d 1044 (1957)

Nichols v. Philadelphia Tribune Company, Inc. 22 F. R. D. 89
    (1958)

November v. Time, Inc. 13 N. Y. 2d 175 (1963)

Ocala Star Banner Company v. Damron 401 U. S. 295 (1971)

Oswalt v. State-Record Company 158 S. E. 2d 204 (1967)

People v. Spielman 149 N. E. 466 (1925)

Powers v. Durgin-Snow Publishing Company, Inc.; Powers v.
    Olesen 144 A. 2d 294 (1958)

Rosenblatt v. Baer 383 U. S. 75 (1966)

Rosenbloom v. Metromedia 403 U. S. 29 (1971)

Roth v. Greensboro News Company 6 S. E. 2d 882 (1940)

St. Amant v. Thompson 390 U. S. 727 (1968)

Sally v. Brown 295 S. W. 890 (1927)

Stice v. Beacon Newspaper Corporation, Inc. 340 P. 2d 396
    (1959)

Szalay v. New York American 254 App. Div. 249 (1938)

Time, Inc. v. Firestone 424 U. S. 448 (1976)

Time, Inc. v. Pape 410 U. S. 279 (1971)

United Press International, Inc. v. Mohs 381 S. W. 2d 104
    (1964)

Wood v. Constitution Publishing Company 194 S. E. 760 (1937)

Zbyszko v. New York American, Inc. 228 App. Div. 277 (1930)

CHAPTER III

PRIVACY

When the U. S. Constitution was adopted, most people lived in homes that were scattered throughout the country. In the America of the late 1700s, people felt secure in their privacy. It is not surprising, then, that the framers of the Constitution did not provide for a "right to privacy."

The legal basis for a right to privacy in America had its foundation in an 1890 Harvard Law Review article written by two law partners, Samuel D. Warren and Louis D. Brandeis. Irritated by the press coverage of parties given by his wife and himself, Warren started collecting information from various court decisions regarding defamation and trespass. With Brandeis, he put the information together in an article entitled "The Right to Privacy." Since that time, the right to privacy has become generally recognized and is supported by legislatures and courts in several states.

According to the late Professor William L. Prosser, privacy torts include: 1) appropriation of some element of an individual's personality for commercial use, 2) intrusion of physical solitude, 3) publication of private matters, and 4) putting an individual in a false position in the public eye.

APPROPRIATION

Appropriation involves taking an individual's name, picture, photograph, or likeness without that person's permission and using it for commercial gain.

Advertising

In most states, laws forbid a person from using the name or picture of any living person for advertising purposes without first obtaining written consent from that person. Over

the years, the courts have heard several cases involving alleged violations of such laws. In 1937, a New York court
handed down a decision that set forth specific guidelines concerning the use of photographs in newspaper advertising.

Sarat Lahiri v. Daily Mirror Inc. 295 N. Y. S. 382 (1937)

In the magazine section of the September 16, 1934,
issue of the Sunday Mirror (New York), there appeared an
article entitled "I Saw the Famous Rope Trick (But It Didn't
Really Happen). " The article was inspired by the offer of
the "Magic Circle, " a British society of mystics, to pay a
large amount of money to anybody who would cause a coil
of rope to rise unaided until one end would be suspended in
mid-air. This feat was known as the Hindu "rope trick. "
The article claimed that Hindu mystics, by the exercise of
hypnotic powers and the creation of an illusion, convinced
viewers that the rope was rising into the air, although it actually remained coiled upon the ground. The article was illustrated by several specially posed color photographs. One
was a reproduction of a photograph of Sarat Lahiri, a well-
known Hindu musician, playing a musical instrument as ac-
companiment for a female Indian dancer. Appearing beneath
the photograph were the words: "MYSTIC. Something of the
Occult Philosophy Which Dominates the Far East May Be Seen,
Even in the Gestures and Postures of Indian Dancers, Such
as Those Portrayed Above. " Lahiri initiated action, claiming invasion of privacy.

The court set forth some specific rules applicable to
unauthorized publication of photographs in a single issue of
a newspaper. The court determined that it was illegal to
publish, without permission, a photograph as part of an advertisement. It was also illegal to use such a photograph in
connection with a fictional article in any part of a newspaper.
However, there was no violation for publication of a photograph in connection with an article of current news or immediate public interest. The court recognized that newspapers
publish some articles that are neither strictly news items nor
strictly fictional in nature, but that serve to satisfy an educational need. Articles involving travel stories, tales of an-
cient places, accounts of historic people and events, the reproduction of past news items, and surveys of social conditions are educational and informative in character. Publishing a photograph in connection with such stories was not forbidden. Turning to the specifics of Lahiri's claim, the court

noted that the article was not one of fiction. It clearly concerned a matter having a legitimate news interest. A British society had offered a substantial prize to any person able to perform the famous rope trick. The author explained how the trick was allegedly performed in India and discussed the possibility that the society would have to pay the prize. The court noted that the only issue was whether the picture had too tenuous a connection with the article. The court thought the photograph illustrated one of the points made by the author--the mystical quality of the East. In the court's opinion, "it would be farfetched to hold in this case that the picture was not used in an illustrative sense, but merely to promote the sale of the paper." There was nothing to warrant a finding that the photograph was used solely to increase the commercial value of the newspaper.

Booth v. Curtis Publishing Company 15 A. D. 2d 343 (1962)

Another New York case involved Shirley Booth, a well-known actress in the theatre, films, and television. While Booth was vacationing at a prominent resort called "Round Hill" in Jamaica, a photographer for Holiday magazine was also present. He was taking photographs to use with an article concerning Round Hill and its guests. Booth was photographed, to her knowledge and without her objection. Booth never gave written consent for publication. In February, 1959, the article appeared in Holiday. A photograph showing Booth in the water up to her neck wearing a brimmed, high-crowned street hat of straw was given a prominent place in the article. The publication in Holiday did not violate Booth's right of privacy because this was reproduction for news purposes. In June, 1959, Curtis published the same photograph in full-page advertisements of Holiday, The New Yorker, and Advertising Age. The advertisements presented Booth's photograph as a sample of the contents of Holiday. Booth initiated court action, claiming that the procedure invaded her right to privacy. After a jury trial, she was awarded $17,500. Curtis Publishing appealed.

The issue facing the court was whether a person's photograph, originally published in one issue of a periodical as a newsworthy subject, may be republished later in another issue or another medium as an advertisement for the periodical itself, without the person's expressed permission. In this case, the court differentiated between collateral and incidental advertising. Collateral advertising involves the sale

of a product completely unconnected with the promotion of a
news medium. Incidental advertising, on the other hand, involves the sale and dissemination of the news medium itself.
The court noted that "contemporaneous or proximate advertising of the news medium, by way of extract, cover, dust
jacket, or poster, using relevant but otherwise personal matter, does not violate the statute." The court found "that so
long as the reproduction was used to illustrate the quality
and content of the periodical in which it originally appeared,
the statute was not violated." Also essential to the decision
was the fact that there was nothing in the reproduction which
suggested that Booth had endorsed the magazine. Accordingly, the judgment in favor of Booth was reversed.

Palmer v. Schonhorn Enterprises, Inc. 232 A. 2d 458 (1967)

In 1967, the Superior Court of New Jersey heard a
case involving action by well-known professional golfers who
objected to the use of their names by a corporation, Schonhorn Enterprises, for the purpose of marketing the Pro-Am
Golf Game. The contents of the game included twenty-three
individual sheets of paper, each entitled "Profile and Playing
Chart, " on which appeared the name of a well-known professional golfer accompanied by a short biography or profile.
Each of the profiles contained accurate facts concerning their
respective professional careers. Four of these twenty-three
sheets contained the names and profiles of Arnold Palmer,
Gary Player, Doug Sanders, and Jack Nicklaus. The golfers
never gave their permission for the use of their names
and profiles by the company. As a matter of fact, each of
them had requested that the information and his name be removed from the game. Schonhorn Enterprises refused to do
so. The golfers sought an injunction, claiming that such use
constituted an invasion of their privacy and an unfair exploitation and commercialization of their names and reputations.

The court noted that the use of the golfer's names and
biographies enhanced the marketability of the game. Schonhorn argued that the players "waived their rights of privacy
because of their being well-known athletes who have deliberately invited publicity in furtherance of their careers." Since
the information contained in the profiles was readily obtainable public data, the company should not be denied the privilege of reproducing that which was set forth in newspapers,
magazine articles, and other periodicals. But the court concluded,

although the publication of biographical data of a
well-known figure does not per se constitute an
invasion of privacy, the use of that same data for
the purpose of a commercial project other than the
dissemination of news or articles or biographies
does.

According to the court, it was unfair for a company to com-
mercialize, exploit, or capitalize upon a person's name, reputation, or accomplishments merely because the accomplishments had been highly publicized.   Finally, the court ruled
that privacy had been invaded even though the golfers' names
were not advertised on the cover of the game box, so that
purchasers did not know who the "23 famous golfers" were
until they purchased and saw the contents.   An injunction was
issued.

Uhlaender v. Henricksen 316 F. Supp. 1277 (1970)

A similar case was decided in 1970.   Keith and Kent
Henricksen manufactured and sold games called "Negamco's
Major League Baseball" and "Big League Manager Baseball. "
The game used the names and such professional statistical
information as batting, fielding, earned run, and other aver-
ages of some five hundred to seven hundred major league
baseball players identified by team, uniform number, and
playing position.   The Henricksens had not obtained the players' permission to use their names or statistics.   In 1966,
most major league baseball players had banded together to
form the Association of Major League Baseball Players.   The
Association acted for the players in marketing and licensing
the use of group names or for group endorsement purposes.
By 1970, the Association had issued twenty-seven contracts
or agreements for group licenses, including five with game
manufacturers calling for payments of 5 percent of gross sales
with a minimum royalty of $2, 500 per year.   These agree-
ments generated over $400, 000 income in 1969, all of which
was distributed equally and not according to the prominence
of the various members.   Since 1967, the Association had
written to the Henricksens, notifying them that they were ex-
ploiting a claimed property right and offering to enter into a
licensing agreement.   The Henricksens refused to do so.   The
players sought an injunction, claiming that the Henricksens
were guilty of "misappropriation and use for commercial profit of the names of professional major league baseball players
without the payment of royalties. "

The district court supported the legitimate proprietary interest a celebrity has in his or her public personality.

> A celebrity must be considered to have invested his years of practice and competition in a public personality which eventually may reach marketable status. That identity, embodied in his name, likeness, statistics and other personal characteristics, is the fruit of his labors and is a type of property.

Accordingly, the Association was awarded injuctive relief.

The cases considered in this section, Sarat Lahiri, Booth, Palmer, and Uhlaender, clearly establish that an action can be brought against a person who uses the name and/ or picture of any other person for commercial purposes without first obtaining permission from that person. Palmer and Uhlaender establish that a person cannot use a celebrity's name or biographical data, even though the data is public and readily obtainable by all, as an aid in marketing a game without first obtaining that celebrity's permission. Other cases do, however, protect legitimate journalistic interests. Sarat Lahiri specifies that journalists may indeed use a person's name and/or picture in connection with an article of current news, immediate public interest, or educational value. In Booth, a New York court held that reproducing a celebrity's picture in order to illustrate the quality and content of the magazine in which it originally appeared constituted a legitimate use of that reproduction. Such advertising was directly related to the sale and dissemination of the news medium itself. In all of the cases cited, the courts restricted the use of a person's name and/or picture for advertising purposes but upheld the right of journalists to use these items in order to illustrate news stories.

Right of Publicity

Celebrities from the worlds of sports, politics, and entertainment, as well as other public figures and public officials, have often found it difficult to control their own publicity. In such cases, the issue of right to publicity has been brought before the courts.

Spahn v. Julian Messner, Inc. 233 N.E. 2d 840 (1967)

Author Milton J. Shapiro and publisher Julian Messner

collaborated on the book The Warren Spahn Story, a biography of professional baseball pitcher Warren Spahn. The book
was based on secondary sources. Shapiro never talked with
Spahn, his family or friends, or even other baseball players.
The book contained several inaccuracies, usually exaggerating
Spahn's successes. Specific inaccuracies included attempts
to make Spahn appear to be a war hero, descriptions of the
influences of Spahn's father in directing Spahn toward baseball, and accounts of the impact of a shoulder injury on
Spahn's career. Spahn had an elbow injury in reality, but
not a shoulder injury. Overall, the writer used imaginary
incidents, manufactured dialogue, and manipulated chronology.
The work was fictionalized.

    In court, Shapiro and Messner admitted fictionaliza-
tion, but argued that it was necessary because the book was
written for children. They also contended that Spahn was a
public figure who enjoyed no right to privacy according to the
New York Times rule. The court, however, ruled Spahn was
not a public official, Messner and Shapiro were liable for
invasion of privacy, and Spahn was entitled to $10,000 dam-
ages. Dissenting judge Francis Bergan suggested that in
light of Time, Inc. v. Hill, a case in which the U.S. Supreme Court applied the actual malice rule to invasion of privacy, the New York privacy law gave no protection against
fictionalization unless it could be shown that the book was
designed to harm Spahn. With these issues generally un-
settled, the U.S. Supreme Court agreed to hear the case.
The litigants, however, settled out of court prior to a decision.

Paulsen v. Personality Posters, Inc. 299 N.Y.S. 2d 501 (1968)

    The right of publicity was also the issue in a case
that involved Pat Paulsen, a well-known television performer
and comedian who conducted a mock campaign prior to the
1968 Presidential election. Claiming to be the "Put-On Presidential Candidate of 1968," Paulsen ran under the banner
of the Stag Party. Paulsen's satirical and provocative comments on various current issues were aired with regularity
on the nationally televised Smothers Brothers program. Paulsen received several votes in primary elections and he participated in various activities traditionally associated with
political campaigning. In conjunction with this comedy routine, Paulsen granted an exclusive license to a California
company in connection with all campaign buttons, stickers,

and posters relating to the "Pat Paulsen for President" campaign. Without obtaining Paulsen's permission, Personality Posters, Inc. , prepared for sale an enlargement of a photograph of Paulsen. In the photograph, Paulsen was attired in beruffled cap and prim frock and held an unlit candle in one hand while his other arm cradled a rubber tire which was hoisted onto his right shoulder. A banner, draped across Paulsen's chest in the manner of a beauty pageant contestant, contained the legend "1968. " Added to the poster were the words "FOR PRESIDENT" at the bottom in two-and-one-half-inch letters. Paulsen initiated action, claiming that distribution of the posters infringed upon and interfered with the license agreement with the California company. Paulsen's application for injunctive relief was based on an alleged invasion of the right of privacy.

The court noted that the privacy statute was not intended to limit the dissemination of news or information concerning matters of public interest. Even though Paulsen was "only kidding" and his Presidential activities were really only a "publicity stunt, " they fell within the scope of constitutionally protected matters of public interest. According to the court, "when a well-known entertainer enters the presidential ring, tongue in cheek or otherwise, it is clearly newsworthy and of public interest. " The poster, which reflected the spirit in which Paulsen approached the role, was a form of public interest presentation entitled to constitutional protection. The court pointed out that Paulsen was less concerned with the "right of privacy" than with the "right of publicity"--that is, the ability to control the financial benefits that attach to a person's name and picture. The court ruled that the right of publicity had no application in this case, which involved a matter of public interest. The use of the poster was constitutionally protected and superseded any privacy or publicity claims.

Man v. Warner Brothers, Inc. 317 F. Supp. 50 (1970)

In 1970, the courts heard another case involving the right of publicity. Frank Man, a professional musician, mounted the stage at the Woodstock Festival, held at Bethel, New York, in August, 1969, and played "Mess Call" on his Flugelhorn before 400, 000 people. The festival was of wide public interest and was extensively reported in newspapers, magazines, radio, television, and other news media. Over 120 hours of sound track and motion pictures of the event

were recorded and later reduced to a length suitable for exhibition as a motion picture in theatres under the title Woodstock. Man brought action, claiming that the producers and
distributors of the film included his performance in the film
without his consent, thereby violating his right to privacy.

According to the district court, "there can be no
question that the Woodstock Festival was and is a matter of
valid public interest. " Furthermore, the New York Privacy
Statute was never intended to apply to professional entertainers
who are shown giving a performance before a public audience.
Man, by his own volition, placed himself in the spotlight of
a sensational event that exposed him to publicity. That fact
alone made him newsworthy and deprived him of any right
to complain of a violation of his privacy. The complaint
was dismissed.

Zacchini v. Scripps-Howard Broadcasting Company
429 U. S. 1037 (1977)

In 1977, the U. S. Supreme Court upheld the right of
a celebrity to control his own publicity. Hugo Zacchini, an
entertainer, performed a "human cannonball" act in which he
was shot from a cannon into a net some two hundred feet
away. In August and September, 1972, Zacchini performed
his act on a regular basis at the Geauga County Fair in Burton, Ohio. Members of the public attending the fair were
not charged a separate admission fee to observe his act. A
free-lance reporter for Scripps-Howard Broadcasting Company, the operator of a television station, videotaped the entire act even though Zacchini had asked him not to do so.
This film clip, approximately 15 seconds in length, was shown
on the 11 o'clock news program that evening along with favorable commentary. Zacchini brought action for damages, alleging that Scripps-Howard "showed and commercialized the
film of his act without his consent" and that such conduct
constituted an "unlawful appropriation of plaintiff's professional
property. " The case reached the U. S. Supreme Court.

In this case, Zacchini acknowledged that his appearance
at the fair and his performance could be reported by the press
as newsworthy items. However, he complained that the reporter filmed his entire act and then displayed that film on
television for the public to see and enjoy. This was an appropriation of his professional property. The Court noted
that the broadcast of a film of Zacchini's entire act posed a
substantial threat to the economic value of that performance.

This act was the product of Zacchini's own talents and ener-gy--the result of considerable time, effort, and expense. Much of its economic value stemmed from the "right of ex-clusive control over the publicity given to his performance"; if the public could see the act for free on television they would be less willing to pay to see it performed elsewhere. The Court noted that public broadcast of the performance was similar to preventing Zacchini from charging an admission fee. The Court stipulated (5-4) that:

> There is no doubt that entertainment, as well as news, enjoys First Amendment protection. It is also true that entertainment itself can be import-ant news.... But it is important to note that neither the public nor respondent will be deprived of the benefit of petitioner's performance as long as his commercial stake in his act is appropriately recognized. Petitioner does not seek to enjoin the broadcast of his performance; he simply wants to be paid for it.

The minority justices held that since the film clip was treated as news the station's action was constitutionally privileged. The majority, however, concluded that in the circumstances of this case the press was not automatically privileged under the First and Fourteenth Amendment.

In Spahn, the court noted the right of celebrities to control their own publicity. That right was affirmed by the U. S. Supreme Court in Zacchini. Yet, as was clearly dem-onstrated in Paulsen and Man, when celebrities engage in an activity of legitimate public interest, they surrender the right to control their own publicity regarding that specific activity.

INTRUSION

Intrusion is the act of thrusting oneself upon the peace and into the private life of an individual. Intrusion can be accomplished through a variety of techniques, which include physical removal, hidden devices, and physical harassment.

Physical Removal

Cases discussed in this section involve accusations that a newspaper reporter and/or publisher received stolen property that was subsequently used in a published article or story. Such a case came before the courts in 1969.

Pearson v. Dodd 410 F. 2d 701 (1969)

On several occasions in June and July, 1965, employ-ees of Senator Thomas J. Dodd entered his offices without permission and took documents from his files, duplicated copies, replaced the originals, and turned the copies over to journalists Drew Pearson and Jack Anderson. The re-porters knew how the copies had been obtained. Pearson and Anderson then used information from the copies in publish-ing articles about Dodd's alleged relationship with certain lobbyists for foreign interests. Dodd sued.

Dodd argued his case on three grounds. First, he claimed he had been libeled. But, applying the New York Times rule, the court disallowed the libel action, as there was no "actual malice." Then, Dodd claimed invasion of privacy. The court, however, ruled that a news medium that published information received through intrusion cannot be held responsible for the behavior of the intruders. The court stressed that in analyzing a claimed breach of privacy, injuries from intrusion and injuries from publication should be kept clearly separate. Pearson and Anderson had not com-mitted an act of physical intrusion. The question was whether they had published information that was genuinely private, thereby committing invasion by publication. In this instance, the columns Dodd complained about were of general public interest. They bore on Dodd's qualifications as a United States Senator and as such amounted to a case of published communication not subject to suit for invasion of privacy. Finally, Dodd tried an inventive argument based on property law. It involved the common law notion of conversion and trover which applied to the unauthorized assumption of owner-ship over property belonging to someone else. The court also denied this claim, noting that the documents in Dodd's files were photocopies and the originals were then returned so that Dodd was not deprived of his files. Since Dodd was not substantially deprived of the use of the files, no conver-sion had occurred. Dodd's case was rejected on all three grounds.

People v. Kunkin 107 Cal. Rptr. 184 (1973)

The Los Angeles Free Press, its editor and owner

Arthur Kunkin, and reporter Gerald Applebaum were indicted
for receiving stolen property by taking possession of a document that had been stolen from the office of the Attorney
General, by Jerry Reznick, a mail clerk in the office. Reznick had taken a copy of the personnel roster of the Bureau
of Narcotic Enforcement. The roster listed the names, home
addresses, and home telephone numbers of undercover narcotics agents throughout the state. It was not marked "secret" or "confidential." Subsequently, Reznick took the roster
to the office of the Free Press, where he gave the roster to
Applebaum. On August 8, 1969, the Free Press published
the roster verbatim in a feature article under the headlines
"Narcotics Agents Listed." "There should be no secret police, " and "Know your local Narc. " The text editorialized
that police should live openly in the community which they
serve. On a television interview, Kunkin acknowledged his
role in publishing the list and stated that he was satisfied
as to its authenticity. At trial, the defendants were convicted
of receiving stolen property. They appealed.

The California Supreme Court noted that a conviction
for receiving stolen property could not stand unless substantial evidence was presented to demonstrate that 1) the property was received, concealed, or withheld by the accused;
2) such property had been obtained by theft or extortion; and
3) the accused knew that the property had been so obtained.
The court decided that the first two requirements were satisfied, then turned to the question of whether there was also
substantial evidence from which the jury could reasonably
draw an inference that the defendants knew the roster was
stolen when Reznick gave it to them. The Attorney General
cited circumstances that he argued established the defendant's
knowledge that the roster was stolen--for example, the sensitive nature of the information; Reznick's appearance and
desire to remain anonymous; and the defendants' awareness
that the publication might cause trouble, willingness to pay
a small sum for the roster, and refusal to surrender the
roster. In the court's opinion, this evidence was insufficient
to sustain a conviction. The sensitive nature of the information contained in the roster, although cause for outrage
at the defendants' gross irresponsibility in publishing it, gave
no basis for presuming that the defendants knew the roster
was stolen. The list of inferences that might reasonably be
drawn from the appearance of a person who hands over a
list of names of undercover narcotics agents and wishes to
remain anonymous does not include the inference of theft.
Recognition that the publication may cause trouble likewise
does not permit an inference of theft. Defendants' willingness

to pay for the information is likewise without significance as
they were willing to pay similar amounts for other information.   The court was also unable to discern any knowledge
of the theft of the roster by the defendants' initial refusal to
surrender the roster after its publication.   The court concluded that there was no substantial evidence to support the
jury's finding that the defendants knew the roster was stolen.
The convictions were reversed.

        The courts sided with the press in Dodd and Kunkin.
In so doing, the courts made it difficult to obtain the conviction of a reporter who publishes information obtained
through physical intrusion.

Hidden Devices

        In 1971, a court of appeals heard a case involving al-
leged invasion of privacy by persons who gained entrance to
the office portion of another's home, where they photographed
him and electronically recorded and transmitted to third persons his conversation without his consent.   The case was
Dietemann v. Time, Inc.

Dietemann v. Time, Inc. 449 F. 2d 245 (1971)

        A. A. Dietemann, a disabled veteran with little edu-
cation, engaged in the practice of healing with clay, minerals,
and herbs.   Sometime during 1963, Life magazine entered
into an arrangement with the District Attorney's Office of Los
Angeles County whereby Life's employees would visit Dietemann and obtain facts and pictures concerning his activities.
Two employees, Jackie Metcalf and William Ray, went to
Dietemann's home on September 20, 1963.   Dietemann, while
examining Mrs. Metcalf, was photographed by Ray with a
hidden camera.   One of the pictures taken by him showed
Dietemann with his hand on the upper portion of Metcalf's
breast while he was looking at some gadgets and holding what
appeared to be a wand in his right hand.   Metcalf had told
Dietemann that she had a lump in her breast.   Dietemann
concluded that she had eaten some rancid butter eleven years,
nine months, and seven days prior to that time.   The conversation between Mrs. Metcalf and Dietemann was carried
by radio transmitter hidden in Metcalf's purse to a tape recorder in a parked automobile occupied by a Life employee
and a member of the District Attorney's Office.   On October

15, Dietemann was arrested at his home on a charge of practicing medicine without a license, a charge to which he later pled nolo contendere. The November 1, issue of _Life_ carried an article entitled "Crackdown on Quackery." The article depicted Dietemann as a quack. Pictures and information obtained by Metcalf and Ray were used in the preparation of the article. Dietemann initiated an invasion of privacy suit against _Life._ He claimed that he administered his treatments to people who visited him, but he was not a doctor. He did not advertise nor did he have a phone. He had a lock on his gate. To obtain entrance it was necessary to ring a bell. He conducted his activities in a building that was his home and that was not open to the public. _Life's_ employees had gained entrance by a subterfuge. The court concluded that the action on the part of _Life_ constituted an invasion of privacy under California law, for which Dietemann was entitled to damages. The court awarded $1,000 general damages for injury to Dietemann's feelings and peace of mind. The case was appealed.

Before the court of appeals, _Life_ claimed that the First Amendment immunized it from liability for invading Dietemann's home with a hidden camera and its concealed electronic instruments because its employees were gathering news. Life argued that its instrumentalities were indispensable tools for investigative reporting. The court agreed that newsgathering was an integral part of news dissemination. However, the court disagreed that the hidden mechanical contrivances were "indispensable tools" of newsgathering. The First Amendment was not a license to trespass, steal, or intrude by electronic means into another's home or office even if the person subjected to the intrusion was suspected of committing a crime. The lower court judgment was affirmed.

Physical Harassment

In 1973, a court acknowledged the right of freedom from physical intrusion that results in harassment.

Galella v. Onassis 487 F. 2d 986 (1973)

Freelance photographer Ronald Galella made a modest living photographing celebrities. His favorite subject was Jacqueline Onassis. Galella initiated a $1.3-million damage suit on the ground that he had been roughed up by Secret Service and police officers whom Onassis had asked to intervene on her behalf.   Also, Galella asked for an injunction against interference with his making a living.   He claimed a right to photograph his subject, a camera-shy and uncooperative public person.   Onassis and the United States then filed a counterclaim for $1.5-million, seeking injunctive relief against Galella's interference with the activities of Secret Service agents assigned to protect the former First Lady and her children.   According to Onassis, Galella continually stalked her, popped up everywhere, and emitted a curious "grunting" sound that terrified her.   She provided specific examples. On separate occasions, Galella had rushed up to her limousine; pursued her and her children at the horse show in Gladstone, New Jersey; appeared behind bursting flash bulbs at two o'clock in the morning at Oliver Smith's home in Brooklyn Heights; observed her in the theatre at the showing of 40 Carats; cruised around her in a power boat as she was swimming off Ischia; dogged her footsteps throughout her shopping trip in Capri; chased her in a taxicab; jumped from behind the wall in Central Park, which frightened her son John and caused him to lose control of his bicycle; and pursued her on the night she attended the play Two Gentlemen of Verona.   According to the Secret Service, Galella followed cars in which the children were passengers, driving at dangerous speeds, and violating the rules of the road.   All of these actions left Onassis "anguished, " "humiliated, " and "terribly upset. "

        The court held that Galella's snooping was not protected by the First Amendment and violated Onassis's right of privacy.   Galella had no right under the First Amendment to trespass inside private buildings, romance maids and bribe employees, or maintain surveillance in order to monitor Onassis's whereabouts.

> Of course legitimate countervailing social needs may warrant some intrusion despite an individual's reasonable expectation of privacy and freedom from harassment.   However, the interference allowed may be no greater than that necessary to protect the overriding public interest.   Mrs. Onassis was properly found to be a public figure and thus subject to news coverage.   Nonetheless, Galella's action went far beyond the reasonable bounds of news gathering.

The court enjoined Galella from approaching within three

hundred feet of the Onassis and Kennedy homes as well as the school attended by the children. He was also required to remain 225 feet from the children and 150 feet from Onassis at all other places. Galella was also instructed not to put the family under surveillance or to attempt to communicate with them. The court of appeals upheld the lower courts decision but reduced the distances Galella was required to keep away from Mrs. Onassis to twenty-five feet and from her children to thirty feet. In Galella, the court upheld the right of freedom from physical intrusion.

PUBLICATION OF PRIVATE INFORMATION

Invasion of privacy can also involve the publication of truthful, private information about an individual. Such situations may involve the publication of private information concerning tragedy, embarrassment, and intimacy.

Tragedy

In the two cases considered in this section the courts rejected invasion of privacy suits that involved publication of photographs of children who died as a result of accidents. The courts protected the journalists because the photographs illustrated accurate news stories about events of legitimate public interest.

Kelley v. Post Publishing Company 98 N. E. 2d 286 (1951)

In 1951, the Supreme Judicial Court of Massachusetts ruled that publishing a picture of the dead body of an automobile accident victim, with a caption referring to the body as being that of the daughter of the parents, was not an invasion of privacy that entitled the parents to sue. On August 25, 1948, the fifteen-year-old daughter of Mr. and Mrs. James Kelley was killed while riding as a passenger in an automobile. The next day, the Post Publishing Company printed an article in a wide-circulation Boston newspaper about the traffic accident. The story included a picture of the disfigured, dead body of the girl, referring to her in the accompanying caption as being the daughter of the Kelleys. The parents brought suit, claiming an invasion of privacy that caused them to suffer bodily pain and mental anguish. They claimed to have incurred medical expenses.

The court noted that the parents at this time were obviously distressed and annoyed by the publication of their
daughter's picture. It was a time above all others when the
parents preferred to be spared the anguish of sensational or
extensive publicity. However, if the right asserted by the
Kelleys was sustained it would be difficult to fix its boundaries.

> A Newspaper account or a radio broadcast setting
> forth in detail the harrowing circumstances of the
> accident might well be as distressing to the mem-
> bers of the victim's family as a photograph of the
> sort described in the declaration. A newspaper
> could not safely publish the picture of a train wreck
> or of an airplane crash if any of the bodies of the
> victims were recognizable.

The court noted that many things that are distressing or that
lack propriety or good taste are not actionable. If the Kelleys
had a cause for action, so did other members of the immediate family--the brothers and sisters whose sensibilities may
also have been offended. The only reference to the Kelleys
was that the girl whose body appeared in the photograph was
their daughter. This did not interfere with their privacy.
The court concluded that the publication of the photograph,
while probably indelicate or lacking in good taste, did not
constitute an actionable invasion of the Kelley's privacy.

Costlow v. Cusimano 311 N. Y. S. 2d 92 (1970)

The courts heard a similar case two decades later.
On June 2, 1964, three-year-old Robert Costlow and his two-
year-old sister Marion died by suffocation when they trapped
themselves inside a refrigerator located at the family's home.
Frederick Cusimano, Jr., employed by Trend Radio, Inc.,
arrived at the scene and photographed the premises and the
dead children. Cusimano then wrote and published an article,
which he illustrated with the photographs. Mr. and Mrs.
Robert Costlow alleged that Cusimano acted without their
consent and with the intent to exploit them for financial profit
and to enhance his reputation as a photographer. According
to the Costlows, Cusimano acted maliciously, with knowledge
of the existing grief of the parents, and intentionally, to hold
the parents up to public shame and to cause mental anguish
and emotional shock. The parents argued that through exhibition of the photographs they received uncomplimentary

comments from persons who read the article. They claimed that they became sick, nervous, unable to sleep, unable to eat, and that they suffered severe mental anguish and emotional disturbance. Mrs. Costlow claimed that she required medical and psychiatric care at a cost in excess of $250. The Costlows initiated action, claiming an invasion of privacy.

In this case, the court denied the invasion of privacy claim because the subject matter was within the area of legitimate public interest; publication and exhibition of the story and photographs of the incident accurately portrayed the events. The article about two children who suffocated by trapping themselves within a refrigerator, while necessarily unpleasant to the children's parents, was a matter of legitimate public concern. The tragedy was a legitimate subject of public concern because the death of two children becomes a matter of public record. Furthermore, the cause of these deaths, a trap created by a common household appliance, would be brought to the attention of the public so that similar deaths might be prevented. The court also noted that the Costlow's complaint contained no allegation that the publication falsely represented the actual occurrence. The court acknowledged that Cusimano probably had exhibited his article with disregard for the emotional distress caused by the pictures, but the court concluded that his main purpose was to make a financial profit and to enhance his professional reputation. The complaint was dismissed.

Embarrassment

On several occasions, the courts have heard cases in which it was alleged that the publication of private information constituted an invasion of privacy that had caused considerable embarrassment. In 1964, the Supreme Court of Alabama ruled that an action constituted an invasion of privacy by causing embarrassment to an ordinary person of reasonable sensitivity.

Daily Times Democrat v. Graham 162 So. 2d 474 (1964)

Flora Bell Graham, a forty-four-year-old woman, led the normal life of a housewife in her Alabama community, participating in church and community activities. On October 9, 1961, she took her two sons to the Cullman County Fair. After going on some of the rides, Graham accompanied the boys through the Fun House. She had no knowledge that there was a device that blew jets of air up from the platform at the exit of the Fun House. As she was leaving, her dress was blown up by the air jets and her body was exposed from the waist down, with the exception of that portion covered by her "panties." At that moment, the photographer for the Daily Times Democrat snapped a picture of the situation. This was done without Graham's knowledge or consent. Four days later, the picture was published on the front page of the newspaper. Graham sued, contending that as a result of this invasion of privacy she became embarrassed, self-conscious, upset, and was known to cry on occasions. The court awarded her damages of $4,166. The newspaper appealed.

The Supreme Court of Alabama noted that an actionable invasion of one's privacy accrued upon "the wrongful intrusion into one's private activities, in such manner as to outrage or cause mental suffering, shame or humiliation to a person of ordinary sensibilities." An exception occurred in cases that involved the interest of the public to be informed. In this case, the court saw nothing of legitimate news value in the photograph. It disclosed nothing about which the public was entitled to be informed. The court stressed that "not only was this photograph embarrassing to one of normal sensibilities" but it could also be classified as obscene because it was "offensive to modesty or decency" and expressed "something which delicacy, purity, or decency forbid to be expressed." The court also argued:

> One who is a part of a public scene may be lawfully photographed as an incidental part of that scene in his ordinary status. Where the status he expects to occupy is changed without his volition to a status embarrassing to an ordinary person of reasonable sensitivity, then he should not be deemed to have forfeited his right to be protected from an indecent and vulgar intrusion of his right of privacy merely because misfortune overtakes him in a public place.

The finding of the lower court was affirmed.

Jacova v. Southern Radio and Television Company
83 S. 2d 34 (1955)

In 1955, the Supreme Court of Florida heard a case

involving alleged invasion of privacy that caused embarrassment. In a news telecast presented to the television audience, Southern Radio and Television Company showed a film
depicting raids on a restaurant and a hotel in Miami Beach.
John Jacova initiated an invasion of privacy suit, claiming
that during the news film Jacova's picture had been shown to
the viewing audience. Jacova said that he was an innocent
bystander. He was present at the cigar shop at the hotel
during the time of the raid because he had stopped for a
newspaper on his way home. The film showed Jacova standing against the wall with one or two men, presumably police
officers, talking to him. The scenes consumed twelve to
fifteen seconds. While Jacova's picture was being shown an
announcer said:

> [John] Tronolone's [operator of the restaurant who
> was arrested by police] cousin Carmen was arrested
> at his apartment by other officers. Then raiders
> visited the cigar shop of the Casablanca Hotel look-
> ing for a man reputedly accepting bets there.

Jacova claimed that his right to privacy had been invaded and
that the broadcasting company had failed to exercise reasonable care in exhibiting the film. He claimed damages for
personal injuries and for injury to his business. The company argued that since the telecast did not falsely depict
Jacova as "being arrested as a gambler" or "tag" him as a
gambler it was privileged to publish his photograph because
he became an actor in a newsworthy event.

The court agreed--a communication medium had a
qualified privilege to use in its telecast the name or photograph of a person who had become an "actor" in a newsworthy event. In this case, though, the court noted that no reasonable person could have inferred that Jacova was being arrested as a gambler.

> But certainly those of his friends and acquaintances
> who saw his picture on the screen would know that
> there was nothing sinister about his presence there.
> Further, the background of his picture clearly
> showed him to be at a newsstand and not at some
> residential apartment, and that he occupied the role
> that, in fact, was his. If not, a simple explana-
> tion by him would make this clear. We see nothing
> humiliating or embarrassing in such a role--shop-
> ping at a newsstand--nor anything that would offend
> a person of "ordinary sensibilities. "

The court also noted that it often took months of diligent
searching to determine the facts of a controversial situation.
Since news reporters were expected to determine such facts
in a matter of minutes or hours, it was only reasonable to
expect that occasional errors would occur. The court concluded that it was vital that no unreasonable restraints be
placed upon the news reporter.

Williams v. KCMO Broadcasting Division--
Meredith Corporation 472 S.W. 2d 1 (1971)

In 1971, the Kansas City Court of Appeals heard a
similar case. On January 16, 1969, high school senior
Charles Williams went downtown in Kansas City, Missouri,
to answer an ad for a job. He met two fellow students, and
since it was too early to apply for the job, they went to the
courthouse to observe a trial. Williams and five other youths
were arrested by police officers and taken out the back door
of the courthouse into the parking lot with their hands above
their heads. They were searched with their hands against
a police vehicle. News personnel for television station KCMO
filmed the events. Williams was then booked at the police
station and placed in a "line-up." He was released several
hours later without any charges being filed. He had not committed any crime. The film was shown on the evening television newscast together with the following commentary:

> Kansas City police surrounded the Jackson
> County Court House today, and took six young men
> into custody following a search of the building.
> Three of them have since been released, but
> two adults and one juvenile remain in custody, and
> will be charged tomorrow in connection with last
> week's holdup of a finance company office at 219
> East 12th. All six walked past that office today
> and three were recognized by the manager as the
> holdup men. He followed them to the Court House,
> and then alerted police. Why the six went to the
> Court House isn't known.

Williams sued, charging that the film showed him in a humiliating position and that even though the event was a matter of legitimate public interest, Williams's right of privacy
was invaded by showing him in an unnatural, offensive, and
humiliating position that would offend a person of normal sensibilities. The court noted that where the publication concerns a matter of legitimate public interest there was no

cause of action for invasion of privacy. The journalist's right to publicize matters of general public interest applied "even though the individual publicized may have been drawn out of his seclusion and become involved in a noteworthy event involuntarily and against his will and over his protest. " Matters concerning crime and subsequent police action and apprehension of suspected criminals are matters of proper public concern. The court decided that Williams's contention that he was "shown in an unnatural or offensive and humiliating pose which would offend a person of normal sensibilities" applied only to cases in which "publicity was given to matters which were not the subject of legitimate public interest. " That doctrine did not apply to publicity concerning newsworthy events. Unlike Graham, where there was no publication of an item of legitimate public interest, in this case, Williams was involved in a noteworthy event about which the public had a right to be informed. The court found this to be true even though Williams's involvement was purely involuntary and against his will. The court concluded that Williams, for reasons like those stated in Jacova, had no cause for action against KCMO for invasion of privacy.

Virgil v. Sports Illustrated 424 F. Supp. 1286 (1976)

In 1976, the courts heard another case involving alleged embarrassment. The February 22, 1971, issue of Sports Illustrated described certain behavior of Mike Virgil--putting out cigarettes in his mouth and diving off stairs to impress women, hurting himself in order to collect unemployment so as to have time for bodysurfing during summer, fighting in gang fights as a youngster, and eating insects. Virgil initiated court action on the ground of invasion of privacy.

The case reached a California district court, where the judges applied the following standard of newsworthiness:

> In determining what is a matter of legitimate public interest, account must be taken of the customs and conventions of the community; and in the last analysis what is proper becomes a matter of the community mores. The line is to be drawn when the publicity ceases to be the giving of information to which the public is entitled, and becomes a morbid and sensational prying into private lives for its own sake, with which a reasonable member of the public, with decent standards, would say that he had no concern.

The court ruled that the article was "not sufficiently offensive to reach the very high level of offensiveness necessary
... to lose newsworthiness protection. " The facts were
generally unflattering and perhaps embarrassing, but they
were not offensive to the degree of morbidity or sensational-
ism.

> In fact they connote nearly as strong a positive
> image as they do a negative one.   On the one
> hand Mr. Virgil can be seen as a juvenile exhibi-
> tionist, but on the other hand he also comes across
> as the tough, aggressive maverick, an archetypal
> character occupying a respected place in the Ameri-
> can consciousness.   Given this ambiguity as to
> whether or not the facts disclosed are offensive at
> all, no reasonable juror could conclude that they
> were highly offensive.

The court emphasized that any reasonable person reading the
Sports Illustrated article would conclude that the personal
facts concerning Virgil were included as a legitimate journalistic effort to explain Virgil's extremely daring style of bodysurfing.   There was "no possibility that a juror could conclude that the personal facts were included for any inherent
morbid, sensational, or curiosity appeal they might have. "
The court concluded that disclosure of these private facts
and the identity of Mike Virgil was privileged as newsworthy
under the First Amendment.

Intimacy

In a recent case, the U.S. Supreme Court heard arguments concerning the publication of private information of
an intimate nature.   In this case, as in most of those already
cited in this section, the Court sided with the press and upheld its right to publish news of a noteworthy public interest.

Cox Broadcasting Corporation v. Cohn 420 U.S. 469 (1975)

In August, 1971, Martin Cohn's seventeen-year-old
daughter Cynthia was raped.   She suffocated in the course
of the attack.   While covering the criminal proceedings against
six youths who were indicted for her rape and murder, a news
reporter for station WSB-TV learned the victim's name by
examining the indictments--public records available for inspection.   He broadcasted her name as part of a news report

over the television station, which was owned and operated by
the Cox Broadcasting Corporation. Georgia law makes it a
misdemeanor to publicize the name of a rape victim. Cohn
cited that statute in alleging that his privacy had been invaded. The trial court agreed and awarded a summary judgment to Cohn with damages to be determined later by jury
trial. The case was appealed.

The case presented one issue to the United States Supreme Court--whether a state could impose sanctions on the
accurate publication of the name of a rape victim obtained
from public judicial records that were maintained in connection with a public prosecution and that were open to public
inspection. The Court concluded (8-1) that the state could
not do so. Great responsibility was placed upon the news
media to report fully and accurately the proceedings of government. Concerning judicial matters in particular, "The
function of the press serves to guarantee the fairness of trials
and to bring to bear the beneficial effects of public scrutiny
upon the administration of justice. " The Court refused to
uphold a system that made public records generally available
to the media while at the same time it forbade their publication when offensive to the sensibilities of reasonable people.
Such a policy made it very difficult for the press to inform
their readers about public events while yet remaining within
the law. The rule invited self-censorship and would very
likely lead to the suppression of items that would otherwise
be put into print, and that should be made available to the
public. According to the Court, "The prevailing law of invasion of privacy generally recognizes that the interests in
privacy fade when the information involved already appears
on the public record. " The protection of freedom of the press
provided by the First and Fourteenth Amendments barred
Georgia from making the WSB-TV news broadcast the basis
of civil liability. The lower court judgment was reversed.

The Graham case confirms that publication of private
information can constitute an invasion of privacy that is subject to civil liability. However, the other cases discussed
in this section indicate that the courts uphold freedom of the
press in invasion of privacy suits when the matter is newsworthy and of public interest. In Kelley and Costlow, the
courts ruled that publication of photographs to illustrate an
article that accurately represented the facts surrounding ac-
cidental death constituted a matter of legitimate public interest. In Jacova and Williams, the court determined that publication of information concerning crime and the apprehension
of suspected criminals constituted a matter of public concern.

In Virgil, the court ruled that even though the published facts were unflattering and embarrassing, since they were not offensive to the degree of morbidity or sensationalism--the "newsworthiness" protection of the press was not lost.   In Cox, the U. S. Supreme Court decided that a state cannot bar the publication of public records regarding the rape and murder of a young girl.   Such a policy would contradict the freedom of the press provided by the First and Fourteenth Amendments.

PUBLICATION OF FALSE INFORMATION

The final type of invasion of privacy involves the publication of any false information about an individual, whether the material is defamatory or not.   There are two types of false reports--fictionalization and false light.

Fictionalization

Fictionalization usually involves a radio or television writer who employs exaggeration in dramatizing a true happening.   In 1958, a district court decided a case of this type.

Strickler v. National Broadcasting Company, Inc.
167 F. Supp. 68 (1958)

During October, 1956, Kenneth Strickler, a commander on active duty with the U. S. Navy, was a passenger on a commercial airliner flying from Honolulu to San Francisco. The airliner developed engine trouble and was forced to make an emergency landing.   Strickler and other passengers were rescued by a Coast Guard cutter.   In 1957, NBC telecast a show depicting in dramatized form the experiences that happened to Strickler.   Strickler claimed the telecast, made without his consent, violated his right of privacy.   His complaint alleged that the television program portrayed him in the highly personal and private act of praying during the course of emergency landing, that it showed him out of uniform and wearing a Hawaiian shirt, that the program depicted him as smoking a pipe and cigarettes, and that the program did not indicate the valuable assistance provided by him in the evacuation of the occupants of the plane.   Strickler claimed that he was placed in a false position by the telecasts and as a result he experienced humiliation, embarrassment, and great mental pain and suffering.   NBC introduced a motion to dismiss the suit.

The court considered two issues. First, what was the proper jurisdiction for this case. Strickler claimed to have causes for action in several states--in fact, all the states where the program was produced and telecast. The court rejected this claim and held that the cause of action was applicable only to California laws because that is the state of Strickler's residence and the state in which he sustained the alleged damage. Second, the court decided whether the telecast by NBC was actionable. The court ruled that the network, by depicting Strickler in the personal act of praying, showing him out of uniform, failing to indicate that he assisted in the evacuation, and showing him as a smoker, had embellished the incident in such a way as to constitute sufficient fictionalization to warrant a cause for invasion of privacy.

Aquino v. Bulletin Company 190 Pa. Super 528 (1959)

In 1959, the courts heard another case involving fictionalization. Theresa Allizza, daughter of Michael and Nancy Aquino, secretly married John Masciocchi on August 19, 1949, before a Justice of the Peace. John promised that at a later date he would provide a home for her and marry her in a church. After the ceremony, they each returned to their parents' homes. Theresa's parents learned about the marriage the next day. Later, when Theresa pressed her husband to carry out his promises, he told her that he did not intend to keep them and that he had married her only to spite her parents who had been opposed to his courting her. Subsequently, Theresa obtained a divorce. The press published numerous news stories regarding both the marriage and divorce. One such story appeared in the December 3, 1950, issue of the American Weekly, a supplement to the Philadelphia Sunday Bulletin. This publication, of which 695, 423 copies were distributed, became the source of an invasion of privacy suit brought by Theresa and her parents. A jury awarded them $10, 000. The case was appealed.

The court noted that Theresa's marriage and her divorce were newsworthy events; newspapers had a right to publish such information. However, the article in question was in the nature of a story and not a news article. It was in a Sunday supplement and not in the news section. It was bedecked with an "illustrated" drawing covering over half of the page. The title of the article was written across the illustration and was entitled "Marriage for Spite. " The illustration was a drawing of a girl standing in front of a theatre.

Her arms were placed around a man who had a hat on the back of his head, a drooping cigarette in his mouth, a hand and a newspaper in his jacket pocket, and his eyes to the ground away from the girl. The figures pictured bore no resemblance to Theresa and John, whom they illustrated. Appearing under the illustration was "Since John Was Barred from Her Home, Theresa Met Him Secretly on a Street Corner." According to the court, the author had permitted his imagination to roam through the facts so that "newsworthy events were presented in a style used almost exclusively by writers of fiction." Although the basic facts of the story were admittedly true, the author embellished and fictionalized them. Therefore, the court upheld the jury verdict against the Bulletin Company.

Carlisle v. Fawcett Publications, Inc. 20 Cal. Rptr. 405 (1962)

In a 1962 case, the courts indicated that minor fictionalization did not constitute an invasion of privacy. The leading article in the December, 1960, issue of Motion Picture was entitled "Janet Leigh's Own Story--'I Was a Child Bride at 14!' " The article included the following excerpts:

> For the small tawny-haired blonde and the
> lean, dark boy their world was coming to an end
> that desperate summer. They put their arms
> around each other in the dark and held tight, afraid.
> The world itself was headed for disaster those
> warm days in 1941--to Pearl Harbor and World
> War II, to Hiroshima and the atomic bomb--but the
> boy and the girl were in love and frightened....
> That summer in Merced, a small town south of
> San Francisco with only one motion picture theatre,
> Jeanette Morrison--the girl who was to become Janet
> Leigh--was 14. The dark boy we'll call "John" was 18.
> They went through the next step, the marriage
> itself, like robots. Later, neither Jeanette nor
> John could recall where they were married, by
> whom, or who stood up with them as a witness.
> They know that a justice of the peace mumbled a
> hurried ceremony, declared them man and wife according to the laws of the state of Nevada, and pocketed
> John's crumpled three dollars with a grunt....
> It was, for a short frustrating time they had, a marriage. One night, and they had to return to Merced
> and face adult authority. They began to have misgivings.
> The annulment followed.

John Kenneth Carlisle initiated action for invasion of privacy.

The California District Court of Appeal noted that there was a public interest that attached to people who by their accomplishments created a widespread attention to their activities. Such public figures as actors and actresses, professional athletes, noted inventors, explorers, war heroes, and the like have to some extent lost their right of privacy. Furthermore, people closely associated with such public figures "also to some extent lose their right to the privacy that one unconnected with the famous or notorious would have." Carlisle claimed that the article contained errors, the two principal ones being that the date of the marriage was put back approximately a year to the attack at Pearl Harbor and the age of the actress at the time of marriage was reduced a year. These elements were altered, apparently for dramatic effect. But, the mere fact that there were errors in the account did not constitute an invasion of privacy. It was further contended that the article was fictionalized and that because the publication was not restricted to a "cold recital of the skeletal fact of the marriage and the annulment but fills in the gaps with the supposed conversations and thoughts of the participants," the article invaded Carlisle's privacy. The court disagreed; the article contained no "so-called revelations of any intimate details which would tend to outrage public [decency]." The circumstances in Carlisle differed sufficiently from Strickler and Aquino. The fictionalization in this case was minor and did not constitute an invasion of privacy.

False Light

False light concerns the creation of a false impression, even if the impression is not unfavorable. In most cases, the plaintiffs allege that the publication places them in an unfavorable light. In 1967, the U. S. Supreme Court handed down the decision in the case of Time, Inc. v. Hill. The Court applied the New York Times standard to the area of privacy, ruling that the First Amendment shields the press from invasion of privacy suits involving matters of public interest unless there is proof of actual malice.

Time, Inc. v. Hill 385 U.S. 374 (1967)

James J. Hill, his wife, and five children became a

front-page news story after being held hostage by three escaped convicts in their suburban home in Whitemarch, Pennsylvania, for nineteen hours on September 11-12, 1952. The
family was subsequently released unharmed. In an interview
with journalists, Hill stressed that the convicts had not been
violent, and in fact had treated the family courteously. Eventually, the convicts were tracked down and in a battle with
the police two of the convicts were killed. Hill sought to
keep his family out of the public spotlight by discouraging
interviews with magazine writers or appearances on television.
In an effort to preserve their privacy, the family moved to
Connecticut. In 1953, Joseph Hayes published The Desperate
Hours, a novel depicting the experience of a family of four
held hostage by three escaped convicts in the family's suburban home. But contrary to Hill's experience in Hayes's
story the father and son are beaten and the daughter is subjected to verbal sexual insult. The book was made into a
play, which was also entitled The Desperate Hours.

In February, 1955, an article appeared in Life magazine that was entitled "True Crime Inspires Tense Play,"
with the subtitle "The ordeal of a family trapped by convicts
gives Broadway a new thriller, 'The Desperate Hours.'" The
article noted that the Hill family had experienced a "desperate ordeal" by being held prisoners in their home by three
escaped convicts. The article noted that people throughout
the country

> read about it in Joseph Hayes' novel, The Desper-
> ate Hours, inspired by the family's experience.
> Now they can see the story re-enacted in Hayes'
> broadway play, based on the book, and the next
> year will see it in his movie, which has been film-
> ed but is being held up until the play has had a chance
> to pay off.

The article described the play as "a heart-stopping account of
how a family rose to heroism in a crisis." Life claimed to
transport "some of the actors to the actual house where the
Hills were besieged." Pictures on the following two pages
included an enactment of the son being "roughed up" by one
of the convicts entitled "brutish convict," a picture of the
daughter biting the hand of a convict to make him drop a gun
entitled "daring daughter," and a picture of the father toss-
ing his gun through the door after a "brave try" to save his
family had failed. Hill sued on the ground that the article
intentionally and falsely gave the impression that the play

portrayed the Hill family experience. The courts determined that even though the play was fictionalized, Life's article portrayed it as a reenactment of the Hill's experience in order to advertise and sell magazines. The jury awarded Hill $50,000 compensatory and $25,000 punitive damages, but the amount was later reduced to $30,000 compensatory damages without punitive damages.

Before the U.S. Supreme Court, attorneys for Life argued that the article concerned a topic of legitimate news interest, a subject of value and concern to the public at the time of publication, and that it was "published in good faith without any malice whatsoever." In balancing the right to privacy against the freedom of the press, the Court held (6-3) on the side of the press. The subject of the article, the opening of the new play linked to an actual interest, was a matter of public interest. The Court also noted that sanctions against either innocent or negligent misstatements would instill in the press a fear of large verdicts in damage suits, which would inevitably cause publishers to "steer far wide of the unlawful zone" and thus "create the danger that the legitimate utterance will be penalized." The Court concluded that the First Amendment shields the press from invasion of privacy suits involving matters of public interest unless there is proof of actual malice, that is, proof that the material was published with deliberate falsehood or reckless disregard of the truth. In Hill, there was an absence of such proof. In subsequent cases, however, such proof was evident.

Varnish v. Best Medium Publishing Company, Inc.
405 F. 2d 608 (1968)

In September, 1963, Melvin Varnish's wife killed their three young children and committed suicide. In March, 1964, the Best Medium Publishing Company published an article entitled "'Happiest Mother' Kills Her Three Children and Herself" in its weekly, the National Enquirer. The article was based upon newspaper reports and police records that author James Donahue had examined. On the basis of this article, Varnish initiated an action for invasion of privacy, claiming that the portrayal of his wife and his relationship with her was fictionalized and placed him in a false and unfavorable light. He claimed that the "happy wife and mother" theme used throughout the article was fictitious and was intended to be ironic to indicate Varnish's insensitivity and lack of caring for his wife. Varnish claimed that, as a result of

the article, he attempted suicide, required psychiatric attention, suffered unemployment, was shunned in his community,
and became the victim of severe mental suffering.   The case
was tried before a jury, which awarded $5,000 compensatory
and $15,000 punitive damages.   The case was appealed.

       The court determined that Varnish had to establish
that the article was false and that it was published with knowledge that it was false or in reckless disregard for the truth.
The court found that Varnish had met this burden.   The record showed that Mrs. Varnish, far from being the happiest
mother, was in reality a despondent, depressed, and extremely unhappy woman.   A suicide note addressed to her mother
expressed her extreme unhappiness.   This note was distorted
in the article.

> ... police found a note left by Mrs. Varnish for
> her mother.   It said:
> > "Just a note in explanation to let you know I
> > am going to put the three children and myself
> > to sleep forever.   I can't go on. "
> It was an explanation that explained nothing, least
> of all to the shocked Varnish.

The actual note explained the suicide in more detail.

> Just a note and explanation to let you know that I
> am going to put the three children and myself to
> sleep forever.   I can't go on any longer.   I see no
> future for the children or myself.   Mitch [plaintiff]
> is impossible and this is the only way to get away
> from him.   Tell Uncle Chris and Uncle Butch I'm
> sorry about the money they each loaned me in
> 1961....   I owe so much I'll never have to bother
> anyone anymore.

The story also contained fictionalized dialogue and some minor inaccuracies.   It concluded:

> ... it would be easier for Varnish if he could only
> understand why the happiest wife and mother in the
> neighborhood suddenly decided to kill her three
> children and herself.

During the trial, Varnish had testified that his wife was not
a happy person, but he claimed that he understood her and
her problems and that he did what he could for her.   The

court noted that minor inaccuracies and fictionalized dialogue
would not alone defeat the privilege granted to truthful publications of public interest.   However, the article presented
a substantially false and distorted picture.   The court found
sufficient evidence of recklessness because of the author's
testimony that he had no basis except his own "presumption"
for labeling Mrs. Varnish a happy wife and mother.   Both
the suicide note and the police reports that the author had
in his possession indicated that the Varnishes did not have a
happy home life.   The article was published with knowledge
that it was false or with reckless disregard for the truth.
The finding of the lower court was affirmed.   The U. S. Supreme Court denied certiorari in April, 1969.

Cantrell v. Forest City Publishing Company 419 U. S. 245 (1974)

        In a recent case, the U. S. Supreme Court held a re-
porter guilty of invasion of privacy when he, through actual
malice, placed a family in a false light.   In December, 1967,
Margaret Cantrell's husband Melvin was killed along with
forty-three other people when the Silver Bridge across the
Ohio River at Point Pleasant, West Virginia, collapsed. Joseph Eszterhas, a reporter assigned by the Cleveland Plain
Dealer to cover the story of the disaster, wrote a "news
feature" focusing on the funeral of Melvin Cantrell and the
impact of his death on the Cantrell family.   Five months
later, Eszterhas and photographer Richard Conway returned
to the Point Pleasant area to write a follow-up feature.   The
two men went to the Cantrell residence, where they talked
with the children and took fifty pictures.   Mrs. Cantrell
was not at home at any time during the sixty to ninety minutes that the men were at the Cantrell home.   The story appeared as the lead feature in the August 4, 1968, edition of
the Sunday Magazine section of the Plain Dealer.   The article
stressed the family's abject poverty; the children's old, ill-
fitting clothes and the deteriorating conditions of their home
were detailed in both the text and accompanying photographs.
Mrs. Cantrell brought action for invasion of privacy against
the Forest City Publishing Company, publisher of the newspaper.   She alleged that the article unreasonably placed the
family in a false light before the public through its many
inaccuracies and untruths.   The story actually contained a
number of false statements.   Most conspicuously: although
Mrs. Cantrell was not present during the reporter's visit,
Eszterhas wrote:

        Margaret Cantrell will talk neither about what

happened nor about how they are doing. She wears
the same mask of non-expression she wore at the
funeral. She is a proud woman. She says that
after it happened, the people in town offered to
help them out with money and they refused to take
it.

Other misrepresentations involved Eszterhas's descriptions of
the poverty in which the Cantrells were living and the dirty
and dilapidated conditions of the Cantrell home. Mrs. Cantrell claimed the story made the family objects of pity and
ridicule and caused them to suffer outrage, mental distress,
shame, and humiliation. The jury returned a verdict against
the paper, the reporter, and the photographer for compensatory monetary damages. The case reached the Supreme Court.

The Court decided (8-1) that the Forest City Publishing
Company had published knowing or reckless falsehoods about
the Cantrells. Eszterhas must have known that a number of
the statements in the feature story were untrue. His article
plainly implied that Mrs. Cantrell had been present during
his visit to her home and that Eszterhas had observed her
wearing "the same mask of non-expression" she wore at her
husband's funeral. These were "calculated falsehoods." The
jury was correct in finding that Eszterhas had portrayed the
Cantrells in a false light through knowing or reckless untruth.
It appears, as seen in Cantrell and Varnish, that the Court
is willing to punish any publication that, through actual malice, places an individual in false light.

As the cases cited in this chapter have demonstrated,
the courts have consistently sided with journalists in balancing
the right of privacy with the freedom of the press. Published
accounts of newsworthy events are protected if they are vested with a legitimate public interest. The four privacy torts--
appropriation, intrusion, publication of private matters, and
publication of false information--must be sufficiently demonstrated to outweigh journalistic considerations.

Bibliography

Books

Pember, Don R. Privacy and the Press: The Law, the Mass
Media, and the First Amendment. Seattle: University of
Washington Press, 1972.

Articles

McKeever, Joyce. "Right to Privacy: Publication of True Information on the Public Record," Duquesne Law Review 14 (Spring, 1976), 507-20.

Prosser, William L. "Privacy," California Law Review 48 (August, 1960), 383-423.

Cases

Aquino v. Bulletin Company 190 Pa. Super 528 (1959)

Booth v. Curtis Publishing Company 15 A. D. 2d 343 (1962)

Cantrell v. Forest City Publishing Company 419 U. S. 245 (1974)

Carlisle v. Fawcett Publications, Inc. 20 Cal. Rptr. 405 (1962)

Costlow v. Cusimano 311 N. Y. S. 2d 92 (1970)

Cox Broadcasting Corporation v. Cohn 420 U. S. 469 (1975)

Daily Times Democrat v. Graham 162 So. 2d 474 (1964)

Dietemann v. Time, Inc. 449 F. 2d 245 (1971)

Galella v. Onassis 487 F. 2d 986 (1973)

Kelley v. Post Publishing Company 98 N. E. 2d 286 (1951)

Jacova v. Southern Radio and Television Company 83 S. 2d 34 (1955)

Man v. Warner Brothers, Inc. 317 F. Supp. 50 (1970)

Palmer v. Schonhorn Enterprises, Inc. 232 A. 2d 458 (1967)

Paulsen v. Personality Posters, Inc. 299 N. Y. S. 2d 501 (1968)

Pearson v. Dodd 410 F. 2d 701 (1969)

People v. Kunkin 107 Cal. Rptr. 184 (1973)

Sarat Lahiri v. Daily Mirror, Inc. 295 N. Y. S. 382 (1937)

Spahn v. Julian Messner, Inc. 233 N. E. 2d 840 (1967)

Strickler v. National Broadcasting Company, Inc. 167 F.
  Supp. 68 (1958)

Time, Inc. v. Hill 385 U. S. 374 (1967)

Uhlaender v. Henricksen 316 F. Supp. 1277 (1970)

Varnish v. Best Medium Publishing Company, Inc. 405 F.
  2d 608 (1968)

Virgil v. Sports Illustrated 424 F. Supp. 1286 (1976)

Williams v. KCMO Broadcasting Division--Meredith Corporation 472 S. W. 2d 1 (1971)

Zacchini v. Scripps-Howard Broadcasting Company 429 U. S.
  1037 (1977)

CHAPTER IV

COPYRIGHT

There was little need to protect an author's literary
property prior to the advent of the printing press.   After
all, each hand-copied manuscript was the original work of
a single copyist.   Each copy was protected by the law of
personal property.   With the development of mechanical printing, mass copying became greatly simplified.   Authors had
no recourse to control the piracy of their works.   After two
centuries of dispute and litigation over the authorship and
ownership of written works, England recognized the need for
comprehensive copyright law.   In 1710, Parliament passed
the Statute of Eight Anne, a law that closely resembled the
first copyright law adopted in America.   The law granted
authors certain exclusive rights to their works and restricted
unauthorized reproduction and distribution of those works.
Under a system of copyright law, authors were encouraged
to continue writing, safe in the knowledge that the originality
and creativity of their efforts would be protected.   Without
it, the quantity and diversity of original works would be impeded.

HISTORY OF COPYRIGHT LAW

Copyright law in America has two sources, common
and statutory.   Each may have a significant impact on the
protection of an author's work.

Common-Law Copyright

Common-law copyright is in effect prior to publication.
There is automatic protection for authors as soon as they
create the work--no one may publish it without the authors'
permission--but it lasts only as long as the work remains
unpublished.   It can last forever, but it ceases if and when

108

the work is first published. Common-law copyright ends
when statutory copyright begins. The practical value of
common-law copyright is limited; it remains useful, however,
for authors who choose not to disseminate their work. Common-law copyright has been recognized by the courts.

Pushman v. New York Graphic Society, Inc. 287 N. Y. 302 (1942)

Hovsep Pushman was an artist of international reputation for painting color still life subjects. He was able to
command substantial prices for his works, many of which
were held by museums and collectors. In 1930, he completed a painting entitled "When Autumn Is Here. " Acting as
Pushman's agent, Grand Central Art Galleries sold the painting outright to the University of Illinois for $3,600. At the
time, Pushman did not state that he wanted to reserve reproduction rights for this painting. Whenever the gallery sold
a painting to a purchaser who was in the reproduction business, the gallery negotiated a separate written agreement
between the artist and the purchaser covering reproduction
rights. In this case, involving a university rather than a
reproduction firm, Pushman never expressly authorized the
gallery to sell the rights to reproduce his painting, nor did
he forbid it. The University of Illinois exhibited the painting until 1940, when it sold the right to make reproductions
to the New York Graphic Society. The reproductions were
about to be put on the market when Pushman learned of the
project. He sued in an effort to stop the reproduction of
his painting.

Since the painting was not legally copyrighted, the
issue to be decided by the court was whether an artist, after
giving an absolute and unconditional bill of sale of a painting,
still retained a common-law copyright that enabled her or
him to prevent commercial reproduction. The court recognized that the common-law copyright belonged to an artist
or author until disposed of by him. In this case, the issue
was whether it had passed with the sale of the painting. Pushman argued that the right to reproduce his work was separate
and apart from the work itself and therefore had a separate
and distinct value. Since no specific permission to reproduce accompanied the original sale, the common-law copyright did not pass from Pushman to the University of Illinois.
The court held that artists must, if they wish to retain reproduction right, reserve that right when they sell the painting. A straight out bill of sale showed an intention to convey

the artist's whole property in his picture. The court concluded
that the unconditional sale carried with it the transfer of the
common-law copyright and the right to reproduce. Pushman
had taken no steps to withhold or control that right. Even
though the court acknowledged the principle of a common-law
copyright, it judged that the right had passed when the painting was sold.

Chamberlain v. Feldman 300 N. Y. 135 (1949)

Another common-law copyright case involved Samuel
L. Clemens, who, under the pen name "Mark Twain" wrote
a story entitled "A Murder, a Mystery and a Marriage. " He
offered the manuscript to William Dean Howells, editor of
the Atlantic Monthly, for publication. During the ensuing
correspondence between Twain and Howells, Twain suggested
an unusual project. He proposed that several famous writers
of the period be enlisted to write their own final chapter for
a mystery work. Twain would set forth a common plot in
the first few chapters and each author would compose a solution, in addition to Twain's own ending. There would be
a common story line with several different endings. However, Twain's idea never developed. When Twain died in
1910, the manuscript of "A Murder, a Mystery and a Marriage" was not found among his effects and had never been
published anywhere, by anyone. In 1945, Lew Feldman bought
the original manuscript at an auction sale. Feldman contacted
Thomas Chamberlain, the owner of all literary property formerly belonging to Mark Twain. Feldman sought permission
to publish the work, but permission was refused. He initiated court action.

The trial court presumed that Twain had transferred
the manuscript and such an unrestricted transfer of this fictional manuscript probably carried with it a transfer of the
common-law copyright. The court of appeals, however, noted that in Twain's lifetime no basis could be found for presuming such a transfer. During Twain's lifetime, the manuscript had been rejected for publication by the Atlantic Monthly and it could be inferred that Twain finally decided that the
manuscript was unsuitable, and never intended it for publication. Thus, the author never granted to anyone the literary
property in "A Murder, a Mystery and a Marriage. " The
court claimed:

> The common-law copyright, or right of first publi-
> cation, is a right different from that of ownership

of the physical paper; the first of those rights does not necessarily pass with the second; and the separate common law copyright or control of the right to reproduce belongs to the artist or author until disposed of by him....

In Chamberlain, the court decided that Twain had never parted with the publication rights to the plot and therefore nobody else ever acquired them. The common-law copyright does not necessarily pass with the ownership of the physical paper. It belongs to the author until disposed of by him. No matter how the manuscript left Twain's possession, he apparently never intended that it be published. Feldman could not have purchased the publication rights.

Estate of Hemingway v. Random House 23 N. Y. 2d 341 (1968)

In this case, the courts again considered the right of common-law copyright. During the thirteen years prior to his death in 1961, a close friendship developed between Ernest Hemingway and a young writer, A. E. Hotchner. Hotchner became a favored drinking and traveling companion of the famous author. In his conversations with Hotchner, Hemingway disclosed personal reminiscences, literary views, and revealed information about actual persons on whom some of the famous writer's characters had been based. Hotchner made careful notes of the conversations in writing or on a portable tape recorder. During Hemingway's lifetime, Hotchner published several articles in which he quoted material from the conversations. Hemingway approved of this practice. In 1966, Random House published Papa Hemingway, a work authored by Hotchner in which there was heavy reliance on the conversations. The work, intended as a serious and revealing biography, contained two chapters on Hemingway's final illness and suicide. Hotchner mentioned events as well as medical information to which he was privileged as an intimate of the family. A suit was initiated, seeking an injunction and damages, that alleged that Papa Hemingway consisted primarily of literary matter composed by Hemingway in which he had a common-law copyright. It was argued that Hemingway was entitled to a common-law copyright because his directly quoted opinions were his "literary creations, " his "literary property, " and Hotchner's note taking only performed the mechanics of recording. Hemingway's conversations constituted not just a statement of his ideas but the very manner in which he conceived them and were as much entitled to common-law copyright as anything he might have written on paper. What Hemingway said one day could become a written manuscript the next day.

The court noted that common-law copyright enabled the author to control the first publication of his work or to prevent publication entirely. The key issue in this case was whether the common-law copyright extended to conversational speech. The court noted that because speech was easily captured by electronic devices, the law should not necessarily exclude protection of words a speaker might utter in private dialogue which may or may not be published eventually. There could be situations in which an individual brought forth oral statements from another person that both understood to be the unique intellectual product of the principal speaker--statements that would clearly qualify for common-law copyright if they were made in writing. The court noted that in Hemingway's later years it had become a continuing practice for Hotchner to write stories, about and approved by Hemingway, that were based largely on conversations between the two men. In these circumstances, authority to publish was implied, thus negating any common-law copyright. The court noted that it was possible to reserve the common-law copyright. It could be stated in prefatory words or inferred from the circumstances in which the dialogue occurred. But as a general rule regarding conversational speech, "There should be a presumption that the speaker has not reserved any common-law rights unless the contrary strongly appears. " In this case, Hemingway's words and behavior, "far from making any such reservation, left no doubt of his willingness to permit Hotchner to draw freely on their conversation in writing about him and to publish such material. " In Hemingway, Chamberlain, and Pushman, the courts noted that works of artists and authors, written or spoken, fall under the protection of common-law copyright.

Statutory Copyright

Article I, Section 8, of the Constitution provides the basic authority for a law of copyright. It gives Congress power "to promote the Progress of Science and useful Arts, by securing for limited Times to Authors and Inventors the exclusive Right to their respective Writings and Discoveries. "

Congress first exercised this constitutional power by enacting the Copyright Act of 1790. The act provided that any author or legal owner of a map, chart, or book printed in the United States could legally affirm the sole right to print, reprint, publish, or sell the work. The term of the copyright was fourteen years with the privilege of obtaining a renewal for an additional fourteen years. In order to copyright a work, a copy of the title had to be deposited and recorded in the clerk's office of the district court where the author or owner lived. The author had to pay the clerk a fee of sixty cents. The author had to publish a copy of the record in a newspaper printed in the United States and had to deposit a copy of the record with the Secretary of State. Any violation was subject to penalties that included forfeiture of all copies to the owner to be destroyed, as well as a fine of fifty cents per page of the work found in the violator's possession. Half of the fine was given to the copyright owner and the other half was used by the government. Court action had to begin within one year of the violation.

Over the next century, few changes occurred in the copyright law. The law was amended to give protection to prints, musical compositions, photographs, and works of fine art. The term of protection was lengthened; the original term was set at twenty-eight years with the owner having the right to a renewal period of an additional fourteen years. During this period, the main aspects of the law remained unchanged.

A revision of the copyright law was enacted in 1909. Copyrightable material included all original books, periodicals, lectures, dramas, musical compositions, maps, works of art, reproductions, scientific drawings, photographs, prints, and motion pictures. Material generally not eligible for statutory copyright protection included titles, phrases, names, slogans, designs, lettering, coloring, ideas, plans, diaries, time cards, scoreboards, calendars, rulers, and schedules of sporting events. Application for copyright had to be made to the Registrar of Copyrights in Washington, D.C. Two complete copies "of the best edition" of the work had to be "promptly deposited in the copyright office" or mailed to the Registrar of Copyrights. The application fee for registration was $6. A published work had to contain a notice of copyright. The first part of the notice contains the symbol ©, the word "copyright," or the abbreviation "copr." The second part gives the name of the copyright proprietor. The third part identifies the year in which the copyright was secured, that is, the date of publication. The initial copyright period remained twenty-eight years but the renewal period was increased to an additional twenty-eight years provided that a "proper and timely" application for renewal was made. Punitive damages for infringement were fixed; the minimum amount was $250 and the maximum amount was $5,000. Compensatory damages could also be awarded. The act also protected the right of an individual to use copyrighted works without obtaining permission so long as the use constituted a "fair use" of the work.

Between 1909 and 1976, technological advancements necessitated piecemeal amendments to the act. During these years, radio, film, tape recorders, television, computers, photocopying, cable television, and even satellite communications systems came under the scope of copyright law.

The current law, which was passed in 1976, retains much of the content and structure of the 1909 act. There are, however, some significant revisions. The 1909 act left it up to the states to protect unpublished works; the 1976 act provides for federal protection from the time the work is fixed in a tangible form. Under the law, a work is "fixed in a tangible medium" when it is "sufficiently permanent or stable to permit it to be perceived, reproduced, or otherwise communicated for a period of more than transitory duration." Under the new law, publication is less of a legal criterion for inclusion of a work under statutory copyright. The 1976 law also establishes a single term of copyright, generally lasting for the author's lifetime plus fifty years. Under the new law, the fee for registration of most works is $10. The new law sets forth some specific provisions regarding reproduction rights of libraries and cable broadcasting systems. The law also clarifies the doctrine of fair use, specifying that reproduction "for purposes such as criticism, comment, news reporting, teaching (including multiple copies for classroom use), scholarship, or research, is not an infringement of copyright." In addition, the act set forth the following factors to be considered in determining when a particular use is a "fair use."

1. the purpose and character of the use, including whether such use is of a commercial nature or is for nonprofit educational purposes;
2. the nature of the copyrighted work;
3. the amount and substantiality of the portion used in relation to the copyrighted work as a whole; and
4. the effect of the use upon the potential market for or value of the copyrighted work.

The courts will apply these criteria in determining whether a use is an infringement or a fair use. The 1976 law also established that statutory damages for infringement may be between not less than $250 and not more than $10,000. However, if a copyright owner proves that an infringement was committed "willfully," the amount may be increased to as much as $50,000. If the infringers prove that they were unaware that their act was an infringement, the fine may be as low as $100. The court has wide discretion.

While the basic concepts of copyright law have remained unchanged in the 1790, 1909, and 1976 enactments, frequent amendments have been necessary in order to enlarge the scope of materials covered by copyright law. As technology continues to expand the media of communication, additional changes in statutory copyright law can be expected.

STANDARDS OF COPYRIGHT LAW

Disputes have arisen over the specific requirements and procedures a work must satisfy to comply with copyright law. In such instances, the courts have had to resolve the matter and in so doing have clarified specific standards of the law.

Originality

Originality is the fundamental requirement of copyrightable material. This standard implies that an author or artist created the work through her or his own skill and effort. The exact meaning of the term "originality" has been a subject for the courts. An early interpretation was provided by Judge Joseph Story of Massachusetts in Emerson v. Davies in 1845.

> In truth, in literature, in science and in art, there are and can be, few, if any, things, which, in an abstract sense, are strictly new and original throughout. Every book in literature, science, and art, borrows, and must necessarily borrow, and use much which was well known and used before. No man creates a new language for himself, at least if he be a wise man, in writing a book. He contents himself with the use of language already known and used and understood by others. No man writes

exclusively from his own thoughts, unaided and un-
instructed by the thoughts of others. The thoughts
of every man are, more or less, a combination of
what other men have thought and expressed, although
they may be modified, exalted, or improved by his
own genius or reflection. If no book could be the
subject of copyright which was not new and original
in the elements of which it is composed, there could
be no ground for any copyright in modern times,
and we should be obliged to ascend very high, even
in antiquity, to find a work entitled to such emi-
nence. . . .

In Story's opinion, authors necessarily incorporate parts of the
content, style, and/or arrangement of another's work into
their own. Such an effort constitutes a new and unique treatment and is entitled to copyright protection. Story's concept
has been generally adhered to by the courts. In most cases,
it is relatively easy to determine if a work is original. Some
provide a more challenging question for the courts.

Bleistein v. Donaldson Lithographing Company 188 U. S. 239 (1903)

In this case, the alleged copyright violation consisted
of the copying in reduced form, by Donaldson Lithographing
Company, of three chromolithographs prepared by George
Bleistein's employees for advertisements of a circus owned
by a Mrs. Wallace. Each of the posters contained a por-
trait of Wallace in the corner and printing related to the designs that indicated that the subjects of the designs could
actually be seen at the circus. One design was of an ordinary ballet, another pictured a number of men and women performing on bicycles, and the third consisted of groups of men
and women whitened to represent statues. The lower courts
returned a verdict for Donaldson on the ground that the chromolithographs were not within the protection of the copyright
law and could thus be copied. Bleistein appealed.

The U. S. Supreme Court reversed (7-2) the lower
court. The Court noted that the material could be copyrighted
because it met the requirement of originality. The designs
belonged to Bleistein because they had been produced by persons employed and paid by Bleistein. According to the opinion of Justice Oliver Wendell Holmes, "these prints in their
ensemble and in all their details, in their design and particular combinations of figures, lines, and colors, are the original work" of Bleistein's designer. Holmes claimed that "the

least pretentious picture has more originality in it than directories and the like, which may be copyrighted. " The Court also noted that the designs were properly copyrighted before publication. The judgment of the lower court was reversed and a new trial was ordered. In <u>Bleistein</u>, the Court noted that printing and engraving were not excluded from protection of copyright law. In addition, this case was significant because it marked the first time the Court applied copyright law to advertising. Holmes noted:

> A picture is none the less a picture and none the less a subject of copyright, that it is used for an advertisement. And if pictures may be used to advertise soap, or the theatre, or monthly magazines, as they are, they may be used to advertise a circus.

<u>Jewelers' Circular Publishing Company v.</u>
<u>Keystone Publishing Company 281 F. 83 (1922)</u>

This case also involved the question of originality. In 1915, Jewelers' Circular Publishing Company copyrighted a third edition of <u>Trade-Marks of the Jewelry and Kindred Trades</u>. Large quantities of the work sold for $5 per copy. This book contained the names and addresses of jewelers classified under various headings, arranged in alphabetical order, and opposite the name of each jeweler appeared the trade names and trademarks the jeweler used. Information contained in the book was obtained by direct inquiry with the jewelers and the illustrations of the trademarks were printed from cuts usually prepared by Jewelers' Circular Publishing Company. In 1920, Keystone Publishing Company prepared <u>Jewelers' Index,</u> a book that achieved the same purpose as the book published by Jewelers' Circular Publishing Company. To acquire the information necessary for publication, Keystone sent a letter to various jewelers asking if enclosed illustrations represented the appropriate trademarks. Fastened to the letter in each case was a printed illustration of a trademark that had been clipped directly from Jewelers book. After verifying the information, Keystone published their work, often making cuts of trademarks from the illustrations clipped from Jewelers' book. In some instances, errors in drawings of trademarks found in Jewelers' book were not corrected when they were mechanically reproduced and placed in Keystone's book. Jewelers' Circular Publishing Company sued.

Keystone argued that Jewelers' book was not protected

by copyright as it was only a list of prints or labels designed to be used for articles of manufacture. The court ruled that Jewelers' book met the requirement of originality. It was clearly a "directory" or an "other compilation" and validly fell within the copyright law. It was not necessary that the matter compiled should itself be copyrighted; it may be in the public domain. It was immaterial that the trademarks themselves could not be copyrighted. Keystone also argued that the Index was not an infringement because Keystone was entitled to research Jewelers' book. After verifying the accuracy of the information contained in Jewelers' book, Keystone should be free to repeat that information. The court conceded that a second compiler may check an independent work against an original compilation, but there was some dispute whether the second compiler may use the original compilation after simply verifying its contents or whether he or she must disregard the original except for verification. According to the Court, it seemed clear that the Index was a copyright infringement because the cuts used to print it were made from illustrations of the same trademarks published in Jewelers' book. The illustrations were protected by copyright. Keystone was enjoined from publishing and distributing the trademark section of the Index and directed to recall all copies possible within twenty days.

Triangle Publications, Inc. v. New England Newspaper Publishing Company 46 F. Supp. 198 (1942)

In 1942, the courts heard another case involving questions of originality. Triangle Publications published periodicals specializing in information about race horses. Triangle's Daily Racing Form and The Morning Telegraph carried race result charts for every race run on the previous day on each track in North America and also carried for every horse scheduled to run the following day a "Past Performance" table. Monthly periodicals carried an accumulation of all the race result charts for the previous month, together with an index of horses. Triangle secured information for their periodicals through their own representatives stationed at every licensed track in North America. Triangle spent more than half a million dollars annually to gather this information. In Massachusetts, Triangle competed with New England Newspaper Publishing Company, which published daily newspapers of general circulation that contained data about race horses. New England Newspaper Publishing Company did not compile any race result charts on their own. They published the race result charts of the Associated Press, and for New England tracks only, the race result charts of Triangle in an abbreviated form, acknowledging their copyright line. Between 1939 and 1941, New England's publications printed a "Last Performance" for race horses, a narrative account of the horse's preceding race. New England obtained its information for preparing the narratives almost exclusively from Triangle's monthly periodicals. Triangle sued.

The first issue for the courts was whether the Triangle periodicals were copyrightable. The court admitted that a daily race chart viewed in isolation could not be regarded as copyrightable as a compilation under the Copyright Act.

> ... the arrangement includes only about a hundred items with reference to a single event that takes less than two minutes to observe and record, and the majority of those items could be collected without labor, skill or judgment by any spectator. To constitute a copyrightable compilation, a compendium must ordinarily result from the labor of assembling, connecting and categorizing disparate facts which in nature occurred in isolation. A compilation, in short, is a synthesis. It is rare indeed that an analysis of any one actual occurrence could be regarded as a compilation. For an account of a single event to be subject to copyright, it must have individuality of expression or must reflect peculiar skill and judgment.

Yet, in this case the requirement of originality was satisfied. Even though individual race charts were subject to very limited protection, the arrangement of charts for all races run anywhere in North America during the previous day, together with past performance tables for all horses scheduled to run anywhere in North America during the day of publication, together with miscellaneous information about race horses, constituted a compilation and was copyrightable. The copyright covered the whole compilation.

The second issue for the courts was whether a copyright infringement occurred when New England used Triangle's periodicals to find where and when a horse raced and then used that information to prepare information on race results in their publication. The court noted that none of Triangle's work was reproduced or cribbed. Admittedly, New England

benefited from their competitior's labor. In analyzing whether
this constituted unfair competition, the court examined <u>Inter-
national News Service v. Associated Press,</u> a case in which
it was held to be fair competition for one news agency to use
the news published by another agency as a "tip" to be independently investigated. In the present case, New England
used Triangle's periodicals to get clues to New England's
own material, a practice similar to the use by one news
agency of tips gathered from a competitor and used for independent investigation. The court concluded that New England's
use of Triangle's periodicals solely for the purpose of securing clues concerning where horses previously ran was
neither an infringement of copyright law nor a condition of
unfair competition. However, the court enjoined New England
from that use because of New England's extensive previous
record of infringement of Triangle's publications.

<u>Amsterdam v. Triangle Publications, Inc. 189 F. 2d 104 (1951)</u>

This case concerned the copyrightability of maps. In
the Sunday, January 13, 1946, issue of the <u>Philadelphia In-
quirer</u>, a historical article included a map of Delaware County.
Lewis Amsterdam, a publisher of maps, initiated a court
action on the ground that this map was copied from his previously copyrighted map. The newspaper conceded the copying but contended that the map was not entitled to copyright.

The court examined the manner in which Amsterdam's
map was prepared. The court stressed that "to be copyrightable a map must be the result of some original work." Amsterdam had made no actual surveys of any roads, county
lines, township lines, creeks, rivers, or railroad tracks; all
such information had been obtained from other maps. The
actual original work of surveying, calculating, and investigating that was done by Amsterdam "was so negligible that it
may be discounted entirely." The court concluded that, because Amsterdam's map lacked originality, it was not copyrightable. The suit was dismissed.

<u>Donald v. Zack Meyer's T. V. Sales and Service
426 F. 2d 1027 (1970)</u>

In this case, a court of appeals considered the originality of a business form. In 1961, O. W. Donald registered
with the copyright office the following paragraph.

Agreement

> For value received, the undersigned jointly and
> severally promise to pay to the Dealer, or order,
> the unpaid balance shown on this invoice according
> to the agreed terms. Title to said Chattel, des-
> cribed hereon by model, make and serial number,
> is hereby retained, or transferred to Dealer until
> Customer has paid in cash all amounts owing said
> Dealer. Customer shall not misuse, secrete, sell,
> encumber, remove or otherwise dispose of or lose
> possession of said Chattel. There is no outstanding
> lien, mortgage, or other encumbrance against said
> Chattel. Should Customer fail to pay its indebted-
> ness when due, or breach this contract, the entire
> unpaid balance shall at once become due and pay-
> able, and Dealer may without notice or demand,
> by process of law, or otherwise, take possession
> of said Chattel wherever located and retain all mon-
> ies paid thereon for use of said Chattel. This
> agreement may be assigned.

This language was printed at the bottom of standard invoice
forms that Donald printed and sold to television dealers and
repairmen. Moore Business Forms, Inc., used the same
language on its forms when Zack Meyer T. V. Sales and Service, one of its customers, ordered a set of invoices. Donald brought suit, claiming that Moore's use of the language
contained in the "Agreement" infringed Donald's copyright.
The trial court expressed doubt concerning the originality
of the "Agreement" but found that Moore had infringed the
copyright by printing and selling the forms. Moore appealed.

The court of appeals noted that to obtain a valid copyright an applicant did not have to show that the material was
unique or novel, only that it was original. A work could be
protected by copyright even though it was based on a prior
copyrighted work if the author contributed a distinguishable
variation from the older work. The author had to add "some
substantial, not merely trivial, originality." The court did
not find the required originality in Donald's "Agreement."
It contained nothing of substance which resulted from Donald's
creative work. The order and arrangement of the subject
matter was identical with prior works. Donald did no original legal research that resulted in any significant change in
the form. The word arrangement used was at most only a
paraphrase of various portions of earlier forms and in copyright law paraphrasing is equivalent to outright copying. According to the court:

> The Copyright Act was not designed to protect such
> negligible efforts. We reward creativity and origi-
> nality with a copyright but we do not accord copy-
> right protection to a mere copycat.

The court concluded that Donald's copyright was invalid for
lack of originality. Thus, Moore's use of the form language
was not an infringement.

Lipman v. Commonwealth of Massachusetts 475 F. 2d 565 (1973)

This case concerned the copyrightability of a court
transcript. On the night of July 18, 1969, Mary Jo Kopechne
was accidently drowned at Chappaquiddick Island, Massachusetts, under circumstances that attracted national, and indeed
international attention. Soon thereafter, a district court inquest was ordered. Sidney Lipman, an experienced free-
lance court stenographer, was hired by the County District
Attorney to record and transcribe the testimony. Realizing
the marketable value to wire services, newspapers, and magazines, of copies of the transcript, Lipman prepared substantial numbers of copies of the report and incurred various expenses in so doing. Senator Edward Kennedy, who had been
driving the car in which Kopechne died, became apprehensive
that the publicity associated with the inquest might be detrimental to him in connection with subsequent criminal proceedings, if such should occur. He instituted proceedings in
the Massachusetts Supreme Judicial Court. The court ordered the inquest to be held in camera, and the transcript
impounded. When the inquest was completed, the transcript
was transferred to the office of the Superior Court Clerk for
Suffolk County.

Edward Keating, clerk of the superior court, planned
to have the Xerox Corporation make a large number of copies
of the transcript, which he intended to sell to the public when
the impounding order was eventually lifted. Keating proposed
to require a deposit of $75 per copy. Lipman's charge for
the 794-page transcript he had prepared would have been much
higher, approximately $560 per copy at customary free-lance
rates or $320 per copy at rates charged by official superior
court reporters. Lipman initiated court action, asking permission to sell the transcript. He also applied for an injunction against Keating's sale of the report. The court authorized Keating to sell the report to all comers for $75,
but to retain in escrow any balance of receipts over expenses
pending the outcome of the litigation. Lipman appealed.

Lipman claimed both a property right and a common-law copyright in the transcript. Concerning the latter, the court noted that "since transcription is by definition a verbatim recording of other persons' statements, there can be no originality in the reporter's product." The report was not copyrightable. With respect to the claim of a property right, the court realized that Lipman took the job of court reporter with the expectation of selling the reports to the print media. Lipman's expectations of a large profit were originally consented to by the district attorney who hired him. However, the district attorney lacked the necessary authority to allow Lipman to sell the transcripts. The court ordered that Lipman be reimbursed for expenses he incurred in the preparation of the reports. The court concluded:

> We would consider that a court has inherent power to prevent the sale of transcripts at an exorbitant profit--public confidence in administration of the courts demands no less. The fact--if it be the fact--that the Dukes County District Court originally consented to an exorbitant profit does not prevent the Supreme Judicial Court from taking a second look.

Lipman received some monetary consideration, but the court rejected his scheme to make an exorbitant profit from the sale of the transcript. The cases cited in this section--Bleistein, Jewelers' Circular, Triangle, Amsterdam, Donald, and Lipman--strongly confirm the principle that originality is the fundamental requirement of copyrightability.

Procedural Formalities

The copyright law describes certain procedural formalities. Two such procedures are that the work should bear a copyright notice and that the copyright should be registered. Arguments regarding these procedural technicalities have been decided by the courts.

Notice--When a work is published, it should bear a notice of copyright. Failure to provide notice can result in loss of copyright. In three cases decided at the turn of the century, the U.S. Supreme Court demanded strict adherence to the notice requirement.

Holmes v. Hurst 174 U. S. 82 (1899)

Oliver Wendell Holmes was the author of The Autocrat of the Breakfast Table, a work that was published during 1857 and 1858, in twelve successive issues of the Atlantic Monthly. No copyright was secured. Later in 1858, Holmes sought to publish the work in a bound book form. He obtained a proper copyright. Holmes deposited a printed copy of the book in the clerk's office of the district court in the Massachusetts district where he lived. A notice was printed in every copy of every edition of the work that was subsequently published. Several years later, another publisher printed copies of the work, taken directly from the version of Holmes's work that was published in the Atlantic Monthly. Holmes sued, claiming that the publication of the work constituted a violation of copyright.

The U. S. Supreme Court agreed (9-0) that the work was copyrighted. The bound volume was copyrighted. The original serialized version from Atlantic Monthly, however, was not. By failing both to provide notice and to deposit copies, Holmes forfeited ownership of that work. It fell into the public domain. In this case, the copying did not constitute an infringement. The copied work stated on the title page that the words were taken from the Atlantic Monthly. That version of the work had never been copyrighted. Holmes's suit was dismissed.

Mifflin v. White 190 U. S. 260 (1903)

Oliver Wendell Holmes also wrote Professor at the Breakfast Table, which was published serially during the year 1859, in the Atlantic Monthly. The first ten parts were published from January to October, without any copyright protection being secured. The remaining two issues for the months of November and December were entered for copyright. After the serial had been completed, Holmes published the entire work in one volume which contained a proper notice of copyright. When another publisher sought to publish a copy of the work, Holmes sued for violation of his copyright.

The issue facing the Court was whether entering for copyright only the last two parts of the Professor at the Breakfast Table in the November and December issues of the Atlantic Monthly was adequate to save the rights of the author for Holmes. In this case, the Court noted that the Copyright Act, as amended in 1831, set forth a specific procedure for giving any reader proper notice of copyright. That was the only method the Court would accept. The Court noted:

> It is incorrect to say that any form of notice is good which calls attention to the person to whom inquiry can be made and information obtained, since, the right being purely statutory, the public may justly demand that the person claiming a monopoly of publication shall pursue, in substance, at least, the statutory method of securing it.

The Court found (9-0) it "impossible to say that the entry of a book under one title by the publisher can validate the entry of another book of a different title by another person. " The Court felt that since the law declared a specific way an author could give a reader proper notice, that was the method that the courts should require.

Mifflin v. Dutton 190 U.S. 265 (1903)

In the same year, the Court heard another case involving improper copyright notice. The Minister's Wooing, by Harriet Beecher Stowe, appeared serially in the Atlantic Monthly. After the first twenty-nine chapters had appeared in the first ten issues of the Atlantic Monthly, for the year 1859, Stowe published the whole work in book form on October 15, 1859, and took proper steps to secure copyright, notice of which was given in the name of Harriet Beecher Stowe. At the date of this publication, the last thirteen chapters had not been published anywhere else, but they subsequently appeared in the November and December issues of the Atlantic Monthly. A court action was initiated when a publishing company sought to copy the work.

The U.S. Supreme Court ruled (9-0) that since the first twenty-nine chapters of The Minister's Wooing appeared in the Atlantic Monthly before any steps were taken either by the publishers or by Stowe to obtain a copyright, those chapters became public property. Stowe's copyright of the last thirteen chapters would doubtless have been valid except for the fact that they subsequently appeared in the November and December issues of the Atlantic Monthly without notice of such copyright. The work fell into the public domain for failure to provide proper copyright notice. Regarding both Mifflin cases, Justice Henry Brown lamented:

It is exceedingly unfortunate that, with the pains
taken by the authors of these works to protect themselves against republication, they should have failed
in accomplishing their object: but the right being
purely statutory, we see no escape from the conclusion that, unless the substance as well as the
form of the statute be disregarded, the right has
been lost in both of these cases.

Wrench v. Universal Pictures Company, Inc.
104 F. Supp. 374 (1952)

About fifty years later, a court was less rigid about
the notice requirement. In 1948, Emily Kimbrough Wrench
sold to Universal Pictures all motion picture rights to three
of her stories based upon her experiences as a lecturer. The
story "My Heart's in My Mouth" was published by the Atlantic Monthly in June, 1944: "Luggage for the South" appeared
in the May 5, 1945, New Yorker; and "Cincinnati and I" was
unpublished. These stories were known collectively as It
Gives Me Great Pleasure. Universal was also given the right
to use the title for any motion picture production based on
the same theme. Wrench agreed that she would protect the
copyright on the stories from coming into the public domain
by seeing that each story was published with proper copyright
notice and that the work was duly registered. Wrench received from Universal a down payment of $10,000. She was
to receive futher payment of $25,000 when work on a photo-
play was begun and up to an additional $25,000 when a full-
length compilation of the stories was published.

In November, 1948, a book entitled It Gives Me Great
Pleasure was published by Dodd, Mead. It contained eight
stories previously published and copyrighted by the Atlantic
Monthly and New Yorker magazines, and four unpublished
stories. The book was based entirely on the idea of Wrench's
experiences as a lecturer, each chapter relating a separate
incident. The copyright notice read "Copyright, 1945, 1948
by Emily Kimbrough." There appeared beneath this a further
notation that several of the specific chapters "originally appeared in somewhat different form as stories in the New Yorker." Neither "1944," the year of the Atlantic Monthly copyright of the chapter entitled "My Heart's in My Mouth," nor
the fact that it had once appeared in that magazine as a story
was mentioned. At the time the book was published, the
copyright on the story "My Heart's in My Mouth" belonged to

the Atlantic Monthly. Because it retained no interest in the
story after its publication, the Atlantic Monthly reassigned
the copyright to Wrench upon her request. Universal felt
the copyright was incorrect and insufficient, so they notified
Wrench that they were rescinding the contract. Universal
offered to return to Wrench everything of value received under the contract if Wrench repayed the $10,000. Wrench re-
fused and sued Universal for breach of contract for failure
to pay the remaining $50,000. Universal alleged that Wrench
had failed to preserve the copyright and because of this failure the contracted material had become "unmarketable."

The court had to decide whether the copyright on the
book It Gives Me Great Pleasure was sufficient to protect
the copyright on that part of it which consisted of the story
"My Heart's in My Mouth." The book contained as a chapter this story, which was originally published and copyrighted
in the July, 1944, issue of the Atlantic Monthly. Universal
claimed that the notice of copyright was faulty because 1) the
year "1945" was claimed as the year of the prior copyright
but the actual year of copyright on the chapter "My Heart's
in My Mouth" was "1944," and 2) the existing copyright for
this chapter was not owned by Wrench as claimed, but rather
by the Atlantic Monthly. The position taken by Universal was
that a substantial portion of the property sold by Wrench to
Universal had lost copyright protection and had fallen into
the public domain. Universal claimed justification for not
abiding by the terms of its contract. The court concluded
that the copyright was valid and that no part of it had fallen
into the public domain. If the story published and copyrighted
in 1944 had been republished and copyrighted alone and with
no changes in 1948 without mention of the 1944 copyright, the
material would have fallen into the public domain. But, revision of the original story was substantial and sufficient to
constitute a new work. In addition, it had been republished
in chapter form as a part of a book which contained new material. The publication of a new work with its own copyright
notice made it unnecessary to list any prior copyright in order to protect it. Since the only copyright date necessary
to protect the property was 1948, the insertion of "1945" in
the copyright notice in the book was superfluous. Even though
publishers tend to list all prior copyrights in a republication,
that practice is not necessary. The judge rejected Universal's
claim that the notice was sufficiently defective to prevent the
marketability of the material.

Under the old copyright laws, those operative when

the U. S. Supreme Court decided <u>Holmes</u> and the <u>Mifflin</u> cases, copyright notice had to adhere to a specific procedure, otherwise the protection was lost.   Under the 1976 law, the rules for notice are not nearly so rigid.   The notice can be placed anywhere that it "can be visually perceived. " And, omission of the proper notice does not necessarily destroy protection if an effort is made within five years to correct the omission.

Registration--Another procedural formality covered by copyright law is registration of copyright claims.   Although registration is not mandatory, failure to register can mean that full protection will not be available against an infringer.

In 1899, in <u>Holmes v. Hurst,</u> the U. S. Supreme Court stressed that in order to receive protection under copyright law, an author had to deposit, prior to publication, a printed copy of the title of the work in the clerk's office of the district court of the district where the author resided.   The author also had to, within three months from publication of the work, deposit a copy of the work with the clerk's office. Failure to comply with this requirement resulted in the loss of any right to copyright protection.   More recently, the courts have been less rigid about copyright registration.

<u>Washingtonian Publishing Company, Inc. v. Pearson</u>
<u>306 U. S. 30 (1939)</u>

On December 10, 1931, an issue of the monthly magazine The Washingtonian was published and copyright was claimed by printing the required notice.   On February 21, 1933, copies were first deposited in the Copyright Office and a certificate of registration secured.   In August, 1932, the Liverright Company published a book written by Drew Pearson and an associate that contained material almost identical with an article contained in The Washingtonian of December, 1931. The usual notice claimed copyright of this book, and on August 26, 1932, copies were deposited in the Copyright Office and a certificate of registration was issued.   Washingtonian Publishing Company sued.   At trial, Pearson conceded that Washingtonian secured upon publication a valid copyright but although prompt deposit of copies was not required by copyright, no action could be maintained because of infringement prior in date to a tardy deposit.   Pearson maintained that "if copies were not deposited promptly after publication the opportunity to comply with the requirement of promptness was gone forever as to that particular work. " In this case, the

courts were called upon to interpret the language of the copyright law, which stated that copies should be "promptly deposited. "

The Court noted that the Copyright Act of 1909 completely revised copyright law.   Under the old act, deposit of
the work was essential to the existence of copyright.   Since
this requirement caused serious difficulties and unfortunate
losses, it was no longer required that anything be deposited
to secure a copyright of a published work, but only to publish with the notice of copyright.   The Court acknowledged
that the 1909 law nowhere defined the term "promptly" and
to make copyright depend upon promptness would produce
confusion.   The Court pointed out that section thirteen of the
act authorized the Register of Copyrights to give notice in
cases of undue delay and to require deposit of copies.   Upon
failure to comply within three months, the copyright became
void and a fine could be levied.   Mere delay did not necessarily invalidate the copyright; its existence for three months
following notice was recognized in the law.   According to
the Court, the penalty specified in section thirteen was sufficient to deal with delinquents.   The Court concluded (6-3)
that section thirteen showed that

> the Congress intended that prompt deposit when
> deemed necessary should be enforced through actu-
> al notice by the register; also that while no action
> can be maintained before copies are actually de-
> posited, mere delay will not destroy the right to
> sue.   Such forfeitures are never to be inferred
> from doubtful language.

During the past century, both judicial and legislative
bodies have eased the procedural requirements associated
with copyright.   At the turn of the century, in Holmes and
Mifflin, the courts demanded that authors adhere to specific
procedures in providing proper notice and in obtaining registration of copyright.   In more recent cases, Wrench and
Washingtonian, the courts allowed more flexibility in comply-
ing with procedural formalities.   Nonetheless, authors should
comply with all contemporary copyright requirements in order
to be assured that their works are subject to full copyright
protection.

Infringement

The 1976 Copyright Act states that "anyone who vio-

lates any of the exclusive rights of the copyright owner ...
is an infringer of the copyright. " The Act does not specify
types of infringement. Frequently, that determination has
been left to the courts. The court cases discussed in this
section illustrate types of alleged infringement involving several different media.

News Stories--There is little interest among newspaper
publishers in copyrighting their papers. After all, who would
be interested in publishing outdated news stories? The Court
has ruled, nonetheless, that while the news itself cannot be
copyrighted, the style or manner in which the news is presented can be protected.

International News Service v. Associated Press
248 U.S. 215 (1918)

Associated Press and International News Service were
competitiors in the gathering and distribution of news. Newspaper companies throughout the United States subscribed to
these corporations. For a fee, members obtained news and
information about current and recent events of interest to
newspaper readers. Under the corporations' bylaws, members
agreed that any news received through the service was to be
used exclusively by that member and no other use of it was
permitted. In this case, AP sought to restrain INS from
pirating news. INS had induced AP employees to furnish
news prior to publication. INS had also copied parts of news
stories from early newspaper editions of AP members.

In deciding this case, the U. S. Supreme Court examined the question of property in news. In the Court's opinion, it was necessary to distinguish between the substance
of the information and the particular form in which the writer communicated it. The literary form was undoubtedly subject to common-law protection, but the news element itself
was not.

> ... the news element--the information respecting
> current events contained in the literary production--
> is not the creation of the writer, but is a report
> of matters that ordinarily are publici juris, it is
> the history of the day. It is not to be supposed
> that the framers of the Constitution ... intended
> to confer upon one who might happen to be the first
> to report a historic event the exclusive right for any
> period to spread the knowledge of it.

The Court also examined the question of unfair competition in business. The Court noted that a purchaser of a newspaper could spread its contents gratuitously, but not for commercial gain in competition with the publisher of the newspaper. In this case, INS did just that by taking material acquired by the skill and labor of AP and distributing it as its own to newspapers that were competitors of AP's membership news- papers. The Court held that such "pirating" of news was prohibited. To copy a copyrighted news story was an infringe- ment. The Court acknowledged that first-published news items may be used as "tips" for other newspapers or press associations, but it concluded (5-3) that while the news ele- ment of a story was not subject to copyright, the style in which an individual story was written could be protected from infringement.

Chicago Record-Herald v. Tribune Association
275 F. 797 (1921)

In 1921, the courts decided a similar case. The New York Tribune copyrighted a special news story on Germany's reliance upon submarines. This story was printed in the Tribune on February 3, 1917. It was offered for simultane- ous publication in the Chicago Herald, which declined, and the Chicago Daily News, which purchased. With full knowl- edge that the story was copyrighted, the Herald nevertheless ran a condensed version of the story. Both versions appear below.

Chicago Herald	New York Tribune
GERMANY PINS HOPE OF FLEET ON 300 FAST SUB- MARINES.	By Louis Durant Edwards Copyright, 1917, by The Tribune Association (New York Tribune).

Chicago Herald — New York Tribune

GERMANY PINS HOPE OF FLEET ON 300 FAST SUB- MARINES.

By Louis Durant Edwards Copyright, 1917, by The Tribune Association (New York Tribune).
GERMANY PLAYS HER TRUMPS.

New York, Feb. 3--3 a. m. (special). --The Tribune this morning in a copyrighted ar- ticle of Louis Durant Ed- wards, a correspondent in Germany, says that Germany to make the final effort against Great Britain has plunged 300 or more submers- ibles into the North Sea. These, according to this writ- er, were mobilized from Kiel,

Three hundred or more sub- mersibles have plunged into the waters of the North Sea to make the final effort against Great Britain. They mobilized from Kiel, Ham- burg, Wilhelmshaven, Brem- erhaven, where, for months, picked crews have trained. . . .

Hamburg, Wilhelmshaven, and Bremerhaven, where for months picked crews were trained.

"They form the world's first diving battle fleet," he says, "a navy equally prepared to fight above or beneath the waves."

There are two types of these new boats now in commission, one of 2,400 tons and one of 5,000 tons displacement.

They dive beneath the water in a fraction of the time that it takes the older types to submerge. They mount powerful guns, are capable of great surface speeds, and are protected by a heavy armor of tough steel plate.

The motors develop 7,000 horsepower and drive the boats under the surface at 22 knots an hour. These smaller cruisers carry a crew of from 60 to 80 men.

The submersibles have a radius of action of 8,000 miles.

They form the world's first diving battle fleet, a navy equally prepared to fight above or beneath the waves....

There are two types of these new boats now in commission, one of 2,400 tons and one of 5,000 tons displacement....

They dive beneath the water in a fraction of the time that it took the older types to submerge. They mount powerful guns, are capable of great surface speeds, and are protected by a heavy armor of tough steel plate....

The motors develop 7,000 horsepower, and drive the boats over the surface at a speed of 22 knots an hour. These smaller cruisers carry a crew of 60 to 80 men.

They have a radius of action of 8,000 miles....

The Tribune Association sued the Record-Herald Company.

The court affirmed that news, as such, was not subject to copyright protection, but insofar as an "article involves authorship and literary quality and style, apart from the bare recital of the facts or statement of news, it is protected by the copyright law." The court indicated that the copying of a copyrighted news story exactly or the substantial copying or paraphrasing of a copyrighted story constituted an infringement. In this case, the Herald presented the essential facts of the Tribune article "in the very garb wherein the author clothed them, together with some of his deductions and comments thereon in his precise words." The court ruled for the Tribune Association.

Books--The courts have heard several cases involving alleged copyright infringement of books. In 1938, a Pennsylvania district court heard a case involving alleged infringement through paraphrasing only a small part of a book.

Henry Holt & Company, Inc. v. Liggett &
Myers Tobacco Company 23 F. Supp. 302 (1938)

In 1931, Henry Holt & Company published and copyrighted Dr. Leon Felderman's book The Human Voice, Its Care and Development. The book was a scientific study designed to convey to vocal teachers and students an understanding of the human vocal mechanism. Shortly after publication of Felderman's work, Liggett & Myers Tobacco Company, in an effort to bolster sales of Chesterfield cigarettes, published and widely circulated a pamphlet entitled "Some Facts About Cigarettes, " in which under the heading "Do cigarettes affect the throat?" appeared the following:

> Dr. Leon Felderman, noted oto-laryngologist,
> Philadelphia, is quoted (1931) as follows:
> "Statistics have it that 80 per cent of
> physicians are smokers.... It appears
> unanimous that smoking is not nearly so
> injurious as over-eating.... From my
> experience with ear, nose and throat cases,
> I firmly believe that tobacco, when properly
> used, has no ill effect upon the auditory
> passages. "

These quotations were copied, although not exactly, from matter appearing in Felderman's book. Henry Holt and Company claimed that the use of Felderman's work cast reflections upon his professional ethics and brought down upon him the term "commercialist, " all of which hampered the sale of this book. The company sought an injunction restraining Liggett and Myers from infringing the copyright. They also asked for an accounting of profits, and damages.

The district court noted that the whole, or even a large portion of a book, need not be copied to constitute an infringement. It was sufficient if a material and substantial part had been copied, even though it was but a small part of the whole. In this case, three sentences had been taken from Dr. Felderman's book. An examination showed that the material taken made up about one-twentieth of the pamphlet. Under these circumstances, the court could not decide that the copied matter was unsubstantial. That the pamphlet acknowledged the source from which this matter was taken did not excuse the infringement. The court, finding a copyright infringement, ruled against the tobacco company.

College Entrance Book Company, Inc. v.
Amsco Book Company, Inc. 119 F. 2d 874 (1941)

In 1941, the courts found that copying word lists from a book constituted copyright infringement. College Entrance Book Company published and copyrighted two paperback booklets--High Points French: Two Years and High Points French: Three Years. These works were compiled especially to facilitate review by New York High school students of their two or three years of French study in preparation for examinations given by the New York Board of Regents. The books were also used by students preparing for college entrance board exams. The books, 127 and 160 pages respectively, included lessons and exercises in grammar and composition, sample copies of previous exams, lists of commonly used French words, and articles in French with English translations. College Entrance Book Company had hired two high school French teachers to compile and arrange the booklets. Shortly after publication of these books, Amsco Book Company published French Two Years and French Three Years. These books, which were offered at a substantially lower price, contained very similar content and design and were intended for the same market as College Entrance Book Company's works. The president of Amsco, Albert Beller, admitted that he owned his competitor's books and that he had used them in preparing his own works. He claimed, however, that he relied primarily on the Regent's syllabi for his selection of French words; on Heath's and Longman-Green's French-English dictionary for French articles; and on a list of English translations compiled by a French teacher, Mr. Louis Goodman. He contended that similarities should be expected in a compilation of such sterotyped material. College Entrance Book Company initiated court action.

The court found Beller guilty of copyright violation. The books contained almost the identical words. Seven commonly used French words were omitted from the works of both companies. Interpretations of grammatical rules were the same in both works. In many cases, Beller gave exactly the same translations as those found in College Entrance Book Company's books. In nine instances, the translations were

not found at all in the sources Beller claimed to have used.
In all, 96 percent of the items of High Points French: Two
Years and 82 percent of the items in High Points French:
Three Years were exactly reproduced in Beller's books. According to the court, the accumulation of evidence indicated
that Beller had copied the books. The court speculated that
Beller's "copying was unquestionably to avoid the trouble or
expense of independent work." This constituted an "unfair
use." The court ruled for College Entrance Book Company,
granting an injunction, damages, and an accounting of profits.

Toksvig v. Bruce Publishing Company 181 F. 2d 664 (1950)

    In this case, the courts found copyright infringement
where a writer failed to do her own independent research.
In 1934, after three years of research done exclusively from
Danish sources that included the original works and letters
of Hans Christian Andersen, Signe Toksvig published and copyrighted a book entitled The Life of Hans Christian Andersen.
In 1946, Margaret Ann Hubbard wrote the book Flight of the
Swan, a novel based on Andersen's life. Hubbard did not
speak or read Danish. Her research, which lasted about a
year, was confined to English sources, including Toksvig's
book. Toksvig claimed copyright violation and initiated a
court procedure.

    The court found that Hubbard had copied certain gene-
ral concepts about Andersen, his life, and his friends, that
were set down for the first time in Toksvig's work. The
court also found that Hubbard had copied twenty-four specific
passages of the work. Hubbard argued that she copied only
the facts of Andersen's life, which were in the public domain.
The court ruled that the copied materials were original translations made by Toksvig from Danish sources--materials subject to copyright protection. Hubbard's intention was immaterial where infringement had occurred, and the fact that Hubbard acknowledged the source from which the materials were
taken did not excuse the infringement. Hubbard also claimed
that she could have obtained the same information from works
other than Toksvig's. She could have gone to the works which
were originally researched by Toksvig. The court noted:

        The question is not whether Hubbard could have
        obtained the same information by going to the same
        sources, but rather did she go to the same sources
        and do her own independent research? In other words,

the test is whether the one charged with the infringement has made an independent production, or made
a substantial and unfair use of the complainant's
work.

The court recognized that Hubbard obtained much value from
the use of Toksvig's book. Since Hubbard could not read
Danish, the use of the specific passages enabled her to complete the book in less than one-third the time it took Toksvig.
The work was clearly an infringement.

Eisenschiml v. Fawcett Publications 246 F. 2d 598 (1957)

In 1957, the courts considered a case of alleged infringement involving books that contained historical facts and
ideas. Civil War historian Otto Eisenschiml published two
scholarly works based on his extensive research of the death
of Abraham Lincoln. Eisenschiml's book, Why Was Lincoln
Murdered?, a scholarly, extensively documented, hardcovered,
503-page work, suggested that Secretary of War Edwin Stanton had knowledge of the conspiracy behind Lincoln's assassination. Some 22,000 copies of this book were sold. The
second book, In the Shadow of Lincoln's Death, was a hardcovered, 415-page supplement to the earlier work. Some
3,600 copies were sold. In the February, 1953, issue of
True magazine appeared an article entitled "America's Greatest Unsolved Murder," written by Joseph Millard, a free-
lance author who had written and sold over one thousand stories to popular media. The article contained about 20,000
words. It contained no footnotes, bibliography, or other doc-
umentation. Neither Fawcett Publications, the publisher of
True, nor Millard, ever sought or received permission to
use material from Eisenschiml's books. Nowhere in the article was Eisenschiml credited or referred to. Eisenschiml
initiated court action, insisting that Millard's article imitated,
paraphrased, and copied substantial portions of the two copyrighted books and that Millard substantially appropriated his
research. Eisenschiml insisted that Millard's article not
only pirated the underlying theme of the books--that Stanton
may have been implicated in the assassination--but also that
the article treated the ideas, characters, scenes, and events
in the same way that Eisenschiml did. He further claimed
that Millard's article so paralleled the two books that it was
actually a condensation of several chapters. Millard freely
admitted that some of the material and ideas used in his article came from Eisenschiml's books. But, he claimed that
he did not copy, that he worked independently of the books.

The court agreed that a large portion of Millard's article resulted from his independent work. The court also recognized that a number of extracts from Eisenschiml's book were used in the article. The court indicated that

> an infringement is not confined to literal and exact repetition or reproduction; it includes also the various modes in which the matter of any work may be adopted with more or less colorable alterations to disguise the piracy. Paraphrasing is copying and an infringement, if carried to a sufficient extent.

The court stressed that ideas, as such, were not protected by the law of copyright. But the mode of expression used by the author could be protected. The arrangement of ideas and their form of expression could comprise a particular literary composition that was entitled to protection. The question before the court was--did Millard make a substantial copy of Eisenschiml's books? The court concluded that Millard did not substantially copy the books. The use that Millard made of the books was a fair use. In historical writings, such as the events immediately before and after Lincoln's assassination, both authors described the same personages during a very limited period of time. It had to be expected that some similarity of treatment would result. Millard's article did not constitute copyright infringement.

The cases presented in this section set forth regulations applicable to copyright infringement of books. In Holt, the court held that the whole, or even a large portion of a book, need not be copied to constitute an infringement. It was sufficient if a material and substantial part had been copied. In College Entrance Book Company, the court ruled that copying word lists from a book constituted copyright infringement. In Toksvig, the court found copyright infringement where a writer failed to do independent research. And, in Eisemschiml, the court noted that while historical facts, as such, were not protected under copyright, the author's mode of expression could be protected.

Characters--To what extent are a writer's characters copyrightable? Does the character of a story pass with the transfer of a copyright? These questions were considered by the courts.

Warner Brothers Pictures, Inc. v. Columbia Broadcasting System, Inc. 216 F. 2d 945 (1954)

Dashiell Hammett wrote, published, and copyrighted a mystery-detective story entitled The Maltese Falcon. In 1930, Hammett sold for $8,500 certain defined rights to the book to Warner Brothers. Warner claimed that it had acquired the exclusive right to use the work--including the individual characters and their names, together with the title--in any motion pictures, radio, and television programming. Use of the title was not an issue because the contract had specifically included it. However, Hammett argued that the exclusive right to use the characters and/or their names was not granted to Warner Brothers; thus, Hammett could use them in other stories. In fact, Hammett did use the characters and their names following the contract. He granted permission for the use of the name of a detective character in weekly half-hour radio broadcasts of "Adventures of Sam Spade" between 1946 and 1950. Warner Brothers sued, claiming infringement of copyright.

The court noted that the tendency of authors to compose sequels to stories was well established, and the copyright statute failed to cover that matter specifically. The court concluded that even if Hammett had assigned the complete copyright to Warner Brothers, such assignment did not prevent Hammett "from using the characters used therein, in other stories. The characters were vehicles for the story told, and the vehicles did not go with the sale of the story." Regarding this specific case, the court found that since the use of characters and character names was nowhere specifically mentioned in the agreements, but that other items--including the title "The Maltese Falcon"--were specifically mentioned as being granted, "the character rights with the names cannot be held to be within the grants." Hammett retained the right to use his characters and their names.

Walt Disney Productions v. The Air Pirates 345 F. Supp. 108 (1972)

In 1972, the courts heard another case involving copyright protection for characters. Walt Disney Productions held valid copyrights for several cartoon drawings. Most of the cartoons depicted the antics of animal characters that Disney had created and developed. A California company, The Air

Pirates, published two cartoon magazines. Their characters bore considerable similarity to those created by Disney. In fact, Air Pirates artist Dan O'Neill admitted that he "chose to parody exactly the style of drawing and the characters to evoke the response created by Disney. " While the "Mickey Mouse" character was not copied in the sense that it was photographically reproduced, it was drawn as nearly like Disney's drawing as O'Neill could make it. The name given to the character was the same name used in Disney's works. The theme and plot of the Air Pirates' publications differed markedly from Disney's cartoons. Walt Disney Productions initiated an action for infringement of copyright.

Before the district court, Air Pirates admitted that Disney's copyright covered the complete work--that is, a book in its entirety. Yet, because Air Pirates had extracted characters from the work, the isolated characters were not protectible. They cited Warner Brothers, in which the court ruled that "the characters were vehicles for the story told, and the vehicles did not go with the sale of the story. " In light of this decision, characters were not entitled to copyright protection. The district court analyzed Warner Brothers, noting that the case did not "shut the door entirely on protection to characters"--it was "conceivable that the character really constitutes the story being told. " In Disney's works, the characters tended to constitute the story being told. After all, the characters were graphically represented numerous times in the course of each cartoon. In addition:

> The facial expressions, position and movement
> represented may convey far more than the words
> set out as dialogue in the "balloon" hovering over
> the character's head, or the explanatory material
> appended. It is not simply one particular drawing,
> in one isolated cartoon "panel" for which plaintiff
> seeks protection, but rather it is the common fea-
> tures of all of the drawings of that character ap-
> pearing in the copyrighted work.

The principal appeal of each of Disney's works was to children, primarily through the use of "the characters and nothing else. " Disney's characters were copyrightable, and by copying the substance of the characters Air Pirates had infringed on Disney's copyright. The findings in Warner Brothers and Walt Disney were consistent--a character that actually constitutes the story being told falls within the protection afforded by the copyright.

Music--Copyright law provides some general guidelines governing the copying and recording of musical selections. Determining specific instances of infringement has been left to the courts.

Herbert v. Shanley Company
John Church Company v. Hilliard Hotel Company
242 U. S. 591 (1917)

These two cases presented the same issue--whether the performance of a copyrighted musical composition in a restaurant or hotel, without charging for admission to hear it, infringed the exclusive right of the owner of the copyright to perform the work publicly for profit. In the first case, Victor Herbert's copyrighted song "Sweethearts" was performed at Shanley's restaurant by musicians employed to play at mealtimes. No arrangement had been made with Herbert to use the song. In the second case, John Church owned the copyright for a march entitled "From Maine to Georgia." The Hilliard Hotel Company hired an orchestra of musicians who performed the march in the dining room of the Vanderbilt Hotel as a means of entertaining guests during mealtimes. No arrangement had been made with Church to use the march. In court, both Shanley and Hilliard Hotel argued that they had not infringed upon any copyright because no profit came from music that was played merely to lend atmosphere to the restaurant. The case reached the U. S. Supreme Court.

The Court held (9-0) that "if the rights under the copyright are infringed only by a performance where money is taken at the door, they are very imperfectly protected." Shanley and Hilliard Hotel benefited financially by playing the music; it provided "a luxurious pleasure not to be had from eating a silent meal." The Court emphasized that the music was part of the total for which the public paid. Certainly, the music was not the sole object, but neither was the food, "which probably could be got cheaper elsewhere."

> If music did not pay, it would be given up. If it pays it pays out of the public's pocket. Whether it pays or not, the purpose of employing it is profit, and that is enough.

According to the Court, the action of Shanley and Hilliard Hotel constituted a copyright infringement.

Heim v. Universal Pictures Company 154 F. 2d 480 (1946)

In 1946, a court of appeals indicated some specific factors that were relevant to proving copyright infringement in the case of musical selections. Emery Heim, a successful Hungarian composer, sued Universal Pictures for infringement of the copyright to his song "Ma Este Meg Boldog Vagyok." The alleged infringement consisted of the use of a portion of the song in Universal Picture's song "Perhaps, " written by Aldo Franchetti, which was sung by Deanna Durbin in the motion picture Nice Girl. Heim did not claim that the lyrics of Universal's song infringed upon his composition, only that the verse infringed upon the chorus of his composition. The verse of Universal's song was the same as the chorus of Heim's song.

In determining this case, Judge Jerome N. Frank indicated that to win a lawsuit, Heim had to show 1) that the alleged infringer copied from Heim's work, and 2) that if copying was proven, it had to be so "material" or "substantial" as to constitute unlawful appropriation. Concerning the first criterion, it was admitted that similarity existed. In fact, parts of "Perhaps" were identical with "Ma Este Meg Boldog Vagyok. " The similarity was explained by Universal Pictures. Independently, both composers utilized the same source--Dvořak's "Humoresque"--which had long been in the public domain. Since Heim failed to demonstrate that Universal Pictures copied from his work, Heim had to lose the suit. Concerning the second criterion, it was found, based on expert testimony, that Heim's "method of dealing with the common trite note sequence did not possess enough originality, raising it above the level of the banal, to preclude coincidence as an adequate explanation of the identity. " Because Heim failed to satisfy the criteria, the court could not find Universal Pictures guilty of copyright infringement.

Berlin v. E. C. Publications, Inc. 329 F. 2d 541 (1964)

In 1964, the courts held that musical lyrics, in the form of parody, did not constitute copyright infringement. When Mad magazine published satiric parody lyrics for twenty-five popular songs, the copyright holders initiated court procedures. Mad's publication failed to reproduce the music of the famous compositions in any form whatsoever, but it did contain parody lyrics that were written in the same meter as the original lyrics.

The district court noted that the theme and content of the parodies differed markedly from those of the originals. For example, "The Last Time I Saw Paris, " originally written as a nostalgic ballad that described pre-war France became "The First Time I Saw Maris, " a caustic commentary upon a baseball hero. "A Pretty Girl Is Like a Melody" became "Louella Schwartz Described Her Malady"; what was originally a tribute to feminine beauty became a burlesque of a female hypochondriac. The court noted:

> We believe in any event that the parody lyrics involved in this appeal would be permissible under the most rigorous application of the "substantiality" requirement. The disparities in theme, content and style between the original lyrics and the alleged infringements could hardly be greater.... The fact that defendants' parodies were written in the same meter as plaintiffs' compositions would seem inevitable if the original was to be recognized, but such a justification is not even necessary; we doubt that even so eminent a composer as plaintiff Irving Berlin should be permitted to claim a property interest in iambic pentameter.

The court concluded that the use made by Mad magazine fell far short of the "substantiality" requirement. Furthermore, the parody had neither the intent nor the effect of fulfilling the demand for the original. Since the parodist did not appropriate a greater amount of the original work than was necessary to "recall or conjure up" the object of his satire, an infringement had not occurred.

Film--During the 1950s, two claims of alleged copyright infringement involved clashes between the economic interests of the established motion picture industry and the youthful television industry. At stake was the issue of whether television could use matter from motion pictures in preparing shorter, burlesque productions.

Columbia Pictures Corporation v. National Broadcasting Company 137 F. Supp. 348 (1955)

In 1951, James Jones published and had copyrighted an original novel entitled From Here to Eternity. That same year, Jones granted permission to Columbia Pictures Corporation to create and produce a motion picture based on the novel.

The film, having a running time of approximately one hour and forty minutes, was completed in 1953. Subsequently, NBC broadcast over its national television network a twenty-minute skit entitled "From Here to Obscurity. " The skit was telecast without the knowledge or consent of Columbia Pictures. The skit was designed as a burlesque of the film From Here to Eternity. Burlesque is an accepted form of literary art in which a part of the content is used to conjure up an image of the original work. Of necessity, there were several similarities between the film and the burlesque skit. The locale was the same. There was similarity in the principal members of the cast of characters. There was also a resemblance in some of the details of the development, treatment, and expression. Columbia Pictures initiated court action.

According to the court, the burlesque used new, original, and different literary material as compared with the motion picture. The use of material from the original work

> was of only sufficient material to cause the viewer of the burlesque to recall and conjure up the motion picture, or the novel "From Here to Eternity" upon which said motion picture was based, and thus provide the necessary element of burlesque.

The use made of the original work was permissible and did not constitute the taking of a substantial portion of Jones's protected material. The telecast did not intend to deceive the viewer that the telecast was, in any way, a telecast of the motion picture. The court concluded that since a burlesque had to make sufficient use of the original to conjure up the subject matter being burlesqued, the law permitted more extensive utilization of the "protectible portion of a copyrighted work in the creation of a burlesque of that work than in the creation of other fictional or dramatic works not intended as a burlesque of the original. " The televised skit did not violate copyright protection.

Benny v. Loew's Incorporated 239 F. 2d 532 (1956)
Columbia Broadcasting System, Inc. v. Loew's Incorporated 356 U. S. 43 (1958)

A similar case reached the courts about the same time. English author Patrick Hamilton published and copyrighted an original play entitled Gaslight sometime during 1939.

Shortly thereafter, it was publicly performed in England. In 1941, it was produced as a play in New York under the name Angel Street and had a successful run of 1, 295 consecutive performances extending over a period of more than thirty-seven months. In 1942, the exclusive motion picture rights for Gaslight were acquired by Loew's, better known under the trade name of Metro-Goldwyn-Mayer. Loew's spent $2, 458, 000 on the production and distribution of the motion picture. The actual making of the film extended over a period of more than two and a half years. In producing the film, Loew's acquired the services of three outstanding artists, Charles Boyer, Ingrid Bergman, and Joseph Cotten. The film was shown in the United States and abroad. Approximately 52 million persons paid admission to see the film. The gross receipts for the film amounted to $4, 857, 000.

On October 14, 1945, Jack Benny, after securing Loew's permission, presented a fifteen-minute parody of Gaslight over a national radio network. Six years later, the Columbia Broadcasting System produced a half-hour-long television show burlesquing Gaslight, with Jack Benny in the leading role. Neither Benny nor CBS secured consent from Loew's to broadcast the television burlesque. Loew's initiated court action for copyright infringement. The district court found that the television play was copied in substantial part from Loew's motion picture. The television presentation was an infringement of the copyright. The court granted injunctive relief, restraining the showing of the television play. Benny appealed.

The court of appeals also found substantial evidence of copying.

> A comparison of the photoplay and the television play indicates how much was copied. If the material taken by appellants from Gaslight is eliminated, there are left only a few gags, and some disconnected and incoherent dialogue. If the television play were presented without appellants' contribution, there would be left the plot, story, principal incidents, and same sequence of events as in the photoplay.

The court concluded that the NBC television play copied a substantial part of the film. The court then emphasized:

> ... a "parodized or burlesque" taking is to be treated no differently from any other appropriation;

that, as in all other cases of alleged taking, the issue becomes first one of fact, i. e. , what was taken and how substantial was the taking; and if it determined that there was a substantial taking, infringement exists.

The court was not willing to afford burlesque the special status granted by the court in <u>Columbia Pictures</u>. In 1958, in a <u>per curiam</u>, the judgment of the court of appeals was affirmed (4-4) by a divided U. S. Supreme Court.

<u>Speeches</u>--The courts have provided some discussion of the copyrighting of public speeches.

<u>Public Affairs Associates, Inc. v. Rickover 369 U. S. 111 (1962)</u>

During 1955 to 1958, Vice Admiral Hyman Rickover delivered several important public addresses on subjects ranging from atomic submarines to secondary education in the United States. For most of them, he prepared a mimeographed copy in advance and distributed copies to the press. Other people who wrote for copies after the speech was delivered received a copy through the Department of Defense as long as the supply lasted. Each speech had been cleared by the Department of Defense, as required by a regulation governing publications by Navy personnel. Late in 1958, Rickover started to compile texts of his speeches for publication in a book. From that point on, he secured copyright protection for his speeches. At the same time, a Washington, D. C. , publisher, Public Affairs Associates, asked Rickover if they could publish some of his past speeches. He refused. Public Affairs brought suit seeking declaration that Rickover's previous speeches were in "the public domain" and not subject to any curtailment as to use. Public Affairs also claimed that the speeches were "government documents" and not entitled to copyright protection.

The district court ruled for Rickover; the speeches were not government documents. The court of appeals decided for Public Affairs Associates, saying Rickover forfeited protection by distributing the speeches without copyright--an act that equals publication, and that use of government machines and materials made the speeches uncopyrightable "government publications. " The U. S. Supreme Court vacated (6-3) this judgment on a technical, procedural ground, and returned the case to the district court. No further proceedings were held, probably because of the following case.

King v. Mister Maestro, Inc. 224 F. Supp. 101 (1963)

On June 23, 1963, in an auditorium at Detroit, Dr. Martin Luther King delivered a speech to which he gave no title, but in the course of which he used the words "I have a dream." Thereafter, a march for civil rights was held in Washington, D. C., on August 28, 1963. King delivered a speech that contained some of the ideas and words of the Detroit speech, but it was much longer and had a great deal not contained in the Detroit speech. Prior to delivery, Dr. King made his speech available to the press. King did not intend his speech to be distributed to the public at large; he specifically limited the use to assisting press coverage of the march. King's speech stirred and impressed the crowd, especially his repetition of the words "I have a dream." King's speech, along with the speeches of others made at the same time, was broadcast by television and radio, recorded, and later shown in movie houses, and, of course widely reported in the press. Twentieth Century-Fox Film Corporation produced a newsreel for movie theatres. It contained pictures and a sound record of King's speech. The New York Post published the complete text of the speech under the title "I Have a Dream." The Post also offered for sale reprints of the speech. Mister Maestro sold a record entitled "The March on Washington," which contained the speech; it had both the voice and words of King. The company sold the records without the consent of Dr. King and without paying anything to him. King also claimed that he had not consented in any way to any of the reprinting and sale of the speech.

After the Washington speech, a record of some of King's speeches was sold with King's consent by Motown Record Company. This record was entitled "The Great March to Freedom--Rev. Martin Luther King Speaks--Detroit June 23, 1963." The record did not contain the Washington speech; it contained the much shorter Detroit speech under the title "I Have a Dream." On September 30, 1963, Dr. King sent a copy of this speech to the Copyright Office for deposit, and, at the same time, sent an application form for a certificate of registration. Subsequently, King filed a complaint, charging Mister Maestro and Twentieth Century-Fox with violation of his copyright.

The court considered the two main arguments of the defendants--that the speech lacked originality and that it had been published. According to the court, the Washington speech was sufficiently original to be the subject of copyright; it differed significantly from the similar speech delivered in Detroit.

The speeches were "sufficiently different in length, content and otherwise that the former does not destroy the originality for copyright purposes of the latter. " The court also decided that King's delivering the speech did not constitute a general publication of the speech so as to place it in the public domain.

> The word "general" with respect to publication in this sense is of greatest significance. There can be a limited publication, which is a communication of the work to others under circumstances showing no dedication of the work to the public. A general publication is one which shows a dedication to the public so as to lose copyright.

The oral delivery of this speech, no matter how vast the audience, did not amount to a general publication. The court then noted the difference in this case as compared with Rickover. Rickover made a wide distribution, not only to the press, but also to members of the public who desired copies. Dr. King had made his speech available only to the press. The court issued an injunction against further use of King's speech without his permission.

Cable Television--Considerable controversy transpired during the past decade concerning the extent to which secondary broadcast transmissions infringed on copyright. Again, determining the specific criteria for infringement was left to the courts.

Fortnightly Corporation v. United Artists Television, Inc.
392 U. S. 390 (1968)

In 1968, the U. S. Supreme Court examined the issue of whether cable television "performed. " Fortnightly Corporation owned and operated community antenna television (CATV) systems in Clarksburg and Fairmont, West Virginia. There were two local television broadcasting stations in the vicinity, but because of hilly terrain most residents of the area could not receive the broadcasts of any additional stations by ordinary rooftop antennas. Some residents joined together and erected larger cooperative antennas in order to receive more distant stations, but a majority of the householders solved the problem by becoming customers of Fortnightly. Fortnightly's systems provided customers with signals of five television stations: three located in Pittsburgh, Pennsylvania;

one in Steubenville, Ohio; and one in Wheeling, West Virginia. The distance between those cities and Clarksburg and Fairmont ranged from fifty-two to eighty-two miles. The systems carried all the programming of each of the stations. Customers could choose any program they wished to view by simply turning the knob on their own television sets. Fortnightly's customers were charged a flat monthly rate regardless of the amount of time they used their television sets.

United Artists held copyrights on several motion pictures, some of which were shown on the five television stations received by Fortnightly and carried to its customers. Fortnightly did not obtain permission to receive the films from United Artists or from any of the five television stations. United sued Fortnightly for copyright infringement, and the case came to the U.S. Supreme Court. United's contention was that Fortnightly's CATV systems infringed United's exclusive right to "perform ... in public for profit." Fortnightly maintained that the CATV systems did not "perform" the copyrighted works at all.

The Court decided (5-1) that Fortnightly's systems did not "perform" United's copyrighted works in any conventional sense of that term. The Court went on to note:

> ... while both broadcaster and viewer play crucial roles in the total television process, a line is drawn between them. One is treated as active performer, the other, as passive beneficiary.
> When CATV is considered in this framework, we conclude that it falls on the viewer's side of the line. Essentially, a CATV system no more than enhances the viewer's capacity to receive the broadcaster's signals; it provides a well-located antenna with an efficient connection to the viewer's television set.... If an individual erected an antenna on a hill, strung a cable to his house, and installed the necessary amplifying equipment, he would not be "performing" the programs he received on his television set. The result would be no different if several people combined to erect a cooperative antenna for the same purpose. The only difference in the case of CATV is that the antenna system is erected and owned not by its users but by an entrepreneur.

Based on this reasoning, the Court found in favor of Fortnightly.

Teleprompter Corporation v. Columbia Broadcasting
System, Inc. 415 U. S. 394 (1974)

  Six years later, the principle established in Fortnightly
was affirmed. In 1964, CBS started a copyright infringement
action against Teleprompter Corporation, claiming that Teleprompter CATV systems intercepted copyrighted programs
and channeled them to Teleprompter's customers without authorization. The alleged copyright violations involved Teleprompter's systems in five cities at stated periods: Elmira,
New York, in November, 1964; Farmington, New Mexico, in
November, 1964, June 1969, and March, 1971; Rawlins, Wyoming, in June, 1969; Great Falls, Montana, in June 1969;
and New York City, in June, 1969, and March, 1971. In
this case, the lower court distinguished two distinct functions
of CATV systems:

> CATV systems perform either or both of two
> functions. First, they may supplement broadcasting
> by facilitating satisfactory reception of local stations
> in adjacent areas in which such reception would not
> otherwise be possible; and second, they may trans-
> mit to subscribers the signals of distant stations
> entirely beyond the range of local antennae.

The Fortnightly system brought television signals to viewers
who could not otherwise have received them. The signals
were already in the community and were not imported long
distances. It was only because of topographical conditions
in the area that residents could not receive the signals by
usual methods. The court noted that when CATV systems
performed the second function of distributing signals beyond
the range of local antennae, it functioned like a broadcaster
and tended to "perform" the programming distributed to subscribers on these imported signals. The system's function
was no longer merely to enhance the customers chances of
receiving signals that were in the area; it acted to bring new
signals into the area. The court found that Teleprompter's
Elmira and New York City CATV systems did not infringe
CBS's rights, but the Rawlins, Great Falls, and Farmington
CATV systems constituted infringements.

  The U. S. Supreme Court disagreed (6-3) with the
lower court's opinion. The justices maintained that importation of distant programs from one area into another did not
constitute a "performance" under the Copyright Act.

  Importation of "distant signals" from one community

into another does not constitute a "performance" under the Copyright Act; thus, a community antenna television system does not lose its status as a non-broadcaster and thus a non "performer" for copyright purposes when the signals it carries are those from distant rather than local sources.

Such activity was "essentially a viewer function, irrespective of the distance between the broadcasting station and the ultimate viewer." Teleprompter, like Fortnightly, had not violated copyright protection.

Photocopy--A current controversial issue in the field of copyright law concerns photocopying by libraries. This issue reached the courts during the 1970s. The courts were asked to decide when the use of photocopying machines constituted copyright infringement.

Williams & Wilkins Company v. United States
487 F. 2d 1345 (1973); 420 U.S. 376 (1975)

During the twentieth century, technology placed great strains on the Copyright Act of 1909. By 1970, photocopy machines were located in almost every library, and the use of such machines to copy printed materials became commonplace. The National Institute of Health (NIH) and the National Library of Medicine (NLM) adopted a practice of providing photocopies of entire articles of medical and scientific periodicals, free of charge, upon the request of medical and scientific researchers. In 1970, NIH copied 85,744, and NLM, 93,746, articles. NIH and NLM considered this service to be part of their library loan programs, in lieu of the actual loan of a copy of the requested journal. Limitations were imposed upon the number of requests an individual researcher could make, and both libraries maintained a policy of not photocopying an entire issue of any journal in answer to a single request.

The Williams and Wilkins Company, publisher of several medical journals, initiated an action for damages for copyright infringement through illegal massive photocopying. The company specifically cited eight articles from four periodicals--Medicine, Journal of Immunology, Gastroenterology, and Pharmacological Review. The trial judge found that the "wholesale copying" of the copyrighted works failed to meet the criteria for fair use because the photocopies were exact

duplicates of the originals, they served as substitutes for
the originals, and they diminished the publisher's market because copies were made for the benefit of potential subscribers.   The court awarded damages to Williams & Wilkins Company.

     The court of claims reversed.   The court found that
the suggestion that copying of an entire copyrighted work
could never be a "fair use" was "an overbroad generaliza-
tion, unsupported by the decisions and rejected by years of
accepted practice. "   The court noted that it was common for
courts to use photocopies of recent decisions during court
proceedings.   The court felt that "the extent of the copying
is one important factor, but only one, to be taken into account, along with several others. "   The court offered three
reasons why the practices of NIH and NLM did not constitute
infringement.   First, Williams & Wilkins had not shown that
it was being, or will be, harmed substantially by the specific
practices of NIH and NLM.   On the other hand, libraries
were scientific, non-profit institutions that did not operate
for commercial gain.   The copying, in this case, was for
scientific use.   Second, medicine and medical research would
be injured by holding these particular practices to be an infringement.   Scientists would simply not use the articles needed in their work.   Third, the problem called for legislative
guidance, and the court should not, during the period before
congressional action was forthcoming, impose a risk of harm
upon science and medicine.   The court carefully placed a
narrow sweep on the decision, stressing that no question of
"vending" the works arose and that the purpose of the copying was "scientific progress, untainted by any commercial
gain. "   The U. S. Supreme Court agreed to review the case.
In 1975, an equally divided Court, without opinion, affirmed
(4-4) the opinion of the court of claims.

     Section 108 of the Copyright Act of 1976 provided some
clarity to the photocopying issue.   Under the law, a library
may reproduce and distribute a copy of specified types of
works without the permission of the copyright owner and without infringing the copyright.   Under certain conditions, a
library may copy an entire work.   But, the law did not approve of multiple or systematic photocopying.   And, the rights
provided in Section 108 apply only to copies prepared "without any purpose of direct or indirect commercial advantage. "
Congress intended Section 108 to be an experiment.   The
Register of Copyrights has to report on it to Congress by
January, 1983.

Remedies

The primary remedies for copyright infringement include: 1) an injunction to curtail the infringing activity, 2) recovery of actual damages, 3) recovery of the infringer's profits, 4) awarding of statutory damages, and 5) recovery of attorney's fees in the court action. The nature and amount of the remedy was a major issue in a case decided by the U. S. Supreme Court in 1940.

Sheldon v. Metro-Goldwyn Pictures Corporation
309 U. S. 390 (1940)

Edward Sheldon's play Dishonored Lady was based upon the trial in Scotland, in 1857, of Madeleine Smith, for the murder of her lover. The play was copyrighted as an unpublished work in 1930, and was produced in the United States and abroad. When making their motion picture Letty Lynton, Metro-Goldwyn Pictures took the title from a 1930 novel of that name written by the English author, Belloc Lowndes. That novel was also based upon the story of Madeleine Smith, and the motion picture rights were bought by Metro-Goldwyn Pictures. Negotiations were conducted for the motion picture rights to Sheldon's play and the price had been fixed at $30,000, but the negotiations fell through. The plot of Letty Lynton covered old material--"the general skeleton was already in the public demesne." A girl kills her lover to free herself for a better match; she is brought to trial and eventually escapes. Metro-Goldwyn Pictures, however, was not content to use the basic plot but also used Sheldon's copyrighted play in the manner of "deliberate plagiarism." Sheldon charged copyright infringement of his play Dishonored Lady by Metro-Goldwyn's motion picture Letty Lynton. Sheldon sought an injunction and an accounting of profits. The court awarded Sheldon all the profits, which amounted to $587,604.37. The circuit court of appeals reversed, holding that Sheldon's share of the profits should be one-fifth. After all, if Sheldon got all the profits, he would receive the benefit that motion picture stars, directors, and technicians brought to the picture.

The U. S. Supreme Court upheld (8-0) the decision. The issue was whether, in determining an award of profits against an infringer of a copyright, there may be an apportionment that gives to the owner of a copyright only that part of the profits that derived from the use of the copyrighted material, as distinguished from the profits that derived from what the infringer had supplied. The Court found no justification for making "an award of profits which have been shown not to be due to the infringement. That would be not to do equity but to inflict unauthorized penalty. " The Court concluded that an

> apportionment of profits can be had where it is clear that all the profits are not due to the use of the copyrighted material, and the evidence is sufficient to provide a fair basis for division so as to give to the copyright proprietor all the profits that can be deemed to have resulted from the use of what belonged to him.

The Court noted that the profits from a motion picture are derived mainly from the talent and popularity of the "motion picture stars. " In this case, "the portion of the profits attributable to the use of the copyrighted play ... was very small. " An apportionment of 20 percent was considered extremely fair. Sheldon and his associates were awarded in excess of $100,000. It would have been cheaper for Metro-Goldwyn to simply buy Sheldon's script.

Fair Use

Fair use of a copyrighted work is not an infringement. According to the 1976 Copyright Act, determining whether a use is indeed a fair use involves consideration of: 1) the purpose and character of the use, 2) the nature of the copyrighted work, 3) the amount used, and 4) the effect of the use upon the value of the copyrighted work. The 1976 law represents the first formal legislative statement of the fair use doctrine. The courts have, however, applied and interpreted the doctrine for many years. The following cases illustrate the nature of the "fair use" doctrine.

Rosemont Enterprises, Inc. v. Random House, Inc.
366 F. 2d 303 (1966)

The famous recluse Howard Hughes had a passionate desire to remain out of the public eye. But, in January, 1954, Look published a series, "The Howard Hughes Story, " and in 1962, Random House hired John Keats to write a biography, eventually published as Howard Hughes--A Biography

by John Keats. In 1965, Rosemont Enterprises, a Hughes-
owned company, purchased the copyright to the Look articles.
Rosemont then brought a copyright infringement suit against
Random House, claiming that Keats had copied and paraphrased
several sentences from the Look articles in preparing the
biography. Over the years, the courts had acknowledged the
doctrine of fair use, but the doctrine had not been precisely
defined. Generally, the courts had been lenient with quotations used in scholarly works and less lenient toward use of
copyrighted materials for commercial purposes. In this case,
the district court found that Hughes's biography by Keats was
prepared for commercial purposes and therefore was not a
fair use. It was a violation of copyright. Random House
appealed.

Judge Leonard B. Moore, writing for the court of appeals, expressed doubt that Keats had substantially copied
from the three 1954 Look articles. The articles contained
some 13, 500 words and would have filled only thirty-six to
thirty-nine book-size pages. The 1966 biography consisted
of some 116, 000 words and 304 pages. The Look articles
did not purport to be a biography, but only narrated certain
highlights in Hughes's career. Naturally, any biography was
bound to touch on the same events. Keats was free to draw
upon Look, like any other sources, for information about
Hughes's life. Two direct quotations and a short paraphrase
taken from the Look articles were attributed to Stephen White,
the author of the articles. In Judge Moore's opinion, there
was "considerable doubt as to whether the copied and paraphrased matter constitutes a material and substantial portion
of those articles. " Judge Moore then considered the issue
of "fair use. " He rejected any dichotomy based on whether
the use was commercial or scholarly. Such a consideration
was "irrelevant to a determination of whether a particular use
of copyrighted material in a work which offers some benefit
to the public constitutes a fair use. " The public was entitled
to the opportunity of becoming acquainted with the life of an
extraordinary man. It would be contrary to the public interest to permit anybody "to buy up the copyright ownership to
restrain others from publishing biographical material concerning him. " The court ruled that John Keats's biography of Howard Hughes was an instance of fair use.

Time Inc. v. Bernard Geis Associates 293 F. Supp. 130 (1968)

In 1968, a court applied specific criteria in deciding
the issue of "fair use. " When President John F. Kennedy

was killed in Dallas, on November 22, 1963, Abraham Zapruder, a Dallas dress manufacturer, was at the scene taking
home movie pictures with his camera. His film, the most
important photographic evidence concerning the fatal shots,
was bought a few days later and eventually copyrighted by
Life magazine. Parts of the film were printed in several
issues of the magazine. In addition, the film was used extensively by the Warren Commission and was cited as evidence
in support of the Commission's findings. Josiah Thompson,
who was skeptical of the official version of the assassination,
wrote Six Seconds in Dallas, a book that critically analyzed
the assassination. The book contained a number of what were
called "sketches, " but which were in fact copies of parts of
the Zapruder film. Life had persistently refused to give
Thompson permission to reproduce the Zapruder pictures.
In fact, Life had refused an offer by Bernard Geis Associates,
Thompson's publisher, to pay a royalty equal to the profits
from publication of the book in return for permission to use
frames from the Zapruder film. Time Incorporated brought
suit, charging that certain frames of the Zapruder film were
"stolen surreptitiously" from Life by Thompson.

The court was impressed by the offer Geis Associates
had made to pay all its profits to Life for permission to use
the pictures. But, the court noted that Thompson was guilty
of a copyright infringement unless the use of the copyrighted
material in the book was a "fair use. " The court noted that,
according to legislation currently before the Congress, determination of fair use depended upon 1) the purpose and character of the use, 2) the nature of the copyrighted work, 3) the
amount and substantiality of the portion used in relation to
the copyrighted work as a whole, and 4) the effect of the use
upon the potential market for or value of the copyrighted work.
In this case, the court decided that in determining the issue
of fair use the balance seemed to be in favor of Thompson
and Bernard Geis Associates. There was a public interest
in having the fullest information available about the Kennedy
assassination. Thompson did serious work on the subject
and had a theory entitled to public consideration. While the
theory could be explained with sketches, the explanation actually made in the book with photographic copies was easier to
understand. The court stressed that the book was not bought
because it contained the Zapruder pictures; it was purchased
because of Thompson's theory and its explanation, supported
by Zapruder's pictures. In addition, there seemed to be little,
if any, injury to Life, the copyright owner. This was a case of
fair use. The four criteria for determining fair use applied in
this case ultimately became the specific criteria set forth in the
1976 Copyright Law.

Bibliography

Books

Crawford, Tad. The Writer's Legal Guide. New York: Hawthorn Books, 1977.

Johnston, Donald F. Copyright Handbook. New York: R. R. Bowker Company, 1978.

Kaplan, Benjamin, and Ralph S. Brown, Jr. Cases on Copyright, Unfair Competition, and Other Topics Bearing on the Protection of Literary, Musical and Artistic Works. 2nd Ed. Mineola, N. Y.: Foundation Press, 1974.

Nasri, William Z. Crisis in Copyright. New York: Marcel Dekker, 1976.

Articles

Conine, Gary B. "Copyright: Unfair Use in Fair Competition--A Search for a Logical Rationale for the Protection of Investigative News Reporting, " Oklahoma Law Review 30 (Winter, 1977), 214-38.

Dannay, Richard. "An Overview of Teleprompter v. CBS and other Recent Developments--Ominous Signals for Copyright Law, " Bulletin of the Copyright Society of the U. S. A. 22 (October, 1974), 10-18.

Patterson, Lyman R. "Private Copyright and Public Communication: Free Speech Endangered, " Vanderbilt Law Review 28 (November, 1975), 1161-1211.

Sobel, Lionel S. "Copyright and the First Amendment: A Gathering Storm?" Copyright Law Symposium 19 (1971), 43-80.

Cases

Amsterdam v. Triangle Publications, Inc. 189 F. 2d 104 (1951)

Benny v. Loew's Incorporated 239 F. 2d 532 (1956)

Berlin v. E. C. Publications, Inc. 329 F. 2d 541 (1964)

Bleistein v. Donaldson Lithographing Company 188 U. S. 239 (1903)

Chamberlain v. Feldman 300 N. Y. 135 (1949)

Chicago Record-Herald v. Tribune Association 275 F. 797 (1921)

College Entrance Book Company, Inc. v. Amsco Book Company, Inc. 119 F. 2d 874 (1941)

Columbia Broadcasting System, Inc., v. Loew's Incorporated 356 U. S. 43 (1958)

Columbia Pictures Corporation v. National Broadcasting Company 137 F. Supp. 348 (1955)

Donald v. Zack Meyer's T. V. Sales and Service 426 F. 2d 1027 (1970)

Eisenschiml v. Fawcett Publications 246 F. 2d 598 (1957)

Emerson v. Davies 8 Fed. Cas. 615 (1845)

Estate of Hemingway v. Random House 23 N. Y. 2d 341 (1968)

Fortnightly Corporation v. United Artists Television, Inc. 392 U. S. 390 (1968)

Heim v. Universal Pictures Company 154 F. 2d 480 (1946)

Henry Holt & Company, Inc. v. Liggett & Myers Tobacco Company 23 F. Supp. 302 (1938)

Herbert v. Shanley Company; John Church Company v. Hilliard Hotel Company 242 U. S. 591 (1917)

Holmes v. Hurst 174 U. S. 82 (1899)

International News Service v. Associated Press 248 U. S. 215 (1918)

Jewelers' Circular Publishing Company v. Keystone Publishing Company 281 F. 83 (1922)

King v. Mister Maestro, Inc. 224 F. Supp. 101 (1963)

Lipman v. Commonwealth of Massachusetts 475 F. 2d 565
(1973)

Mifflin v. Dutton 190 U. S. 265 (1903)

Mifflin v. White 190 U. S. 260 (1903)

Public Affairs Associates Inc. v. Rickover 369 U. S. 111 (1962)

Pushman v. New York Graphic Society, Inc. 287 N. Y. 302
(1942)

Rosemont Enterprises, Inc. v. Random House, Inc. 366 F.
2d 303 (1966)

Sheldon v. Metro-Goldwyn Pictures Corporation 309 U. S. 390
(1940)

Teleprompter Corporation v. Columbia Broadcasting System,
Inc. 415 U. S. 394 (1974)

Time, Inc. v. Bernard Geis Associates 293 F. Supp. 130
(1968)

Toksvig v. Bruce Publishing Company 181 F. 2d 664 (1950)

Triangle Publications, Inc. v. New England Newspaper Publishing Company 46 F. Supp. 198 (1942)

Walt Disney Productions v. The Air Pirates 345 F. Supp.
108 (1972)

Warner Brothers Pictures, Inc. v. Columbia Broadcasting
System Inc. 216 F. 2d 945 (1954)

Washingtonian Publishing Company Inc. v. Pearson 306 U. S. 30
(1939)

Williams & Wilkins Company v. United States 487 F. 2d 1345
(1973); 420 U. S. 376 (1975)

Wrench v. Universal Pictures Company, Inc. 104 F. Supp.
374 (1952)

CHAPTER V

FAIR TRIAL

A vital area of communication law involves two constitutional guarantees--freedom of communication and the
right to a fair trial.   These rights are occasionally in conflict, especially when the public clamors to know the facts
of a case, but the discussion of those facts might place in
jeopardy the defendant's right to a fair trial.   In several instances, the U. S. Supreme Court has been asked to balance
the demands of these rights in conflict.   In this chapter, relevant cases are considered under two main headings--contempt
and pretrial publicity.

CONTEMPT

In 1831, federal judge James H. Peck used the contempt power to suspend from legal practice for eighteen
months an attorney who had criticized Peck's handling of some
Spanish land grant cases.   A political dispute followed; Peck
was subsequently impeached and tried in the U. S. Senate.   The
impeachment attempt failed by one vote, but the dispute associated with this case furthered a widespread resentment of
the common-law method of dealing with constructive contempt
that was currently practiced in the United States.   Within nine
days, Congress enacted the Federal Contempt Act of 1831,
limiting punishable contempt to disobedience of any judicial
process or decree and to misbehavior in the presence of the
court "or so near thereto as to obstruct the administration
of justice. "

"So Near Thereto"

In 1918, the U. S. Supreme Court provided an interpretation of the phrase "so near thereto. "   The Court rendered a causal rather than a geographical interpretation of
the phrase.

Toledo Newspaper Company v. United
States 247 U. S. 402 (1918)

The Toledo Railways & Light Company operated practically all the street railways in Toledo. In 1914, when the
franchise under which the company controlled such local transportation expired, the city and the company engaged in a bitter dispute over the issuance of a new franchise. As part
of an effort to gain a favorable contract with the company,
the city passed an ordinance that stipulated that the company
should charge 3¢ fares from day to day. This action gave
rise to considerable public agitation and discussion on the
issue. Subsequently, the company filed suit seeking to restrain enforcement of the city ordinance. Before any action
was taken by the court, the Toledo News-Bee published editorials that defended the right of the city to enact the ordinance and that assailed any right of the court to grant any
relief to the company. Shortly thereafter, an information for
contempt was issued against the managing editor of the News-
Bee for publications that were made concerning the controversy.
The court found the defendant guilty and imposed a fine. The
case was appealed.

In affirming (5-2) the lower-court decision, the U. S.
Supreme Court noted:

> Newspaper articles, referring to a suit in the feder-
> al court to enjoin municipal ordinances regulating
> street car fares, which held the federal judge up
> to ridicule and hatred in case he should grant an
> injunction, and in advance impeached his motives
> in so doing, and practically urged noncompliance
> with any such order, must be deemed acts tending
> to obstruct the administration of justice ... and
> punishment for contempt cannot be avoided on the
> ground that it did not appear the judge saw the arti-
> cles or that he was unaffected by them.

The Court majority interpreted the 1831 act as recognizing an
inherent power of the courts to punish a newspaper's misbehavior which showed a "reasonable tendency" to obstruct justice. In the Court's interpretation, the phrase "so near thereto" required a causal rather than a geographical construction.
The Court upheld the conviction of the News-Bee for attributing
bias to a judge in a squabble between the city and the transit
company.

Nye v. United States 313 U. S. 33 (1941)

In 1941, the Court reversed the causative interpretation of the "so near thereto" phrase. According to the Court, the "reasonable tendency" rule as applied in Toledo Newspaper contradicted the purposes of the Contempt Act of 1831. The case involved a wrongful death action brought by W. H. Elmore against the B. C. Remedy Company concerning the death of Elmore's son James. Elmore claimed that his son died as a result of taking a medicine manufactured and sold by the company. Shortly thereafter, R. H. Nye used alcoholic beverages and persuasion to coax Elmore, a feeble, illiterate, elderly man, to drop the suit. These events took place more than one hundred miles from Durham, North Carolina, where the court hearing the wrongful death suit was located. Nye was, nonetheless, held in criminal contempt for obstructing justice. The court held that Nye's conduct was "misbehavior so near to the presence of the court as to obstruct the administration of justice. " It ordered Nye to pay the costs of the proceedings and a fine of $500. Nye appealed.

When the case reached the U. S. Supreme Court, the justices interpreted (6-3) "so near thereto" to mean physical proximity. They decided that the phrase should be applied as a geographical rather than a causative standard. According to the Court, the phrase connoted that the misbehavior must be in the vicinity of the court. The term "near" suggested physical proximity, not relevancy. Nye's influence on Elmore had not been perpetrated in the "presence" of the court or "near thereto. " It was insufficient that the misbehavior had some direct relation to the business of the court. The Court reversed Nye's conviction, and by overturning Toledo Newspaper, considerably limited the power of judges to punish contempt that occurred outside of the courtroom.

Bridges Principle

In two 1941 companion cases, the Court expanded the power of the press to comment on pending court cases and court judges.

Bridges v. State of California
Times-Mirror Company v. Superior Court of State of California, In and For Los Angeles County 314 U. S. 252 (1941)

In the first case, a motion for a new trial was pending in a case involving a dispute between two labor unions. Harry Bridges, the president of one of the unions, sent a telegram to the Secretary of Labor that described the court judge's decision in the case as "outrageous"; threatened a strike of the ILWU (longshoremen) that would tie up the port of Los Angeles and affect the entire Pacific Coast if the court decision was enforced; and concluded with the announcement that the CIO Union, representing some 12,000 members, did "not intend to allow state courts to override the majority vote of members in choosing its officers and representatives and to override the National Labor Relations Board." The telegram was published in Los Angeles and San Francisco newspapers. Bridges was tried and found guilty for contempt of court by the Superior Court of Los Angeles. He appealed.

In the second case, the Times-Mirror Company, publisher of the Los Angeles Times, and L. D. Hotchkiss, its managing editor, were cited for contempt for publishing editorials while the outcome of a court case was still pending. An editorial entitled "Sit Strikers Convicted" approved the convictions of twenty-two sitdown strikers. The editorial appeared in the newspaper after the verdict, but prior to sentencing. Another editorial, "Probation for Gorillas?" approved the convictions of two labor leaders who had previously been found guilty of assaulting non-union truck drivers. The article urged the judge to make examples of the labor officials: "Judge A. A. Scott will make a serious mistake if he grants probation to Matthew Shannon and Kennan Holmes. This community needs the example of their assignment to the jute mill." The Times-Mirror Company and Hotchkiss were found to be responsible for the editorials and were fined $500 and $100, respectively.

In these cases, the U. S. Supreme Court applied (5-4) the "clear and present danger" rather than the "bad tendency" test. Writing for the majority, Justice Hugo Black claimed that "the likelihood, however great that a substantive evil will result cannot alone justify a restriction upon freedom of speech or the press. The evil itself must be 'substantial.'" According to Black:

> What finally emerges from the "clear and present danger" cases is a working principle that the substantive evil must be extremely serious and the degree of imminence extremely high before the utterances can be punished.

Specifically, in the Bridges case, the Court found that the

telegram stated that if the court's decision was enforced there
would be a strike.   There was no claim that the strike would
violate the court decision, nor that it would violate California
law in any way.   The telegram was clearly no threat either
by Bridges or the union to follow an illegal course of action.
The Court did not find anything that obstructed the administration of justice.   In Times-Mirror, the Court claimed that
neither "inherent tendency" nor "reasonable tendency" justified the restriction of free expression.   But even if "tendency"
was an appropriate measure, the test was exaggerated in describing the facts of this case.   The Los Angeles Times had
a long-established policy of militancy on labor controversies;
there was no doubt that the paper would adversely criticize
any idea of probation for Shannon and Holmes.   To consider
such criticism a substantial influence upon the course of justice would "impute to judges a lack of firmness, wisdom, or
honor. "   In these two cases, the Court seemed to acknowledge
that, concerning pending court cases, there were greater benefits to be derived from public discussion than from forced
silence.   In Bridges and Times-Mirror, the Court increased
the power of the press to comment on pending court cases
and judges.

Pennekamp v. State of Florida 328 U. S. 331 (1946)

     In 1946, the Court affirmed the Bridges principle.   The
Miami Herald published two editorials and a cartoon accusing
local judges in non-jury proceedings of leniency toward criminals, and especially toward gambling establishments.   The
paper claimed that the judges were using legal technicalities
to delay and subvert swift convictions of criminals.   The newspaper itself and associate editor John Pennekamp were cited
for contempt because the paper allegedly impugned the integrity of the court, tended to create distrust of the court, suppressed the truth, and tended to obstruct the impartial administration of justice in pending cases.   Pennekamp was
fined $250 and the company, $1, 000.

     On appeal, the U. S. Supreme Court found (8-0) no
clear and present danger affecting the administration of justice.   The editorials and the cartoon did not constitute a
"clear and present danger to fair administration of justice"
because the effect on juries that might eventually try alleged
offenders was very remote and the editorials only criticized
court action already taken.   Justice Stanley Reed noted: "The
danger under this record to fair judicial administration had

not the clearness and immediacy necessary to close the door
of permissible public comment. " The Court reversed the
decision of the lower court.

Craig v. Harney 331 U. S. 367 (1947)

One year later, the Court again affirmed the Bridges
principle. During 1946, a court was hearing the forcible de-
tainer case of Jackson v. Mayes, whereby Jackson sought to
regain possession from Mayes of a business building that Mayes claimed under a lease. The case turned on whether Mayes's
lease was forfeited because of non-payment of rent. At the
close of testimony, each side moved for an instructed verdict. The judge instructed the jury to return a verdict for
Jackson. The jury returned with a verdict for Mayes. The
judge refused to accept it and again instructed the jury to return a verdict for Jackson. The jury returned a second time
with a verdict for Mayes. Again, the judge refused to accept it and repeated his previous instruction. Finally, the
jury complied, noting that it acted under coercion of the judge
and against its conscience. Mayes moved for a new trial,
but the motion was denied on June 6. During days of this
trial--May 26, 27, 28, 30, and 31--the Corpus Christi Caller-
Times printed partial reports of what transpired at the trial
and reported news of what certain groups of citizens proposed
to do about the judge's ruling in the case. The judge, who
was a layman and who held an elective office, was criticized
for taking the case away from the jury. That ruling was
called "arbitrary action" and a "travesty on justice. " The
paper deplored the fact that a layman rather than a lawyer
sat as judge. Groups of local citizens were reported as peti-
tioning the judge to grant Mayes a new trial and it was said
that one group had labeled the judge's ruling as a "gross mis-
carriage of justice. " The paper also claimed that the judge's
behavior had properly brought down "the wrath of public opinion upon his head, " that the people were aroused because a
serviceman (Mayes) "seems to be getting a raw deal, " and
that there was "no way of knowing whether justice was done,
because the first rule of justice, giving both sides an opportunity to be heard, was repudiated. " A Texas court determined that the editorials were designed to represent falsely
to the public the nature of the proceedings and to influence
the court in its ruling on the motion for a new trial. The
court maintained that inaccurate reporting had inflamed public feeling against the court and threatened a disturbance in
the courtroom as the trial progressed. The court ruled that

a clear and present danger existed and found the paper in contempt. The publisher, an editorial writer, and a news reporter were sentenced to jail for three days. The case was appealed.

Speaking for the U. S. Supreme Court, Justice William Douglas noted (6-3) that the articles reflected inept reporting because they neglected to indicate the precise issue before the judge. The paper had reported that Mayes had tendered a rental check but did not disclose that the check was post-dated, and hence in the opinion of the judge was not a valid tender. The articles were an unfair report of what transpired. But, according to Douglas, "it takes more imagination than we possess to find in this rather sketchy and one-sided report of a case any imminent or serious threat to a judge of reasonable fortitude.... " In reporting the proposed community action, the paper was merely reporting community events of legitimate public interest. Even if the community citizens who planned the action were guilty of contempt, "freedom of the press may not be denied a newspaper which brings their conduct to the public eye. " Douglas also noted that "a judge may not hold in contempt one who ventures to publish anything that tends to make him unpopular or to belittle him. " The vehemence of the language used does not, alone, constitute the measure of the power to punish for contempt. That language must spark an imminent threat to the administration of justice. Furthermore, the danger must not be remote or even probable; it must immediately imperil. The Court concluded that the articles did not constitute a "clear and present danger" to the administration of justice so as to authorize conviction for contempt of court. The lower court conviction was reversed. The Craig decision is significant because it furnishes press protection against contempt charges when commenting on a trial involving private parties only.

State of Maryland v. Baltimore Radio Show 338 U. S. 912 (1950)

In 1949, the courts heard a case that applied the Bridges principle to the broadcast media. The Baltimore Radio Show and other Baltimore radio stations broadcast news items about a man the police were holding in custody on the suspicion of killing a ten-year-old girl. The broadcasts asserted that the murder suspect had confessed, that he had a long criminal record, and that he had reenacted the crime when police returned him to the scene. The reports claimed that the suspect dug down into some leaves to recover the knife that he had used to kill the little girl. A trial court found that the broadcasts constituted a clear and present danger to the administration of justice. The court found the media guilty of contempt. However, in the tradition of the Bridges principle, the Court of Appeals of Maryland reversed the conviction. In 1950, the U. S. Supreme Court denied certiorari.

Wood v. Georgia 370 U. S. 375 (1962)

In the cases cited thus far, the Bridges principle has been applied to contempt cases involving the print and broadcast media. In all these cases, the courts have upheld the right of the media to criticize court action. In 1962, the U. S. Supreme Court upheld the right of an individual to criticize a court. The case began in 1960, when a judge in Bibb County, Georgia, instructed a grand jury to investigate black block voting to determine if there was any truth to rumors that block voting was being stimulated by illegal payments to black groups and their leaders by political candidates. The judge initiated the inquiry in the middle of a political campaign, and in order to publicize his investigation he read the instructions in front of all local journalists. On the next day, with the grand jury in session, James I. Wood, the sheriff of Bibb County, who was then a candidate for reelection, issued a news release criticizing the judge's action. The release was published and disseminated to the general public. Wood also sent an open letter to the grand jury implying that the judge's charge was false, that the County Democratic Executive Committee was behind the corrupt purchase of votes, and that the grand jury would do well to investigate the committee. A month later, the sheriff was cited for contempt on the grounds that his statement ridiculed the investigation, suggested lack of judicial integrity to the court, and presented a clear and present danger to the investigation and the proper administration of justice. A day later, the sheriff restated his original charges. Again he was cited for contempt on the ground that the second statement presented a clear and present danger to the proper handling of the first contempt citation. Wood was found guilty on three counts of contempt. He was fined $200 and sentenced to twenty days in prison on each count. He appealed.

The U. S. Supreme Court upheld (5-2) Wood's right to engage in the public dialogue. At the time of Wood's criticism, no individual was under investigation. Wood merely contributed to a stream of public discussion at a time when

public interest in the matter was at its peak. The majority
of the Court noted:

> Particularly in matters of local political corrup-
> tion and investigations it is important that free-
> dom of communication be kept open and that the
> real issues not become obscured to the grand jury.
> It cannot effectively operate in a vacuum.

Examination of the content of Wood's statement and the circumstances under which it was published led the Court to
conclude that there was no danger to the administration of
justice. Wood's conviction was reversed.

Goss v. State of Illinois 312 F. 2d 257 (1963)

In Goss, the court upheld a contempt citation. On
July 26, 1955, Carl Champagne filed a complaint for divorce
against his wife, Shirley, charging her with cruelty. At the
same time, he initiated a motion that he be granted custody
of their child. A hearing was held in a Cook County court.
On July 28, Robert Risberg, a private detective employed by
Carl Champagne, testified that on June 3, Mrs. Champagne
had spent the hours from 2:30 a. m. until 6:00 a. m. in the
apartment of Thomas Duggan Goss, and that on June 11, she
had been in the apartment during the hours from 2:00 a. m.
to 5:45 a. m. During 1955, Thomas Duggan Goss appeared
five nights a week on an evening television program watched
by about 200,000 persons within the Chicago area. On July
29, Champagne's complaint for divorce was amended to charge
Mrs. Champagne with having committed adultery with John
Doe on the dates mentioned by Risberg. In his broadcast of
July 28, Goss claimed that Risberg was a "professional sneak
and liar. " Goss also referred to Carl Champagne, his father
Dr. Carl Champagne, and his uncle Anthony Champagne, as
a family "with court-admitted hoodlum connections, " and referred to Dr. Carl Champagne as "a known associate of hoodlums. " He claimed that Anthony Champagne had offered to
keep Goss's name out of the case if he would "lay off the
hoodlums" in his broadcasts. Goss stated that he had promised Mrs. Champagne to do everything in his power "to prevent the legal kidnapping of her child. " Goss also denied
that he had committed adultery with Mrs. Champagne.

Contempt proceedings were initiated against Goss. He
admitted making the statements with knowledge of the pending

divorce action. Goss claimed that his purpose was to defend himself before his television viewers against the charges of adultery that were being made at the trial and which were being reported in Chicago newspapers. Goss disclaimed any intent to influence the court proceedings. Goss was found guilty because, according to the court, his remarks were not limited to criticism of past action. The future of the divorce and custody hearings depended heavily upon testimony to be offered by witnesses Goss attacked. His remarks were "designedly calculated to bring odium upon the testimony of the witnesses produced by the plaintiff and to inspire distrust in their testimony." Goss's words interfered with judicial procedure in both the divorce and custody cases. The words were contemptuous because they were "calculated to impede, embarrass, or obstruct the court in the due administration of justice." Goss was sentenced to ten days in the county jail and fined $100. On appeal, the Illinois Supreme Court held that Goss's statements "constituted a clear and present danger to the administration of justice." The U. S. Supreme Court denied certiorari. Goss was then able to get a district court to reverse on the ground that the Illinois trial court had used the reasonable tendency rather than a clear and present danger test. However, a federal court of appeals ruled that the district court lacked jurisdiction to attack a state criminal contempt conviction that had been affirmed by the highest state court and denied review by the U. S. Supreme Court. The contempt citation against Goss was ultimately upheld.

The cases examined in this section uphold the principle established in Bridges--the clear and present danger test rather than the bad tendency test should be applied to cases involving alleged contempt. Furthermore, the danger must be "substantial" and "imminent." The principle was clearly upheld in Pennekamp, Craig, Baltimore Radio Show, and Wood. In these cases, representatives of the media and the general public were granted the right to engage in extensive discussion of judicial matters, court actions, and the legal process.

Gag Orders

In order to control coverage of court proceedings, judges have imposed restrictive orders concerning the acceptable scope of media coverage. When the news media appealed such orders, the courts faced a conflict between the

First Amendment right of free speech and the Sixth Amendment right to a fair trial. In most cases, the courts gave priority to the right of free expression. An exception occurred in 1967.

Seymour v. United States 373 F. 2d 629 (1967)

William Seymour, a television news photographer, violated a standing district court order by taking photographs regarding a judicial proceeding on the same floor of the courthouse building on which the courtroom was located. Seymour was found guilty of contempt and fined $25. He appealed.

The court of appeals decided that the court order did not represent an unconstitutional prior restraint upon the liberty of the press. The right to gather news is not unconditional. A trial court must ensure that an accused receives a fair trial--a proceeding conducted in an atmosphere as free as possible from the threat of prejudicial publicity. The court noted that defendants should not be required to run a gauntlet of reporters and photographers every time they enter or leave the courtroom. The judgment of the lower court was affirmed.

Schuster v. Bowen 347 F. Supp. 319 (1972)

Another exception occurred in 1972. When Thomas Lee Bean was tried and convicted of first degree murder, the death penalty was imposed. However, the Supreme Court of Nevada decided that the penalty should be retried before another jury. In November, 1970, Judge Grant Bowen presided over the new penalty trial. After the jury was selected, Bowen issued an order prohibiting the publication of the names of the jurors during the trial. The press complied with the order, but at the same time instituted an action for injunctive and declaratory relief.

The district court declared that the two relevant doctrines--no prior restraint and the need for proof of a clear and present danger to the administration of justice--were not absolutes. In most cases involving such prohibitory orders, the Sixth Amendment guarantee of a speedy and public trial by an impartial jury would give way to the First Amendment right to free expression. In this case, however, the clear, explicit command limited to publicizing the names of the jurors

had a minimal if not a non-existent impact upon achieving an effective system of free expression.   The public's right to
know was wholly irrelevant to this situation.   No public purpose was furthered by publication of the jurors' names on the
first day of the trial rather than the last.   The only use any
member of the public might make of such information was an
improper one--jury tampering.   The court concluded that Judge
Bowen's order was constitutional and valid.

Wood v. Goodson 485 S. W. 2d 213 (1972)

        In Seymour and Schuster, the courts upheld the "gag
order. " In ensuing cases, the courts repeatedly held such
orders unconstitutional.   An example is Wood v. Goodson.
Harry Wood, editor of the Texarkana (Arkansas) Gazette, was
ordered by Miller County Circuit Judge John Goodson not to
publish the jury's verdict in a particular criminal case.   Goodson maintained that such information might prejudice the outcome of a pending trial.   Even though the jury had returned
the verdict in open court, Goodson did "not consider it a public record. " Nonetheless, Wood published the information
and Goodson found him in contempt.   Wood was given a $250
fine and a sixty-day jail term, both of which were suspended.
He appealed.

        The Supreme Court of Arkansas decided that no court
had the power to prohibit the news media from publishing that
which transpired in open court.   The order not to publish was
unconstitutional.

Miami Herald Publishing Company v. Rose 271 So. 2d 483 (1972)

        Later that same year, a Florida district court of ap-
peal held in a per curiam decision that an order that prohibited a newspaper from publishing any information about a
case was invalid because it operated as a prior restraint upon constitutionally privileged publication.   A trial judge had
ample power to ensure a fair trial without suppressing First
Amendment rights.

Sun Company of San Bernardino v. Superior Court
Progress-Bulletin Publishing Company v. Superior Court
29 Cal. App. 3d 815 (1973)

        In this case, the court overturned the judge's order.

On April 21, 1972, Frederick Castillo was stabbed to death while confined in the California Institute for Men at Chino. Fred Mendrin and Donald Hale were brought to trial for the murder. The trial judge issued an Order re Publicity prohibiting the news media from publishing the true names or photographs of any state prison inmates scheduled to be called as prosecution witnesses in the trial. The court held that the "gag order" was necessary to ensure the safety of the inmates. If the inmates feared for their lives, they might refuse to testify, thereby denying the administration of justice. Two newspaper publishers initiated action to vacate the order. The main attack on the order was that it violated freedom of the press.

Referring to Bridges, Craig, and Pennekamp, the Court of Appeal, Fourth District, noted that before a court can restrict freedom of speech or press the prohibited communication must constitute a "clear and present danger" to the administration of justice. There must be no doubt that the utterances are a serious and imminent threat. The danger must not be remote or even probable; it must immediately imperil. In this case, not a single inmate had stated that he would not testify. Therefore, there was no proof for establishing the order on fair trial principles. First Amendment rights may not be "sacrificed" on the basis of a possibility. The court vacated the Order re Publicity.

United States v. Dickinson 465 F. 2d 496 (1972)

In United States v. Dickinson, the court established a specific requirement for reporters to follow in dealing with a gag order. In November, 1971, Baton Rouge reporters Larry Dickinson and Gibbs Adams were cited for contempt for publishing testimony given at an open court hearing in violation of a judge's order. The hearing involved a VISTA worker who had been indicted on a charge of conspiring to murder the Mayor of Baton Rouge. The accused contended that the court action was completely groundless and designed to harass him. The purpose of the hearing was to determine if the state's case was legitimate. At the proceeding, the judge ordered that no report of the testimony or details of the evidence should be made in any newspaper, radio, television, or any other news media "in order to avoid undue publicity which could in any way interfere with the right of the litigants in connection with any further proceedings." The judge acknowledged that the press could report the fact that a hearing was being held. He outlawed reporting details of any evidence presented during the hearing. The reporters ignored the order and wrote articles summarizing the court's testimony in detail. They were found guilty of criminal contempt and were fined $300 each.

The court of appeals noted that the public had a right to know the facts brought out in the hearing and affirmed that a newspaper may not be proscribed in advance from reporting to the public those events that occur during an open and public court proceeding. Nonetheless, Judge John Brown wrote:

> The conclusion that the District Court's order was constitutionally invalid does not necessarily end the matter of the validity of the contempt convictions. There remains the very formidable question of whether a person may with impunity violate an order which turns out to be invalid. We hold that in the circumstances of this case he may not.

The court held that even though the judge's order was unconstitutional the reporters should have respected the order until they had exhausted court remedies. The case was remanded back to the district court to determine if the contempt finding and punishment would be deemed appropriate in light of the fact that the order the journalists disobeyed was constitutionally infirm. The judge again convicted the reporters and upheld the fines. The U. S. Supreme Court refused to review the case. Despite the unconstitutionality of the court's gag order, the violating reporters were punished because they didn't pursue available remedies through the courts. The Dickinson principle looms as a serious barrier to free press in the minds of most news journalists.

United States v. Columbia Broadcasting System, Inc.
497 F. 2d 102 (1974)

In 1974, the courts heard another case involving a prohibiting order--this time related to sketches of courtroom participants. CBS News sent correspondent Jed Duvall and artist Aggie Whelan to cover the pretrial stage of the criminal prosecution of the "Gainesville Eight, " who were accused of conspiring to disrupt the Republican National Convention in 1972. In court, the trial judge announced that "no sketches in the courtroom would be permitted to be made for publication. " After attending the court proceedings, Whelan left the courtroom and began sketching outside in the hall. When the judge learned of this activity, he confiscated Whelan's sketches and issued another order--no sketches for publication of proceedings in the courtroom were to be made, even if the sketches were made outside of the courtroom from memory. After this order, Whelan sketched the trial participants from memory. Four of the sketches were televised on the CBS Morning News on June 22, 1973. Subsequently, CBS was judged guilty of having defied the court's order.

The U. S. Court of Appeals for the Fifth Circuit acknowledged that there were problems confronting the trial court in this particular case. The defendants were actively seeking publicity and in so doing were trying to place before the public, including potential jurors, their version of the merits of the case. However, before a prior restraint could be imposed by a judge, there must be "an imminent, not merely a likely, threat to the administration of justice." In this case,

> ... even though the district court was legitimately concerned with preventing prejudicial publicity from poisoning the impartial atmosphere essential to a fair trial, we conclude that the total ban on the publication of sketches is too remotely related to the danger sought to be avoided, and is, moreover, too broadly drawn to withstand constitutional scrutiny.

The court held that both parts of the order, that banning in-court sketching and that prohibiting the publication of such sketches, were unconstitutional.

Times-Picayune Publishing Corporation v. Schulingkamp
419 U. S. 1301 (1974)

During the same year, the U. S. Supreme Court also rejected a gag order. In April, 1973, a young nursing student was raped in one of New Orlean's public housing projects. Shortly thereafter, two suspects were arrested and charged with the crime. The case immediately received media coverage for a number of reasons. The state university program that prompted the student's unescorted visit to the housing project came under attack. The media questioned the adequacy of law enforcement efforts in high crime areas of the city. In addition, the case sparked criticism of the criminal and juvenile justice systems. Much publicity was directed toward one of the suspects, a seventeen-year-old with an extensive history of previous arrest. Some newspapers referred to his previous arrests for murder and armed robbery without simultaneously revealing that the charges had been dropped for insufficient evidence. Within a few days, however, the media coverage diminished and then ceased. In March, 1974, eleven months after the crime, when the case came to trial, the judge imposed restrictions on reporting. The order banned reporting of testimony after the selection of a jury and also placed other selective restrictions on reporting during the trial. The Times-Picayune Publishing Company initiated a suit seeking to have the order stayed.

The Supreme Court issued (9-0) the stay. Justice Lewis Powell noted that the trial court's order imposed "significant prior restraints on media publication. " In Powell's opinion, the record revealed "the absence of any showing of an imminent threat to fair trial. " If necessary, the court had available alternative methods for protecting the defendant's right to a fair trial.

Nebraska Press Association v. Stuart 427 U. S. 539 (1976)

In 1975, the Supreme Court struck down another gag order, ruling that it was in violation of the First Amendment. On October 18, 1975, six members of the Henry Kellie family were found murdered in their home in Sutherland, Nebraska. The following day, Erwin Charles Simants was charged with six counts of first degree murder. In the ensuing court proceeding, which was open to the press, there was testimony that Simants had made several statements, including a confession, to police officers. Nebraska State District Judge Hugh Stuart ordered that the Nebraska Press Association refrain from publishing or broadcasting accounts of these statements. Stuart said that "because of the nature of the crimes charged in the complaint that there is a clear and present danger that pretrial publicity could impinge upon the defendant's right to a fair trial. " The gag order, effective until a jury was selected, prohibited any reporting about the existence or contents of the confession Simants had made to police officers, which had been introduced previously in open court; the fact or nature of statements made by the accused to other persons; the contents of a note written by the accused the night of the crime; portions of medical testimony; the identity of the victims and nature of the assault; and the nature of the restrictive order. Shortly thereafter, several press and broadcast associations initiated court action asking that the restrictive order imposed by Judge Stuart be vacated.

In a unanimous opinion, the Court overturned the gag order. Writing for the Court, Chief Justice Warren Burger argued that "prior restraints on speech and publication are the most serious and least tolerable infringements on First Amendment rights."

> ... there was indeed a risk that pretrial news accounts, true or false, would have some adverse impact on the attitudes of those who might be called as jurors. But on the record now before us it is not clear that further publicity, unchecked, would so distort the views of potential jurors that 12 could not be found who would, under proper instructions, fulfill their sworn duty to render a just verdict exclusively on the evidence presented in open court. We cannot say on this record that alternatives to a prior restraint on petitioners would not have sufficiently mitigated the adverse effects of pretrial publicity so as to make prior restraint unnecessary.

The Court realized that it was a "heavy burden to demonstrate in advance of trial that without prior restraint a fair trial will be denied," but that kind of evidence was necessary in order to demonstrate a "threat to fair trial rights that would possess the requisite degree of certainty to justify restraint." Such evidence was not evident in Nebraska Press Association so the order was vacated.

The cases cited in this section affirm that the courts usually give prominence to First Amendment rights of free speech and press over the Sixth Amendment right to a fair trial. In order for a judge to impose a "gag order" there must be an imminent, not merely a potential threat to the administration of justice. That principle was supported in Wood, Miami Herald, Sun Company, Dickinson, CBS, and before the U. S. Supreme Court in Times-Picayune and Nebraska Press Association. When, as in Schuster, the danger was considered to be imminent, and the order specifically limited the prohibition, the court upheld the fair trial interest. Finally, it appears that the Dickinson requirement that reporters exhaust all available court remedies before violating an unconstitutional gag order poses a potential barrier to thorough news coverage of courtroom proceedings.

TRIAL BY MEDIA

In the age of modern mass media, the task of providing an impartial jury for trials has become exceedingly difficult. Prior to jury selection, the news media have already disseminated information about the crime, the victim, and the accused. Journalists print the results of interviews that they hold with police, lawyers, witnesses, even the accused. The public is aware of facts concerning the parties that will never be presented at the trial because those facts lack any relevance to the issue before the court. The problem of pretrial prejudicial information does not end with selection of the jury. Media reports often continue to be available to jurors after a trial has begun. This section examines two rights in conflict--the right of the accused to a fair and impartial trial by jury versus the right of the media to inform the public about a particular case.

Pretrial Publicity

Occasionally, the news media publish and broadcast prejudicial information about the defendant in a criminal trial. In such instances, the courts are called upon to judge the impact of such material on the conduct of the trial.

Shepherd v. State of Florida 341 U. S. 50 (1951)

In 1949, two black men, Samuel Shepherd and Walter Irvin, were arrested and charged with the rape of a seventeen-year-old white girl in Florida. A local newspaper reported that the men had confessed. Upon reading this information, a furious mob of local citizens stormed the jail in a lynch attempt, burned the house of one of the accused, and forced another suspect's relatives to flee the town because they feared for their lives. The newspaper also printed a cartoon that appeared while the grand jury was deliberating. It pictured three electric chairs with the caption "No Compromise--Supreme Penalty. " Eventually, the National Guard was called out to maintain order in the community. At the trial, the suspects were sentenced to death, although their purported confessions were never introduced as evidence. The defense attorney presented, but the judge rejected as irrelevant, evidence of brutal beating of the suspects while in police custody. Shepherd and Irvin appealed the verdict.

The U. S. Supreme Court, in a per curiam opinion,

reversed the conviction on the ground that blacks had been purposefully excluded from the grand jury. In addition, Justice Robert Jackson found it

> hard to imagine a more prejudicial influence than a press release by the officer of the court charged with defendant's custody stating that they had confessed, and here just such a statement, unsworn to, unseen, uncross-examined, and uncontradicted, was conveyed by the press to the jury.

The Court held that newspapers, in the enjoyment of their constitutional rights, may not deprive accused persons of their right to a fair trial. In this case, the crime had stirred deep feelings, which were exploited to the limit by the press. During the trial, the judge was helpless to provide the accused "any real protection against this out-of-court campaign to convict." Accordingly, the Court reversed the convictions.

Marshall v. United States 360 U. S. 310 (1959)

In 1959, the Court heard another case involving pretrial publicity. Howard Marshall was convicted of unlawfully dispensing dextro amphetamine sulfate tablets without a prescription from a licensed physician. During the trial, two newspapers published information about Marshall's previous convictions for practicing medicine without a license. The defense asked for a mistrial, claiming that the information was available to the jurors. When questioned by the trial judge, seven jurors admitted reading the newspaper accounts. However, each of them told the judge that he would not be influenced by the articles, that he could decide the case on the basis of the evidence presented, and that he felt no prejudice against Marshall as a result of the articles. The judge indicated that he believed that there was no prejudice against Marshall and denied the motion for mistrial. Marshall appealed.

In a per curiam decision, the U. S. Supreme Court noted (8-1) that the jurors were exposed to information which the trial judge had ruled was so prejudicial it could not be directly offered as evidence during the trial. Clearly, the prejudice to Marshall was almost certain to be as great when that evidence reached the jury through news accounts as when it was a part of the prosecution's case. Under such conditions, the Court thought a new trial should be granted.

Irvin v. Dowd 366 U. S. 717 (1961)

Two years later, the Court reversed a conviction on the ground that prejudicial pretrial publicity had precluded a fair trial before an impartial jury. On April 8, 1955, Indiana state police arrested Leslie Irvin on suspicion of burglary and writing bad checks. Within a few days, the Vanderburgh County prosecutor and Evansville police released press reports announcing that "Mad Dog" Irvin had confessed to six killings, including the murders of three members of a single family. In the six or seven months that preceded Irvin's trial, "a barrage of newspaper headlines, articles, cartoons and pictures was unleashed against him. " These accounts revealed the details of his background, including references to crimes committed when a juvenile, convictions for arson almost twenty years previously, conviction by a court-martial on AWOL charges during the war, and charges of being a parole violator. Headlines announced Irvin's police lineup identification, that he had been placed at the scene of the crime, his confession to the six murders, and his offer to plead guilty if promised a ninety-nine-year sentence, as well as the determination of the prosecutor to secure the death penalty. On the day before the trial, the press announced that Irvin had admitted the "robbery-murder" and "slaughter" of the six victims. When the trial began, the papers noted that "strong feelings, often bitter and angry, rumbled to the surface" and the existence of "a pattern of deep and bitter prejudice against the former pipe-fitter. " Spectator comments appeared in the newspapers that suggested "my mind is made up, " "I think he is guilty, " and "he should be hanged. " Headlines reported that "impartial jurors are hard to find. " Irvin's attorney asked for and received a change of venue from Vanderburgh to nearby Gibson County, where the same media were available. Another request for change was denied. During voir dire, 370 of the 430 prospective jurors said they believed Irvin guilty, but his lawyer had exhausted all peremptory challenges. When twelve jurors were finally selected by the court, the defense attorney challenged all of them for bias, complaining that during voir dire four had admitted a belief in Irvin's guilt. The pretrial publicity was published in newspapers that were delivered regularly to about 95 percent of the homes in the area, and local radio and television stations also carried extensive newscasts covering the same incidents. Irvin was tried, found guilty, and sentenced to death. He appealed.

The U. S. Supreme Court concluded (9-0) that because of prejudicial news reporting Irvin had not received a fair trial.

With his life at stake, it is not requiring too much that petitioner be tried in an atmosphere undisturbed by so huge a wave of public passion and by a jury other than one in which two-thirds of the members admit, before hearing any testimony, to possessing a belief in his guilt.

The case was remanded to the district court and Irvin was retried in a less emotional climate. He was found guilty and sentenced to life in prison.

Rideau v. State of Louisiana 373 U. S. 723 (1963)

Rideau v. State of Louisiana provides another instance where the Court set aside a conviction because of pretrial publicity. On February 16, 1961, a man robbed a bank in Lake Charles, Louisiana, while kidnapping three and killing one of the bank's employees. A few hours later, police captured Wilbert Rideau and held him in jail. The next morning, a sound-motion-picture film was made of a twenty-minute "interview" in the jail between Rideau and the Sheriff of Calcasieu Parish. Under interrogation, Rideau admitted that he had perpetrated the bank robbery, kidnapping, and murder. Later the same day, the film was broadcast over television station KLPC in Lake Charles. About 24,000 people in the community saw and heard it on television. The film was again shown on television the next day to an estimated audience of 53,000 people. The following day the film was broadcast by the same station and this time approximately 20,000 people watched the program. Overall, a substantial portion of the total population of approximately 150,000 persons living in Calcasieu Parish viewed the film. Two weeks later, Rideau was charged with armed robbery, kidnapping, and murder. His lawyers promptly filed a motion for a change of venue on the ground that a fair trial was impossible in Calcasieu Parish after the three television broadcasts. Three members of the jury admitted during voir dire that they had watched the television interview. In addition, two members of the jury were deputy sheriffs of Calcasieu Parish. Rideau's counsel had requested that they be excused for cause, but these challenges were denied by the trial judge. The motion for a change of venue was denied. Rideau was convicted and sentenced to death.

The Supreme Court held (7-2) that Rideau was denied due process of law when the court refused to grant a change

of venue "after the people of Calcasieu Parish had been exposed repeatedly and in depth to the spectacle of Rideau personally confessing in detail to the crimes with which he was later
to be charged. "

> For anyone who has ever watched television the
> conclusion cannot be avoided that this spectacle, to
> the tens of thousands of people who saw and heard
> it, in a very real sense was Rideau's trial--at
> which he pleaded guilty to murder. Any subsequent
> court proceedings in a community so pervasively
> exposed to such a spectacle could be but a hollow
> formality.

The conviction was reversed. Rideau was later retried and
convicted.

Sheppard v. Maxwell 384 U. S. 333 (1966)

The classic case of pretrial publicity is Sheppard v.
Maxwell. On July 4, 1954, Marilyn Sheppard, wife of Dr.
Sam Sheppard, was bludgeoned to death in the upstairs bedroom of their lakeshore home in Bay Village, a suburb of
Cleveland. According to Dr. Sheppard, he and his wife were
watching television in the living room when he became drowsy
and dozed off to sleep on the couch. Hearing his wife cry
out, he rushed upstairs and in the dim light saw a "form"
standing next to his wife's bed. A struggle ensued--Sheppard
was struck on the back of the neck and fell unconscious. When
he awoke, he checked his wife's pulse and determined that
Marilyn was dead. He checked his son's bedroom and found
him unmolested. Sheppard notified neighbors, who called
the police as well as Dr. Richard Sheppard, Sam's brother,
who came, checked Sam's injuries, and then took Sam to a
nearby clinic operated by the family. When the Coroner, the
police, and other officials arrived, the house and surrounding
vicinity were thoroughly searched, the rooms of the house
were photographed, and several neighbors were questioned.
From the beginning, law enforcement officials suspected Sheppard of the crime.

Considerable press coverage surrounded the case. On
July 7, a newspaper story appeared in which the chief prosecutor criticized the refusal of the Sheppard family to permit early questioning. From then on, headline stories constantly stressed Sheppard's unwillingness to cooperate with

the police and other officials.   Under the headline "Testify
Now in Death, Bay Doctor Is Ordered, " an article described
a visit to the hospital by the Coroner and four police officers.
The next day Sheppard reenacted the tragedy at his home before the Coroner, police, and a group of journalists, who reported the event in detail, along with photographs.   Headlines
announced that "Doctor Balks at Lie Test; Retells Story. "
Another headline story disclosed that Sheppard had "again
late yesterday refused to take a lie detector test. "   Other
articles appeared when Sheppard refused to allow authorities
to inject him with "truth serum. "   On July 20, a front page
editorial charged that somebody was "getting away with murder. "   The following day another page one editorial was headed "Why No Inquest? Do It Now, Dr. Gerber. "   Dr. Gerber
then called a coroner's inquest and subpoenaed Sheppard, who
was brought into the room by police and searched in full view
of several hundred spectators.   When Sheppard's counsel tried
to place some documents in the record, he was removed from
the room by the coroner, who received cheers, hugs, and
kisses from women in the audience.

        Newspapers emphasized discrepancies in the statements
of Sheppard and the authorities.   One story reported that a
detective "disclosed that scientific tests at the Sheppard home
have definitely established that the killer washed off a trail
of blood from the murder bedroom to the downstairs section, "
a circumstance casting doubt on Sheppard's account of the
murder.   No such evidence was produced at trial.   Newspaper articles also stressed Sheppard's extramarital love affairs as a motive for the crime.   The newspaper fully detailed his relationship with Susan Hayes and named several
other women who were allegedly involved with him.   Testimony at the trial failed to demonstrate that Sheppard had any
illicit relationships other than the one with Hayes.   A front
page editorial in late July inquired "Why Isn't Sam Sheppard
in Jail?"   It demanded "Quit Stalling--Bring Him In. "   On
July 30, Sheppard was arrested and charged with murder.
The publicity increased in intensity.   Headlines announced
that "Doctor Evidence Is Ready for Jury, " "Corrigan Tactics
Stall Quizzing, " "Sheppard 'Gay Set' Is Revealed by Houk, "
"Blood Is Found in Garage, " "New Murder Evidence Is Found,
Police Claim, " and "Dr. Sam Faces Quiz at Jail on Marilyn's
Fear of Him. "

        Jury selection took place in mid-October.   A list of
the names and addresses of seventy-five prospective jurors
was published in all three Cleveland newspapers.   As a conse-
quence, anonymous correspondence concerning the trial was

received by all the prospective jurors. All but one juror admitted at <u>voir dire</u> of being exposed to the case by the media. During the trial, the jurors themselves were constantly exposed to news coverage, and pictures of the jury appeared more than forty times in the Cleveland newspapers.

The trial itself received enormous coverage. Even though the courtroom measured only twenty-six feet by forty-eight feet, an army of news personnel was admitted. Approximately twenty representatives of the news media were seated at a table that ran the width of the courtroom. There were also four rows of benches in the room. The first row was assigned to personnel from television and radio stations, the second and third rows were occupied by reporters from newspapers and magazines, and the last row was assigned to Sam and Marilyn Sheppard's families. Representatives of the news media used all the rooms on the courtroom floor; telegraphic equipment and telephone lines were installed so that reports could be speeded to the papers. Station WSRS set up broadcasting facilities on the third floor next door to the jury room. Newscasts emanated from this room throughout the trial and during jury deliberations. In the corridors outside the courtroom, photographers and television personnel with cameras constantly flashed pictures during court recesses. Outside the building, television and newsreel cameramen took motion pictures of the defendant, judge, jury, and other participants in the trial. The crowded courtroom certainly provided a poor environment for confidential talk between Sheppard and his counsel.

During the trial, anti-Sheppard coverage continued. One story was headlined "Sam Called a 'Jekyll-Hyde' by Marilyn, Cousin to Testify." The story announced that the prosecution had "a 'bombshell witness' on tap who will testify to Dr. Sam's display of fiery temper--countering the defense claim that the defendant is a gentle physician with an even disposition." It claimed that Marilyn had told friends that Sam was a "Dr. Jekyll and Mr. Hyde character." No such testimony was presented at the trial. In the seventh week, Walter Winchell broadcast over television station WXEL and radio station WJW that Carole Beasley, who was under arrest in New York for robbery, had claimed that she had borne Sam Sheppard a child while being his mistress. Two jurors admitted hearing the broadcast, but when they indicated it would have no effect on their verdict the judge accepted their statement. On December 9, Sheppard testified that he had been abused by detectives after his arrest. Although he was not at the trial, Captain Kerr of the Homicide Bureau issued a press statement denying Sheppard's claims. The newspapers printed the detective's story under the headline " 'Barefaced Liar, ' Kerr says of Sam. " Captain Kerr never appeared as a witness in court.

Sheppard was convicted of second degree murder. On appeal, the U. S. Supreme Court denied certiorari. Several years later, Sheppard started proceedings in a district court, which granted that Sheppard had been denied a fair trial. The case ultimately came to the Supreme Court, which agreed (8-1) with the district court and ordered that Sheppard be released unless Ohio tried him again within a reasonable time. Justice Tom Clark's opinion noted that the trial judge failed to protect Sheppard from the inherently prejudicial publicity that saturated the community and neglected to control the disruptive influences in the courtroom. Clark noted that "the carnival atmosphere at trial could easily have been avoided since the courtroom and courthouse premises are subject to the control of the court. " He suggested ways in which the trial atmosphere could have been improved. First, the presence of the press at judicial proceedings could have been restricted when it was clear that the accused could be disadvantaged. Second, the judge should have insulated the witnesses. The media interviewed prospective witnesses at will and on numerous occasions disclosed their testimony. Third, the judge should have controlled the release of information to the press. Much of the data thus disclosed was inaccurate, contributing to groundless rumors and confusion. The Court overturned the verdict. Ohio tried Sheppard again but this time he was acquitted. In November, 1966, Sheppard became a free man.

Murphy v. State of Florida 421 U. S. 794 (1975)

In the cases discussed thus far, the Court overturned several convictions obtained in a trial atmosphere that was corrupted by press and broadcast coverage. In 1975, the Court upheld a conviction in which the jury had been exposed to media coverage regarding prior convictions of the defendant. In 1968, Jack Roland Murphy was arrested in Dade County, Florida, for robbery and assault. Murphy's arrest received extensive press coverage because he had been in the news frequently before. He had made himself notorious for his part in the 1964 theft of the Star of India sapphire from a museum in New York. His flamboyant life-style made him a continuing subject of press interest; he was generally referred to in the media as "Murph the Surf." Before he was tried on the robbery and assault charges, Murphy was indicted for murder in Broward County. Thereafter, the Dade County court declared Murphy mentally incompetent to stand trial, and he was committed to a hospital. After Murphy was judged competent for trial, he was convicted of murder. Then, in 1969, Murphy pleaded guilty to a federal indictment involving stolen securities. All the events of 1968 and 1969 drew extensive press coverage. Each new case against Murphy was considered newsworthy; scores of articles reporting Murphy's trials and tribulations were published during this period.

Jury selection for the robbery and assault charges began in August, 1970. Seventy-eight jurors were questioned. Of these, thirty were excused for miscellaneous personal reasons, twenty were excused peremptorily by the defense or prosecution, twenty were excused by the court because of prejudice against Murphy, and the remaining eight served as the jury. The defense moved to dismiss the chosen jurors on the ground that they were aware of Murphy's previous convictions. The motion was denied, as was a motion for a change of venue based on alleged prejudicial pretrial publicity. Murphy was convicted on both counts. He appealed.

The U. S. Supreme Court noted (8-1) that unlike Marshall, the voir dire in this case indicated no such hostility to Murphy by the jurors who served in this trial "as to suggest a partiality that could not be laid aside." Some of the jurors had a vague recollection of the robbery and some knowledge of Murphy's past crimes, but none indicated any belief in the relevance of the past to the present case. Furthermore, the community and courtroom circumstances surrounding Murphy's trial were not at all inflammatory. An examination revealed that news coverage of Murphy's past experiences was largely factual in nature. The Court concluded:

> ... we are unable to conclude, in the circumstances presented in this case, that petitioner did not receive a fair trial. Petitioner has failed to show that the setting of the trial was inherently prejudicial or that the jury-selection process of which he complains permits an inference of actual prejudice.

In Murphy, the Court based its decision on the notion

that jurors "need not ... be totally ignorant of the acts and issues involved. " It was sufficient that jurors be able to set aside their impressions and render a verdict based on the evidence presented in the specific case. In <u>Murphy</u>, the Court decided that appropriate juror impartiality was evident. Nonetheless, as <u>Shepherd</u>, <u>Marshall</u>, <u>Irvin</u>, <u>Rideau</u>, and <u>Shep-pard</u> indicate, the Court is clearly willing to reverse a conviction in order to offset prejudicial pretrial publicity.

Implied Bias

Cameras and tape recorders are barred from most courtrooms. Canon 35, a judicial rule against permitting photographic and sound equipment in the courtroom, was adopted by most states during the 1930s--a period when photography was a disruptive process. During the 1960s, many journalists complained about the regulations, arguing that modern photographic equipment rendered the ban obsolete. Furthermore, they asserted that broadcasting a trial was a First Amendment freedom. In 1962, a Texas trial was televised. It received nationwide attention.

Estes v. State of Texas 381 U. S. 532 (1965)

In 1962, Texas financier Billie Sol Estes was tried on charges of theft, swindling, and embezzlement. Massive pretrial publicity gave the trial national notoriety. During the two-day pretrial hearing, all available seats in the courtroom were occupied and an additional thirty persons stood in the aisles. A defense motion to prevent telecasting, radio broadcasting, and news photography was denied. So, twelve television camermen and several radio broadcasters carried the court proceedings live. News photography was a constant occurrence. Workers laid cables and wires across the courtroom floor; they placed microphones on the judge's bench and aimed other microphones at the jury box and the counsel table. Activities of the broadcast crews often disrupted the hearing. Witnesses present at the hearing as well as the jury members were clearly aware of the press and television coverage being provided. In fact, they themselves were televised live and their pictures were rebroadcast later.

The actual trial opened in a completely different environment. A booth constructed at the rear of the courtroom blended in with the permanent appearance of the room. Television cameras and news photographers took pictures from this location that provided an unrestricted view of the court-room. Live telecasting was restricted; only the opening and closing arguments of the prosecution and the return of the verdict to the judge were carried live with sound. Various portions of the trial were videotaped without sound for broad-cast on regularly scheduled newscasts later in the day and evening. The judge prohibited coverage of any kind during the defense's summation to the jury. Because of these re-strictions, telecasts of the trial were limited primarily to film clips shown on the various stations' regular newscasts. News commentators used the film as a backdrop for their reports concerning the trial. After Estes was convicted, he appealed on the ground that because of the way the pretrial hearing was conducted, he had been denied a fair trial.

When the case reached the U. S. Supreme Court, the justices agreed that publicity in a pretrial hearing could be detrimental to due process in the ensuing criminal trial. Writing for the majority, Justice Tom Clark argued the doc-trine of "implied bias"--that is, prejudice is inherent in a televised trial. He offered four reasons. First, the poten-tial impact of television on the jurors may be detrimental be-cause, "while it is practically impossible to assess the ef-fect of television on jury attentiveness, those of us who know juries realize the problem of jury 'distraction. ' " Second, the quality of the testimony in criminal trials could be im-paired. The knowledge that she or he is being viewed by a vast audience may have a detrimental impact upon a witness. Some witnesses may be demoralized and frightened while others become cocky and given to overstatement. Memories may falter, as with any type of public speaking, and accuracy of statement may be severely undermined. For some, "em-barrassment may impede the search for the truth, as may a natural tendency toward overdramatization. " Third, the presence of television places additional responsibilities on the judge. His job is to assure that the accused receives a fair trial, but "when television comes into the courtroom he must also supervise it. " Fourth, the presence of courtroom television has an impact on the defendant; "its presence is a form of mental--if not physical--harassment, resembling a police line up or the third degree. " The Court ruled (5-4) that the presence of television could only have impressed the people in the courtroom as well as those in the community at large with the notorious character of Billie Sol Estes and the significance of the trial. Televising the proceedings im-paired due process. The Court closed the courtroom doors to cameras. As a result of Estes, cameras were prohibited

in courtrooms except in those states that did not subscribe
to Canon 35.

In a separate concurring opinion, Justice John Harlan
envisioned the day "when television will have become so commonplace an affair in the daily life of the average person as
to dissipate all reasonable likelihood that its use in courtrooms
may disparage the judicial process." When that day comes,
the opinions set forth in Estes will be "subject to re-exam-
ination." Recently, several states have loosened regulations
pertaining to broadcasting of trials. Under the discretion of
the specific trial judge, increasing numbers of courtroom procedures are taking place in front of television cameras.

Public Trial

As seen in the cases already discussed in this chapter,
the courts have vigorously protected the right to a fair trial.
In so doing, the courts have restricted press publicity prior
to a trial and have recognized an implied bias in the presence
of television in the courtroom. Throughout all the challenges
to fair and impartial courtroom justice, the courts have emphatically preserved the principle of a public trial. At different times, the courts have protected this principle in the
interests of the accused, the public, the victim, and the
press.

United Press Associations v. Valente 123 N.E. 2d 777 (1954)

A 1954 case determined that a public trial is guaranteed in the interest of the accused. Judge Francis Valente
excluded the general public and the press from the courtroom
during a large part of a criminal trial. Subsequently, some
press associations and newspaper publishers brought proceedings to restrain the judge from enforcing the order.

The Court of Appeals of New York ruled that while
the exclusionary order operated to deprive the defendant of
his right to a public trial, it did not deprive members of
the public, including press associations and newspaper publishers, of any right of which they could complain. The court
stressed that the primary function of the doctrine of public
trial in criminal cases has traditionally been to safeguard
the accused against possible unjust persecution and abuse of
judicial authority, and of assuring her or him a fair trial.

The court also stressed that freedom of the press was in no way abridged by an exclusionary ruling that denied to the public generally, including journalists, the opportunity to see and hear what transpired in a courtroom. Actually, the public's interest was adequately protected if the accused was given a fair and public trial.

United States v. Kobli 172 F. 2d 919 (1949)

In another case, the court indicated that the right to a public trial is a right of the public. Elizabeth A. Kobli was arrested and charged with violating the Mann Act. She allegedly transported her eighteen-year-old niece, Mary Kovacs Riviello, from Scranton, Pennsylvania, to Buffalo, New York, in order to place her in a house of prostitution. The case attained some notoriety, and on the day when the trial was to begin the courtroom was filled to overflowing. Included among those who had been attracted by the lurid nature of the expected testimony were several young girls. The trial judge, believing there was not enough room to seat the members of the jury, asked whether Kobli's counsel objected to a court order clearing the courtroom of all people except jurors, witnesses, lawyers, and members of the press. Kobli's lawyer objected and requested "a trial conducted before the public." Nonetheless, the judge directed the courtroom to be cleared. The trial was held and Kobli was convicted. She appealed on the ground that she was not accorded a public trial as guaranteed by the Sixth Amendment.

The court of appeals decided that the Sixth Amendment did not permit a general exclusion of all the members of the public from the trial. The judge's power of exclusion was limited to those members of the public for whom space was not available in the courtroom or whose conduct interfered with the administration of justice or who ought not, in the interest of public morals, to be permitted to hear the testimony.

> We are satisfied that the framers of the Sixth Amendment believed it to be essential to the preservation of the liberty of the individual that, to the extent and within the limits which we have indicated, members of the general public should be admitted to every criminal trial even though it might appear that, in a case such as the one before us, most of them come only out of morbid curiosity.

The "public trial" concept had to be preserved as a protection for the individual and a restraint upon the possible abuse of judicial power. There was a reasonable possibility that persons might voluntarily come forward to testify. In addition, a public trial enables spectators to learn about their government and acquire confidence in their judicial remedies. The court concluded that the trial judge's order clearing the courtroom of all people except the jurors, witnesses, attorneys, and members of the press, over Kobli's objection, denied her the constitutional right to a public trial, notwithstanding that the order was made for the purpose of protecting the public morals of a large group of youthful spectators.

Oxnard Publishing Company v. Superior Court
of Ventura County 68 Cal. Rptr. 83 (1968)

In 1968, a court ruled that a public trial protects several interests. On January 25, 1968, William Clinger came to trial for the murder and robbery of a bartender named Veryl Robert Hays. Prior to selection of a jury, the judge, on a motion of the public defender, excluded the public and the press from the trial. The trial took place during the following two months. Several of the sessions were closed to the public. The judge indicated that the proceedings would be made available at the conclusion of the trial. The Oxnard Publishing Company appealed, contending that the public had a right to attend a trial and scrutinize the administration of justice.

The court of appeals cited some of the undesirable aspects of a closed trial. First, secret sessions tend to aggravate extrajudicial reporting of trials. In Clinger's trial, "the attempted secrecy brought far more publicity to the case than would have resulted from a trial in open court." Second, the therapeutic value a public trial has for the victim seeking justice may be wholly lost and replaced by public suspicion and distrust of the proceedings. Third, making a record of the proceedings available at the conclusion of the trial does not provide a complete record. The appearance, expression, gestures, tone of voice, and hesitations of the judge, attorneys, and witnesses--all important parts of the trial--would be permanently lost to public scrutiny. The court emphasized that all interests--those of the accused in securing a fair trial, those of the victim in obtaining justice, and those of the public in maintaining effective and honest institutions--were entitled to consideration in a criminal trial. In this case, in which the accused had sought a closed trial, there was no showing made to justify the holding of closed sessions.

Oliver v. Postel 282 N. E. 2d 306 (1972)

Four years later, the courts heard another case involving the issue of public versus closed trial. The trial of Carmine Persico for the crimes of conspiracy and extortion began in New York on November 8, 1971. Three days later, prior to the presentation of any evidence, the New York Times and the New York Daily News published stories indicating that Persico had a criminal record and underworld connections. Persico moved for a mistrial on the ground that the articles prejudiced the jury. Judge George Postel said that he considered the articles unfair, polled the jury, and after determining that no juror had been exposed to the information, denied the motion. He then warned the media that he would hold "in contempt" any "individual reporter" who "reported anything other than [what] transpires in this courtroom" because it "would not be fair reporting insofar as this defendant is concerned. " On the next two days, articles and editorials appeared in the Times, the News, and the New York Post that described Postel's denial of the mistrial motion and the previously published stories about Persico's criminal record and associations. The articles also criticized Postel's threats of contempt. On November 15, Persico's lawyer moved for a mistrial or, as an alternative "for the exclusion of the public and the press" for the balance of the trial. The prosecuting attorney opposed the motion, claiming that Persico's rights would be adequately protected and prejudice avoided by warning the jury, polling it, and, if required, sequestering it. Judge Postel said the news reporting constituted "contumacious conduct, " granted the motion, and directed that the courtroom be closed to the press and public for the remainder of the trial. The trial concluded with the acquittal of Persico, but five newspaper journalists appealed the judge's order and continued to pursue the matter after the verdict of acquittal.

The New York Court of Appeals held that it was wrong for the judge to bar the press and the public from the trial. The court said that even if the reporting "was improper and tended to prejudice the defendant, it is manifest that closing the trial was not the means to be employed to cure the prejudice or prevent a continuation of the impropriety. " In fact, since the articles complained of dealt with Persico's alleged criminal record and in no way related to any events that had transpired in the courtroom, their publication would not have been prevented by refusing to allow the press to attend the trial. The court concluded that Postel's order was "an unwarranted effort to punish and censor the press, and the fact that it constituted a novel form of censorship cannot insulate or shield it from constitutional attack." The <u>Oliver</u> decision clearly suggests that closing the courtroom is an unacceptable method of punishing the media. The cases presented in this section, <u>Valente, Kobli, Oxnard,</u> and <u>Oliver,</u> demonstrate that the right to public trial protects many interests--those of the accused, the public, the victim, and the press.

Bibliography

Articles

Alberich, H. Glenn. "<u>Nebraska Press Association vs. Stuart</u>: Balancing Freedom of the Press Against the Right to Fair Trial," <u>New England Law Review</u> 12 (Winter, 1977), 763-88.

Antonelli, Carol S. "Fair Trial/Free Press--<u>Nebraska Press Association vs. Stuart</u>" Defining the Limits of Prior Restraint in the Trial by Newspaper Controversy," <u>Loyola University Law Journal</u> 8 (Winter, 1977), 417-37.

Cases

<u>Bridges v. California; Times-Mirror Company v. Superior Court of State of California, In And For Los Angeles County</u> 314 U. S. 252 (1941)

<u>Craig v. Harney</u> 331 U. S. 367 (1947)

<u>Estes v. State of Texas</u> 381 U. S. 532 (1965)

<u>Goss v. State of Illinois</u> 312 F. 2d 257 (1963)

<u>Irvin v. Dowd</u> 366 U. S. 717 (1961)

<u>Marshall v. United States</u> 360 U. S. 310 (1959)

<u>Miami Herald Publishing Company v. Rose</u> 271 So. 2d 483 (1972)

<u>Murphy v. State of Florida</u> 421 U. S. 794 (1975)

Nebraska Press Association v. Stuart 427 U. S. 539 (1976)

Nye v. United States 313 U. S. 33 (1941)

Oliver v. Postel 282 N. E. 2d 306 (1972)

Oxnard Publishing Company v. Superior Court of Ventura
County 68 Cal. Rptr. 83 (1968)

Pennekamp v. State of Florida 328 U. S. 331 (1946)

Rideau v. State of Louisiana 373 U. S. 723 (1963)

Schuster v. Bowen 347 F. Supp. 319 (1972)

Seymour v. United States 373 F. 2d 629 (1967)

Shepherd v. State of Florida 341 U. S. 50 (1951)

Sheppard v. Maxwell 384 U. S. 333 (1966)

State of Maryland v. Baltimore Radio Show 338 U. S. 912
(1950)

Sun Company of San Bernardino v. Superior Court; Progress-
Bulletin Publishing Company v. Superior Court 29 Cal.
App. 3d 815 (1973)

Times-Picayune Publishing Corporation v. Schulingkamp 419
U. S. 1301 (1974)

Toledo Newspaper Company v. United States 247 U. S. 402
(1918)

United Press Associations v. Valente 123 N. E. 2d 777 (1954)

United States v. Columbia Broadcasting System, Inc. 497 F.
2d 102 (1974)

United States v. Dickinson 465 F. 2d 496 (1972)

United States v. Kobli 172 F. 2d 919 (1949)

Wood v. Georgia 370 U. S. 375 (1962)

Wood v. Goodson 485 S. W. 2d 213 (1972)

CHAPTER VI

MANAGEMENT OF INFORMATION

In 1643, the English Parliament passed a law that required licensing of the press. Any book, pamphlet, or paper had to be registered with the Stationers' Company prior to publication. In this way, all printing was centralized in London under the direct supervision of the Government. No printed material could be published without a license. The Company had the power to search for unlicensed presses and to seize publications that violated the law.

John Milton protested against this system in 1644 when he wrote Areopagitica, a pamphlet that defended freedom of the press. In Milton's view, truth was more likely to emerge from free discussion than from repression. He felt that the lawmakers erred when they doubted the strength of truth to win out against falsehood in a free and open encounter. Milton's work marked the beginning of the marketplace of ideas theory--the notion that free and open discussion of ideas, even those we oppose or hate, encourages a society to meet the stresses of survival and growth. While Milton pleaded for freedom of expression, others defied the law by actually speaking out or publishing their views. Many were brought before the Courts of the Star Chamber and the High Commission, where illegal printers were sentenced to mutilation, life imprisonment, or hanging. Finally, in 1695, the licensing system was ended in England.

Censorship took a different form in the American colonies, where prosecution for criminal or seditious libel replaced licensing as the method of governmental restraint of the press. The most famous prosecution for seditious libel involved John Peter Zenger, editor of the New York Weekly Journal. Politicians constantly used Zenger's paper to criticize the colonial governor of New York, William Cosby. Zenger was arrested in 1734, charged with publishing seditious libels, and jailed for eight months prior to trial. When

Zenger finally came to trial, the jury ignored the judge's instructions and decided that Zenger was not guilty. Winning this case was a tremendous achievement for Zenger's attorney, Andrew Hamilton, because under the common-law, truth of the utterance was an irrelevant defense. The judge rather than the jury had the responsibility for determining if the publication had in fact printed seditious libel. The jury simply ascertained whether the defendant had published the material. Under this system, freedom of expression was extremely restricted indeed. During Zenger's trial, Hamilton asked the jury to recognize truth as a defense and urged the jury to decide both the libelousness of the words and the fact of the printing. The Zenger verdict marked the end of the court trial for seditious libel in the American colonies.

The Sedition Act, which Congress enacted in 1798, permitted truth as a defense, required proof of malice, and allowed the jury to pass on both questions of law and fact. Punishment was set by the law. The Act established as a misdemeanor the publishing of any false or scandalous writings designed to bring the government into disrepute, excite hostility against the government, or incite resistance to the law. Under this statute, leading Republican journalists were punished because of their criticism of the Federalist Administration. For example, Matthew Lyon was sentenced to jail for four months and fined $1,000 when he suggested that under President John Adams the Executive branch showed "an unbounded thirst for ridiculous pomp, foolish adulation, and selfish avarice" and that the public welfare was "swallowed up in a continual grasp for power." While Republicans condemned the ordinance, the Federalists defended it as vital to the self-protection of the government. The constitutionality of the Act was never brought before the United States Supreme Court. The unpopularity of the Act, however, led to the defeat of Adams and the Federalist Party. Under Thomas Jefferson, the Sedition Act expired on March 3, 1801.

The Stationers' Company and the Sedition Act were early legislative efforts at managing information. In this chapter, more recent attempts to regulate the gathering and publication of information are examined.

FREEDOM TO PUBLISH

Legislative efforts have been designed to limit the efforts of publishers to disseminate information and opinion to

the public.   In this section, we will examine ways in which
the courts have dealt with such efforts.

Prior Restraint

The second class mail privilege encouraged the dissemination of current information by affording publishers low
postal rates.   Admission to the second class mail privilege
had to be obtained from the Postmaster General after a hearing that satisfied him that the publication contained only "mailable matter. "   The power to suspend or revoke the privilege
was exercised when the publication printed other than mailable
matter.

Milwaukee Social Democrat Publishing Company v. Burleson 255 U. S. 407 (1921)

In 1917, the second class privilege for the Milwaukee
Leader was revoked because the paper had become "non-mailable" under the provisions of the 1916 National Defense Law,
also known as the Espionage Act.   The Milwaukee Social Democrat Publishing Company, publisher of the Leader, introduced
a suit seeking restoration of the privilege.   The matter came
to the U. S. Supreme Court, where the newspaper charged that
the Espionage Act was unconstitutional because it did not allow
a trial in a court of competent jurisdiction and because the
law hampered the right of free speech and press.

Concerning the first issue, the Court decided that the
hearing provided for the publisher was fairly conducted and
satisfied all the requirements of due process of law.   The
Court then turned to the second issue, free speech and press.
According to the Postmaster General, more than fifty editorial
comments appearing in the Milwaukee Leader between April
14 and September 12, 1917, constituted the basis for the revocation.   These articles were printed during the first five
months of U. S. involvement in World War I.   The articles
claimed that U. S. participation was unjustifiable and dishonor-
able.   It was a capitalistic war, which had been forced upon
the people by a particular class in order to serve their selfish ends.   The paper denounced the government as a "pluto-
cratic republic" and a financial and political autocracy.   Articles denounced the draft law as unconstitutional, arbitrary,
and oppressive, with the implication that the law should not
be obeyed.   The paper referred to the President as an auto-

crat and the war legislation as having been passed by a "rubber stamp Congress. " According to the paper, the government was waging a war of conquest when Germany was ready to make an honorable peace.   The U. S. was fighting for commercial supremacy and world domination.   When the "financial kings" decided that further fighting might endanger their loans to the Allies, they would quickly move for peace.   The paper repeatedly condemned the Allies and frequently praised the enemies of the U. S.

According to the U. S. Supreme Court, the articles in the Leader did not seek the repeal of any laws denounced as arbitrary and oppressive, but rather sought to form hostility toward and to encourage violation of those laws.   The paper contained articles of this type almost daily for five months, thus rendering it "non-mailable. "   It was reasonable to conclude that the paper would continue with its unpatriotic editorial policy.   It was clearly within the power of the Postmaster General to suspend the privilege until a proper showing could be made for its renewal.   It was up to the paper to correct its editorial policy and to publish a paper that conformed to the law.   When it did so, the second class privilege could be restored.   The Court upheld (7-2) the action of the Postmaster General.   In a minority opinion, Justices Louis Brandeis and Oliver Wendell Holmes opposed the action of the Postmaster General as a form of prior restraint.   They argued that the Postmaster could not determine previous to publication that a specific newspaper was going to be "non-mailable" and deny to it the use of the mails at a particular postage rate.   Instead, the only power the Postmaster possessed was to refrain from forwarding any non-mailable papers and to return them to the sender.   He could not ban a paper from second class privilege because he thought that it would contain unpatriotic or obscene material.   This minority view was affirmed by the Court in 1931.

Near v. State of Minnesota 283 U. S. 697 (1931)

Throughout September, October, and November, 1927, the Saturday Press (Minneapolis) published and circulated issues highly critical of law enforcement officers and other public figures in Minneapolis.   The paper contended that a Jewish gangster controlled gambling, bootlegging, and racketeering in Minneapolis and that law enforcement agencies and officers were grossly negligent in the pursuit of their obligations to expose and punish these crimes.   The paper charged Min-

neapolis Chief of Police Frank Brunskill with gross neglect
of duty, illicit relations with gangsters, and with participation in graft. County Attorney Floyd Olson was charged with
knowing the existing conditions and with failing to take adequate measures to remedy them. Mayor George Leach was
accused of inefficiency and dereliction. The article called
for a special grand jury and a special prosecutor to deal with
the situation. Under the provisions of the 1925 Session Laws
of Minnesota, Hennepin County Attorney Olson brought an action
against the periodical for publishing material that was "malicious, scandalous and defamatory. " He secured a temporary
order restraining future publication of the periodical. J. M.
Near, publisher of the Saturday Press, appealed the case on
the ground that the Minnesota law violated freedom of the
press.

The U. S. Supreme Court noted that under the Minnesota law, public officials could bring the publisher of a newspaper before a judge upon a charge of conducting a business
that published scandalous and defamatory statements. Unless
the publisher could satisfy the judge that the statements were
true and published with good motives, the periodical was suppressed and future publication was made punishable as a contempt. The Court noted, historically, during the preceding
century and a half, almost a total absence of efforts to impose prior restraints upon publications regarding misconduct
of public officials. Public officers whose behavior remained
open to free discussion in the media had remedies available
for dealing with false accusations under libel laws. The
Court decided (5-4) that freedom of the press gave immunity
from prior restraints and forbade any proceeding that suppressed publication. The Court noted that

> this decision rests upon the operation and effect of
> the statute, without regard to the question of the
> truth of the charges contained in the particular
> periodical. The fact that the public officers named
> in this case, and those associated with the charges
> of official dereliction, may be deemed to be im-
> peccable, cannot affect the conclusion that the sta-
> tute imposes an unconstitutional restraint upon pub-
> lication.

The Court declared the Minnesota law unconstitutional because
it provided for suppression rather than punishment of publications.

New York Times Company v. United States
United States v. Washington Post Company 403 U. S. 713 (1971)

In 1971, a sharply divided Court decided a case involving the issue of prior restraint. In this case, the U. S. sought to enjoin newspapers from publishing the contents of a classified historical study of Vietnam policy. On June 13, 1971, the New York Times published the first article in a series dealing with the previously secret Pentagon study of the origins and conduct of the Vietnam War. The Pentagon Papers, a classified forty-seven-volume study entitled "History of U. S. Decision-Making Process on Viet Nam Policy," had been made available to the press by Dr. Daniel Ellsberg, an opponent of the war. After the Times had published three installments, the U. S. Government went to court and sought an injunction to prevent further publication. A temporary restraining order was issued and a hearing was ordered to determine if disclosure of any information contained in the document would "pose such grave and immediate danger to the security of the United States as to warrant their publication being enjoined." Meanwhile, the Washington Post began publication of the papers, and the Government initiated an action in which a Washington court denied a preliminary injunction. Both the New York Times and the Government asked the U. S. Supreme Court to consider the case. The Government argued that releasing this information posed a threat to national security; the papers said the society had a right to know about the war and that the Government simply wanted to save the Pentagon from embarrassment. The Court stayed both newspapers from further publication of the Pentagon Papers while a hearing on the matter could be held.

The Court wrote a brief per curiam decision that affirmed the judgment of the Washington court and reversed the finding of the New York court. It also lifted the restraints on publication that had been issued. Each of the justices wrote a separate opinion. Three were identified as dissents-- Warren Burger, John Harlan, and Harry Blackmun. The dissenters accepted the Government's claim that publication of certain papers would cause national harm. The majority rejected (6-3) the Government's claim and supported the newspapers' right to publish. Justice William Douglas cited the absolutist position. The First Amendment provided that "Congress should make no law ... abridging the freedom of speech, or of the press." In his opinion, that left "no room for governmental restraint on the press." Justice William Brennan agreed that the Court had no right to levy prior restraint; in fact, the temporary restraint that had been issued on the ground that it was necessary to give the Court an opportunity to examine the claim more thoroughly should not have been issued. Unless and until the Government had clearly made its case, the Constitution precluded any injunction from being issued. The per curiam opinion acknowledged that the Government carried a heavy burden of showing justification for the imposition of a prior restraint. In New York Times and Washington Post, as in Near, the Court ruled that the Government had not met that burden.

Taxation

In 1936, the U. S. Supreme Court turned back the attempt of a state legislature to control newspaper publication and circulation through unfair taxation.

Grosjean v. American Press Company Inc. 297 U. S. 233 (1936)

On July 12, 1934, the Louisiana legislature passed a law that provided that any newspaper that sold advertising and had a circulation in excess of 20,000 copies per week, would be required to pay a license tax of 2 percent on its gross receipts. Only thirteen out of 163 state newspapers qualified for the tax, but twelve of the thirteen were outspoken critics of Governor Huey Long--at whose request the law had been enacted. The act required that papers subject to the tax had to report the gross receipts and pay the tax every three months. Failure to file the report or pay the tax constituted a misdemeanor and subjected the violator to a fine and/or imprisonment. Nine newspaper publishers sued to stop the enforcement of the statute.

The U. S. Supreme Court determined (8-0) that the First Amendment forbade any form of previous restraint upon publication or circulation of printed material. The Louisiana law operated as a restraint in two ways. First, it curtailed the amount of revenue obtained through advertising. Second, its direct effect was to restrict circulation. Justice George Sutherland wrote:

> The form in which the tax is imposed is in itself suspicious. It is not measured or limited by the volume of advertisements. It is measured alone by the extent of the circulation of the publication in

which the advertisements are carried, with the
plain purpose of penalizing the publishers and curtailing the circulation of a selected group of newspapers.

The Court thus rejected Louisiana's attempt to control newspaper publication through unfair taxation.

Post Office Control

Historically, a unique relationship has existed between
the Post Office and those who disseminate news and information. The Post Office has distributed such materials at low
cost. As an obvious result of this relationship, the Postmaster General has possessed considerable control over the
dissemination of news. The major source of such control
is the second class mailing privilege, which is indispensable
to the distribution of periodicals. When this privilege is denied, a periodical operates at a serious economic disadvantage
with competitors.

Lewis Publishing Company v. Morgan
Journal of Commerce & Commercial Bulletin v.
Burleson 229 U. S. 288 (1913)

In an early case, the U. S. Supreme Court upheld post
office control. The 1912 Newspaper Publicity Law required
the manager of newspapers and magazines to file twice annually the names of the editor, managing editor, publisher,
and stockholders of the publication. Also, all advertising
matter had to be plainly marked. Any failure to comply with
the provisions of the act could result in denial of the mails
for distribution. The Lewis Publishing Company brought suit,
complaining that the law abridged freedom of the press.

The Supreme Court disagreed (9-0) and upheld the requirement that this information be filed. Placing these conditions upon the right to enjoy second class mail privilege
was not repugnant to freedom of the press.

Hannegan v. Esquire, Inc. 327 U. S. 146 (1946)

In a 1946 case, the U. S. Supreme Court restricted
the power of the Post Office. Based on the postal depart-

ment's judgment that the contents of some issues of Esquire did not contribute to the public good and the public welfare, the Postmaster General revoked the magazine's second class privilege. Esquire appealed and the case reached the Supreme Court.

In a unanimous opinion, the Court noted that the postal laws granted the favorable second class rates to periodicals so that the public good might be served through a "dissemination of information of a public character, or devoted to literature, the sciences, arts, or some special industry." Congress did not intend that each applicant for the second class rate must convince the Postmaster General that the publication positively contributed to the public good. In fact, the requirements of the postal laws could be served only by uncensored distribution of literature. Only then could the public choose, according to individual tastes, from the multitude of competing offerings. According to Justice William Douglas, "Congress has left the Postmaster General with no power to prescribe standards for the literature or the art which a mailable periodical disseminates."

Lamont v. Postmaster General
Fixa v. Heilberg 381 U. S. 301 (1965)

In 1965, the Court further restricted the Post Office, this time forbidding the department to screen political mail from abroad. The case involved Section 305 (a) of the Postal Service and Federal Employees Salary Act of 1962, which provided that unsealed mail from a foreign country that was determined by the Secretary of the Treasury to be "communist political propaganda" would be detained by the Postmaster General and the addressee would be notified that the mail would be delivered only upon the addressee's request. To implement the statute, the Post Officer maintained about a dozen screening points through which all unsealed mail from foreign countries was routed and checked by Customs authorities. When a piece of mail was determined to be "communist political propaganda, " a notice was sent to the addressee identifying the mail being detained and advising that it would be destroyed unless delivery was requested by returning an attached reply card within twenty days. Prior to March 1, 1965, the reply card contained a space in which the addressee could request delivery of any "similar publication" in the future. The Post Office maintained a list of the names of those persons who desired to receive the publications. Thereafter, a notice was sent and had to be returned regarding every individual piece of mail.

In 1963, the Post Office detained a copy of the Peking Review # 12 that was addressed to Dr. Corliss Lamont, a publisher and distributor of pamphlets. Lamont did not respond to the notice that was sent to him, but instead instituted a suit to prevent enforcement of the statute. The Post Office thereupon notified Lamont that it considered his institution of the suit as an expression of his desire to receive "communist political propaganda" and thereafter none of his mail would be detained. Lamont amended his complaint to challenge the constitutionality of placing his name on a list of people wishing to receive "communist political propaganda. " Meanwhile, the Post Office initiated the new system under which there was no list. This change in procedure left for the U. S. Supreme Court's consideration solely the issue of the constitutionality of the statute.

The Court concluded (8-0) that the law was unconstitutional because it required an official act--returning the reply card--as a restriction on the unfettered exercise of a person's constitutional rights. Any person was likely to feel some inhibition in sending for material that federal officials had condemned as "communist political progaganda. " The statute violated the concept of an "uninhibited, robust, and wide-open" debate and discussion that characterized the First Amendment. The Court enjoined enforcement of the statute. While in Hannegan the Court clearly protected the publisher's right to send material through the mails, in Lamont the Court affirmed an individual's right to receive information without Post Office infringement or control.

Antitrust Laws

In 1890, Congress enacted the Sherman Antitrust Act. The law declared illegal all monopolistic combinations in restraint of trade between states or with foreign nations. Thereafter, the courts heard several cases involving alleged combinations that restrained trade in the news industry.

Associated Press v. United States
Tribune Company v. United States 326 U. S. 1 (1945)

The Associated Press--a non-profit cooperative association of newspaper publishers--collects, assembles, and distributes news. The information it distributes is originally gathered by direct employees of the Association, employees of the member newspapers, and the employees of foreign independent news agencies with which AP has contractual relations. The news is distributed through interstate channels of communication to the various newspaper members of the Association, who pay for it under an assessment plan. The United States charged in a Federal District Court that AP had violated the Sherman Antitrust Act by restraining trade in news among the states and attempting to monopolize portions of that trade. The main charge was that AP had established a system that prohibited AP members from selling news to non-members and that granted each member power to block its non-member competitiors from membership. Another charge concerned a contract between AP and Canadian Press, a news agency similar to AP, under which AP and the Canadian agency obligated themselves to furnish news exclusively to each other. The district court held that the AP bylaws violated the antitrust laws. The court enjoined AP from observing them. The court further noted that nothing in the decision prevented AP's adoption of new bylaws through which the news would be furnished to competitiors without discrimination. AP appealed.

The U. S. Supreme Court agreed (5-3) with the district court that the

> inability to buy news from the largest news agency,
> or any one of its multitude of members, can have
> most serious effects on the publication of competi-
> tive newspapers, both those presently published
> and those which but for these restrictions, might
> be published in the future.

The Court emphasized that freedom to publish meant freedom for all and not for some. Freedom to publish is a constitutional guarantee, but freedom to combine to prevent others from publishing is not. The First Amendment did not afford any support for a combination to restrain trade in news. The Court stressed that the decision would not restrict AP members as to what they could print, but rather compelled AP to make their dispatches accessible to others. With more outlets, there would be better clash and more varied coverage of news events. In this decision, the Court clearly held newspapers subject to antitrust legislation.

Lorain Journal Company v. United States 342 U. S. 143 (1951)

This case involved another antitrust violation. In 1932,

the Lorain Journal Company, an Ohio corporation that published the Journal, purchased the Times-Herald, the only competing daily paper published in the city. After 1933, the Journal held a commanding position regarding news dissemination in Lorain. The paper had a daily circulation of over 13,000 copies, reaching 99 percent of the families in the city. From 1933 to 1948, the company enjoyed a substantial monopoly of the dissemination of news and advertising in Lorain. In 1948, the Elyria-Lorain Broadcasting Company was licensed by the Federal Communications Commission to operate radio station WEOL in Elyria, eight miles south of Lorain. With the arrival of a competing medium, the Lorain Journal Company devised a plan to eliminate the threat of competition from the radio station. Under the plan, the newspaper refused to accept any local advertisements in the Journal from any Lorain County advertiser who also advertised over WEOL. The U.S. brought suit in district court, alleging that the company engaged in a conspiracy to restrain and monopolize interstate commerce in violation of the Sherman Antitrust Act.

The court found that the plan to prevent advertisers from using the services of WEOL was designed to destroy the broadcasting company. The court characterized the plan as "bold, relentless, and predatory commercial behavior." The publisher had monitored WEOL programs in order to identify the station's local advertisers. Those advertisers then had their contracts with the newspaper terminated until they stopped advertising on WEOL. The plan was effective. Several Lorain merchants testified that they had abandoned their plans to advertise over WEOL. Merchants also maintained that advertising in the Journal was essential for the promotion of their sales in the area.

The U.S. Supreme Court agreed (7-0) with the district court that the newspaper publisher's conduct was an attempt to monopolize interstate commerce. In fact, the plan was aimed at a larger target, the complete elimination of the radio station. The attempt of the Lorain Journal Company to force advertisers to boycott a competitor violated antitrust laws.

Times-Picayune Publishing Company v.
United States 345 U.S. 594 (1953)

Two years later, the Court heard another antitrust case. Prior to 1933, four daily newspapers served the New

Orleans area. The Item Company published the Morning
Tribune and the evening Item. The Times-Picayune Publishing Company published the morning Times-Picayune. The
Daily States Publishing Company distributed the evening States.
In 1933, the Times-Picayune Company purchased the States
and continued to publish it evenings. The Morning Tribune
ceased publication in 1941. As of 1953, the Times-Picayune,
Item, and States remained the only significant newspaper
media in New Orleans. During 1950, the Times-Picayune
had a daily average circulation of 188,402, the Item had
114,660, and the States had 105,235. In 1950, the Times-
Picayune Company instituted the unit plan for selling advertising. As a result, general and classified advertisers could
not buy space in either the Times-Picayune or the States
alone, but had to insert identical copy in both or none. Parties who purchased advertising in the publications could purchase only combined insertions that appeared in both papers
and not in either separately. The U.S. filed suit under the
Sherman Act, challenging these "unit" contracts as unreasonable restraints of trade designed to monopolize an aspect of
interstate commerce.

The district court found violations of the law and entered a decree enjoining the company's use of unit contracts.
The court determined that the system of unit selling caused
a substantial rise in advertising placed in the States, enabling
it to enhance its comparative standing with the Item. The
Times-Picayune Company had instituted the system solely because of the Times-Picayune's "dominant" or "monopoly"
position in order to "restrain general classified advertisers
from making an untrammeled choice between the States and
the Item in purchasing advertising space and also to substantially diminish the competitive vigor of the Item." The
company had attempted to monopolize the afternoon newspaper
general and classified advertising field by eliminating choice
from "those advertisers who also required morning newspaper
space and who could not because of budgetary limitations or
financial inability purchase space in both afternoon newspapers."
On the basis of these findings, the court decided that unit
contracts violated the Sherman Act. The court ordered the
company to stop the unit system of selling advertising space.
The company appealed.

The U.S. Supreme Court reversed the decision; it
found that the paper did not enjoy a dominant position. The
Times-Picayune's sale of advertising over the years was
about 40 percent. If each of the New Orleans newspapers

shared equally in the total volume of advertising, the Times-Picayune would have sold 33 1/3 percent. The small existing increment did not indicate a level of market "dominance" that would indicate a Sherman Act violation. Furthermore, the Item did not suffer. The year 1950 was the Item's peak year for total advertising as well as circulation. Between 1943 and 1949, the Item had earned over $1.4 million net before taxes, enabling the publisher to transfer his equity at a net profit of $600,000. The Item appeared "to be doing well." The Court concluded (5-4) that although the unit rule bene-fited the Times-Picayune because it expanded advertising sales, it did not disadvantage the Item. Since the government's case was based primarily on that supposition, the verdict of the district court was reversed. In 1958, the Times-Picayune Company purchased the Item for a reported $3.4 million and thus became the only daily newspaper publisher in New Or-leans. At the time of the transaction, the Item was experi-encing a financial loss.

Times-Mirror Company v. United States 390 U.S. 712 (1968)

In this case, a combination was broken up because of its adverse effect on independent newspaper publishing. In 1964, the Sun Company, located in San Bernardino, was the largest independent publishing company in Southern California. A newspaper is independent when its owners do not publish another newspaper at another locality. The company was locally owned, primarily by the Gutherie family, and none of its owners had significant interests in other newspapers. The company was in sound financial condition. With three newspapers, the morning Sun, the evening Telegram, and the Sunday Sun-Telegram, the company dominated the newspaper business in San Bernardino County. They were the only news-papers other than Los Angeles papers that were home deliv-ered throughout San Bernardino County.

The Times-Mirror Company, publisher of the Los Angeles Times, the largest daily newspaper in Southern Cali-fornia, began negotiations for the acquisition of the Sun Com-pany. In 1964, an offer was made to James A. Gutherie for $12.5 million in cash, which was refused. Also in 1964, the Pulitzer Publishing Company of St. Louis made a cash offer of $15 million. Gutherie realized that the $15 million offer could not be ignored. However, he preferred that the Sun Company be sold to Times-Mirror because he thought that the interests of the two companies in the development of the

West were similar. Gutherie disapproved of the Pulitzer
Company's politics and policies and he treasured the friend-
ship that existed between the Chandler family, owners of the
Times-Mirror Company, and his family. Gutherie informed
Chandler that he had received an offer of $15 million and
Chandler agreed to meet the price. Shortly thereafter, the
sale was formally completed. On March 5, 1965, the govern-
ment filed a complaint alleging that the acquisition by the
Times-Mirror Company of all the shares of stock of the Sun
Company violated the antitrust laws of the United States. The
effect of the acquisition might be to substantially lessen com-
petition, in violation of the Clayton Act.

        The California District Court observed "a steady de-
cline of independent ownership of newspapers in Southern California. " In 1952, six of the seven daily newspapers in San
Bernardino County were independently owned, but in 1966 only
three of the eight dailies published there remained independent. In Southern California during the same period of time,
the number of daily newspapers increased from sixty-six to
eighty-two, but the number independently owned decreased
from thirty-nine to twenty. In 1952, 59 percent of dailies
were independent; in 1966 only 24 percent were independent.
According to the court, the acquisition of the Sun by the
Times-Mirror Company was especially anticompetitive because
it eliminated one of the few independent papers that had been
able to function successfully in the morning and Sunday fields.
Most newspapers in Southern California had been evening papers largely because of the strength of the Los Angeles Times,
which accounted for 70 percent of Southern California's morning circulation. The court observed that

> the acquisition has raised a barrier to entry of
> newspapers in the San Bernardino County market
> that is almost impossible to overcome. The evi-
> dence discloses the market has now been closed
> tight and no publisher will risk the expense of uni-
> laterally starting a new daily newspaper there.

The court decided that "acquisition which enhances existing
barriers to entry in the market or increases the difficulties
of smaller firms already in the market is particularly anticompetitive. " The court concluded that the acquisition of the
stock of the Sun Company by Times-Mirror violated the Clayton Act and directed the Times-Mirror Company to divest itself of the stock and of all forms of control of the Sun Company. On appeal, the court's judgment was unanimously affirmed in a per curiam by the U. S. Supreme Court.

The cases examined in this section indicate the Court's willingness to break up monopolistic combinations in order to protect freedom of the press. In Associated Press, the Court declared unconstitutional the AP bylaws, which prevented non-member newspapers from acquiring news information. In Lorain, the Court declared that a newspaper company violated antitrust laws when it refused to accept advertising from a customer who also advertised over a specific radio station. In Times-Mirror, the Court ruled that the acquisition of a newspaper company was anticompetitive because the transaction eliminated one of the few independent papers in Southern California. The Court ordered the company to divest itself of the stock. And, in Times-Picayune, the Court sided with the newspaper after it determined that the company did not enjoy a dominant position as a result of unit selling of advertising. In the decisions discussed in this section, the Court clearly held newspapers subject to antitrust legislation.

Failing Company Doctrine

In 1960, in Maryland and Virginia Milk Producers Association v. United States, the U. S. Supreme Court accepted the "failing company" defense as justification for a merger. Nine years later, this defense was argued in a case involving an alleged monopoly of newspaper companies.

Citizen Publishing Company v. United States 394 U. S. 131 (1969)

In 1940, the Citizen Publishing Company, publisher of the only evening daily newspaper in Tucson, Arizona, formed a joint operating agreement with the Star Publishing Company, publisher of the only morning daily newspaper and the only Sunday newspaper in Tucson. Since 1932, the Citizen Publishing Company had operated at a substantial financial loss. Under the provisions of their agreement, the news and editorial departments of the two newspapers would remain separate but a new corporation, Tucson Newspapers, Inc. (TNI), would operate all other departments of these newspapers—primarily printing, advertising, and circulation, as a joint project. Profits would be pooled, and the parties agreed not to engage in any other publishing business in the county. All commercial competition between the two companies ceased. Combined profits before taxes rose from $27,531 in 1940, to $1,727,217 in 1964. In 1965, an out of state publisher offered to purchase the Star Company for $10 million, provided that the joint operating agreement remained in operation. By prior agreement, the Citizen Company was offered the opportunity to purchase the Star at this price, which it did. The transaction resulted in a merger, with the news and editorial staffs of the Star under the direction of the Citizen. The Star continued to be published as a separate paper. The U. S. initiated suit, charging that the joint operating agreement constituted an unreasonable restraint of trade. The operation was held by the district court to violate the Sherman Act and the court directed the divestiture of the evening newspaper and a modification of the joint operating agreement. Citizen Publishing Company appealed.

The U. S. Supreme Court affirmed (7-1) the decision. According to the opinion of Justice William Douglas,

> The purpose of the agreement was to end any business or commercial competiton between the two papers and to that end three types of controls were imposed. First was price fixing. The newspapers were sold and distributed by the circulation department of TNI; commercial advertising placed in the papers was sold only by the advertising department of TNI; the subscription and advertising rates were set jointly. Second was profit pooling. All profits realized were pooled and distributed to the Star and the Citizen by TNI pursuant to an agreed ratio. Third was a market control. It was agreed that neither the Star nor Citizen nor any of their stockholders, officers, and executives would engage in any other business in Pima County-- the metropolitan area of Tucson--in conflict with the agreement. Thus competing publishing operations were foreclosed.

Citizen Publishing argued the "failing company" defense. Justice Douglas, however, explained why the requirements of the doctrine had not been met in this case. First, at the time Star Publishing and Citizen Publishing entered into the joint agreement, Citizen was not on the verge of going out of business, nor was there a strong likelihood that Citizen would terminate its business if the agreement was not formed. In fact, there was "no evidence that the joint operating agreement was the last straw at which Citizen grasped. Indeed the Citizen continued to be a significant threat to the Star. " Second, the failing company doctrine could not be applied in a merger unless it was established that the company that acquired it or brought it under dominion was the only available purchaser. For, if another possible purchaser expressed interest, "a unit in the competitive system could be preserved and not lost to monopoly power." In Citizen Publishing, the Court thus established two prerequisites to the failing company defense: 1) the company must be on the verge of liquidation, and 2) there must be no prospective buyer of the failing company other than its competitor.

Newspaper Preservation Act

Citizen Publishing caused concern among newspaper publishers. When that case was decided, forty-four daily newspapers in twenty-two cities operated under the terms of joint agreements similar to the Citizen-Star arrangement. In 1970, Congress passed the Newspaper Preservation Act, which provided a special exemption from antitrust laws to newspapers in the same city that had preexisting joint operating agreements. As a result of this law, the forty-four newspapers were allowed to maintain joint advertising and subscription rates, which might otherwise have been viewed in violation of the antitrust laws. A 1972 case provided a test of the law.

Bay Guardian Company v. Chronicle Publishing Company 344 F. Supp. 1155 (1972)

In July, 1971, Bruce Brugmann, publisher of the San Francisco Bay Guardian, a monthly newspaper with a circulation of 17,000, claimed that the Newspaper Preservation Act had legitimized the joint advertiser and subscription rates that were charged by the two San Francisco daily newspapers, the Morning Chronicle and the evening San Francisco Examiner. Advertisers who desired to advertise in one San Francisco daily newspaper were required to advertise in both dailies because of the joint advertising rate. Profits were shared by the companies on a fifty-fifty basis. According to Brugmann, the Chronicle and Examiner had eliminated competition between them and had achieved a monopoly position in the San Francisco daily newspaper market. Many advertisers were unable to afford to advertise in other newspapers. The result was that the Bay Guardian had been crippled in efforts to obtain advertisers. The Guardian Company filed suit against the publishers of the Examiner and Chronicle, contending that the Newspaper Preservation Act violated freedom of the press.

The court upheld the Act, noting that much of Brugmann's argument seemed directed at a phantom act that legitimized newspaper monopolies. In describing the Act the
court held:

> ... the Act was designed to preserve independent
> editorial voices. Regardless of the economic or
> social wisdom of such a course, it does not violate
> freedom of the press.... The Act in question does
> not regulate or restrict publishing, rather it merely
> permits newspapers to merge when they might not
> otherwise have been able to do so because of the
> antitrust laws.

According to the court, the Newspaper Preservation Act did
not offend First Amendment freedoms.

Political Campaigns

Occasionally, legislation has been directed at controlling the publication of politically oriented information. In
1966, the Court decided a case involving election day editorials.

Mills v. State of Alabama 384 U. S. 214 (1966)

The city of Birmingham, Alabama, held an election
in November, 1962, to determine whether the people preferred to keep their existing city commission form of government or to replace it with a mayor-council government. On
election day, the Birmingham Post-Herald carried an editorial prepared by the editor, James E. Mills, that strongly
urged the voters to adopt the mayor-council form. Mills was
arrested and charged with violating the Alabama Corrupt Practices Act, which made it a crime to solicit votes in support
of any candidates or propositions "on the day on which the
election affecting such candidates or propositions is being
held. " The case reached the U. S. Supreme Court.

The Court had to determine whether it abridged freedom of the press for a state to punish a newspaper editor
for publishing on election day an editorial that urged people
to vote a particular way in the election. Justice Hugo Black,
speaking for the Court, noted that a major purpose of the
First Amendment was to protect the free discussion of governmental affairs, which "of course includes discussion of

candidates, structures and forms of government, the manner in which government is operated or should be operated, and all such matters relating to political processes. " The Alabama law tended to silence the press at a time when it could be most effective. The Court ruled (9-0) that the law was an "obvious and flagrant abridgement of the constitutionally guaranteed freedom of the press. "

American Civil Liberties Union, Inc. v. Jennings 366 F. Supp. 1041 (1973)

Seven years later, the courts heard a case involving political advertising. In September, 1972, the American Civil Liberties Union and the New York Civil Liberties Union submitted to the New York Times an advertisement that opposed Nixon-Administration-backed legislation aimed at limiting court-ordered busing. The advertisement listed in the form of an "honor roll" the names of 102 members of Congress who had spoken out against this antibusing policy. The ACLU and NYCLU hoped that by publishing the advertisement, public opinion would be influenced to support their side of the issue. The organizations denied any intent to assist in the election campaign of any political candidates. The Times refused to publish this ad because it violated certain certification requirements under the Federal Elections Campaign Act of 1971. Title I of that Act prohibited particular types of media advertising on behalf of candidates for federal office unless the candidates certified that the cost of the advertising would not exceed campaign spending limits. Rather than risk criminal penalties, the Times refused publication. The ACLU and NYCLU filed a suit challenging the constitutionality of the FECA. The organizations further requested the court to stop enforcement of Title III of the Act, which established restriction and filing requirements for organizations engaged in political campaigning. Publishing of the proposed communication would cause the ACLU and NYCLU to be deemed a political committee, thereby compelling them to disclose lists of their contributors. The organizations claimed such disclosures violated their constitutional right to freedom of association. Disclosure provisions had not been threatened against the ACLU or the NYCLU, but the organizations sought to protect themselves in light of the law.

The court found that Title I of the Federal Elections Campaign Act established impermissible prior restraints, discouraged free and open discussion of matters of public concern, and as such was unconstitutional. The court also noted that Title III established a complex system of record keeping and public disclosure of campaign contributions and expenditures. Such public disclosure requirements and reporting of membership lists "cast a chilling effect upon an individual's right to associate freely and to voice personal views through organizational ties." The vagueness surrounding these provisions of the Act had to be removed. In light of the court's findings, on October 27, 1972, the Times published a slightly revised version of the antibusing advertisements submitted by the ACLU and the NYCLU.

Right to Reply

According to the 1913 Florida Election Code, a political candidate had the right to publish free of charge a reply to a newspaper article that assailed his or her personal character or that charged malfeasance in office. In 1974, the U. S. Supreme Court decided a case that involved a claim for the "right to reply."

Miami Herald Publishing Company v. Tornillo 418 U. S. 298 (1974)

In the fall of 1972, Pat L. Tornillo, Jr., the Executive Director of the Classroom Teacher's Association, was a candidate for the Florida House of Representatives. On September 20, and again on September 29, the Miami Herald printed editorials critical of Tornillo's candidacy. The paper referred to Tornillo as a "czar" and a lawbreaker. The Herald also claimed that it would be "inexcusable of the voters" if they sent Tornillo to the legislature in Tallahassee. The reason for the paper's opposition to Tornillo stemmed from the 1960 Dade County Classroom Teacher's Association strike. At the time, a strike by public school teachers was illegal under Florida law. Tornillo had led the strike in Miami. In light of the editorial comments, Tornillo asked for the right to reply under the Florida Election Code. When the Herald refused to print a reply, Tornillo filed a suit to secure the printing of his reply. He also sought damages in excess of $5,000.

The Supreme Court of Florida made two main points. First, the public "need to know" was most critical during an election campaign. In order to assure fairness in campaigns, assailed candidates must have an equivalent opportunity to respond--otherwise the candidates would be harmed and the public would be deprived of both sides of the controversy. First Amendment guarantees were "not for the benefit of the press so much as for the benefit of us all. " Second, the Florida statute here under consideration was designed to add to the flow of information and ideas and did not constitute an incursion upon First Amendment rights against prior restraint since no specified newspaper content was excluded. There was nothing prohibited, but rather the law required, in the interest of full and fair discussion, additional information. The Florida Supreme Court upheld the right to reply.

The U. S. Supreme Court reversed, disagreeing on both points. First, faced with the penalties that would accrue to any newspaper that published commentary that might fall within the reach of the right of reply statute, editors might well conclude that the safe course was to avoid controversy. In such an instance, political and electoral coverage would be blunted or reduced under the operation of the Florida statute. According to the Court: "Government enforced right of access inescapably dampened the vigor and limits and variety of public debate. " Second, the main issue involved requiring publishers to publish that which "reason" told them should not be published. The Florida statute operated as a command in the same sense as a law forbidding a publisher from publishing specified matter. According to the Court: "Governmental restraint on publishing need not fall into familiar or traditional patterns to be subject to constitutional limitations on governmental powers. " The Court concluded (9-0) that the statute violated the First Amendment's guarantee of a free press. The U. S. Supreme Court refused Tornillo the right to reply.

Over the years, the U. S. Supreme Court has emphatically protected the right to publish. In Near and New York Times, the Court protected the press from attempts to suppress publication through prior restraint. In Grosjean, the Court rejected an attempt to suppress publication through unfair taxation. In Hannegan and Lamont, the Court affirmed the publisher's right to send material through the mails as well as the individual's right to receive information. In Associated Press, Lorain, Times-Picayune, and Times-Mirror, the Court applied antitrust laws to the newspaper industry. Any monopolistic combination aimed at the destruction of competition in publishing newspapers was declared unconstitutional. In Citizen Publishing, the Court rejected the "failing company" defense; in this case, the company was not on the verge of liquidation and there was another prospective buyer. Bay Guardian upheld the constitutionality of the Newspaper Preservation Act--a measure designed to protect independent newspaper companies from financial failure. In Mills and American Civil Liberties Union, the Court affirmed the importance of publishing information related to political elections. In Tornillo, the Court rejected a right to reply; operation of this right could blunt the publication of political campaigns and elections. In all these areas, the U. S. Supreme Court consistently protected a specific First Amendment freedom of the press--the right to publish.

FREEDOM TO GATHER NEWS

News journalism succeeds only when the public is informed. Clearly, a newspaper cannot publish information if reporters lack access to it. In several cases, the courts have examined the right to gather news in light of First Amendment considerations.

Journalist's Privilege

In recent years, several news reporters have claimed a privilege to refuse to testify before grand juries and in courts. They argued that when reporters are forced to identify confidential sources of information, their ability to use such sources in the future diminishes. In effect, forcing reporters to reveal such sources ultimately impedes their ability to gather news. In 1972, the U. S. Supreme Court handed down an important ruling on the matter of journalist's privilege.

Branzburg v. Hayes
In the Matter of Pappas
United States v. Caldwell 408 U. S. 665 (1972)

On November 15, 1969, the Louisville Courier-Journal carried an article under staff reporter Paul Branzburg's byline describing in detail his observation of two young people synthesizing hashish from marijuana, an activity that the youths claimed earned them about $5,000 in three weeks. The story contained a photograph of a pair of hands working over a laboratory table on which was a substance identified by the caption as hashish. The article noted that the reporter had promised to keep secret the identity of the two hashish makers. The Jefferson County grand jury subpoenaed Branzburg, but he refused to reveal the identities of any individuals he had seen possessing marijuana or making hashish. A judge ordered Branzburg to answer these questions and denied his claim that the Kentucky reporters' privilege statute, the First Amendment of the Constitution, or the Kentucky Constitution authorized his refusal to answer. The judge construed the Kentucky reporters' privilege statute as affording journalists the privilege of refusing to divulge the identity of informants who supplied them with information, but maintained that the law did not permit a reporter to refuse to testify about events or individuals he had witnessed personally.

On January 10, 1971, Branzburg wrote a story that described in detail the use of drugs in Frankfort, Kentucky. The article reported that in order to provide a comprehensive survey of the "drug scene" in Frankfort, Branzburg had "spent two weeks interviewing several dozen drug users in the capital city" and had observed some of them smoking marijuana. Branzburg recounted conversations with numerous unnamed drug users. He was subsequently subpoenaed to appear before a grand jury "to testify in the matter of violation of statutes concerning use and sale of drugs." Branzburg objected. An order was issued that protected Branzburg from revealing "confidential associations, sources of information," but that required him to "answer questions which concern or pertain to any criminal act, the commission of which was actually observed by him." Prior to the time he was slated to appear, Branzburg argued before the Kentucky Court of Appeals that if he was required to answer questions regarding the identity of informants or reveal information given to him in confidence, his effectiveness as a reporter would be severely damaged. The court rejected his request, reaffirmed its construction of the Kentucky statute, and denied Branzburg's claim of a First Amendment privilege.

On July 30, 1970, Paul Pappas, a television reporter-photographer, was asked to report on civil disorders in New Bedford, Massachusetts. Pappas went to cover a Black Panther news conference at the group's headquarters in a boarded-up store. Pappas found the streets around the store barricaded, but he gained entrance to the area and recorded and photographed a prepared statement presented by a Black Panther leader. Later that evening, Pappas was allowed to enter and remain inside Panther headquarters on the condition that he agree not to disclose anything he saw or heard inside the store except an anticipated police raid, which Pappas "on his own" was free to photograph and report as he wished. Pappas remained inside the headquarters for about three hours but there was no police raid and Pappas wrote no story concerning what transpired in the store while he was there. Two months later, Pappas appeared before a grand jury and answered questions as to his name, address, employment, and what he had observed taking place outside the Panther headquarters, but he refused to respond to questions about what had occurred inside the headquarters. He claimed that the First Amendment afforded him a privilege to protect confidential informants and their information. In this case the judge, noting the absence of a statutory journalist's privilege in Massachusetts, decided that Pappas had no constitutional privilege to refuse to divulge what he had seen and heard, including the identity of persons he had observed.

On February 2, 1970, Earl Caldwell, a reporter for the New York Times assigned to cover the Black Panther Party and other black militant groups, was ordered to appear before a grand jury to testify and to bring with him notes and tape recordings of interviews given him for publication by officers and spokespeople of the Black Panther Party regarding the organization's aims, purposes, and activities. Caldwell objected to the scope of this subpoena. A second subpoena was served that omitted the documentary requirement and simply ordered Caldwell "to appear ... to testify before the Grand Jury." Caldwell objected on the grounds that if he was required to appear in secret before the grand jury it would destroy his working relationship with the Black Panther Party and would "suppress vital First Amendment freedoms ... by driving a wedge of distrust and silence between the news media and the militants." Caldwell argued that "so drastic an incursion upon First Amendment freedoms" should not be permitted "in the absence of a compelling governmental interest--not shown here--in requiring Mr. Caldwell's appearance before the grand jury."

In response, the government pointed out that the grand jury was investigating possible criminal violations including threats against the President, conspiracy to assassinate the President, civil disorders, interstate travel to incite a riot, and mail frauds and swindles. The government noted that on November 15, 1969, a representative of the Black Panther Party, in a publicly televised speech, declared that "we will kill Richard Nixon" and that this threat had been repeated in the Black Panther newspaper. The government referred to various writings by Caldwell about the Black Panther Party, including an article published in the New York Times stating that "in their role as the vanguard in a revolutionary struggle the Panthers have picked up guns" and quoting a Party leader as declaring, "We advocate the very direct overthrow of the Government by way of force and violence" and "By picking up guns and moving against it because we recognize it as being oppressive and ... we know that the only solution to it is armed struggle. " The government also stated that the Chief of Staff of the Black Panther Party had been indicted by the grand jury on December 3, 1969, for uttering threats against the life of President Nixon.

Caldwell objected, but the court noted that "every person within the jurisdiction of the government" was bound to testify upon being properly summoned. The court accepted Caldwell's arguments to the extent of issuing a protective order providing that even though Caldwell must reveal whatever information had been given to him for publication, he would not be required to divulge confidential associations or sources of information established "by him as a professional journalist in the course of his efforts to gather news for dissemination to the public through the press or other news media. " The court held that the First Amendment provided Caldwell a privilege to refuse disclosure of such confidential information until there had been "a showing by the Government of a compelling and overriding national interest requiring Mr. Caldwell's testimony which cannot be served by any alternative means. " When Caldwell refused to appear before the grand jury, he was ordered committed for contempt until such time as he complied with the court's order or until the expiration of the term of the grand jury. Caldwell appealed, and the court of appeals reversed. The court ruled that the First Amendment provided a qualified testimonial privilege to reporters, and forcing them to testify would deter their informants from communicating with them in the future and would encourage them to censor their reports in an effort to avoid being subpoenaed. Without compelling reasons for requiring his testimony, Caldwell was privileged to withhold it.

All of these cases came before the U. S. Supreme Court. The argument presented by the journalists was:

> ... that to gather news it is often necessary to agree either not to identify the source of information published or to publish only part of the facts

revealed, or both; that if the reporter is nevertheless forced to reveal these confidences to a grand
jury, the source so identified and other confidential
sources of other reporters will be measurably de-
terred from furnishing publishable information, all
to the detriment of the free flow of information protected by the First Amendment.

Even though the reporters did not claim an absolute privilege
against interrogation in all circumstances, they maintained
that a reporter should not be forced to testify unless sufficient grounds were shown for believing that she or he possessed information relevant to a crime, that the information
was unavailable from other sources, and that the need for
the information was sufficiently compelling to override First
Amendment protection.

The majority opinion of the Court, prepared by Justice Byron White, noted (5-4) that requiring journalists to
testify before grand juries did not abridge First Amendment
guarantees. A reporter's agreement to conceal criminal conduct of his or her news sources did not enjoy any constitutional safeguard. White observed that Congress had freedom
to determine policy regarding journalist's privilege and suggested that state legislatures were free to fashion shield laws.
The matter of the relations between law enforcement officials
and reporters was left to the legislature. The Court claimed
to be "powerless to erect any bar to state courts responding
in their own way and construing their own constitutions so
as to recognize a newsman's privilege, either qualified or
absolute. "

Concerning the specific cases, the Branzburg decisions
were affirmed. Branzburg had refused to answer questions
that directly related to criminal conduct he had witnessed and
written about. In Kentucky, unlicensed possession or com-
pounding of marijuana was a felony punishable by both fine
and imprisonment. Branzburg "saw the commission of the
statutory felonies and the unlawful conversion of it into hashish. " In both instances, if what Branzburg wrote was true,
"he had direct information to provide the grand jury concerning the commission of serious crimes. " In the Pappas case,
the issue was whether Pappas had to appear before the grand
jury to testify. In Massachusetts, there was no statutory
right to journalist's privilege. The Massachusetts Supreme
Judicial Court, however, had characterized the record as
"meager. " It was unclear as to what Pappas would be asked

by the grand jury. It was also unclear whether he would be asked to divulge information received in confidence. Yet, the U. S. Supreme Court affirmed the decision and held that Pappas had to appear before the grand jury to answer the questions put to him regarding "the propriety, purpose, and scope of the grand jury inquiry and the pertinence of the probable testimony. " The issue was whether a newspaper reporter who had published articles about an organization could refuse to appear before a grand jury investigating possible crimes by members of the organization where the members had been quoted in the published articles. The majority of the Court said "no. " Regarding Caldwell, the Court held that if there was no First Amendment privilege to refuse to answer relevant questions asked during a grand jury investigation, then there was no journalist's privilege to refuse to appear before such a grand jury until the Government had demonstrated some "compelling need" for the reporter's testimony. The lower court ruling was reversed. By the time the Supreme Court finally heard these three cases, the Massachusetts and California grand juries had been dismissed. Pappas and Caldwell were already free. Branzburg had moved to Detroit and the state of Michigan refused to extradite him to Kentucky.

The minority opinion, written by Justice Potter Stewart, suggested that when a reporter was asked to appear before a grand jury to reveal confidences, the government should 1) show cause to believe that the reporter had information that is clearly relevant to the specific probable violation of law, 2) demonstrate that the information sought could not be obtained by alternative means, and 3) demonstrate a compelling and overriding interest in the information. The minority opinion cautioned that

> the sad paradox of the Court's position is that when a grand jury may exercise an unbridled subpoena power, and sources involved in sensitive matters become fearful of disclosing information, the newsman will not only cease to be a useful grand jury witness; he will cease to investigate and publish information about issues of public import.

In Branzburg, the Court was deeply divided about the right of journalist's privilege. The division has also been evident in the lower courts. Following Branzburg, some courts upheld, while others denied the right of newsman's privilege.

Baker v. F. & F. Investment 470 F. 2d 778 (1972)

In this case, the courts recognized the privilege. In the early 1970s, a court action was begun on behalf of all blacks in Chicago who purchased homes from sixty named defendants between 1952 and 1969. The complaint claimed that the defendants sold homes at excessive prices by engaging in racially discriminatory practices, such as "blockbusting." During the conduct of this case, Alfred Balk was called as a witness. Ten years earlier, Balk had written an article entitled "Confessions of a Block-Buster, " which was published in the July 14, 1962, issue of the Saturday Evening Post. The article was based upon information supplied to Balk by an anonymous Chicago real estate agent, who was given the pseudonym "Norris Vitchek. " In court, Balk answered several questions about "blockbusting" and about his article, but he refused to identify "Vitchek" on the ground that he had obtained his information on a confidential basis. The judge weighed the competing public and private interests involved in this case and concluded that Balk should not be forced to reveal "Vitchek's" identity. The case was appealed.

The United States Court of Appeals, Second Circuit, indicated that "federal law on the question of compelled disclosure by journalists of their confidential sources is at best ambiguous. " The court analyzed Branzburg and noted that while federal law did not recognize an absolute or conditional journalist's privilege, neither did it require disclosure of confidential sources in each and every case. The court noted that there were other available sources of information that might have disclosed the real identity of "Vitchek" that had not been exhausted. The court stated that forced disclosure of confidential sources has a deterrent effect on investigative reporting and ultimately "threatens freedom of the press and the public's need to be informed. " The court affirmed the lower court decision.

Democratic National Committee v. McCord
In re Bernstein 356 F. Supp. 1394 (1973)

In this case, the courts again upheld the principle. Reporters for the Washington Evening Star and Daily News, New York Times, and Time magazine were subpoenaed to appear in court for depositions, and to bring with them all documents, papers, letters, photographs, and audiovisual tapes relating to the Watergate "break-in" of June 17, 1972. All of those

summoned moved to quash the subpoenas. In addition, members of the Committee for the Re-election of the President,
and the Finance Committee to Re-Elect the President, all
of whom were parties in civil actions arising out of the break-
in, also moved to quash the subpoenas. The primary issue
was whether the subpoenas were valid under the First Amendment.

The U. S. District Court, District of Columbia, held
that the parties were entitled to at least a qualified privilege
under the First Amendment. The court could not "blind itself to the possible 'chilling effect' the enforcement of these
broad subpoenas would have on the flow of information to the
press, and so to the public." In this case, there had been
no showing that alternative sources of evidence had been exhausted as to the possible gleaning of the facts sought from
the reporters. Nor had there been any positive showing of
the materiality of the documents sought by the subpoenas.
The scales were heavily weighted in favor of the journalists.
The court noted,

> ... the Court in no way wishes to imply that to-
> day's ruling constitutes the implicit recognition
> of an absolute privilege for newsmen. Such would
> clearly be improper under the Branzburg decision.
> It may be that at some future date, the parties
> will be able to demonstrate to the Court that they
> are unable to obtain the same information from
> sources other than Movants, and that they have a
> compelling and overriding interest in the informa-
> tion thus sought. Until that time, however, the
> Court will not require Movants to testify at the
> scheduled depositions or to make any of the re-
> quested materials available to the parties.

The court ordered that the subpoenas be quashed. In McCord,
the court recognized a qualified journalist's privilege.

Bursey v. United States 466 F. 2d 1059 (1972)

In this case, the courts rejected claims of newsman's
privilege. On November 15, 1969, David Hilliard, Chief of
Staff of the Black Panther Party, delivered a speech before
a large audience in San Francisco, during Moratorium Day
demonstrations. In the course of the televised speech, Hilliard claimed, "We will kill Richard Nixon." Hilliard's speech

was printed in full in the October 22 issue of The Black Panther newspaper. It was also widely reported in the news
media. An investigation was begun to determine whom Hilliard referred to when he said "We" will kill the President.
Later, the probe was expanded to include a general explora-
tion of the affairs of the Black Panther Party. Sherrie Bursey and Brenda Presley, reporters for The Black Panther,
were called, but refused to answer certain questions before
a federal grand jury. Specifically, they both declined to answer questions relating to the internal management of the newspaper and about the identity of persons with whom they worked on the newspaper. They were also asked whether they
had any information about a plot to kill the President or Vice
President or about the acquisition of weapons for that purpose. Bursey responded that she had no such information.
Presley refused to answer. Bursey and Presley were held
in contempt. They appealed.

The court of appeals noted that freedom of the press
was not guaranteed solely to shield news reporters "from unwarranted governmental harassment"; the "larger purpose
was to protect public access to information. " The court determined that questions about the identity of persons with whom
the reporters worked infringed Bursey and Presley's right of
associational privacy and had a chilling effect on the press.
They did not have to answer such questions. But, the court
also determined that the reporters had to answer questions
about Black Panther Party activities concerning possession
of firearms, guerrilla training, and threats against the life
of the President. These questions were vital to the government's investigation, and the impact of such questions "on
lawful association and protected expression" was "so slight
that governmental interests would prevail. " The reporters
could be compelled to answer such inquiries.

U. S. v. Liddy 354 F. Supp. 208 (1972)

The courts again refused to recognize journalist's privi-
lege in U. S. v. Liddy. In its October 5, 1972, issue, the
Los Angeles Times printed four articles headlined "Inside
Watergate, Bugging Witness Tells of Incident, " "Baldwin Says
GOP Unit Disowned Him, " "Gave Memos to Official Baldwin
Says, " and "An Insider's Account of the Watergate Bugging. "
The stories claimed to contain information obtained from Al-
fred C. Baldwin, III, "in more than five hours of tape-re-
corded interviews with the Times. " According to the paper,

Baldwin had "monitored the telephone tap at the Democratic headquarters last May and June from a listening post in the Howard Johnson Motel across the street from the Watergate. " The articles pictured Baldwin as an associate of several of the seven defendants in the Watergate case, the trial of which was to begin in Washington, D. C. , on January 8, 1973. On October 25, 1972, George Gordon Liddy, one of the Watergate defendants, filed a pretrial motion for a subpoena to order Times Bureau Chief John Lawrence and reporters Jack Nelson and Ron Ostrow to produce all documents related to their interview with Baldwin. The Times filed a motion to quash.

The district court noted that the First Amendment right to gather news afforded "no absolute privilege against the compelled revelation of news sources. " In the Liddy case, even though the public had a crucial interest in the investigation and punishment of criminal activity, it had "an even deeper interest in assuring that every defendant receives a fair trial. " The court stressed that Liddy's right to secure evidence to counter Baldwin's testimony outweighed any First Amendment considerations. The court denied the motion to quash.

Dow Jones & Company, Inc. v. Superior
Court 303 N. E. 2d 849 (1973)

The courts also rejected journalist's privilege in this case. On October 17, 1972, the Wall Street Journal published an article written by Liz Gallese concerning the impact on Massachusetts towns of a so-called "anti-snob zoning law. " In the article, an unnamed "Stoneham official" was quoted as stating that real estate developer William D'Annolfo was a "bad word" in Stoneham and that D'Annolfo was in fact using the law to "blackmail" town officials. The article closed with a denial of the charges by "a lawyer for Mr. D'Annolfo. " Five days later, a correction appeared in the Journal. The paper acknowledged that "the inference of 'blackmail' was incorrect. " The Journal stated that it regretted the error. D'Annolfo initiated a libel action. During the court proceedings, Gallese refused to identify the name or the precise office held by the "Stoneham official" whom she had quoted in the article. The court ordered her to identify the source of the allegedly defamatory statements. She appealed.

Before the Supreme Judicial Court, Gallese contended

that First Amendment free press protection, while not providing an absolute privilege, "at least creates a partial shield behind which journalists may conceal their confidential sources. " That shield must stand until it has been demonstrated that the information sought by the court is crucial to the particular judicial proceeding. Thus, the plaintiff in the current case would have to exhaust alternative means of identifying the "Stoneham official, " and demonstrate that the case can succeed only if the identity of the "Stoneham official" is revealed. The Supreme Judicial Court of Massachusetts disagreed; the First Amendment afforded no journalist's privilege, qualified or absolute. The court upheld the order that required Gallese to reveal her source.

The Branzburg Court was deeply divided about the issue of journalist's privilege. Following Branzburg, the lower courts have acted with uncertainty, as indicated by the lack of consistent action in Baker, McCord, Bursey, Liddy, and Dow Jones. The matter of journalist's privilege will undoubtedly be the subject of future court action.

Shield Laws

More than half the states have passed shield laws that set forth the specific conditions under which a journalist's privilege applies. Some laws, for example those in Alabama, Nevada, and New York, are almost absolute. Others are qualified and prohibit use of the privilege in specific situations. In Arkansas, the law provides that a reporter may be compelled to reveal a source of information if it can be demonstrated that her or his article was written, published, or broadcast with malice and not in the interest of the public. In New Mexico, a reporter may be required to disclose a source if disclosure is "essential to prevent injustice. " The Indiana law generally restricts protection to persons connected with a newspaper that has been published for five consecutive years in the same city and that has a paid circulation of 2 percent of the population of the county in which it is published. Overall, the laws are inconsistent from state to state regarding the personnel, media, and information protected, as well as the procedures under which the privilege may be invoked. Several state shield laws have been interpreted by the courts, and, in such cases, the interpretation has been narrow--tending to force reporters to comply with court rulings.

Lightman v. State of Maryland 294 A. 2d 149 (1972)

Newspaper reporter David Lightman was assigned to prepare a story on how open drug use and sales were in Ocean City, Maryland. Through his investigation, Lightman learned that a particular store was selling pipes for smoking marijuana and other drugs, and sometimes the proprietor allowed customers to smoke some marijuana before making a purchase. Lightman spoke with the shopkeeper, and she gave him information that he subsequently used in his article. Lightman indicated in the story that he was a "customer" who had a conversation with the storekeeper. Lightman was called by a grand jury, but he refused to reveal the name of the shopkeeper or the location of the shop. The Circuit Court for Worcester County found Lightman in civil contempt for refusing to answer grand jury inquiries. The court noted that there had been no testimony that Lightman had identified himself to the shopkeeper as a reporter. There was no evidence that the Shopkeeper gave Lightman any information based upon the knowledge that he was a reporter. The court concluded that the shopkeeper was not a "source" of information within the meaning of Maryland's Shield Law. Lightman was a stranger to the shopkeeper, and what he heard was not conveyed to him in confidence. Lightman's constitutional rights of free speech and press would not be violated by requiring that he provide a grand jury with the information. Lightman appealed.

The court of appeals noted that not all news or information published by journalists has as its origin a "source" protected by Maryland's law. Where a reporter, because of her or his own investigative efforts, personally observed illegal activity,

> the newsman, and not the persons observed, is the "source" of the news or information in the sense contemplated by the statute. To conclude otherwise in such circumstances would be to insulate the news itself from disclosure and not merely the source, a result plainly at odds with the Maryland law.

If the substance of Lightman's information had been learned, not by personal observation, but through an informant, the identity of the informant would clearly be protected. The court concluded that Lightman could be directed to disclose the location of the pipe shop and to identify all those persons observed by him, including the shopkeeper, who were engaged in illegal activities. The judgment of the circuit court was affirmed.

In re Bridge 295 A. 2d 3 (1972)

The Bridge case involved a judicial interpretation of the New Jersey shield law. On May 2, 1972, the Newark Evening News published an article written by Peter Bridge concerning an alleged offer of a bribe to Pearl Beatty, a member of the Newark Housing Authority. The article contained the following statements:

> Mrs. Pearl Beatty, a commissioner of the Newark Housing Authority, said yesterday an unknown man offered to pay her $10,000 to influence her vote for the appointment of an executive director of the authority.
>
> Mrs. Beatty said also that at least two other commissioners had been harassed and threatened in efforts to control their votes. . . .
>
> Mrs. Beatty said, "A man walked into my office and offered me $10,000 if I would vote for 'their' choice for executive director. "

The Essex County Grand Jury initiated an investigation of the alleged bribe attempt and, on May 19, subpoenaed Bridge to appear before it. When Bridge appeared, he refused to answer any questions. Eventually, a court determined that Bridge had neither a constitutional privilege nor a statutory privilege to refuse to answer the questions. The judge found Bridge to be in contempt of court and ordered that he be confined to the county jail until he answered the questions or until the grand jury was discharged. Bridge appealed.

Bridge contended that if reporters were required to testify before grand juries concerning unpublished information received from public officials, then government would be able "to prevent its wrongdoings from being brought to the attention of the public. " The court of appeals held that Bridge had waived his statutory journalist's privilege by disclosing the source of his information. Furthermore, compelling his appearance did not abridge his rights under the First Amendment. The order was affirmed.

People v. Dan 41 App. Div. 2d 687 (1973)

In 1973, a New York court heard a case involving that state's shield law. Newscaster Stewart Dan and cameraman Roland Barnes were assigned by television station WGR to cover the Attica prison riots in 1972. They were subsequently called before a grand jury and asked to testify concerning what they had observed while inside Attica during the disturbances. They refused, citing the shield law as a defense.

The appeals court noted that the shield law did not protect the journalists in this case. The questions posed by the grand jury did not require them to disclose news or the sources of news, but merely asked them to testify about events they had personally observed. The shield law granted reporters the privilege of refusing to divulge the identity of any informant who had supplied them with information, but the statute "does not permit them to refuse to testify about events which they observed personally, including the identities of the persons whom they observed."

WBAI-FM v. Proskin 42 App. Div. 2d 5 (1973)

In 1973, the appellate court heard another New York case. On September 17, 1971, radio station WBAI-FM received an anonymous telephone call. The caller claimed that a letter, describing an imminent bomb threat, had been placed in a nearby phone booth. A newscaster from the station found the letter, which stated that the "Weather Underground" was about to bomb the offices of the Commissioner of Correctional Services in the Twin Towers Office Building in Albany. The newscaster notified the police, the letter was read over the air, and the contents were released to other news media. An explosion occurred as threatened, causing considerable property damage. In October, the station was served with a subpoena that requested the production of the letter. The station refused, claiming the shield law as a defense.

The appellate court found that the shield law did not protect the station. The court interpreted the statute to protect a newscaster only when "the information was received under a cloak of confidentiality."

> The author of the letter took pains to conceal his identity by signing the letter "Weather Underground," and to insure that appellant would obtain the letter without learning its author's identity. Clearly, he was not willing to rely upon appellant to shield his identity from the authorities. He

refused to establish a confidential relationship with appellant but preferred to talk with anyone who answered the phone.

Moreover, since the letter was left in a public telephone booth where it might have been found by anyone and turned over to the police, it is clear that the author could not have been relying upon appellant to withhold the letter itself.

The court upheld the order; the station was required to produce the letter. It had not been conveyed to the station or to the newscaster in confidence.

Farr v. Superior Court of the State of California, County of Los Angeles 99 Cal. Rptr. 342 (1971) In re Farr 111 Cal. Rptr. 649 (1974)

This case involved the California shield law. In 1971, during the trial of Charles Manson and his followers for two sets of multiple murders, the court entered an Order re Publicity that prohibited any attorney, court employee, or witness from releasing for public dissemination the content or nature of any testimony that might be given. Shortly thereafter, Deputy District Attorney Stephen R. Kay obtained a written statement from Mrs. Virginia Graham, a potential witness. The statement claimed that Susan Atkins, a codefendant in the prosecution, had confessed the crimes to Mrs. Graham in lurid detail, and had implicated Manson. Atkins purportedly told Mrs. Graham that the Manson group planned to murder a series of show business personalities, including Elizabeth Taylor, Richard Burton, Frank Sinatra, Tom Jones, and Steve McQueen. William Farr, a reporter for the Los Angeles Herald Examiner, learned of the Graham statement. Although aware of the Order re Publicity, Farr obtained two copies of the statement from attorneys of record. Farr told his sources that he would keep their identity confidential. When the court learned that Farr had obtained the statement, the presiding judge asked Farr if the Herald Examiner intended to print a story based upon the statement. The judge also sought the identity of the persons who had given the statement to Farr. While informing the court that he had copies of Graham's statement, Farr refused to reveal his sources. Farr wrote a story headlined "Liz, Sinatra on Slay List--Tate Witness," which appeared in the Herald Examiner. The story repeated the sensational, gory details of the planned murders as well as the statements implicating

Manson in the murders already committed. At the comple-
tion of the trial, Manson, Atkins, and the other codefendants
were found guilty of the murders. The trial court then con-
vened to determine whether there had been a violation of its
Order re Publicity that had jeopardized a fair trial for the
defendants in the case. Farr refused to answer a series of
questions asking the identity of the persons who had furnished
the Graham statement to him. The court held Farr in contempt. It ordered him incarcerated in the county jail until
he answered the question. He appealed.

The court of appeals noted that the California shield
law provided a journalist's privilege to "a publisher, editor,
reporter, or other person connected with or employed upon
a newspaper, or by a press association." However, even
though Farr had been employed by a newspaper when he obtained the Graham statement, he had since taken a different
position. He was no longer a reporter when questioned by
the court. He was no longer entitled to protection under the
law. Farr argued that the law had to be construed broadly
to include within its immunity persons who occupied the reporter's status at the time they acquired the information,
even though they no longer occupied the status when disclosure was required. Otherwise, the purpose of the statute--
the free flow of information to the public--would be impaired
by the reluctance of persons to communicate with a reporter
because of the possibility of the revelation of their identity
if the reporter's status changed. The court rejected Farr's
claim. According to the court, a trial court could control
prejudicial publicity only if that court could compel disclosure of the origins of such publicity. To immunize Farr
from contempt would interfere with that power. The court
concluded:

> Balancing, as we are required to do, the interest
> to be served by disclosure of source against its
> potential inhibition upon the free flow of informa-
> tion, we conclude that petitioner is not privileged
> by the First Amendment to refuse to answer the
> questions put to him in the trial court.

The contempt order was affirmed. Farr went to jail. In
1974, a court of appeals ruled that continuing Farr's imprisonment would become punitive at some point. Soon thereafter, Farr returned to the trial court and convinced the
judge that more time in jail would not achieve disclosure of
the sources. Farr was fined and sentenced to five additional
days in jail. Farr was finally free of the contempt charge.

In Farr, as in Lightman, Bridge, Dan and Proskin, the court upheld an order requiring the reporter to reveal the information. In these cases, the shield laws did not protect the news journalist.

Banning of Reporters

In the 1970s, court actions arose when journalists were banned from specific sources of news. One case involved the banning of all reporters from interviewing prisoners. Another involved the ban against a particular reporter from a mayor's press conferences. The third involved the ban of specific reporters from White House press conferences. The courts had to determine under what conditions such bans are permissible.

Prisoners--A regulation of the Bureau of Prisons states: "Press representatives will not be permitted to interview individual inmates. This rule shall apply even where the inmate requests or seeks an interview." In 1974, the U. S. Supreme Court decided two cases involving challenges against this regulation.

Pell v. Procunier
Procunier v. Hillery 417 U. S. 817 (1974)
Saxbe v. Washington Post Company 417 U. S. 843 (1974)

A California Department of Corrections regulation prohibited members of the press from conducting interviews with specifically designated inmates. This policy was established when violence erupted after face-to-face interviews resulted in some inmates receiving considerable notoriety, which increased their influence over fellow prisioners. Three journalists, including Eve Pell, and four prison inmates, brought suit to prevent Director of the California Department of Corrections, Raymond Procunier, from enforcing the regulation. About the same time, reporters from the Washington Post were denied interviews with specific inmates at federal prisons in Lewisburg, Pennsylvania, and Danbury, Connecticut. The regulations allowing such bans were challenged in court. In these cases, inmates alleged that the regulations curtailed their right to free speech. Journalists contended that the rules constituted an unconstitutional obstacle to newsgathering. Both cases reached the U. S. Supreme Court.

The Court upheld (5-4) the regulations. First of all,

the Court rejected the prisoners' arguments. Prisoners' free
speech rights must be balanced against the legitimate interests
of the state to deter crime and protect internal security.
Since alternative methods of communication were open to inmates, their free speech rights had not been violated. For
example, "The medium of written correspondence affords inmates an open and substantially unimpeded channel for communication with persons outside the prison, including representatives of the news media." Another alternative was visi-
tation policy, which allowed inmates visits with their family
members, friends, clergy, and attorneys. Prisoners thereby "have an unrestricted opportunity to communicate with the
press or any other member of the public through their families, friends, clergy, or attorneys who are permitted to visit
them at the prison." Secondly, the Court ruled against the
claims of the journalists. The rights of the press were not
violated because they still retained access to information
available to the general public. The minority disagreed. In
an opinion prepared by Justice William Douglas, they argued
that the absolute ban on press interviews with specifically
designated prisoners was "far broader than necessary to protect any legitimate governmental interests" and was an "unconstitutional infringement on the public's right to know protected by the free press guarantee of the First Amendment."
The majority, however, held that the First Amendment did
not guarantee the press a constitutional right of special access to information.

Houchins v. KQED, Inc. 438 U. S. 1 (1978)

The Court affirmed the Pell decision four years later.
On March 31, 1975, television station KQED broadcast the
suicide of a prisoner at the jail in Santa Rita, California.
The report contained a statement by a psychiatrist that the
conditions at the facility were responsible for the illness of
patient-prisoners there, and a statement from Thomas Houchins, a local sheriff, denying that prison conditions were
responsible for prisoner illnesses. KQED asked permission
to inspect and take pictures within the jail. After the request was refused, KQED and the Alameda and Oakland Branches of the NAACP filed suit, alleging that such refusal violated the First Amendment right of media access. Refusal
failed to provide an effective means by which the public could
be informed of conditions prevailing in the facility. Houchins
responded that six monthly tours were planned and funded by
the County. Subsequently, a KQED reporter and several

other reporters were on the first tour on July 14, 1975. However, each tour was limited to twenty-five persons and allowed only limited access to the jail.   The tours did not include the disciplinary cells or the portions of the jail that were the scene of alleged rapes, beatings, and adverse physical conditions.   Photographs of some sections of the jail were made available, but no cameras or tape recorders were allowed on the tours.   Persons on the tours were not permitted to interview inmates.   The case reached the U. S. Supreme Court.

The Court noted that inmates may lose many rights when they are jailed, but they do not lose all civil rights.

> Inmates in jails, prisons or mental institutions retain certain fundamental rights of privacy; they are not like animals in a zoo to be filmed and photographed at will by the public or by media reporters, however "educational" the process may be for others.

The Court cited Pell and Saxbe in concluding (4-3) that the "news media have no constitutional right of access to a county jail, over and above that of other persons. "

Press Conferences--One way a government official can control publicity is by banning unfavorable reporters from a press conference.   In some cases, the proper function of the press is thwarted.   In other instances, a government official may legitimately seek to ban a reporter from a press conference in order to maintain accuracy, objectivity, safety, or public order.   In two recent cases, the courts had to balance these conflicting interests.

Borreca v. Fasi 369 F. Supp. 906 (1974)

Richard Borreca, a news reporter for the Honolulu Star-Bulletin, was assigned to cover city hall, which included attending the mayor's press conferences.   During 1973, Mayor Frank Fasi decided that Borreca was "irresponsible, inaccurate, biased, and malicious in reporting on the mayor and the city administration. "   Fasi declared that Borreca was not welcome at city hall and instructed his staff to keep Borreca out of the mayor's office.   Upon the occasion of the next mayor's news conference, Borreca appeared as the representative of the Star-Bulletin.   Borreca was not admitted.

Fasi informed the Star-Bulletin that any other reporter from that newspaper would be welcome, but the paper refused to change Borreca's assignment or to send another reporter to cover the mayor's press conferences. Borreca and the newspaper initiated court proceedings.

The district court noted that First Amendment freedom of the press "includes a limited right of reasonable access to news. " The right included access to public galleries, press rooms, and press conferences dealing with government. The court stressed that any limitations that may be placed by government on this right to access must be determined "by a balancing process in which the importance of the news gathering activity and the degree and type of the restraint sought to be imposed are balanced against the state interest to be served. " The court noted that newspapers take sides, reporters are not always accurate and objective, and the press is always subject to criticism.

> But when criticism transforms into an attempt to use the powers of governmental office to intimidate or to discipline the press or one of its members because of what appears in print, a compelling governmental interest that cannot be served by less restrictive means must be shown for such use to meet Constitutional standards. No compelling governmental interest has been shown or even claimed here.

The court concluded that Mayor Fasi could not prevent Borreca from attending the news conferences.

Forcade v. Knight 416 F. Supp. 1025 (1976)

Thomas Forcade was a news reporter for the Alternate Press Syndicate, an international news service that represented more than two hundred subscribing newspapers. Since 1971, he had been the APS's national affairs correspondent in Washington, and a member of the House and Senate Press Galleries. He held press credentials issued by the Washington, D. C. , police department, and was accredited as a national reporter at the 1972 Democratic and Republican National Conventions. On January 20, 1972, Forcade covered the President's State of the Union message from the press gallery of the House of Representatives. Another reporter, Robert Sherrill, was the Washington correspondent for The

Nation. He had been a member of the House and Senate Periodical Press Galleries since 1966. Sherrill had written more than sixty-six articles and numerous editorials for magazines and newspapers. He had also written six books, two of which were listed on the New York Times list of best books of the year. Since their arrival in Washington, both Forcade and Sherrill applied to Presidential Press Secretary Ronald Ziegler for a pass to attend White House press conferences and briefings. The passes for both men were denied "for reasons of security." The reporters could obtain no more specific information for the denial of their passes. The reporters were offered no opportunity to present evidence on their own behalf. They initiated court action.

When the case reached the district court, some FBI and Secret Service files were offered as evidence for the denials. The files showed that Forcade had been active in leftist student groups, such as the Yippies, SDS, and the May Day Committee. Sherrill had been involved in two cases of assault, which gave rise to charges that he was "mentally unbalanced." It was for these activities that Forcade and Sherrill had been barred entry to the White House. However, there were no established public criteria for determining such bans on reporters. After examining the facts of this case, the court held 1) that the White House's failure to devise specific standards for issuance or denial of press passes infringed on Forcade's and Sherrill's First Amendment right to freedom of the press; 2) that the White House's failure to inform the reporters of the grounds for the denial of the pass, or to permit them an opportunity to respond, violated their Fifth Amendment right to procedural due process; and 3) that the Secret Service should devise and publicize specific standards for the issuance and denial of press pass applications, and then consider Forcade's and Sherrill's applications within the context of those standards. In Forcade, as in Borreca, the court specified that a governmental official could not, without good reasons, ban a reporter from access to press conferences.

Freedom of Information

Information-gathering by journalists, as well as by other citizens, has frequently been impeded by government secrecy. In 1953, the Court decided a case involving conflicting rights--the right of the public to know versus the right of the government to maintain secrecy in the interest of national security.

United States v. Reynolds 345 U. S. 1 (1953)

When some government workers were killed in the
crash of an Air Force plane that was testing secret electronic
equipment, their widows wanted to examine the investigatory
report of the crash as well as statements of surviving crew
members that had been gathered in an official Air Force investigation. The Secretary of the Air Force refused to disclose the information on the ground that military secrets
were involved. He filed a formal "Claim of Privilege." The
district court ruled that the right to withhold documents had
been waived by the Tort Claims Act and ordered the government to produce the documents. The government again declined. The court then concluded that if the government refused to produce the documents, it would enter an order that
would permit it to view the documents. The court would examine the facts concerning the issue of negligence against
the government--the party refusing disclosure. The theory
behind this was that since the party knowing the facts refused
to make them available, it was only reasonable to assume
that the facts were against that party. The government appealed. The question in this case was whether such a rule
could be used against the government.

The U. S. Supreme Court reversed (6-3) the lower
court decision. Chief Justice Frederick Vinson described
the difficult task facing the Court. The justices had to determine whether the circumstances were appropriate for the
claim of privilege, without forcing a disclosure of the information the privilege was designed to protect. Vinson spelled
out the test the Court would use to resolve the issue. The
test would be applied in cases involving the conflicting claims
of the need for public disclosure versus the need for government or military privilege based on national security.

> Judicial control over the evidence in a case cannot
> be abdicated to the caprice of executive officers.
> Yet we will not go so far as to say that the court
> may automatically require a complete disclosure
> to the judge before the claim of privilege will be
> accepted in any case. It may be possible to sat-
> isfy the court, from all the circumstances of the
> case, that there is a reasonable danger that com-
> pulsion of the evidence will expose military matters
> which, in the interest of national security, should
> not be divulged. When this is the case, the oc-
> casion for the privilege is appropriate, and the

court should not jeopardize the security which the privilege is meant to protect by insisting upon an examination of the evidence; even by the judge alone, in chambers.

Regarding this case, the Court noted that air power was a potent weapon in the U. S. Defense arsenal and that newly developed electronic devices had greatly enhanced the use of air power. It was apparent that such devices had to be kept secret if their full military advantage was to benefit the national interest. According to the Court, the accident investigation threatened to uncover information about the secret electronic equipment. The Court upheld the Air Force's Claim of Privilege, thereby protecting the interests of government secrecy. Those interests were somewhat limited with the passage of the Freedom of Information Act.

Freedom of Information Act 5 U. S. C. § 552

In 1966, Congress enacted the Freedom of Information Act (FOIA)--a measure designed to make available to reporters and other members of the public, various types of information long closed to public inspection. The law stated that all persons had access to all federal records except those that fell into nine categories of exemption. Initially, the Act did not provide much improvement in obtaining information. When requests were made for records, federal agencies were reluctant to surrender them. They stalled in releasing requested information. Court action moved slowly, and often the information was no longer "news" or "relevant" by the time it was released.

In 1974, and again in 1976, Congress amended the Act in an effort to facilitate access to information. Significant procedural changes made records considerably more accessible. Under the amendments, federal agencies had to answer requests for records within ten days. If an appeal was filed after a denial, the agency had only twenty days to respond to the appeal. Each agency was required to publish a quarterly index of records. Any charges for searching out or duplicating records had to be reasonable. Agencies had to file an annual report of all records to which access was granted. And, any agency employee who denied access in an arbitrary and capricious manner could be disciplined by the Civil Service Commission. These changes facilitated access to government records under the FOIA.

In addition to the procedural changes, Congress amended exemptions one, three, and seven. The amended FOIA provided access to all government records except the following: 1) material authorized by Executive order to be kept secret in the interest of national defense or foreign policy, 2) information related solely to internal personnel rules, 3) matter exempted from disclosure by another statute, 4) confidential commercial and financial data, 5) interagency and intra-agency memorandums, 6) personnel and medical files, 7) investigatory records compiled for law enforcement purposes, 8) information collected for an agency responsible for the regulation of financial institutions, and 9) geological and geophysical data concerning oil wells.

During the 1970s, several tests of the Freedom of Information Act reached the federal courts. In a 1970 case, a historian sought to obtain U. S. Army files dealing with forced repatriation of Soviet citizens following World War II.

Epstein v. Resor 421 F. 2d 930 (1970)

Julius Epstein, a research associate at Stanford University's Hoover Institution on War, Revolution, and Peace, was preparing a book on the forced repatriation of anticommunist Russians following World War II. He wanted to examine the U. S. Army file designated "Forcible Repatriation of Displaced Soviet Citizens--Operation Keelhaul. " This file was prepared over twenty years earlier by the Allied Force Headquarters of World War II. That agency had classified the file as "top secret. " At the close of the war, the Army maintained the classification. The classification of the file was reviewed by the Army in 1954 and 1967, and the classification was retained. In 1968, Epstein requested release of the file. The Army contended that the material fell within the first of the nine exempted categories under the FOIA. Epstein initiated court action.

Before the U. S. Court of Appeals, Ninth Circuit, Epstein argued that the courts should examine the file in camera to determine whether the file should, after twenty-four years, still be classified as "top secret" in the interests of the national defense or foreign policy. The court noted, however, that "the function of determining whether secrecy is required in the national interest is expressly assigned to the executive. " Such a determination "is not the sort of question that courts are designed to deal with. " The court claimed that "the judiciary has neither the 'aptitude, facilities, nor responsibility' to review these essentially political decisions. " The court decided that in camera examination of the file was not warranted in this case. The court concluded that, under exemption one, the Army had justified withholding the material in question.

Environmental Protection Agency v. Mink 410 U. S. 73 (1973)

In 1973, the U. S. Supreme Court rendered a significant decision regarding the FOIA. An article appeared in a Washington, D. C. , newspaper in July, 1971, that indicated that President Richard Nixon had received conflicting recommendations on the advisability of the underground nuclear test scheduled for that coming fall. In particular, the article noted that the "latest recommendations" were the product of "a departmental undersecretary committee named to investigate the controversy. " Two days later, U. S. Representative Patsy Mink sent a telegram to Nixon urgently requesting the immediate release of the classified reports. The request was denied. Representative Mink and thirty-two of her colleagues in the House inititated court action under the Freedom of Information Act. They contended that the court should examine the reports in private to determine whether they were classified properly or whether the Government was simply trying to keep controversial information from the public.

The Environmental Protection Agency immediately moved for summary judgment on the ground that the reports were exempted from disclosure under the Freedom of Information Act. The Act exempted matters that were, according to subsection (b)(1), "specifically required by Executive order to be kept secret in the interest of the national defense or foreign policy, " or were, under (b)(5), "inter-agency or intra-agency memorandums or letters which would not be available by law to a party other than an agency in litigation with the agency. " To support the motion, the EPA submitted the statement of Undersecretary of State John N. Irwin, II, whom Nixon had appointed to chair the "Undersecretaries Committee, " which was part of the National Security Council system. The Committee was directed by Nixon in 1969 to review the underground nuclear test program. The Committee sent to Nixon a report on the proposed test known as "Cannikin, " scheduled to take place at Amchitka Island, Alaska. The report consisted of a total of ten documents. An Environmental Impact Statement prepared by the Atomic Energy Commission was publicly available and was not in dispute. According to Irwin, the other nine were prepared solely to advise the President of varying viewpoints regarding the proposed test. At least eight of these documents involved highly sensitive matter vital to the national defense and foreign policy and had been classified "Top Secret" and "Secret. "

The district court ruled that each of the documents was exempted from compelled disclosure. However, the court of appeals reversed, concluding that subsection (b)(1) permits the withholding of only the secret portions of the documents. The court instructed the district judge to examine the classified documents "looking toward their possible separation for purposes of disclosure or nondisclosure. " The court of appeals also concluded that the documents fell within subsection (b)(5) but interpreted that exemption as shielding only the "decisional processes" reflected in internal government memorandums, not "factual information, " unless that information was "inextricably intertwined with policymaking processes. " The court ordered the district judge to examine the documents in camera to determine if "factual data" could be separated out and disclosed "wihout impinging on the policymaking decisional processes intended to be protected by this exemption. "

The U. S. Supreme Court reversed the appeals court. The Court indicated (5-3) that exemption one stated "with the utmost directness" that the act exempted matters "specifically required by Executive order to be kept secret. " This made wholly untenable any claim that the Act intended to subject the soundness of executive security classifications to judicial review at the insistence of any objecting citizen. " It also negated the proposition that exemption one authorized in camera inspection of a contested document bearing a single classification so that the court could "separate the secret from the supposedly nonsecret, and order disclosure of the latter. " In the Court's opinion, once information was classified, that classification could not be challenged. Furthermore, the President could delegate his authority to classify documents, as he had done in this case. Regarding exemption five, the implication of the appeals court was that any member of the public could require confidential documents to be brought forward and placed before the district court for in camera inspection, regardless of how little purely factual material they may contain. According to the Court (7-1), exemption five mandated no such result. An agency should be allowed the opportunity to demonstrate to the satisfaction of the court that

the materials sought fall clearly beyond the range of material
that would be available to a private party in litigation with
the agency.   The burden rested with the agency, and if it
failed to meet that burden, the court could order in camera
inspection.

     In Mink, the Court clearly upheld the government's
claims based on national defense and foreign policy considerations.   But the Court broadened the scope of the Freedom
of Information Act in that intra-agency and interagency memos
could in some circumstances be subjected to in camera review.
The ruling suggested that the Court might be sympathetic to
judicial review of exemption challenges apart from the sensitive areas of national defense and foreign policy.   Regarding
the matter covered in exemption one, the Court took the position that once a document was classified under national defense or foreign policy, the classification could not be challenged.

     The Mink decision facilitated government abuse of pow-
er under exemption one, a practice that was used considerably during the Watergate investigation.   The Nixon Administration classified numerous documents under the national security label, thereby precluding the information from public
inspection.   The 1974 FOIA procedural amendments went a
long way to curb such abuse.   Under the changes, the courts
were able to review government decisions to withhold documents.   Specifically, the courts had the power to inspect
classified reports in private to determine if they were classified properly.   And, the Executive Branch had to specify the
criteria used to justify a particular classification.   The courts
were then able to determine whether the classified documents
actually met the criteria.

Vaughn v. Rosen, Executive Director, United States
Civil Service Commission 484 F. 2d 820 (1973)

     In Vaughn v. Rosen, another test of FOIA, a district
court set forth specific guidelines for enforcement.   Robert
Vaughn, a law professor researching the Civil Service Commission, sought disclosure under the Freedom of Information
Act of certain government documents, including evaluations
of certain agencies' personnel management programs.   The
Executive Director of the Civil Service Commission claimed
exemptions from disclosure under subsections (b) (2), (5) and
(6).   Vaughn brought suit.

The district court established some standards for interpreting the Act. Under the present system, enforcement was hampered by certain barriers. First, the current method of resolving disputes actually encouraged the government to contend that large amounts of information were exempt, when in fact part of the data was subject to disclosure. Clearly, there were "no inherent incentives that would affirmatively spur government agencies to disclose information." Second, since the burden of determining the justification of a government claim of exemption ultimately fell on the court system, there was "an innate impetus that encourages agencies automatically to claim the broadest possible grounds for exemption for the greatest amount of information." The court then set standards that were designed to eliminate these barriers to effective operation of the Act.

1. Detailed Justification--Courts would no longer accept conclusionary and generalized allegations of exemptions, but would require a relatively detailed analysis of the situation.

2. Specificity, Separation, and Indexing--In a large document, the agency had to specify in detail which portions of the document were considered disclosable and which were allegedly exempt.

3. Adequate Adversary Testing--A trial court could designate a special master to examine documents and evaluate claims of exemption. This person would assume much of the burden of examining and evaluating documents that currently fell on the trial judge.

The case was remanded for additional proceedings consistent with these standards.

Administrator, Federal Aviation Administration
v. Robertson 422 U. S. 255 (1975)

In 1975, a test of exemption three of FOIA reached the U. S. Supreme Court. Reuben Robertson, III, requested the Federal Aviation Administration (FAA) to make available Systems Worthiness Analysis Program Reports, which consisted of the FAA's analyses of the operation and maintenance performance of commercial airlines. Section 1104 of the

Federal Aviation Act of 1958 permitted the FAA Administrator, upon receiving an objection to public disclosure, to withhold disclosure when in the Administrator's judgment it was not required in the public's interest. The Administrator declined to make the reports available upon receiving an objection from the Air Transport Association, which claimed that confidentiality was necessary for the effectiveness of the program. Robertson sued, claiming the records were non-exempt under the Freedom of Information Act.

The U. S. Supreme Court, in an opinion prepared by Chief Justice Warren Burger, noted that exemption three, which prohibited the disclosure of "matters specifically exempted from disclosure by statute," was ambiguously worded and lacked clear standards for application. The Court felt that if "specifically" was meant to apply only to documents specified--either by naming them precisely or by identifying the category into which they fell--such an interpretation would require of Congress a virtually impossible task. The Court also indicated that the FOIA had not repealed any existing statutes that restricted public access to specific government records. Congress had vested in the FAA the power to withhold from public disclosure information that, in the judgment of the Administrator, would adversely affect the public interest. The Court concluded (7-2) that, in this case, the records were exempt from disclosure under exemption three.

In 1976, Congress amended exemption three, acknowledging that matter could be exempted from disclosure when a statute required the matter to be withheld from the public, established particular criteria for withholding the matter, or referred to particular types of information to be withheld. As amended, the Court cannot give exemption three as broad an interpretation as it did in Robertson.

Alfred A. Knopf, Inc. v. Colby 509 F. 2d 1362 (1975)

The 1974 FOIA amendments designated specific actions courts could take. In a 1975 case, a court refused to take such action. A former employee of the State Department, who had bound himself not to disclose classified information acquired during the course of his employment, prepared the manuscript of a book that Alfred A. Knopf, Inc., intended to publish. The CIA objected to the publication, arguing that much of the material was classified information.

The court noted that the October, 1974, FOIA amendments specifically provided that the judge could examine the contents of agency records in camera to determine whether such records could be withheld under any of the FOIA exemptions. In this case the court noted:

> There is a presumption of regularity in the performance by a public official of his public duty. The presumption of regularity supports the official acts of public officers, and, in the absence of clear evidence to the contrary, courts presume that they have properly discharged their official duties.

Satisfied in the "presumption of regularity," the court rejected Knopf's request that the materials be examined in private to see if they had been classified properly.

This section considered the Freedom of Information Act, its amendments, and court interpretations. In the 1953 Reynolds case, the Court upheld the government's claim of privilege to refuse disclosure of information in the interest of national security. Since that time, the Freedom of Information Act of 1966, amendments to that measure in 1974 and 1976, and court interpretations of FOIA in Mink, Vaughn, and Robertson have slowly shaped a public freedom of information. In the process, the power of enforcing FOIA has been placed largely with the courts. Recently, however, in Knopf, the court refused to exercise that power. It appears that information will become accessible under FOIA only when court judges assume their responsibility for assuring such access.

Executive Privilege

The U. S. Supreme Court acknowledged the concept of executive privilege in 1802. In Marbury v. Madison, the Court held that the President did not have to reveal matters communicated to him in confidence.

> By the Constitution of the U. S., the President is invested with certain important political powers, in the exercise of which he is to use his own discretion, and is accountable only to the country in his political character and to his own conscience.

Throughout history, this concept has been expanded and has

been called upon by various Presidents.   Recently, the concept has been discussed by the courts in several cases involving President Richard Nixon.

Nixon v. Sirica 487 F. 2d 700 (1973)

On July 23, 1973, at the recommendation of Special
Prosecutor Archibald Cox, a subpoena was issued by Judge
John Sirica calling upon President Nixon to produce tape recordings of specific meetings and telephone conversations between himself and his advisors.   Nixon declined.   He appealed.   The issue in the case was whether the President could,
at his sole discretion, disobey the subpoena and thereby withhold relevant evidence in his possession from a grand jury
investigation.   The President specifically argued that Judge
Sirica lacked jurisdiction to order submission of the tapes for
inspection because, first, the President was immune from
compulsory court process, and second, executive privilege
was absolute regarding presidential communications.

The court examined both of Nixon's arguments.   First,
the court held that the President was not above the law.   The
people did not forfeit through election the right to have the
law applied to any citizen.   Second, concerning executive privilege, the court noted that if the President's claim to absolute
privilege was affirmed, the President could deny access to
all documents in Executive departments and thereby nullify
the intent of the Freedom of Information Act.   In this case,
the confidentiality privilege had to recede before the grand
jury's showing of need.   The court felt that in camera judicial inspection was an appropriate manner of protecting the
grand jury's purpose of obtaining relevant evidence.   Any
interference with the President's confidentiality privilege depended solely on the grand jury's ability to demonstrate the
relevancy of the evidence to its investigation.   During the
hearings, "privileged" material could be deleted so that only
"unprivileged" matter would go to the grand jury.   According to the court, executive privilege was not absolute.   A
year later, the U. S. Supreme Court reached the same conclusion.

United States v. Nixon 418 U. S. 683 (1974)

On March 1, 1974, a District of Columbia federal
grand jury indicted former Attorney General John Mitchell

and six other persons for conspiracy to defraud the United States and for obstruction of justice. The charges stemmed from the cover-up of the Watergate incident. The grand jury also named President Nixon as an unindicated co-conspirator. Soon thereafter, at the request of Special Prosecutor Leon Jaworski, Judge John Sirica directed a subpoena toward the President to produce certain tape recordings of conversations with specific advisors on particular dates that were relevant to the trials of the Watergate conspirators. On April 30, Nixon released to the public edited transcripts of forty-three conversations, twenty of which had been subpoenaed. The President refused to release additional material and asserted that the court had exceeded its authority since the controversy was an internal dispute between a superior officer and his subordinate within the Executive Branch, and because any judicial action was precluded by the claim of executive privilege.

The case came to the U. S. Supreme Court, which ruled (8-0) against Nixon. The Court noted that Nixon did not claim executive privilege on the ground that the tapes involved military or diplomatic secrets. Rather, Nixon had declined releasing the tapes on the claim of absolute executive privilege. The Court recognized that, in the matter of criminal justice, "the very integrity of the judicial system and public confidence in the system depend on full disclosure of all the facts, within the framework of the rules of evidence. " In weighing the importance of the privilege of confidentiality of Presidential communications against the fair administration of criminal justice, the Court concluded that

> when the ground for asserting privilege as to subpoenaed materials sought for use in a criminal trial is based only on the generalized interest in confidentiality, it cannot prevail over the fundamental demands of due process of law in the fair administration of criminal justice. The generalized assertion of privilege must yield to the demonstrated, specific need for evidence in a pending criminal trial.

In this case, the Court indicated that absolute privilege could be claimed when the information related to military or diplomatic secrets. When other kinds of information were involved, the need for privilege had to be weighed against the need for the information. The Court ordered that the subpoenaed materials be made available to the district court to determine by in camera inspection what evidence would be potentially relevant to the conduct of the trial.

Nixon v. Administrator of General Services 433 U. S. 425 (1977)

After Richard Nixon resigned as President, he made a depository agreement with the General Services Administration for the storage of 42 million documents and 880 tape recordings accumulated during his tenure in office. The agreement detailed conditions of access to the materials and provided for the eventual destruction of the tape recordings. Three months later, Congress passed the Presidential Recordings and Materials Preservation Act, which directed the Administrator of the GSA to 1) take custody of the materials, 2) screen the materials and return to the former President those that were personal and private in nature, 3) preserve materials of historical value, and 4) maintain the availability of any materials for possible use in judicial proceedings. The Administrator was also directed to draw up regulations regarding public access to the materials, taking into consideration guidelines specified by the Act. Nixon sued in federal court, alleging that the act violated the separation of powers, executive privilege, personal privacy, and First Amendment guarantees of freedom of association. The case ultimately reached the U. S. Supreme Court, which, in the opinion prepared by Justice William Brennan, analyzed each of Nixon's arguments.

The Court rejected Nixon's claim that the Act's regulation of the disposition of Presidential materials violated the principle of separation of powers. Actually, the control over the materials remained in the Executive Branch. The Administrator of the General Services Administration was an official appointed by the President. Statutory justification existed in the Freedom of Information Act for the required disclosure of documents in the possession of the Executive Branch.

The Court then turned to the alleged violation of executive privilege. Nixon based his claim on the assertion that the potential disclosure of communications given to the President in confidence would adversely affect the ability of future Presidents to obtain the candid advice necessary for effective decision making. However, the Court had to adjudicate that claim only as it applied to the screening and cataloging of the materials by professional archivists since any eventual public access would be governed by guidelines established by the Presidential Recordings and Materials Preservation Act--guidelines designed to protect any constitutionally based executive privilege. According to the Court:

> The screening constitutes a very limited intrusion
> by personnel in the Executive Branch sensitive to
> executive concerns. These very personnel have
> performed the identical task in each of the Presi-
> dential libraries without any suggestion that such
> activity has in any way interfered with executive
> confidentiality.

Furthermore, the legitimate purpose of the Act was

> to preserve the materials for legitimate historical
> and governmental purposes. An incumbent Presi-
> dent should not be dependent on happenstance or
> the whim of a prior President when he seeks ac-
> cess to records of past decisions that define or
> channel current governmental obligations. Nor
> should the American people's ability to reconstruct
> and come to terms with their history be truncated
> by an analysis of Presidential privilege that focuses
> only on the needs of the present.

The Court concluded that the screening process contemplated
by the Act would not constitute a more severe intrusion into
Presidential confidentiality than the in camera inspection by
the district court approved in United States v. Nixon.

Concerning the alleged invasion of privacy, the Court
reasoned that the proportion of the 42 million pages of documents and 880 tape recordings involving Nixon's privacy interests was minimal because the major portion of the materials
related to Nixon's conduct as President and were therefore
materials of considerable public interest. Nixon could not
claim any privacy rights as to documents and tape recordings
that he had already disclosed to the public. The Court noted
that the Act did not authorize a general search and seizure
of all Nixon's papers, but rather it provided procedures expressly for the purpose of minimizing the intrusion into
Nixon's private and personal materials.

Nixon also argued that the Act violated the First
Amendment freedoms of associational privacy and political
speech. Nixon claimed that as President he has served as
head of his national political party and spent time on partisan
political matters. Records relating to his political activities
could not be screened without violating the First Amendment.
In response, the Court noted that "only a fraction of the
materials can be said to raise a First Amendment claim. "

Again, the Act's screening procedures safeguarded the President's papers from such an intrusion. In <u>Nixon v. Administrator of General Services,</u> the Court supported a limited interpretation of the doctrine of executive privilege and confidentiality of Presidential communications. The Court upheld (7-2) the constitutionality of the Presidential Recordings and Materials Preservation Act. In this case, as in <u>Nixon v. Sirica</u> and <u>U. S. v. Nixon,</u> the courts ruled that executive privilege was not absolute.

<u>Nixon v. Warner Communications, Inc. 435 U. S. 589 (1978)</u>

In a recent case, the Court refused to release Nixon's tapes for commercial use. On July 16, 1973, testimony before the Senate Select Committee on Presidential Campaign Activities revealed that President Nixon tape-recorded conversations in the White House Oval Office. A week later, the Watergate Special Prosecutor subpoenaed Nixon to produce tapes of eight meetings and one telephone conversation. In March, 1974, a grand jury indicted seven individuals for conspiring to obstruct justice in connection with the investigation of the 1972 burglary of the Democratic National Committee headquarters. In preparation for this trial, the Special Prosecutor subpoenaed Nixon to produce tape recordings and documents relating to sixty-four Presidential meetings and conversations. During the course of the trial, twenty-two hours of taped conversations were played for the jury and the public in the courtroom. The district court furnished the jurors, reporters, and members of the public in attendance with earphones and with written transcripts. Six weeks after the trial had begun, Warner Communications sought permission to copy, broadcast, and sell to the public the portions of the tapes played at the trial. In April, 1975, Judge Sirica denied Warner Communications' petition for immediate access to the tapes. Such access might

> result in the manufacture of permanent phonograph records and tape recordings, perhaps with commentary by entertainers; marketing of the tapes would probably involve mass merchandising techniques designed to generate excitement in an air of ridicule to stimulate sales.

The court of appeals reversed. It stressed the importance of the common-law privilege to inspect and copy judicial records. In the court's view, the mere possibility of prejudice to defendants' rights in the event of a retrial did not outweigh the public's right of access. The district court had "abused its discretion in allowing those diminished interests in confidentiality to interfere with the public's right to inspect and copy the tapes." The case reached the U.S. Supreme Court.

The Court noted that the right to inspect and copy judicial records is not absolute. Every court has supervisory power over its own records, and access can be denied where court files might become a vehicle for improper purposes. Nixon challenged the accuracy of any reproduction of the tapes. He emphasized that the tapes required twenty-two hours to be played. If they were commercially recorded, only fractions of the tapes, necessarily taken out of context, would be presented. Nor would there be any safeguard against distortion through cutting, erasing, and splicing of tapes. Nixon insisted that such use would infringe his privacy, resulting in embarrassment and anguish to himself. The Court examined the procedures established by the Presidential Recordings and Materials Preservation Act, noting that it created a centralized custodian for the preservation and "orderly processing" of Nixon's historical materials. Immediate release of the tapes to Warner Communications would probably violate such safeguards.

Warner Communications then argued that release of the tapes was required by the First Amendment guarantee of free press. The Court, however, noted that the contents of the tapes were given wide publicity by all elements of the media. The issue was not whether the press had been denied access to information that the public had a right to know, but whether copies of the tapes--to which the public had never had physical access-should be made available for copying. The Court emphasized that the First Amendment "generally grants the press no right to information about a trial superior to that of the general public." The Court refused (7-2) to release the tapes to Warner Communications.

On the basis of cases examined in this chapter, it seems that the courts are considerably more reluctant to uphold the freedom to gather news than they are willing to protect the freedom to publish. In the first half of this chapter, several cases indicated the Court's desire to preserve the freedom of newspapers to publish. The Court has not shown an equal enthusiasm for the freedom to gather news. The Branzburg ruling clearly rejected the notion of a national journalist's privilege. Interpretation of state shield laws, as in <u>Lightman</u>, <u>Bridge</u>, <u>Dan</u>, <u>Proskin</u>, and <u>Farr</u> has tended to be narrow, requiring reporters to comply with court rulings. In <u>Pell</u> and <u>Saxbe</u>, the Court denied the press any special access to prisoners. Congress, by enacting and amending the Freedom of Information Act, has made information more accessible to the public. While the courts have been granted considerable enforcement power for FOIA, in <u>Knopf</u> the court refused to use that power. Recently, in three cases involving Richard Nixon, the courts ruled that executive privilege is not absolute, and in so doing, restricted exemption five of the FOIA. In <u>Nixon v. Warner Communications</u>, the Court ruled that, under the First Amendment, the press had no right to information about a trial superior to that of the general public. Overall, the Court has made certain information accessible to the public but has refused to grant news reporters the unqualified freedom to gather news.

Bibliography

Books

Francois, William E. <u>Mass Media Law and Regulation</u>. 2nd ed. Columbus, Ohio: Grid, 1978.

Hachten, William A. <u>The Supreme Court on Freedom of the Press: Decisions and Dissents</u>. Ames: Iowa State University Press, 1968.

Schmidt, Benno C., Jr. <u>Freedom of the Press vs. Public Access</u>. New York: Praeger, 1976.

Shapiro, Martin, ed. <u>The Pentagon Papers and the Courts: A Study in Foreign Policy-Making and Freedom of the Press.</u> San Francisco: Chandler, 1972.

Smith, James M. <u>Freedom's Fetters</u>. Ithaca, N.Y.: Cornell University Press, 1956.

Articles

Bennett, Richard V. "<u>Branzburg v. Hayes</u>--Must Newsmen Reveal Their Confidential Sources to Grand Juries?," <u>Wake Forest Law Review</u> 8 (October, 1972), 567-80.

Goodale, James C. "Branzburg v. Hayes and the Developing Qualified Privilege for Newsmen, " Hastings Law Journal 26 (January, 1975), 709-43.

Gorski, James M. "Access to Information? Exemptions from Disclosure Under the Freedom of Information Act and the Privacy Act of 1974, " Willamette Law Journal 13 (Winter, 1976), 135-71.

Teplitzky, Sanford V. , and Kenneth A. Weiss. "Newsman's Privilege Two Years After Branzburg v. Hayes: The First Amendment in Jeopardy, " Tulane Law Review 49 (January, 1975), 417-38.

Cases

Administrator, Federal Aviation Administration v. Robertson 422 U. S. 255 (1975)

Alfred A. Knopf, Inc. v. Colby 509 F. 2d 1362 (1975)

American Civil Liberties Union, Inc. v. Jennings 366 F. Supp. 1041 (1973)

Associated Press v. United States; Tribune Company v. United States 326 U. S. 1 (1945)

Baker v. F. & F. Investment 470 F. 2d 778 (1972)

Bay Guardian Company v. Chronicle Publishing Company 344 F. Supp. 1155 (1972)

Borreca v. Fasi 369 F. Supp. 906 (1974)

Branzburg v. Hayes; In the Matter of Pappas: United States v. Caldwell 408 U. S. 665 (1972)

Bursey v. United States 466 F. 2d 1059 (1972)

Citizen Publishing Company v. United States 394 U. S. 131 (1969)

Democratic National Committee v. McCord; In re Bernstein 356 F. Supp. 1394 (1973)

Dow Jones & Company, Inc. v. Superior Court 303 N. E. 2d 849 (1973)

Environmental Protection Agency v. Mink 410 U. S. 73 (1973)

Epstein v. Resor 421 F. 2d 930 (1970)

Farr v. Superior Court of the State of California, County of Los Angeles 99 Cal. Rptr. 342 (1971)

Forcade v. Knight 416 F. Supp. 1025 (1976)

Grosjean v. American Press Company, Inc. 297 U. S. 233 (1936)

Hannegan v. Esquire, Inc. 327 U. S. 146 (1946)

Houchins v. KQED, Inc. 438 U. S. 1 (1978)

In re Bridge 295 A. 2d 3 (1972)

In re Farr 111 Cal. Rptr. 649 (1974)

Lamont v. Postmaster General: Fixa v. Heilberg 381 U. S. 301 (1965)

Lewis Publishing Company v. Morgan; Journal of Commerce & Commercial Bulletin v. Burleson 229 U. S. 288 (1913)

Lightman v. State of Maryland 294 A. 2d 149 (1972)

Lorain Journal Company v. United States 342 U. S. 143 (1951)

Marbury v. Madison 1 U. S. 137 (1802)

Maryland and Virginia Milk Producers Association, Inc. v. United States 362 U. S. 458 (1960)

Miami Herald Publishing Company v. Tornillo 418 U. S. 298 (1974)

Mills v. State of Alabama 384 U. S. 214 (1966)

Milwaukee Social Democrat Publishing Company v. Burleson 255 U. S. 407 (1921)

Near v. State of Minnesota 283 U. S. 697 (1931)

New York Times Company v. United States; United States v. Washington Post Company 403 U. S. 713 (1971)

Nixon v. Administrator of General Services 433 U. S. 425 (1977)

Nixon v. Sirica 487 F. 2d 700 (1973)

Nixon v. Warner Communications, Inc. 435 U. S. 589 (1978)

Pell v. Procunier; Procunier v. Hillery 417 U. S. 817 (1974)

People v. Dan 41 App. Div. 2d 687 (1973)

Saxbe v. Washington Post Company 417 U. S. 843 (1974)

Times-Mirror Company v. United States 390 U. S. 712 (1968)

Times-Picayune Publishing Company v. United States 345 U. S. 594 (1953)

U. S. v. Liddy 354 F. Supp. 208 (1972)

United States v. Nixon 418 U. S. 683 (1974)

United States v. Reynolds 345 U. S. 1 (1953)

Vaughn v. Rosen, Executive Director, United States Civil Service Commission 484 F. 2d 820 (1973)

WBAI-FM v. Proskin 42 App. Div. 2d 5 (1973)

CHAPTER VII

BROADCASTING

In an age when new and better systems of communication are constantly being developed, social and cultural differences between nations have been steadily eroded. Relationships among peoples have grown increasingly complex. As the world progresses from the tribal isolation of years past to the organic unity of a global community, the bonds of international interdependence multiply and strengthen. The increased effectiveness and complexity of communication that has occurred within the past half-century have been met by a multitude of laws and regulations. The broadcasting media in particular have become so important and pervasive that the government has recognized the necessity for regulation.

HISTORY OF REGULATION

From its outset, government regulation of broadcasting has been and will continue to be based ostensibly on the public interest, convenience, and necessity. In this section, the history of broadcast regulation will be traced from its formulation to the present time.

Regulation of Radio

When the radio was first introduced at the turn of the century, there were no problems requiring government intervention. Not many people owned a radio or attempted broadcasting on their own. By 1912, however, electrical interference from stations using the same frequency required congressional action.

Radio Act of 1912

The Radio Act of 1912 placed radio licensing under the

control of the Secretary of Commerce and Labor. Electrical interference was avoided by giving each station a separate call number. In applying for a license, each station had to specify its 1) ownership, 2) location, 3) purpose, 4) hours of operation, and 5) authorized frequency. Once allowed to broadcast, the station had to be continuously supervised by an authorized agent. Violators were subject to imprisonment and a fine not to exceed $500. Section 2 of the Act provided that the President, in time of war or public peril, could close any station or authorize use of a station by the government with just compensation of the owners. Section 4 listed a total of twenty regulations relating to appropriate wavelengths, broadcasting of distress signals, division of time, uses of power, secrecy of messages, and broadcasting control of vicinities. Though soon to become obsolete due to the increased use of radio, the Act was one of the first instances of government regulation of mass communication. Americans, however, were reluctant to accept widespread intrusion by the government into the traditionally inviolate domain of communication. The Supreme Court, generally reflecting this laissez-faire philosophy, was at first hesitant to grant the Secretary of Commerce broad discretion in radio licensing.

Hoover v. Intercity Radio Company, Inc. 286 F. 1003 (1923)

One of the first court interpretations of the Radio Act occurred in 1923. Intercity Radio Company was licensed in 1920 for one year under the Radio Act of 1912. The following year, Secretary of Commerce Herbert Hoover refused to renew the license because he was unable to assign a wavelength that would not interfere with government and private stations. Hoover claimed that issuing or refusing a license was left solely to his discretion.

The court disagreed. The duty of assigning a wavelength was "mandatory upon the Secretary." The only discretionary act left to the Secretary was to select a wavelength that would result in the least possible interference. Issuing of a license was not dependent upon the fixing of a wavelength. According to the court, "the duty of issuing licenses to persons or corporations coming within the classification designated in the act reposed no discretion whatever in the Secretary of Commerce. The duty is mandatory."

Radio Act of 1927

Obviously, as more and more stations began to broadcast, the standard of "least possible interference" became impractical. So, Congress passed the Radio Act of 1927. The primary purpose of the legislation was to regulate all forms of interstate and foreign radio transmissions and communications. Dividing the United States into five geographic zones, the Act created a Federal Radio Commission composed of five commissioners appointed for six-year terms by the President. Each Commissioner represented a different zone and not more than three could be from the same political party. The Commission was to regulate broadcasting "as public convenience, interest or necessity requires." The numerous duties of the Commission included: 1) classifying radio stations as to power ratings, 2) prescribing the nature of service to be rendered by each class and each station within a class, 3) assigning wavelengths to stations, 4) determining station locations, 5) regulating the apparatus to be used, 6) preventing electrical interference, 7) establishing areas to be served by each station, 8) regulating stations involved in chain (network) broadcasting, 9) establishing regulations governing records that a station must keep, and 10) holding meetings to investigate stations regarding their performance.

One year from the passage of the Act, all powers vested in the Commission except the power to revoke licenses reverted to the Secretary of Commerce. Several of the more important duties included: 1) issuing licenses to qualified individuals or groups, 2) referring all applications for licenses or renewal to the Commission, 3) referring any disputes or protests to the Commission, 4) prescribing qualifications of station operators and delineating their duties, 5) suspending licenses for up to two years when a specific regulation was violated, 6) inspecting transmission facilities for compliance with federal requirements, 7) designating call letters for all radio stations, and 8) publishing relevant announcements and data as is necessary for efficient station operation. Ultimate authority rested with the Commission. Any party or organization aggrieved by an action by the Secretary could appeal to the Commission. In addition, any station the application of which was refused had the right to appeal to the Court of Appeals of the District of Columbia. All potential or incumbent licensees were afforded strict procedural safeguards, including the opportunity to be heard at a formal hearing. In all cases, the license was granted for no longer than three years. Licenses were to be automatically denied to any station attempting illegally to monopolize radio communication.

Moreover, licenses were granted only conditionally. The Commission retained discretion to revoke licenses when the station made false statements, used profane, obscene, or indecent language, or failed to operate substantially within the limitations set forth by the license.

The Act retained many of the essential features of the 1912 Act, including the special privileges of government stations and the right of the President in time of national peril to authorize the use of broadcasting facilities. As under the 1912 Act, no person could transmit a false signal of distress. Violators of any regulation were subject to imprisonment and a $500 fine. The Act, however, included new areas of station operation that were subject to government control. Section 18, for example, was a prototype of the "Equal Time Doctrine" concerning political broadcasts. According to the Act,

> ... if any licensee shall permit any person who is a legally qualified candidate for any public office to use a broadcasting station, he shall afford equal opportunities to all other such candidates for that office.

The Act also specified that any broadcast by a station for which money or other consideration was paid had to be properly identified. The name of the person or company had to be announced during or after the broadcast. Though the Act gave the government significant power to regulate radio communication, it specifically banned any form of censorship or prior restraint by the licensing authority.

For the next four years the Federal Radio Commission went about its work quietly and without major incident. Its ultimate authority to license stations in the public interest, convenience, and necessity was largely unquestioned. Not until 1931 was this authority tested before the courts.

KFKB Broadcasting Association, Inc. v. Federal Radio Commission 47 F. 2d 670 (1931)

KFKB, a radio station located in Milford, Kansas, was first licensed by the Secretary of Commerce on September 20, 1923, in the name of the Brinkley-Jones Hospital Association, and intermittently operated until June 3, 1925. In 1926, it was relicensed to Dr. J. R. Brinkley. In early

1930, the station filed for renewal of its license. Upon consideration of evidence presented at a hearing, the Commission found that public interest, convenience, or necessity would not be served by granting the application. The Commission denied renewal. The evidence tended to show that Brinkley, founder of Station KFKB, the Brinkley Hospital, and the Brinkley Pharmaceutical Association, controlled the policy of the station. The hospital paid the station from $5,000 to $7,000 per month for advertising. Each day, Brinkley broadcast three half-hour programs entitled the "Medical Question Box." Without ever personally diagnosing the callers, Brinkley prescribed patent medicines produced by his drug company. The Commission noted that the practice of physicians prescribing treatment for patients they have never seen, and basing their diagnosis upon what symptoms may be recited by the patients in a letter, "is inimical to the public health and safety, and for that reason is not in the public interest." The Commission held that

> the testimony in this case shows conclusively that the operation of Station KFKB is conducted only in the personal interest of Dr. John R. Brinkley. While it is to be expected that a license of a radio broadcasting station will receive some remuneration for serving the public with radio programs, at the same time the interest of the listening public is paramount, and may not be subordinated to the interests of the station licensee.

KFKB appealed the decision to the Court of Appeals, District of Columbia.

The court unanimously affirmed the Commission's decision. The court argued that such radio broadcasting was a form of interstate commerce and was therefore subject to government regulation. The court also ruled that the burden was upon the applicant to show that such renewal would be in the public interest, convenience, and necessity. Generally accepting the Commission's findings, the court provided the first judicial support and acknowledgement of the Commission's right to consider a station's past programming with relation to the public interest, convenience, and necessity.

Trinity Methodist Church, South v. Federal
Radio Commission 62 F. 2d 850 (1932)

One year later, the court of appeals strengthened its

position taken in the Brinkley case. Trinity Methodist Church, South was the lessee and operator of the Los Angeles radio station KGEF. The station had been in operation for several years. The Commission's findings showed that, though in the name of the church, the station was in fact owned by the Reverend Doctor Shuler and its operation was dominated by him. In September, 1930, KGEF filed an application for renewal of its station license. Numerous citizens of Los Angeles protested, and the Commission, unable to determine that public interest, convenience, and necessity would be served, denied the application for renewal. Some of the factors urging it to this conclusion were that the station had been used to attack the Roman Catholic Church, that the broadcasts by Dr. Shuler were sensational rather than instructive, and that in two instances Shuler had been convicted of attempting in his radio talks to obstruct the orderly administration of public justice. Specifically, Shuler attacked the integrity of many members of the judiciary and bar. He made defamatory statements against the Board of Health. He charged that the Los Angeles Labor Temple was a bootlegging and gambling joint. In addition, he attacked Jews and Roman Catholics. His numerous defamations were of his own sentiments and were not provable. Appealing the decision, KGEF argued that the Commission's decision was unconstitutional in that it violated the guarantee of free speech and deprived the station of property without due process of law.

The court disagreed. Again the court affirmed the authority of government to regulate broadcasting.

> Everyone interested in radio legislation approved the principle of limiting the number of broadcasting stations, or, perhaps, it would be more nearly correct to say, recognized the inevitable necessity. In these circumstances Congress intervened and asserted its paramount authority, and, if it be admitted, as we think it must be, that, in the present condition of the science with its limited facilities, the regulatory provisions of the Radio Act are a reasonable exercise by Congress of its powers, the exercise of these powers is no more restricted by the First Amendment than are the police powers of the States under the Fourteenth Amendment.

The court reaffirmed earlier rulings that established broadcasting as an instance of interstate commerce. Most importantly, it rejected Shuler's claims that First Amendment privileges were abridged. Though individuals can legitimately claim constitutional protection from prior restraints on expression, the continued use of a public radio station as a forum for personal sentiments was not guaranteed. The court also rejected Shuler's claim that he was deprived of property without due process of law. The court ruled that injury merely incidental to the legitimate exercise of government powers for the public good does not apply under the Constitution. The authority of government to license radio broadcasting in the public interest was firmly established in the KFKB and Trinity Methodist cases. Legitimate good-faith actions by the Commission were upheld. In effect, Federal Radio Commission rulings attained presumptive validity.

Regualtion of Broadcast Media

By 1934, government regulation of broadcasting had been largely accepted by all segments of society. The products of communication technology had become widely accessible to the general public. During the Depression years, the vast majority of American families owned at least one radio. Television, first demonstrated in 1920, was soon to become a major force in the American way of life. Congress, aware of the increasing complexity of broadcasting, modified the 1927 Radio Act. The expanding activities and responsibilities of the Radio Commission required a more timely and realistic elucidation than that provided in previous legislation.

Federal Communications Act of 1934

The Federal Communications Act of 1934, based largely on the 1912 and 1927 acts, became the basis of modern broadcast regulation. The Radio Commission was replaced by a seven-member Federal Communications Commission. The Commission's chairman and members were to be appointed by the President for seven-year terms. The Commission, in effect, had been granted semiautonomous status and exclusive authority to regulate the broadcasting industry. The Secretary of Commerce was divested of any real authority in Commission activities. Penalties for violators were increased to a maximum of $10,000 and/or one year imprisonment. The Commission retained all of the responsibilities and powers enunciated in the 1927 act and was, in addition, provided with more effective means of enforcement.

Chain Broadcasting--The emergence of chain, or network, broadcasting presented the Commission with one of its
first major challenges. Chain broadcasting was defined in
the Communications Act of 1934 as the "simultaneous broadcasting of an identical program by two or more connected
stations. " In 1938, the Federal Communications Commission
began an investigation to determine whether special regulations
applicable to radio stations engaged in chain broadcasting were
required in the "public interest, convenience, or necessity. "

National Broadcasting Company v. United States
Columbia Broadcasting System, Inc. v. United
States 319 U. S. 190 (1943)

On May 2, 1941, the findings were published in the
Commission's Report on Chain Broadcasting. The Commission
found that at the end of 1938 there were 660 commercial stations in the United States and that 341 of those were affiliated
with national networks. Some 135 stations were affiliated
exclusively with the National Broadcasting Company, which
operated two national networks called the "Red" and the "Blue. "
NBC was also the licensee of ten stations, including seven
that operated on "clear" channels with the maximum power
available--50 kilowatts. In addition, NBC operated five other
stations, four of which had power of 50 kilowatts, under management contracts with their licensees. Some 120 stations
were affiliated exclusively with the Columbia Broadcasting
System. CBS was the licensee of eight stations, seven of
which were clear-channel stations. Seventy-four stations
were under exclusive affiliation with the Mutual Broadcasting
System. Moreover, twenty-five stations were affiliated with
both NBC and Mutual, and five with both CBS and Mutual.
These figures, the Commission noted, did not accurately reflect the relative prominence of the three companies, since
the stations affiliated with Mutual were generally inferior in
frequency, power, and coverage. The report pointed out
that the stations affiliated with the national networks utilized
more than 97 percent of the total nighttime broadcasting power
of all the stations in the country. NBC and CBS together
controlled more than 85 percent of the total nighttime wattage,
and the broadcast business of the three national networks
amounted to almost half of the total business of all stations
in the United States.

The Commission recognized that network broadcasting
had played and would continue to play an important part in the
development of radio.

Chain broadcasting makes possible a wider reception for expensive entertainment and cultural programs, and also for programs of national or regional significance which would otherwise have coverage only in the locality of origin.

In addition, "access to greatly enlarged audiences made possible by chain broadcasting has been a strong incentive to advertisers to finance the production of expensive programs. "

The Commission discovered network abuses that it felt were in its power to remedy: 1) Exclusive affiliation of station. The Commission found that the network affiliation agreements between NBC and CBS usually contained a provision that prevented the station from broadcasting the programs of another network. The effect was to hinder the growth of new networks. 2) Territorial exclusivity. Networks bound themselves not to sell programs to any other station in the same area. The effect of this agreement, designed to protect the affiliate from the competition of other stations serving the same territory, was to deprive the listening public of many programs that might otherwise be available. 3) Term of affiliation. The standard NBC and CBS affiliation contracts bound the station for a period of five years, with the network having the exclusive right to terminate the contracts upon one year's notice. The Commission, citing section 307 (d) of the 1934 act, noted that no license could be granted for a term longer than three years. 4) Option time. The Commission found that network affiliation contracts usually contained "network optional time" clauses. Under these provisions, the network could, upon twenty-eight days notice, call upon its affiliates to carry a commercial program during any of the hours specified in the agreement as "network optional time. " For CBS affiliates, network optional time meant the entire broadcast day. The Commission argued that these provisions created serious obstacles for new networks and hindered stations in developing local programming. 5) Right to reject programs. The Commission found that most network contracts contained a clause defining the right of the station to reject network commercial programs that would not be in the public interest, convenience, and necessity. As a practical matter, the licensee often could not determine in advance whether any particular network program would be in the public interest. In practice, stations delegated to the networks a large part of their programming function. It was the station, though, not the network, that was licensed to serve the public interest. 6) Network ownership of station. The Commission found that the eighteen stations owned by NBC and CBS were among the most powerful and superior in the country, and were permanently inaccessible to competing networks. The Commission thought it was contrary to the public interest for networks to own stations in areas where available facilities were so few or of such unequal coverage that competition would thereby be substantially restricted. 7) <u>Control by networks of station rates</u>. Under this agreement, the station could not sell time to a national advertiser for less than it cost the advertiser to buy the time from the network. Clearly, such network domination of advertising pricing policy was not in the public interest.

On October 30, 1941, the networks sought to enjoin the enforcement of the regulations, arguing that the FCC had exceeded its authority. According to the U. S. Supreme Court, the provisions of the Federal Communications Act precluded the notion that the Commission was empowered to deal only with technical and engineering impediments to the larger and more effective use of radio in the public interest. The Court went on to note:

> With the number of radio channels limited by natural factors, the public interest demands that those who are entrusted with the available channels shall make the fullest and most effective use of them. If a licensee enters into a contract with a network organization which limits his ability to make the best use of the radio facility assigned him, he is not serving the public interest.

The network also argued that the First Amendment was violated. But, according to the Court, "unlike other modes of expression, radio inherently is not available to all. That is its unique characteristic. " That was why radio was subject to government regulation. Because it could not be used by all, "some who wish to use it must be denied. ... " The Court's reasoning was based on the assumption that broadcasting was a limited access medium. As the Court wrote, "Since the spectrum is finite and the frequencies are not available to all who might like them, some regulation is necessary. " The Court stressed that the licensing system established by Congress in the Communications Act of 1934 was a proper exercise of its power over commerce. Thus, a valid denial of a station license on that ground was not a denial of free speech. In <u>NBC</u>, the Court vigorously upheld (5-2) the Commission's authority to regulate network broadcasting in the public interest, convenience, and necessity.

Cable Television--Other more recent challenges to the Commission's authority have occurred in a series of decisions dealing with community antenna television (CATV) regulation. CATV systems receive signals from television broadcasting stations, amplify the signals, transmit them by cable or microwave, and ultimately distribute them to subscriber's receiving units. The systems charge their subscribers installation and miscellaneous fees. Orginally used in sparsely populated areas, CATV has spread rapidly to metropolitan centers. The systems perform either or both of two functions. First, they may supplement broadcasting in a locality by facilitating satisfactory reception of the adjacent stations. Second, they may transmit to subscribers the signals of distant stations. Such importation of distant signals has increasingly become the dominant function of CATV systems. Since the cable television industry merely redistributes signals and does not, in general, produce its own programming, it is not subject to the same FCC regulation as other conventional stations. Most importantly, cable television systems do not have to be licensed by the FCC. Anyone wishing to start a CATV system need only apply to the appropriate municipality for a franchise. In 1962, in the Carter Mountain case, the FCC decided that cable television, though not subject to traditional guidelines, could nonetheless be denied the necessary facilities if operation of the system would provide dangerous competition to license holders to a degree inconsistent with the public interest.

Carter Mountain Transmission Corporation v.
Federal Communications Commission 321 F. 2d 359 (1963)

Carter Mountain Transmission Corporation filed an application with the Federal Communications Commission for permission to construct a microwave radio communication system to transmit signals received from television stations located in several distant cities to CATV systems established in Riverton, Lander, and Thermopolie, Wyoming. The Commission denied Carter Mountain's application, concluding that it would not serve the public interest, convenience, and necessity. The FCC reasoned that to permit Carter Mountain to bring in outside programs for the community antenna systems would result in the "demise" of local television station KWRB-TV, and the loss of service to a substantial rural population not served by the community antenna systems and to many other persons who did not pay the cost of subscribing to the systems. Further, the need for the local outlet outweighed the improved service that the proposed facilities would bring to those who subscribe to the systems. Carter Mountain appealed, arguing that under the criteria applied to common carriers, the Commission was obliged to grant a certificate of convenience and necessity authorizing construction of the requested facilities.

The court of appeals disagreed. In rejecting Carter Mountain's arguments, the court pointed out that competition is a relevant factor in weighing the public interest.

> Federal Communications Commission, in carrying out its obligation to make such distribution of licenses, frequencies and power among the states and communities as to provide a fair, efficient and equitable distribution of service, may weigh the net effect on the community or communities to be served.

In such a weighing, the court agreed with the Commission's finding that a grant of the license would result in the demise of station KWRB-TV, contrary to the public interest. The court felt that the FCC's exercise of power in this case was not capricious or arbitrary, or that it exceeded the FCC's statutory jurisdiction to regulate CATV systems. In 1963, the U. S. Supreme Court denied certiorari. In so doing, the Court expanded the role of regulation into the domain of CATV-- in effect making CATV substantially the same as other broadcasting modes in the eyes of the law.

United States v. Southwestern Cable Company
Midwestern Television, Inc. v. Southwestern
Cable Company 392 U. S. 157 (1968)

In 1968, the Supreme Court confirmed its support for FCC regulation of the cable television industry. Midwestern Television claimed that Southwestern Cable Company, a CATV system, transmitted the signals of Los Angeles broadcasting stations into the San Diego area and thereby had, inconsistent with the public interest, adversely affected Midwestern's San Diego station. Midwestern further claimed that Southwestern's importation of Los Angeles signals had fragmented the San Diego audience, that such fragmentation reduced the advertising revenues of local stations, and that the station would have to eventually terminate or reduce the service provided in the San Diego area by local broadcasting stations. Midwestern

sought an appropriate order limiting the carriage of such signals by Southwestern's systems. The FCC restricted the ex-
pansion of Southwestern's service area to that in effect on
February 15, 1966. On petition for review, the Court of
Appeals for the Ninth Circuit held that the Commission lacked
authority under the Communications Act of 1934 to issue such
an order.

In an important victory for the FCC, the U. S. Supreme
Court overturned (7-0) the decision.

> The Commission has been charged with broader
> responsibilities for the orderly development of an
> appropriate system of local television broadcasting.
> The significance of its effects can scarcely be ex-
> aggerated, for broadcasting is demonstrably a prin-
> cipal source of information and entertainment for a
> great part of the Nation's population. The Com-
> mission has reasonably found that the successful
> performance of these duties demands prompt and
> efficacious regulation of community antenna tele-
> vision systems. . . . We therefore hold that the
> Commission's authority over "all interstate . . .
> communication by wire or radio" permits the reg-
> ulation of CATV systems.

The Court broadly interpreted the type and extent of communication that came under FCC jurisdiction. Another important concern expressed by the Court in this case was that
the ability of CATV to provide many channels to viewers receiving the service conflicted with the emphasis the FCC had
placed on local service programming. The Court stressed
that "the ability of listeners to view channels far from their
homes erodes the audience of the locally based channel and
therefore shrinks its appeal to local advertisers. " By utilizing a pragmatic, economic argument for limited competition,
the Court assured its continued support of incumbent license
holders who by their past performance have indicated their
concern for the public interest. The Court not only upheld
the authority of the FCC to regulate cable television under
the Federal Communications Act of 1934 and the commerce
clause, but also showed its approval for the local programming requirement.

United States v. Midwest Video Corporation 406 U. S. 649 (1972)

On October 24, 1969, the Federal Communications

Commission adopted a rule providing that

> no CATV system having 3, 500 or more subscribers
> shall carry the signal of any television broadcast
> station unless the system also operates to a signi-
> ficant extent as a local outlet by cablecasting and
> has available facilities for local production and pre-
> sentation of programs other than automated services.

Obviously, such a regulation was open to diverse interpretations. To provide some reasonable understanding of its outer
limits, certain key terms must be defined. Operation to a
"significant extent, " for example, means something more
than the origination of automated services (i. e. , time, weather, news, and stock tickers) and aural services (i. e. , music
and announcements). "Cablecasting" is programming distributed on a CATV system that has been originated by the CATV
operator or by another entity exclusive of broadcast signals
carried on the system. Cablecasting may include not only
programs produced by the CATV operator, but films and
tapes produced by others, and CATV network programming
as well. On June 24, 1970, the FCC ordered all CATV systems having 3, 500 or more subscribers to originate their
own programming. This FCC ruling was viewed as a significant step toward providing an alternative to commercial
television. The hope was that the development of local television programming by CATV systems in communities throughout the country might provide an opportunity for local participation in community affairs through cable television. Upon
the challenge of Midwest Video Corporation, an operator of
CATV systems subject to the new cablecasting requirement,
the United States Court of Appeals for the Eighth Circuit set
aside the regulation on the ground that the FCC "is without
authority to impose it. "

The U. S. Supreme Court reversed (5-4) the lower
court. The decision sustained the program origination rule,
thereby approving a doctrine of FCC jurisdiction that was
far more encompassing than that enunciated in Southwestern.
The Court ruled that the program origination rule was within
the Commission's authority recognized in Southwestern and
that the cablecasting requirement thus applied would promote
the public interest. One of the dissenters, Justice William
Douglas, claimed that "the fact that the Commission has
authority to regulate origination of programs if CATV decides
to enter the field does not mean that it can compel CATV to
originate programs. " Douglas also noted "that to entrust the
Commission with the power to enforce some, a few, or all CATV
operators into the broadcast business is to give it a forbidding
authority. "

Carter Mountain, Southwestern, and Midwest Video firmly established the authority of the FCC to regulate cable television. Moreover, specific regulations designed to promote the public interest, convenience, and necessity have been affirmed. In short, as these cases have demonstrated, all mass communication is vested with a public interest to some degree. As such, broadcasters utilizing any technical means already developed should expect that their activities will not proceed without the watchful guidance of the FCC.

Public Broadcasting--Another significant development in the history of radio and television was the passage of the Public Broadcasting Act of 1967. The FCC thereby became responsible for regulating a new breed of broadcasting facility. In January, 1967, the Carnegie Foundation, under the chairmanship of Dr. James R. Killian, Jr., recommended the development of a non-profit corporation to encourage the development of non-commercial television. The Carnegie Report provided much of the impetus towards government-financed public broadcasting and helped to secure passage of the Public Broadcasting Act. The Act itself authorized financial appropriations to stimulate the development of non-commercial educational broadcasting. Such development began immediately.

To become certified by the Corporation for Public Broadcasting (CPB), a station had to possess an FCC non-commercial education license, the appropriate facilities for local program origination, and a regular schedule of local programming. In addition, certain minimum requirements concerning air time and size of staff had to be met. Certification under the CPB was limited to one station in an area. If there was a population reached by two stations, each one had to show that it broadcast to a sizable, otherwise unreached population. In 1970, the CPB formed the Public Broadcasting Service (PBS)--a network for public programs. It was formed as an instrument through which the local stations could work in close collaboration with the CPB, but removed from the federal funding source. In short, the government began to phase out funding of these stations as they became more able to meet their economic and programming needs. As an alternative to traditional network programming, the educational and public service broadcasting of local PBS stations has come of age.

State of Maine v. University of Maine 266 A. 2d 863 (1970)

Public television related issues have been the subject of few court actions. One such case involved a challenge to the University of Maine's public television system. On April 28, 1970, the University broadcast a program that consisted of comments by State Senator Robert Stuart, an active and legally qualified candidate for the office of United States Representative for the First District. The program, which lasted approximately forty minutes, consisted of the candidate answering questions telephoned in by the public. The station accepted the calls on a collect basis. The State of Main initiated a court action, seeking to enjoin the University from using its educational television system for political interviews with candidates for political office. The State cited a statute that held:

> None of the facilities, plant or personnel of any educational television system which is supported in whole or in part by state funds shall be used directly or indirectly for the promotion, advertisement or advancement of any political candidate for any municipal, county, state or federal office....
> Any person convicted of a violation of any provision of this section shall be punished by a fine of not more than $5,000 or by imprisonment for not more than 11 months, or by both.

The University contended that the statute conflicted with Section 315 of the Federal Communications Act of 1934.

The Supreme Judicial Court of Maine agreed with the University; the "public interest" standard was as binding upon non-commercial licenses as it was upon those that operated for profit. According to the court:

> The designation of their licensed activities as "educational television broadcasting" would indeed be a misnomer if state law would effectively preclude them from presenting programs which are by their very nature essential to the educational process.

The court concluded that the Maine statute prohibiting state educational television systems from promoting any political candidates violated the supremacy clause of the federal Constitution in that it would be impossible for the educational television system to obey the rigid censoring requirements of the statute and, at the same time, satisfy the FCC licensing requirement that programs be shown that are in the public interest. The court upheld the position of the University of Maine.

THE LICENSING DECISION

The courts have accepted the general premise that government regulation of broadcasting is essential. However, how does the Federal Communications Commission exercise the regulatory powers entrusted to it by the government? Specifically, what considerations are taken into account in licensing new broadcasting facilities or renewing the licenses of existing ones? In this section, consideration is given to the programming, economic, and procedural considerations that come into play in making such decisions.

Programming Considerations

Several decisions handed down by both the FCC and the courts have concerned programming matters. In particular, important decisions have related to the issues of local service programming, lotteries, superior service, obscentiy, and format.

Local Service Programming--One of the first cases to deal with programming standards and desirable broadcasting activities was heard in 1948 by the United States Appeals Court, District of Columbia.

Simmons v. Federal Communications Commission
169 F. 2d 670 (1948)

In April, 1947, the Federal Communications Commission denied Allen Simmons's application to increase the power of station WADC at Akron, Ohio, from 5 kw to 50 kw and to change the station's frequency from 1350 kc to 1220 kc. The FCC also granted the mutually exclusive application of Cleveland station WGAR to increase its power from 5 kw to 50 kw. The Commission found that in the event that the Simmons's application was granted, WADC intended "to broadcast all programs, commercial and sustaining, offered by the CBS network." The Commission noted in its conclusions that

the application of WADC thus raises squarely the
issue of whether the public interest, convenience
and necessity would be served by a station which
during by far the largest and most important part
of the broadcast day 'plugs' into the network line
and, thereafter, acts as a mere relay station of
program material piped in from outside the community. We are of the opinion that such a program
policy which makes no effort whatsoever to tailor
the programs offered by the national network organization to the particular needs of the community
served by the radio station does not meet the public service responsibilities of a radio broadcast
licensee.

This ruling stressed that a licensee was compelled to provide
programming adapted to the interests of the local community.

In agreeing with the FCC's findings, the court emphasized that the FCC's power was not limited to regulating frequencies. The Commission could influence, to an extent consistent with the public interest, the actual content of the broadcasts. Simmons further argued that the FCC's policy amounted to censorship. The court disagreed.

Even if the National Broadcasting Company case
had not foreclosed any such contention, censorship
would be a curious term to apply to the requirement that licensees select their own programs by
applying their own judgment to the conditions that
arise from time to time.

Even though the FCC's ruling might be viewed as a precedent for control of program content, the decision in no way
determined which individual programs best suited the local
needs of each community.

Henry v. Federal Communications
Commission 302 F. 2d 191 (1962)

The desirability of local service programming was
again affirmed in 1962. Suburban Broadcasters filed the only
application for a permit to construct the first commercial
FM station in Elizabeth, New Jersey. However, none of
Suburban's principals were residents of Elizabeth, and they
did not inquire into the characteristics or programming needs

of that community. Suburban's program proposals were identical with those submitted in its application for an FM facility
in Berwyn, Illinois, and in the application for a FM facility
in Alameda, California. Although the Federal Communications Commission found Suburban Broadcasters legally, tech-
nically, and financially qualified, it set up a hearing on the
issues raised by Metropolitan Broadcasting Company, the licensee of WNEW in New York. Metropolitan claimed that
a grant would result in objectionable interference. At Metropolitan's request, the FCC added another issue for hearing:
"To determine whether the program proposals of Suburban
Broadcasters are designed to and would be expected to serve
the needs of the proposed service area. " The trial examiner
found for Suburban on both issues. Although the trial examiner resolved the program planning issue in favor of Suburban,
he stated that its approach might be characterized as "cava-
lier. " Referring to the Program Policy Statement released
by the Commission on July 29, 1960, the examiner argued
that the broadcaster's programming responsibility was measured by the statutory standard of "public interest, convenience
or necessity. " In meeting such a standard, the broadcaster
was obliged to show "a positive, dilligent and continuing effort in good faith, to determine the tastes, needs and desires
of the public in his community and to provide programming to
meet those needs and interests. " The examiner noted, however, that these standards were intended for existing licensees
rather than for applicants for new stations, and were inapplicable in this case.

Upon appeal, the FCC reversed the examiner. The
Commission found that the "program proposals were not 'designed' to serve the needs of Elizabeth" and that it was not
known whether the proposals could be expected to serve those
needs since no evidence was offered. In essence, the Commission was asked to grant an application prepared by individuals who were totally without knowledge of the area they
sought to serve. The Commission felt that "the public deserves something more in the way of preparation for the responsibilities sought by applicant than was demonstrated on
this record. " The Commission denied the permit. The courts
affirmed the FCC decision, ruling that the Commission could
require that an applicant demonstrate an earnest interest in
serving a local community by evidencing a familiarity with
its particular needs.

Lotteries--According to accepted legal definition, a
lottery is a scheme in which there is a distribution of a prize

by chance for a consideration. Obviously, a prize is anything of value. Chance is a condition of winning over which the participant has no control. The inability of a person to determine the value of a prize may also constitute chance. Other uncontrollable factors contributing to chance are the number of persons entering a contest, the number of store sales, the earliest postmarks, the earliest customers to arrive at a store, the random selection of contest entries, or the random drawing of names, even when subsequent questions require skill of knowledge. Consideration, the third element of a lottery, is more difficult to define. Generally, it means an effort in time or money must be made by a participant. Having to buy something to become eligible for a prize is an example of a consideration. In 1954, the U.S. Supreme Court handed down a decision that related to the broadcasting of lotteries.

Federal Communications Commission v.
American Broadcasting Company, Inc.
Federal Communications Commission v.
National Broadcasting Company, Inc.
Federal Communications Commission v.
Columbia Broadcasting System, Inc. 347 U.S. 284 (1954)

Postal regulations passed by Congress in 1868 (18 USCA Section 1304, 1306) prohibited the use of the mails to advertise or promote lotteries. Violation could result in the loss of a publication's second class mailing privileges. The FCC applied this federal law to the broadcast media. Violation could lead to loss of license, fines, and/or imprisonment. In 1953, the Post Office relaxed the rule and stipulated that consideration was present even though some individuals play free while others pay. Specifically, the Post Office exempted from lottery regulation those schemes permitting entry by submission of only a plain piece of paper or a coupon from an ad with an individual's name and the name of a product. Soon thereafter, the three major networks began to broadcast giveaway programs (Stop the Music, What's My Name, Sing It Again) that were based on participation by viewers and listeners at home. The FCC sought to ban the programs on the grounds that they were lotteries and were illegal for broadcast purposes. The networks appealed.

Speaking for the U.S. Supreme Court, Chief Justice Earl Warren defined consideration in a permissive way.

To be eligible for a prize on the "give away"

programs involved here, not a single home contestant is required to purchase anything or pay an
admission price or leave his home to visit the pro-
moter's place of business; the only effort required
for participation is listening.

The Court believed (8-0) "that it would be stretching the statute to the breaking point to give it an interpretation that
would make such programs a crime. " The Court held that
the third element, consideration, was lacking from the programs. According to the Court, the FCC had overstepped
the boundaries of interpretation and had exceeded its rule
making power. Giveaway shows did not constitute a pernici-
ous evil. Indeed, they did not come under the province of
lotteries.

New York State Broadcasters Association v.
United States 414 F. 2d 990 (1969)

Fifteen years later, the court ruled that newsworthiness was a defense against lottery law violations. In 1967,
the question of where to draw the line between lottery promotion and genuine news reporting became an issue. The
New York State Broadcasting Association challenged the FCC
lottery rules on First Amendment grounds. Their arguments
were rejected by the Commission. Broadcasting of information about lotteries was prohibited except for "ordinary news
reports concerning legislation authorizing the institution of a
state lottery, or of public debate on the course state policy
should take, " or "any good-faith coverage which is reasonably
related to audiences' right and desire to know and be informed
of the day-to-day happenings within the community. " New
York State Broadcasters appealed, arguing that the people of
New York were being denied access to news, opinions, and
other information in violation of their right to receive information.

The court of appeals upheld the FCC. In so ruling,
though, the court sent the question of conditional broadcast
of lottery information back to the Commission for resolution.
The court noted:

> Petitioners contend that section 1304 is unconstitu-
> tional on its face, arguing that its broad terms
> improperly inhibit "lawful communication unconnected
> with the operating of a lottery. " It is obvious that

> a literal reading of the statute would support pe-
> titioners' challenge, since by its terms it punishes
> the broadcasting of "any ... information concern-
> ing any lottery. "

However, the court did not believe that such a broad construction of Section 1304 was warranted. The court interpreted the phrase "information concerning any lottery" to refer only to information that directly promoted a particular
existing lottery.

Though Section 1304 was upheld by the court, it was
clear that any broad construction of the questionable clause
in violation of the public's right to be informed was impermissible. In 1970, Congress amended the lottery laws by
specifying that Section 1304 did not apply to the advertisement, list of prizes, or information concerning a legally
conducted state lottery. As both ABC and New York State
Broadcasting illustrate, the broadcasting of lottery information is regulated but not prohibited. Clearly, lottery programming is generally outside the control of the FCC.

Superior Service--A third area into which the courts
have ventured deals specifically with the licensing decision
itself. In an unusual reversal of FCC policy, the Court of
Appeals, District of Columbia, substituted its own programming policy for that enunciated in an FCC statement. A 1971
case introduced the doctrine of superior service.

Citizens Communications Center v.
Federal Communications Commission
Hampton Roads Television Corporation v.
Federal Communications Commission
Citizens Communications Center v. Burch 447 F. 2d 1201 (1971)

On January 15, 1970, the FCC introduced its Policy
Statement on Comparative Hearings Involving Regular Renewal
Applicants. Actually, the statement tended to entrench existing ownership and make it difficult for citizen groups to secure a hearing to show that an existing licensee had not performed in the public interest. According to the statement,
when there was a hearing in which an applicant sought the
license of an incumbent licensee, the incumbent was preferred if he or she could demonstrate substantial past performance not characterized by serious deficiencies. The
criterion for renewal--"substantial service to the public"--

rather than choosing the applicant most likely to render the best possible service was justified by the FCC on the basis of "considerations of predictability and stability. " It was feared that if there was no stability in the industry it would not be possible for a station to render even substantial service. Citizen groups, led by Albert Kramer of the Citizens Communication Center and William Wright of Black Efforts for Soul in Television (BEST), challenged the legality of the statement.

In June, 1970, the United States Court of Appeals for the District of Columbia directed the FCC to stop applying the policy statement. The citizen groups had won the case on three grounds. First, the Ashbacker rule requiring a comparative hearing for mutually exclusive applicants was violated by depriving an applicant of such a hearing if the incumbent made a showing of substantial service. Further, the statement unlawfully deprived a competing applicant of a hearing. Second, the statement violated the Administrative Procedure Act. Third, the statement unlawfully chilled the exercise of First Amendment rights. In the opinion of the court, the statement had produced rigor mortis instead of stability. The court intended to restore healthy competition "by repudiating a Commission policy which is unreasonably weighted in favor of the licensees it is meant to regulate, to the great detriment of the listening and viewing public. " The court, however, recognized the value of a good incumbent and established a different criteria--the court recognized that the public would suffer if incumbent licensees could not reasonably expect renewal when they had rendered superior service. Given such an incentive, "an incumbent will naturally strive to achieve a level of performance which gives him a clear edge on challengers at renewal time. " By basing the licensing decision on merit of programming rather than continued compliance of the incumbent with some minimum standard the court introduced competition into a system heretofore characterized by an all-too-often automatic renewal of license.

Yale Broadcasting Company v. Federal
Communications Commission 478 F. 2d 594 (1973)

In 1973, the courts established the license holder's responsibility for knowledge, evaluation, and control of programming consistent with the public interest. The controversy involved a Notice issued by the FCC regarding "drug-oriented music" allegedly played by some radio stations. The Notice, as well as subsequent Order, required licensees to have knowledge of the content of their programming, and on the basis of this knowledge, to evaluate the desirability of broadcasting music dealing with drug use. The FCC set up certain guidelines. In order to remove any excuse for misunderstanding, the FCC suggested ways a broadcaster could obtain the requisite knowledge. A licensee could fulfill its obligation by 1) prescreening by a responsible station employee, 2) monitoring selections while they were being played, or 3) considering and responding to complaints made by the public. The Order made it clear that these procedures were merely suggestions; they were "not to be regarded as either absolute requirements or the exclusive means of fulfilling public interest obligations." The FCC did not mandate any particular form of screening that was required but merely offered suggestions as to how the licensee might meet its obligation.

On the grounds that the license holder failed to meet its responsibility, the FCC denied renewal to the Yale Broadcasting Company. Yale argued that the Notice and the Order constituted an unconstitutional infringement of the right of free expression. They also claimed that the statements were impermissibly vague and that the FCC abused its discretion in refusing to clarify them. Finding none of these arguments to be valid, the Appeals Court, District of Columbia, affirmed the action of the FCC. The Yale case points to the concern the courts have in guaranteeing programming that is conscientiously chosen, aired, and evaluated. Though reluctant to assume the functions of the FCC, the court was nonetheless willing to provide meaning and clarity to licensing guidelines. The presumption of sufficient performance by incumbent license holders no longer holds. All applicants have a positive responsibility to control and evaluate their programs in the public interest, convenience, and necessity.

Obscenity--A fourth area of programming considerations concerns the broadcasting of obscenity. One of the premiere cases involving the competing claims of free speech and control of obscenity was the Palmetto decision.

In re Palmetto Broadcasting Company 33 FCC 250 (1962)

Though the Commission recognized the grave constitutional question involved in prior restraints on communication, it also acknowledged its responsibility for guaranteeing that

the license be granted in the public interest. Radio station
WDKD devoted up to 25 percent of its programming to off-
color jokes and statements that the FCC examiner concluded
were "coarse, vulgar, suggestive, and susceptible of indecent,
double meaning." The record indicated that a preponderance
of witnesses in WDKD's service area were especially offended by the Charlie Walker Show. The examiner denied renewal
of the license.

On appeal, the Commission affirmed the original decision and noted that though censorship was not permissible,
denial of renewal could be countenanced if based on public
interest grounds. Referring to the programming statement
of July 29, 1960, which forbade censorship on the basis of
personal opinion and taste, the Commission stated:

> But this does not mean that the Commission has
> no authority to act under the public-interest stand-
> ard. Rather, it means that the Commission can-
> not substitute its taste for that of the broadcaster
> or his public--that it cannot set itself up as a na-
> tional arbiter of taste.... It follows that in deal-
> ing with the issue before us, we cannot act to deny
> renewal where the matter is a close one, susceptible
> to reasonable interpretation either way. We can
> only act where the record evidence establishes a
> patently offensive course of broadcasters.

The Commission denied renewal on the basis that such a
large portion of broadcast time devoted to such material represented "an intolerable waste of the only operating broadcast
facilities in the community...."

In re Pacifica Foundation 36 FCC 147 (1964)

In 1964, however, the Commission significantly modified its stance. In deciding whether to grant a license to the
Los Angeles station KPFK, and renew the licenses of Berke-
ley's KPFB and KPFA-FM, and New York's WBAI-FM, all
owned by Pacifica Corporation, the Commission considered
certain programming complaints as well as the question of
possible Communist Party affiliation of Pacifica members.
Five programs broadcast over a four-year period were considered offensive or "filthy" by a group of listeners. Unlike
Palmetto, the licensees did not devote a substantial part of
the broadcast day to such programs. Pacifica Corporation

argued that the programs served the needs and interests of
the listening public. In voiding the complaints, the Commission argued:

> We recognize that as shown by the complaints here,
> such provocative programming as here involved
> may offend some listeners. But this does not mean
> that those offended have the right, through the Com-
> mission's licensing power, to rule such programming
> off the airwaves. Were this the case, only the
> wholly inoffensive, the bland, could gain access to
> the radio microphone or TV camera.

In fact, the complaints did not even "pose a close question
in the case: Pacifica's judgments as to the above programs
clearly fall within the very great discretion which the act
wisely grants to the licensee. " The Commission gave the
licensee the benefit of the doubt.

> The standard of public interest is not so rigid that
> an honest mistake or error on the part of a licensee
> results in drastic action against him when his over-
> all record demonstrates a reasonable effort to serve
> the needs and interests of his community.

As for the communist affiliation issue, the Commission argued that the relevant question was not whether the principals
of the applicants were communists but whether the applicants
themselves were. Since there was no evidence of such affiliation the Commission disregarded the issue. The Pacifica
decision signaled an observable philosophical shift by the Commission. License holders would have wide discretion in programming considerations. In effect, the Commission set itself up not as an arbiter of programming standards but as a
public tribunal of sorts in which matters of public interest
could be weighed.

In re WUHY-FM, Eastern Educational Radio 24 FCC 2d 408 (1970)

Six years later, the Commission seemed to have some
reservations about its decision. The Commission, though reluctant aggressively to shape individual programming decisions
of its licensees, was not willing to condone the broadcasting
of obscenity. WUHY-FM, a non-commercial educational radio
station, broadcast the program CYCLE II weekly between
10:00 and 11:00 p.m. On January 4, 1970, Jerry Garcia of

the musical group The Grateful Dead was interviewed on the air by WUHY. In the interview, he frequently used offensive words. The FCC subsequently investigated WUHY. In a notice of liability, the Commission demanded forfeiture of $100 because of WUHY's indecent programming. The notice indicated that during the interview, about 50 minutes in length, Garcia expressed his views on ecology, music, philosophy, and interpersonal relations. His comments were frequently interspersed with the words "fuck" and "shit." In a letter of response, the licensee indicated that "internal procedures to insure against a similar incident are being strengthened" and that CYCLE II had been suspended, pending review. The FCC concluded, however, that the language had "no redeeming social value" and was "patently offensive by contemporary community standards"--having "very serious consequences to the 'public interest in the larger and more effective use of radio.'" The Commission also noted the inherent distinction between radio and other communication media.

> Unlike a book which requires the deliberate act of purchasing and reading (or a motion picture where admission to public exhibition must be actively sought), broadcasting is disseminated generally to the public under circumstances where reception requires no activity of this nature. Thus, it comes directly into the home and frequently without any advance warning of its content.

Ruling against the station, the FCC declared that the material was obscene and that it was presented willfully. Even though the material was presented without obtaining the station manager's approval--contrary to station policy--the licensee was not resolved of responsibility.

Since the station chose to pay its fine, there was no opportunity for judicial support or clarification of the obscenity standard set up by the FCC. Indeed, the FCC's definition differed significantly from either the Supreme Court's Roth or Miller tests. The FCC banned specific words instead of judging the expression in its totality and determining whether it possessed intrinsic value as judged by contemporary community standards. The broadcasting of obscenity was subject to a completely different standard than obscenity that was merely communicated by non-broadcast means.

Sonderling Broadcasting Corporation, WGLD-FM
27 P. & F. Rad. Regs. 2d 285 (1973)

In 1973, the FCC clarified its approach in an attempt
to conform more closely with judicial doctrine regarding obscenity. Station WGLD-FM, Oak Park, Illinois, licensed
to Sonderling Broadcasting Corporation, was one of a number
of broadcast stations that used a format sometimes called
"topless radio, " in which an announcer took calls from the
audience and discussed primarily sexual topics. The program, called Femme Forum, ran from 10:00 a. m. to 3:00
p. m. on Monday through Friday. On February 23, 1973,
the topic was "oral sex. " The program consisted of very
explicit exchanges in which female callers spoke of their
oral-sexual experiences. The FCC found the station guilty
of willful violations and demanded forfeiture of $2, 000. The
FCC emphasized that sex per se was not a forbidden subject
on the broadcast medium. But, in distinguishing this decision from Pacifica, the FCC noted that "we are not dealing
with works of dramatic or literary art as we were in Pacifica. "

Two tests were applied in this case: First, the
Commission applied Roth. In making some attempt to apply
the Supreme Court's 1957 test of obscenity, the FCC argued
that Femme Forum contained explicit material that was "patently offensive to contemporary standards for broadcast matter. " Special emphasis was placed on the fact that minors
compose a significant segment of a radio audience.

> Our conclusions here are based on the pervasive
> and intrusive nature of broadcast radio, even if
> children were left completely out of the picture.
> However, the presence of children in the broad-
> cast audience makes this an a fortiori matter.
> There are signigicant numbers of children in the
> audience during these afternoon hours--and not all
> of a pre-school age. Thus, there is always a
> significant percentage of school age children out of
> school on any given day. Many listen to radio;
> indeed it is almost the constant companion of the
> teenager.

Second, the Commission considered WUHY. In this decision,
the FCC set forth its construction of the term "indecent" as
defined in 18 U. S. C. 1464, which provided a different standard than "obscene. "

It is sufficient to note that to contravene the standard proscribing broadcast of indecent material, it
must be shown that the matter broadcast is a) patently offensive by contemporary community standards; and b) is utterly without redeeming social
value.

In effect, the Sonderling decision granted the FCC authority
to ban not only obscene speech as defined in Roth, but indecent speech as defined in WUHY as well.

Federal Communications Commission v. Pacifica
Foundation 98 S. Ct. 3026 (1978)

While the Sonderling decision placed considerable limitation on the broadcasting of indecent material, the courts had
not dealt definitively with the issue. Nonetheless, the FCC
fashioned its own definition of "indecency" and applied it to
a George Carlin recording aired by New York station WBAI-
FM. On October 30, 1973, station WBAI, as part of its
general discussion of society's attitude toward language, aired
a segment of the album "George Carlin, Occupation: Foole."
Listeners were warned beforehand that some of the language
might be regarded as offensive. The album devotes considerable time to a discussion of the use of seven "four-letter"
words: "shit," "piss," "fuck," "cunt," "cocksucker," "moth-
erfucker," and "tits." A complaint was received from a
father claiming that his young son had heard the broadcast.
The FCC responded by defining as indecent any language that
described in terms patently offensive as measured by contemporary community standards for the broadcasting medium,
sexual or excretary activities and organs, at times of the
day when there was a reasonable risk that children may be
present. The seven words were found to be indecent and
were prohibited. According to the Commission, one of the
most important characteristics of the broadcasting media was
its intrusive nature. This was important because 1) children
had access to radios and in some cases were unsupervised
by parents, 2) radios were in the home, a place where privacy was entitled to additional deference, 3) unconsenting adults might tune in to a station where offensive language was
or would be used, and 4) there was a scarcity of available
frequencies, the use of which the government had to license
in the public interest. The Commission wanted to channel
the broadcast to another time of the day when it would be
less likely that children would be present.

Pacifica Foundation, the license holder of the station, challenged the ruling in the district court. The FCC argued that its ruling was constitutional and sufficiently precise. The Commission sought not to absolutely prohibit indecent broadcasts but merely to channel them to another time of the day. Pacifica argued that the FCC had overstepped its power. The Carlin recording did not appeal to any prurient interest, had literary and political value, and was therefore not obscene. Pacifica argued that the FCC ruling would severely jeopardize the airing of certain programs of serious literary, artistic, political, or scientific value.

The court overruled the Commission's decision. It argued that despite professed intentions, the direct effect of the Commission's order was to "inhibit the free and robust exchange of ideas on a wide range of issues and subjects by means of radio and television communications." According to the court,

> The Commission claims that its Order does not censor indecent language but rather channels it to certain times of the day. In fact the Order is censorship regardless of what the Commission chooses to call it.... The Commission expressly states that this language has "no place on radio," and that when children are in the audience a claim that it has literary, artistic, political, or scientific value will not redeem it.

The court criticized the FCC for not allowing licensees to set their own programming standards.

The U.S. Supreme Court claimed that the content of Pacifica's broadcast was "vulgar," "offensive," and "shocking." Because content of that nature was not entitled to absolute constitutional protection under all circumstances, the judges had to consider its context in order to determine whether the Commission's action was constitutionally permissable. The Court noted, first, that:

> Patently offensive, indecent material presented over the airwaves confronts the citizen, not only in public, but also in the privacy of the home, where the individual's right to be let alone plainly outweighs the First Amendment rights of an intruder.

In addition, broadcasting was uniquely accessible to children.

The Court supported (5-4) the FCC's "nuisance rationale, " under which context was all-important.

> The concept requires consideration of a host of variables. The time of day was emphasized by the Commission. The content of the program in which the language is used will also affect the composition of the audience, and differences between radio, television, and perhaps closed-circuit transmissions, may also be relevant.

The Court concluded that "when the Commission finds that a pig has entered the parlor, the exercise of its regulatory power does not depend on proof that the pig is obscene. " In this decision, the Court upheld the FCC's power to regulate obscene speech.

Format--A change in a radio station's programming format affects the public interest. Can a citizen's committee that raises substantial and material questions concerning the transfer of an ownership application that will ultimately result in a change of format demand a formal hearing before the FCC? This issue was dealt with in the 1974 WEFM case.

Citizens Committee to Save WEFM v. Federal Communications Commission 506 F. 2d 246 (1974)

Since it was first licensed to Zenith Corporation in 1940, Chicago radio station WEFM had broadcast a classical musical format. In March, 1972, Zenith contracted to sell WEFM to GCC, a corporation organized for the purpose of the purchase, for $1 million. Zenith was suffering financial losses and wanted to make the transaction as soon as possible. GCC proposed to present a format of contemporary music approximately 70 percent of the time. A citizens committee was organized to contest the transfer of application. It felt that the loss of the classical music format would be sorely missed by a sizeable audience and would thus not be in the public interest. The FCC rejected the petition to deny without a hearing. The FCC ruled that programming decisions had traditionally been left to the licensee's or applicant's judgment and competitive marketplace forces. The FCC sought to strike a balance between the "preservation of a free competitive broadcasting system, on the one hand, and the reasonable restriction of freedom inherent in the public interest standard provided in the Communications Act, on the other. " In Chicago, only stations WEFM, WFMT, and WNIB presented classical music formats. By far, WEFM provided for the largest share of the area's classical music listening needs. The issue for the FCC was whether the assignee, without a hearing, could change the musical format from classical to contemporary music where there were two other classical music stations serving Chicago. In approving the transfer application and rejecting the petition to deny, the FCC in effect disregarded some 1, 000 letters protesting the format change. In the FCC's view, abandonment of a non-unique format was "not a matter affected with the public interest but a business decision within the licensee's discretion. "

On appeal, the Circuit Court of Appeals, District of Columbia, felt that the citizens committee had raised substantial and material questions of fact concerning the public interest, Zenith's financial position, and the community leader survey taken by GCC to ascertain community needs. Such issues required that the FCC grant a formal hearing. The court disagreed that changes in program format should be left to the competitive forces of the marketplace.

> Moreover, there is no longer any room for doubt that, if the FCC is to pursue the public interest, it may not be able at the same time to pursue a policy of free competition.... There is, in the familiar sense, no free market in radio entertainment because over-the-air broadcasters do not deal directly with their listeners.

The court implied that the Commission had an affirmative responsibility to ensure that programming changes were in the public interest. According to the court, the FCC should have granted a formal hearing in order to ascertain the community's needs.

Economic Considerations

The licensing decision is also affected substantially by two economic considerations: 1) the effect of competition on incumbent license holders, and 2) the extent to which ownership of broadcasting facilities is diversified among different groups and individuals. These considerations are considered in this section.

Incumbent Licensee--The Sanders Brothers case represents one of the first important attempts by the Court to

provide some guidance in matters regarding the economic
well-being of incumbent license holders.

Federal Communications Commission v. Sanders Brothers Radio Station 309 U. S. 470 (1940)

In 1936, the Telegraph Herald, a newspaper published
in Dubuque, Iowa, filed an application for a construction permit to build a broadcasting station in that city. The incumbent license holder, Sanders Brothers radio station (WKBB),
sought to prevent the Telegraph Herald from building the station, arguing that the loss in advertising revenue would harm
WKBB and that the public interest, convenience, and necessity was already being adequately served. The Commission denied the request, noting that two stations were necessary and
that no electrical interference would result from building the
new station. The Court of Appeals, District of Columbia, reversed the decision. The court held that the Commission
should have investigated the alleged economic injury to Sanders Brothers that might result from the establishment
of an additional station.

Appealing to the Supreme Court, the Telegraph Herald
argued that economic injury to a competitor was not a ground
for refusal to grant a license. The Court agreed:

> We hold that resulting economic injury to a rival
> station is not, in and of itself, and apart from con-
> siderations of public convenience, interest, or ne-
> cessity, an element the petitioner must weigh, and
> as to which it must make findings, in passing on
> an application for a broadcasting license.

The Court recognized that the incumbent by no means had a
vested property right to continue broadcasting. The 1934
Act was intended to protect the public, not the broadcaster.
The Court noted, however, that the question of competition
between a proposed station and one operating under an existing license could not be disregarded. The issue of incumbent well-being was relevant if it tangentially affected the
public interest, convenience, and necessity. Perhaps by
granting a license both stations would provide inadequate service, or because of loss of revenue the incumbent would be
forced off the air. The Court noted that in the present case
the attack against the FCC ruling was not that the public interest was insufficiently protected, but only that the financial

interests of Sanders Brothers had not been considered. The
Court reaffirmed (8-1) the FCC's original decision that granted the Telegraph Herald a license to broadcast. From 1940
to 1958, the FCC interpreted Sanders Brothers to mean that
possible economic injury to an incumbent was no basis for
refusing to license a potential competitor. This was not an
entirely accurate interpretation.

Carroll Broadcasting Company v. Federal Communications Commission 258 F. 2d 440 (1958)

In 1958, the court of appeals rejected the FCC's interpretation of the Sanders Brothers decision and emphasized
that economic considerations were relevant when potential
competition seemed likely to affect the public interest adversely. Carroll Broadcasting Company, a radio station in Car-
rollton, Georgia, sought to prevent West Georgia Broadcasting
Company from broadcasting from a nearby city. The FCC
granted the license to West Georgia, arguing that the issue
of competition was not relevant and that the burden of proof
in demonstrating the harm to the public interest rested with
Carroll.

On appeal, the decision was reversed. The Court of
Appeals, District of Columbia, noted that competiton indeed
was relevant if it adversely affected the public interest.

> But if the situation in a given area is such that
> available revenue will not support good service in
> more than one station, the public interest may well
> be in the licensing of one rather than two stations.

The court did not really overturn the Sanders doctrine, but
rather elaborated it.

> We hold that, when an existing licensee offers to
> prove that the economic effect of another station
> would be detrimental to the public interest, the
> Commission should afford an opportunity for the
> presentation of such proof and, if the evidence is
> substantial (i.e. if the protestant does not fail en-
> tirely to meet his burden), should make a finding
> or findings.

The incumbent license holder now had legal standing even
though actual economic harm was not suffered. Nonetheless,

the main concern was for the public interest. The harmful effects of competition on an incumbent were relevant only in this context. The court emphasized that the Commission was not required to "evaluate the economic results of every license grant. " Indeed, such a formulation of the decision would be unworkable and undesirable. According to the court, "The public interest is affected when service is affected. " In this case, the court was willing to give Carroll the benefit of doubt.

Diversification of Ownership--Another economic consideration relevant to the licensing decision is the extent to which ownership of broadcasting facilities is diversified among different groups and individuals. The Mansfield Journal case illustrates the problems involved with concentrated ownership.

Mansfield Journal Company v. Federal Communications Commission Lorain Journal Company v. Federal Communications Commission 180 F. 2d 28 (1950)

The Mansfield Journal was the only newspaper in Mansfield, Ohio. The only other medium of mass communication in Mansfield, radio station WMAN, competed with the paper for local advertising. The Mansfield Journal Company used its position as sole newspaper in the community to coerce its advertisers to enter into exclusive advertising contracts with the newspaper and to refrain from advertising on WMAN. It did this by refusing to permit advertisers who also used the radio to sell their products from advertising in the paper. In addition, the company demonstrated a marked hostility to station WMAN's program log and failed to print any comments about the station unless unfavorable. The FCC concluded that such actions were taken with the intent of suppressing competition and of securing a monopoly of mass advertising and news dissemination. When the Mansfield Journal Company applied for a radio broadcasting license, the FCC denied the application. The FCC ruled that the company's practices were likely to continue and would be reinforced by the acquisition of a radio station. Granting a license would be inconsistent with the public interest.

The court affirmed the FCC ruling. The court agreed that it was contrary to the public interest to grant a license to a newspaper that attempted to suppress competition.

This would not appear to be a consideration conceived in whimsey but rather a sound application
of what has long been the general policy of the
United States. Congress intended that there be
competition in the radio broadcasting industry. It
is certainly not in the public interest that a radio
station be used to achieve monopoly.

Greater Boston Television Corporation v. Federal
Communications Commission 444 F. 2d 841 (1970)

Twenty years after the Mansfield case, the court once
again took a strong stand against monopolistic control and
ownership of broadcasting facilities. WHDH Inc. had broadcast from Channel 5 in Boston, Massachusetts, since it obtained its original license in 1957. However, in 1969, the
FCC announced that BBI (Boston Broadcasters, Inc.) was
granted the license instead of WHDH or the other applicants--
Charles River Broadcasting Company and Greater Boston T.
V. Company Inc. BBI was cited in the decision for superior
service due to its diversification of communications media
control and integration of ownership with management. WHDH
Inc., by contrast, was licensee of WHDH-AM, the incumbent
licensee, and was owned by the Boston Herald-Traveler Cor-
poration. The Herald-Traveler, a daily newspaper, also had
a controlling interest in Entron Inc., a CATV equipment manufacturer and system operator. The Commission gave BBI
a slight preference on the question of diversification over
Charles River Civil Television Inc. The president-elect of
Charles River was Theodore Jones, president of Charles
River Broadcasting Company, which was the licensee of WCRB-
AM-FM, Waltham, Massachusetts, and owner of WCRQ-FM,
Providence, Rhode Island. Both BBI and Charles River were
given preference by the Commission on the question of integration of ownership over WHDH. The Commission, in addition, faulted WHDH's unauthorized transfers of control. The
transfers first took place with the death of Sidney W. Winslow, Jr., and his subsequent replacement as president of
the Herald Traveler Corporation by Robert B. Choate, then
the president of WHDH. With the death of Choate, George
E. Akerson replaced him in both presidencies. The FCC
noted: "Diversification is a factor of first significance since
it constitutes a primary objective in the Commission's licensing scheme." According to the Commission, WHDH mani-
festly ranked a poor third because of its ownership of a powerful standard broadcast station, an FM station, and a newspaper in the city of Boston itself.

A grant to either Charles River or BBI would clearly result in a maximum diffusion of control of the media of mass communications as compared with a grant of the renewal application of WHDH. A new voice would be brought to the Boston community as compared with continuing the service of WHDH-TV. We believe that the widest possible dissemination of information from diverse and antagonistic sources is in the public interest, and this principle will be significantly advanced by a grant of either the Charles River or the BBI application.

The Commission concluded that the public interest would be served by granting the license to BBI and denying it to the WHDH, Charles River, and Greater Boston broadcasting stations. The matter was affirmed by the Court of Appeals, District of Columbia.

Federal Communications Commission v. National Citizens Committee for Broadcasting
Channel Two Television Company v. National Citizens Committee for Broadcasting
National Association of Broadcasters v. Federal Communications Commission
American Newspaper Publishers Association v. National Citizens Committee for Broadcasting
Illinois Broadcasting Company, Inc. v. National Citizens Committee for Broadcasting
Post Company v. National Citizens Committee for Broadcasting 436 U.S. 775 (1978)

In 1978, the Supreme Court consolidated six cases that concerned the FCC's regulations governing the permissibility of common ownership of a radio or television station, and a daily newspaper located in the same community. The Commission believed that diversification of mass media ownership served the public interest by promoting a diversity of viewpoints and preventing concentration of economic power. Each of the cases heard by the Court involved the FCC's prospective barring of "co-located combinations" by rejecting the application for licensing. The FCC, however, did not require divestiture, except in sixteen "egregious cases" where the combination involved the sole newspaper published in a community and either the sole television or sole radio station for that community. The Court of Appeals, District of Columbia, upheld the bans, but ordered adoption of regulations requiring, in effect, automatic divestiture of unacceptable combinations, arguing that limited divestiture was arbitrary and capricious.

The Supreme Court ruled (8-0) that the limited divestiture requirement was not arbitrary or capricious since such a rule reflected a rational weighing of competing policies. Automatic divestiture would unduly disrupt the industry in certain cases, causing needless hardship or harming the public interest. The Court also upheld the constitutionality of the FCC's regulations and rejected the newspaper owners claims that First Amendment rights were violated. The Court argued that there is no unabridgeable right to broadcast comparable to the right of every individual to speak, write, or publish.

> In view of the limited broadcast spectrum, allocation and regulation of frequencies is essential. Nothing in the First Amendment prevents such allocation as will promote the "public interest" in diversification of the mass communications media.

The regulations, moreover, were based on public interest goals that fell within the FCC's rule making authority. The FCC had made a rational judgment in concluding that the need for diversification was especially great in cases of local monopoly.

The Mansfield, Greater Boston, and National Citizens Committee cases clearly emphasize the preeminent concern for the public interest. The concentration of the media-- both electronic and printed--was looked upon with great disfavor by the courts. The greater the diversity and scope of information presented the better the chance that the public will be served. Not only is concentration of media control unhealthy, but any attempts to suppress competition are weighted against the incumbent licensees. The economic "rights" of broadcasters are limited indeed.

Procedural Considerations

Procedural guarantees constitute a third consideration that bears heavily on the licensing decision. Does the incumbent license holder have an advantage over potential competitors? If so, to what extent? How can non-incumbent applicants successfully protest the renewal of a license? What is their legal standing? Who has the burden of proof? These questions have been recently confronted by the courts. The 1966 United Church case, the first in a series of cases addressing various issues, formally established the requirement of an evidentiary hearing in granting licenses and set forth that legal standing to bring action is not absolute.

Office of Communication of the United Church of Christ v. Federal Communications Commission 359 F. 2d 994 (1966)

In 1955, the FCC received a complaint that station WLBT had deliberately cut off a network program about racial problems. During the program, on which the general counsel of the NAACP appeared, a "Sorry, Cable Trouble" message appeared on viewers' screens. In 1957, another complaint to the Commission alleged that WLBT had presented a program urging the maintenance of racial segregation and had refused requests for time to present the opposing viewpoint. Subsequently, numerous other complaints were brought. When WLBT sought a renewal of its license in 1958, the Commission eventually granted a three-year renewal. The Commission found that while there had been failures to comply with the Fairness Doctrine, the failures were isolated instances of improper behavior and did not warrant denial of WLBT's renewal. In 1962, shortly after the outbreak of prolonged civil disturbances, the Commission again received complaints that various Mississippi radio and television stations, including WLBT, had presented only one viewpoint concerning racial integration. In 1963, the Commission investigated and requested the stations to submit factual reports on their programs concerning racial issues. In 1964, while the FCC was considering WLBT's response, the station again filed a license renewal application.

Enraged citizens and groups, under the organization of the Office of Communication of the United Church of Christ, filed a petition urging denial of WLBT's application. The group asked the Commission to intervene in their behalf as representatives of "all other television viewers in the State of Mississippi. " The petition argued that WLBT failed to serve the general public because the station provided a disproportionate amount of commercials and entertainment and did not give a fair and balanced presentation of controversial issues--especially those concerning blacks, who comprised almost 45 percent of the total population within the station's prime service area. In brief, the petition claimed that blacks were given much less television exposure than others and that programs were generally disrespectful. The allegations were accompanied by a detailed presentation of the results of United Church's monitoring of a typical week's programming.

The FCC denied the petition on the ground that legal standing to bring suit was predicated upon the invasion of a legally protected interest or an injury that was direct and substantial. The Commission argued that "petitioners ... can assert no greater interest or claim of injury than members of the general public. " The Commission stated in its denial, however, that as a general practice it considered "the contentions advanced in circumstances such as these, irrespective of any questions of standing or related matters. " Upon considering United Church's claims and WLBT's answers, the Commission concluded that

> serious issues are presented whether the licensee's operations have fully met the public interest standard. Indeed, it is a closed question whether to designate for hearing these applications for renewal of license.

Nevertheless, the Commission conducted no hearing and granted a license renewal, asserting that renewal would be in the public interest since broadcast stations were in a position to make worthwhile contributions to the resolution of pressing racial problems. Further, this contribution was "needed immediately" in the Jackson area and WLBT, if operated properly, could make such a contribution. The renewal period was explicitly made a test of WLBT's qualifications in this respect.

> We are granting a renewal of license, so that the licensee can demonstrate and carry out its stated willingness to serve fully and fairly the needs and interests of its entire area--so that it can, in short, meet and resolve the questions raised.

The one-year renewal was in the nature of a probationary grant. The conditions were stated as follows: 1) that the licensee comply strictly with the established requirements of the Fairness Doctrine; 2) that the licensee observe strictly its representations to the Commission in this area; 3) that the licensee immediately have discussions with community leaders, including those active in the civil rights movement, as to whether its programming is fully meeting the needs and interests of its area; 4) that the licensee immediately cease discriminatory programming patterns; and 5) that the licensee make a detailed report as to its effort in the above four respects.

On appeal, United Church contended that against the background of complaints since 1955 and the FCC's conclusion that WLBT was guilty of "discriminatory programming" the Commission could not properly renew the license even for one year without a hearing to resolve factual issues raised by the petition. The Commission argued, however, that it in effect accepted United Church's view of the facts and took all necessary steps to ensure that the practices complained of would cease. For this reason, the Commission granted a short-term renewal as a "political decision." The decision was based on a hope that WLBT would improve and on the view that the station was needed. The Commission's denial of legal standing to the appellants was based on the theory that

> absent a potential direct, substantial injury or adverse effect from the administrative action under consideration, a petitioner has no standing before the Commission and that the only types of effects sufficient to support standing are economic injury and electrical interference.

The FCC asserted that members of the listening public did not suffer any injury peculiar to them and that allowing them standing would pose great administrative burdens. However, according to the court,

> In order to safeguard the public interest in broadcasting, therefore, we hold that some "audience participation" must be allowed in license renewal proceedings. We recognize this will create problems for the Commission but it does not necessarily follow that "hosts" of protestors must be granted standing to challenge a renewal application or that the Commission need allow the administrative process to be obstructed or overwhelmed by captious or purely obstructive protests. The Commission can avoid such results by developing appropriate regulation by statutory rulemaking.

The court noted that the FCC must be granted "broad discretion" in setting rules for such hearings--including the number and type of witnesses required and the extent of "audience participation" allowed. In establishing the requirement of audience participation at renewal proceedings, the court emphasized that the legal standing of any petitioner must be judged in relation to other petitioners' claims. The right to petition is not absolute. Legal standing can be granted only after weighing the claims of other petitioners and the nature of the claims themselves.

Office of Communication of the United Church of Christ v. Federal Communications Commission 425 F. 2d 543 (1969)

Another procedural consideration concerns the burden of proof. Does the incumbent have to prove that it alone can provide service in the best interests of the public? Does a potential competitor have to prove that the incumbent is not as well qualified to serve the public as itself? This issue was presented to the courts in the second United Church case. After a hearing, the FCC granted a full-term, three-year renewal to WLBT. Once again, the United Church of Christ took the FCC to court. The basis for the decision in this case related to the FCC Examiner's treatment of evidence and the burden of proof. The court observed:

> The Examiner seems to have regarded Appellants as "plaintiffs" and the licensee as "defendant, " with burden of proof allocated accordingly. This tack, though possibly fostered by the Commission's own action, was a grave misreading of our holding on this question. We did not intend that intervenors representing a public interest be treated as interlopers. Rather, if analogues can be useful, a "Public Intervenor" who is seeking no license or private right is, in this context, more nearly like a complaining witness who presents evidence to police or a prosecutor whose duty it is to conduct an affirmative and objective investigation of all the facts and to pursue his prosecutorial or regulatory function if there is probable cause to believe a violation had occurred.

The court strongly emphasized that the intervenor (United Church) protested WLBT's renewal not for selfish reasons but to provide information to the Commission to aid in the determination of whether the public interest was being served.

The "presumption of innocence, " in effect, rested with WLBT. The court stressed that it was not the correct duty of the Examiner or the Commission to sit back and simply provide a forum for the intervenors. In fact, the Commission's duties did not end by allowing appellants to intervene; its duties began at that stage.

The court noted that a neutrality that favored the licensee had guided the Examiner in his conduct of the evidentiary hearing. For example, the Examiner failed to view objectively United Church's 1964 monitoring study. The Examiner concluded that the playback had "virtually no meaning for the simple reason that it was not ... fair and equitable. " It was dismissed as worthless by the Commission. The Examiner also disregarded the claim that WLBT had cut off a network program in violation of the Fairness Doctrine. The Examiner found that "there is not one iota of evidence in the record that supports any such allegation. " However, the court found testimony identifying the program that was admittedly cut off. Concerning allegations that at least two of the licensee's commentators used disparaging remarks with reference to blacks, there was testimony that listeners had heard such terms, yet the Examiner belittled this evidence. In this case, the court revoked the license renewal grant to WLBT and directed the FCC to invite applicants to apply for the license. In reversing the FCC's decision, the court established that the burden of proof rested with the incumbent licensee.

Hale v. Federal Communications Commission
425 F. 2d 556 (1970)

One year later, the Court of Appeals, District of Columbia, rejected the requirement of an evidentiary hearing except in certain cases. The court also reversed the burden of proof. Two citizens of Salt Lake City challenged the renewal application of station KSL-AM. KSL was wholly owned by the Mormon Church as was one of the daily newspapers in Salt Lake City, the Desert News. The citizens seeking to defeat the renewal application initially had to wage a tough battle for a hearing. Without a hearing, it would be difficult for the citizens to obtain testimony showing the poor programming response by the licensee to community needs. Proof of the actual programming presented by KSL-AM was difficult to determine because the station did not even publish its daily program log in any Salt Lake daily newspaper. The FCC adamantly refused to grant a hearing on the matter; the Commission interpreted Sections 309 (d) and (e) of the Federal Communications Act to require a hearing only when the petition to deny revealed a substantial issue of fact requiring a resolution by hearing. Such an interpretation effectively contradicted the United Church decision. Actually, the FCC resolution of the issue in Hale involved a victory for circular reasoning. Without a hearing, the citizen group found it nearly impossible to demonstrate the material issue of fact concerning the licensee's performance, which alone would have produced a hearing. The citizens took the FCC to court because of its refusal to grant a hearing.

The court of appeals affirmed the FCC's determination not to grant a hearing. The court said:

> To establish a violation of this doctrine [Fairness], appellants must show that specific programs have dealt with controversial issues partially, and, if so, that other programs on the station have not balanced the coverage by presenting the alternative viewpoints. Appellants claim their inability to survey KSL-AM's general programming is due to the fact that the station does not publish a daily log of its programming in any newspaper. Such logs, however, are required to be kept by the licensee and could have been made available upon request.

The appellants, in short, were not even given the chance to present their testimony bearing on "substantial issues of fact." The court, in effect, accepted the FCC's interpretation of the 1934 Federal Communications Act that a hearing was required only when the petition brings out a new issue of fact requiring resolution by a hearing. Further, in protesting the renewal, appellants had to carry the burden of proof. According to the court, even though the Fairness Doctrine required the Commission to look to the general balance of a station's programming, proof of a violation must be based on specific facts.

> Where complaint is made to the Commission, the Commission expects a complainant to submit specific information indicating 1) the particular station involved, 2) the particular issue of a controversial nature discussed over the air, 3) the date and time when the program was carried, 4) the basis for the

claim that the station has presented only one side
of the question, and 5) whether the station had afforded, or has plans to afford an opportunity for
the presentation of contrasting viewpoints.

The strict guidelines of proof established in Hale obviously
made it considerably more difficult for citizens to obtain a
hearing from the FCC through a petition to deny.   The road
of the incumbent licensee was thus made much smoother
and obstacle-free.

Stone v. Federal Communications Commission 466 F. 2d 316 (1972)

        In 1972, a circuit court of appeals affirmed the FCC's
decision to dismiss a citizen group's petition to deny renewal
of a television station's license.   The case raised a number
of fundamental issues that affect broadcasters.   One of the
most important was how a citizen group could obtain an evidentiary hearing.   Precisely, what constituted legitimate
grounds for such a hearing? In September, 1969, sixteen
Washington, D. C., community leaders filed a petition to deny
renewal of the television license for station WMAL-TV.   The
committee argued that 1) the station did not adequately survey the black community in an effort to ascertain the needs
of the Washington, D. C., area, 2) the station misrepresented
facts concerning contacts between the licensee and certain
Washington, D. C., leaders, 3) programming did not serve
the public interest, 4) the station's employment practices
were discriminatory against blacks, and 5) the renewal would
lead to excessive concentration in the Washington media.   The
FCC dismissed the petition, arguing that the committee had
not proven their allegations or that the allegations themselves
were of such a substantial and material nature as to require
a hearing.

        The court agreed with the FCC's ruling.   WMAL had
met the Commission's ascertainment requirements and had
not intentionally misrepresented any facts.   The committee
failed to make a prima facie case that WMAL's programming
did not come within the discretion afforded licensees or that
WMAL used discriminatory employment practices.   Furthermore, the renewal "would not result in excessive concentration in the communications media and that in any event, this
was a subject for rulemaking, then under progress."   According to the court,

> In the event, then, that a petition to deny does not
> make substantial and specific allegations of fact
> which, if true, would indicate that a grant of the
> application would be prima facie inconsistent with
> the public interest, the petition may be denied with-
> out hearing on the basis of a concise statement of
> the Commission's reasons for denial.

Citizens groups had to clear several important and comparatively rigorous obstacles in order to obtain an evidentiary
hearing. Aside from the sufficiency of a petition to deny,
the FCC was not required to hold a hearing where it found,
on the basis of the application and other pleadings submitted,
no substantial and material questions of fact to exist and that
granting the application would serve the public interest. Secondly, a hearing was not required when facts necessary to
resolve a particular question were not disputed and when the
case turned not on a determination of fact but rather on inferences from facts already shown. Thirdly, a hearing was
not required to resolve issues the Commission finds are
either not "substantial" or "material." In this case, the
citizen's group did not, to either the court's or Commission's
satisfaction, raise questions of fact of such a nature as to
require a hearing, and did not sufficiently prove their allegations. At base, the committee did not demonstrate WMAL's
lack of responsiveness to community, especially black community, needs and interests. According to the court, the
objections raised as to this question lacked the required specificity; they were largely conclusionary and usually not tied
to specific programming considerations. The court noted
that "such generalized criticisms run the risk of turning the
FCC into a censorship board, a goal clearly not in the public interest." The court went on to rule that the plaintiff
bears a substantial burden of specificity:

> In the absence of a competing broadcast application
> situation, where a hearing is required, plaintiffs
> bear a substantial burden of specificity, a burden
> they have not met in the case at bar.

This case demonstrated that in order for a citizen's group to
obtain an evidentiary hearing, it must first raise sufficient
and material questions of fact and sufficiently prove specific
allegations. In Stone, as in Hale, the court established procedures favorable to the incumbent licensee.

BROADCASTING REGULATION DOCTRINES

The FCC, in addition to its influence on broadcasting through the authority to license, exercises direct control over programming through the Equal Time and Fairness Doctrines. The first of these was enunciated in Section 315 of the Federal Communications Act of 1934.

Equal Time

The Equal Time rule placed several important responsibilities on broadcasters. Most importantly, Section 315 required a broadcaster to provide equal opportunity to all legally qualified candidates for use of a station's facilities if the station afforded such opportunity to any one candidate. Such opportunity required equal time, equal facilities, and comparable costs for such candidates. Though the station was under no obligation to solicit appearance by every candidate, it had to afford equal opportunity for use of the facilities if so requested within one week of the original appearance. Section 315, however, clearly provided an "out" for the broadcaster. Under the rule, the broadcaster was not required to provide air time to any candidate, thereby preventing the operation of Section 315. Thus, the Equal Time rule has not been entirely successful in providing a forum for public debate.

Another provision of Section 315 prohibited broadcasters from censoring materials in political broadcasts. Congress recognized the necessity of a free and unhindered discussion of issues. It didn't, however, fully take into account the question of libel. Could a station be sued for libel for merely presenting the views of a political candidate--in accord with the Equal Time rule? The question was resolved in 1959.

Farmers Educational & Cooperative Union of America, North Dakota Division v. WDAY, Inc. 360 U.S. 525 (1959)

A libel suit arose as a result of a speech made over the radio and television facilities of station WDAY, by A. C. Townley, a legally qualified candidate in the 1956 United States Senate race in North Dakota. WDAY permitted Townley to broadcast his speech, uncensored in any respect, as a reply to previous speeches made over WDAY by two other senatorial candidates. Townley's speech accused his opponents,

302 / JOURNALISTIC FREEDOM

together with the Farmers Educational and Cooperative Union, of conspiring to "establish a Communist Farmers Union Soviet right here in North Dakota." Farmers Union sued Townley and WDAY for libel. The court dismissed the complaint against WDAY on the ground that Section 315 rendered the station immune from liability. The Supreme Court of North Dakota agreed.

> Section 315 imposes a mandatory duty upon broadcasting stations to permit all candidates for the same office to use their facilities if they have permitted one candidate to use them. Since power of censorship of political broadcasts is prohibited it must follow as a corollary that the mandate prohibiting censorship includes the privilege of immunity from liability for defamatory statements made by the speakers.

On appeal, the case presented a dilemma to the U. S. Supreme Court--whether to uphold Section 315 or to negate substantially the right of private citizens and groups to seek redress from libelous statements made against them over the airwaves. In such cases, should the station remove the libelous material? If not, should the station be immune from liability from defamatory statements made by candidates for public office? Regarding the first question, the Court decided that any system of station censorship would undermine the purpose for which Section 315 was passed--providing unhampered discussion of political issues by legally qualified candidates. The Court noted:

> Quite possibly, if a station were held responsible for the broadcast of libelous material, all remarks even faintly objectionable would be excluded out of an excess of caution. Moreover, if any censorship were permissible, a station so inclined could intentionally inhibit a candidate's legitimate presentation under the guise of lawful censorship in libelous matter. Because of the time limitation inherent in a political campaign, erroneous decisions by a station could not be corrected by the courts promptly enough to permit the candidate to bring improperly excluded matter before the public. It follows from all this that allowing censorship ... would almost inevitably force a candidate to avoid controversial issues during political debates over radio and television, and hence restrict the coverage of consideration relevant to intelligent political decision.

Regarding the second question, the Court granted (5-4) broadcasters immunity from defamation suits based on remarks
made by the candidates over the air. This decision, though
necessary to legitimate enforcement of the Equal Time rule,
was not sufficient to guarantee broadcasters' compliance with
the rule's underlying purposes.

Federal Election Campaign Act (1971)

Recognizing the pitfalls of the Equal Time rule, Congress passed the Federal Election Campaign Act of 1971
(FECA). Under the law, a broadcaster was subject to license
revocation if she or he willfully or repeatedly failed to "allow
reasonable access to or to permit purchase of reasonable
amounts of time for the use of a broadcasting station by a
legally qualified candidate for federal elective office on behalf
of his candidacy." The act only applied to federal offices.
Candidates for state and local offices were still subject to
the same abuses prevalent before 1971. The FECA also controlled the amount that broadcasters could charge political
candidates. Every candidate was to pay either the lowest
rate charged to the station's advertisers or the rate charged
to the original candidate making use of the facilities--which-
ever was lower.

The 1971 act, though a significant step in the right
direction, did not stem the problems in applying and enforcing the Equal Time rule. One problematic term found in
Section 315 is "use." What constitutes "use" of facilities by
candidates? The courts have generally determined that an
appearance by a candidate does not constitute a use when the
program is 1) a bona fide newscast, 2) a bona fide news
interview, 3) spot news coverage, or 4) news documentary
when the appearance is incidental to the presentation of the
relevant topic. Also, such events as press conferences or
political debates are legitimate news events; they are not of
a partisan nature, per se. Other events, including spot announcements, paid advertisements, and even brief appearances
on talk shows come under the aegis of Section 315.

A second problematic term is "legally qualified candidate." In providing a definition, the FCC set forth four
characteristics. A legally qualified candidate is a person
1) who publicly announces that he/she is a candidate for nomination or election to any local, county, state, or national
office, and 2) who meets the qualifications prescribed by law

for that office, and 3) who qualifies for a place on the ballot or is eligible to be voted for by sticker or write-in methods, and 4) who was duly nominated by a political party that is commonly known and regarded as such or makes a substantial showing that he/she is a bona fide candidate. Obviously, the fourth characteristic provides the FCC with the most problems in interpretation. What is a "substantial showing" ? What is a "political party, " for that matter?

McCarthy v. Federal Communications Commission 390 F. 2d 471 (1968)

One of the most recent cases to deal with the question of who is a legally qualified candidate was McCarthy. On December 19, 1967, the three major television networks carried a joint hour-long interview of President Lyndon Johnson. Senator Eugene McCarthy, who had prior to the broadcast announced his own candidacy for the Democratic nomination, requested "equal time" on the ground that President Johnson was a legally qualified candidate for the same nomination within the intent of Section 315 of the Communications Act. The FCC denied the Senator's request. The ruling was based on the definition of a legally qualified candidate. President Johnson had not announced his candidacy for the nomination, and thus did not fulfill the first requirement. McCarthy did not contend that it was unreasonable to require, as a condition prior to invoking the section, that claimants to equal treatment announce their candidacies. McCarthy argued that it was unreasonable if candidates deprived their opponents of the benefit of the section simply by withholding an announcement of their own candidacy. If the President had announced his candidacy prior to the December 19 program, McCarthy would have been entitled to equal time irrespective of the content of that program. His argument was rejected on the ground that Section 315 did not apply to interviews.

On appeal, the decision was affirmed. "Considering the content and the timing of the ... year-end interview with the President, " the court could not "say that the application of the Commission's rule in this case without the requested hearing produced an unreasonable result. " By rejecting McCarthy's arguments, the court made it easier for incumbents to achieve the advantage of media exposure through bona fide news coverage without suffering the disadvantages owing to equal coverage of the opponent's campaign under

Section 315. By delaying formal announcement of candidacy, an incumbent may still successfully forestall operation of the Equal Time clause.

A third problem is applying Section 315 arises during political primary campaigns. Can a candidate in a primary election claim equal time if a broadcaster provides coverage of a potential opponent from the other party? The FCC has decided that during primaries, Section 315 applies to intra-party rather than interparty disputes. A candidate cannot claim equal time privileges against candidates of different parties during a primary. Section 315 applies only to contests within the party.

A fourth problem with the Equal Time Rule is that it operates only when the actual candidate makes use of broadcasting facilities. Relatives, friends, and other supporters are not covered under Section 315. A candidate has to appear in person before the rule may be invoked. If a spokesperson for or supporter of the candidate broadcasts a campaign message, the Equal Time rule is not applicable. In order to offset the impact of such a partisan campaign broadcast, the FCC developed its "Political Party Doctrine."

Letter to Nicholas Zapple 23 FCC 2d 707 (1970)

The doctrine set forth in the Zapple letter holds that when, during a political campaign for elected public office, a broadcaster sells air time to a candidate's spokespeople or supporters who use that time to discuss issues in the campaign, urge the candidate's election, criticize the candidate's opponent, or criticize positions taken by the candidate's opponent--then the spokespeople or supporters of the candidate's opponent are entitled to purchase comparable air time for a reply broadcast. The doctrine does not require free reply time if the original broadcast was paid for. All Zapple stipulates is that the opposing candidate's supporters must be sold comparable time if they want it. Free reply time is available only when the original time was given without charge. The Political Party Doctrine is not available to all parties. The Commission indicated that the doctrine was designed to provide responses by major political parties only. The FCC affirmed this doctrine in its 1972 Report Regarding the Handling of Political Broadcasts, which claimed that stations must provide equal opportunity for reply in the event of non-candidate appearances.

Fairness Doctrine

Unlike the Equal Time rule, the Fairness Doctrine does not place a burden on broadcasters to provide a precise quantitative equivalence of air time to rival political candidates. Rather, the emphasis is on the broadcaster's affirmative responsibility to fairly and adequately cover issues of public importance. As has been noted, Section 315 had occasionally operated to stifle debate and chill the discussion of political issues. The broadcaster could fulfill the letter of the law by refusing air time to all candidates. The Fairness Doctrine, by contrast, was formulated by the FCC in response to public complaints regarding editorial policy and the coverage of controversial issues.

Controversial Issues--One of the most important cases that has dealt with editorial policy, and that ultimately led to the formal announcement of the Fairness Doctrine, was the Mayflower decision.

In the Matter of the Mayflower Broadcasting Corporation and the Yankee Network, Inc. (WAAB) 8 FCC 333, 338 (1941)

In 1938, Yankee Network Inc. applied for renewal of its licenses for the main and auxiliary transmitters of Boston station WAAB. Mayflower Broadcasting Inc. challenged the renewal and applied for a construction permit. The FCC hearing revealed that Yankee Broadcasting had since early 1937 broadcast "editorials" urging the election of various candidates to public office. No pretense of impartiality was made by the editor-in-chief of the station news service in announcing the choices. The FCC, in noting the large number of broadcasts devoted to such partisan appeals, sharply condemned Yankee's practices.

Under the American system of broadcasting it is clear that responsibility for the conduct of a broadcast station must rest initially with the broadcaster. It is equally clear that with the limitations in frequencies inherent in the nature of radio, the public interest can never be served by a dedication of any broadcast facility to the support of his own partisan ends. Radio can serve as an instrument of democracy only when devoted to the communication of information and the exchange of ideas fairly and objectively presented. A truly free radio cannot

> be used to advocate the causes of the licensee. It
> cannot be used to support the candidacies of his
> friends. It cannot be devoted to the support of
> principles he happens to regard most favorably.
> In brief, the broadcaster cannot be an advocate.

Despite its firm position against editorializing by broadcasters,
the FCC denied Mayflower's application on the ground that
the company was not financially qualified to construct and
operate the proposed station. The FCC also pointed to certain misrepresentations of fact made by Mayflower. The real
importance of the decision, though, was that stations were
effectively discouraged from editorializing. Stations decided
not to risk losing their licenses by broadcasting what the FCC
could possibly consider "unfair editorials. " The Commission
noted in Mayflower that "freedom of speech on the radio must
be broad enough to provide full and equal opportunity for the
presentation to the public of all sides of public issues. " Even
though Mayflower recognized the importance of fairness and
balance, the FCC did not require broadcasters affirmatively
to seek out opposing viewpoints and fairly and adequately present these views. Subsequent rulings in the WHKC and Scott
decisions signaled a new approach to the coverage of controversial issues--an approach that contained within it the founda-
tions of the Fairness Doctrine.

In re United Broadcasting Company (WHKC) 10 FCC 515 (1945)

In a petition to deny renewal of license to United Broadcasting Company for station WHKC, two labor unions argued
that United had throttled free speech and was not operating
in the public interest. Specifically, the unions pointed to
1) the station policy not to permit the sale of time for programs that solicited memberships or discussed controversial
subjects (race, religion, politics), 2) non-uniform application
of the policy "strictly to those with whom the management
of Station WHKC disagrees ... and loosely or not at all with
respect to others, " and 3) censorship of scripts submitted
by the unions. United had complied with the Code of the
National Association of Broadcasters, which provided that at
no time should air time be sold for the presentation of controversial issues with the exception of political issues and
the public forum type of programs. While conceding that
stations are not common carriers and do not have to sell
time to all who want it, the FCC argued that strict rules
against such sales did not justify a policy of unfair or inadequate coverage of controversial issues.

> The Commission recognizes that good program
> balance may not permit the sale or donation of
> time to all who may seek it for such purposes and
> that difficult problems calling for careful judgment
> on the part of station management may be involved
> in deciding among applicants for time when all
> cannot be accommodated. However, competent man-
> agement should be able to meet such problems in
> the public interest and with fairness to all con-
> cerned. The fact that it places an arduous task
> on management should not be made a reason for
> evading the issue by a strict rule against the sale
> of time for any program of the type mentioned.

The FCC's decision, by no means a liberal mandate for
broadcasters to provide fair coverage of controversial issues,
merely denounced the absolute banning of sales of air time
for such issues.

In re Petition of Robert Harold Scott for Revocation of Licenses of Radio Stations KQW, KPO and KFRC 11 FCC 372 (1946)

The Scott case was more in line with the emerging
concept of "fairness." It provided a consideration of religious liberty as related to freedom of expression in broadcasting. In 1945, Robert Scott filed a petition requesting
that the Commission revoke the licenses of radio stations
KQW, San Jose, and KPO and KFRC, both of San Francisco.
Scott was denied air time to broadcast talks on the subject
of atheism while the stations permitted the use of their facilities for arguments against atheism as well as for church services, prayers, Bible reading, and other kinds of religious
programs. Scott argued that the stations did not present all
sides of the issue and therefore were not operating in the
public interest.

The Commission denied the petition on the ground that
Scott's complaint was so broad as not to be unique to any
one of the three stations. Yet, the fundamental questions
of freedom of expression and religion were not ignored. For
the Commission, the fact that a majority of the public did
not accept a particular point of view was no reason to deny
airing that view.

Freedom of religious belief necessarily carries

with it freedom to disbelieve, and freedom of
speech means freedom to express disbeliefs as
well as beliefs.   If freedom of speech is to have
meaning, it cannot be predicated on the mere popularity or public acceptance of the ideas sought to
be advanced.   It must be extended as readily to
ideas which we disapprove or abhor as to ideas
which we approve.   Moreover, freedom of speech
can be as effectively denied by denying access to
the public means of making expression effective--
whether public streets, parks, meeting halls, or
the radio--as by legal restraints or punishments
of the speaker.

According to the Commission, the diverse conceptions of God
are such that the God of one person does not exist for another.
The Commission noted that the demands of time made on the
broadcaster may be such that a difficult selection among competing interests must be made.   The final decision rests with
the broadcaster.   Admittedly, much opportunity exists for
prejudicial selling of air time.   The ultimate test is whether
the decision is in the public interest--that the available air
time is allocated among those who would use it to the best
advantage of society.

The vagaries existing in both the Scott and WHKC
decisions led the FCC in 1949 to specifically delineate the
broadcaster's responsibilities concerning the coverage of
controversial issues.   The FCC report, In the Matter of
Editorializing by Broadcast Licensees, was the result of a
study of the impact of the Mayflower decision.   The report
stated that 1) the broadcaster has an affirmative responsibility for providing a reasonable amount of time for the presentation of programs devoted to the discussion of public issues,
and 2) it is contingent upon the broadcaster to afford a reasonable opportunity for the presentation of all responsible
positions on the matter.   In 1959, Congress adopted almost
the same wording as that provided in the report when it
amended the Federal Communications Act.

The Fairness Doctrine, though straightforward and
seemingly clear, contains several ambiguous terms.   Such
words and phrases as "fair, " "reasonable opportunity, " and
"public issues" must be defined almost on a case-by case
basis.   In general, however, the FCC has left much of the
implementation of the doctrine to the individual license holders.   Broadcasters typically retain discretion in determining

how much time to devote to discussion of an issue, what constitutes a "reasonable opportunity for opposing viewpoints, "
and what is a controversial issue.   The FCC considers a
public issue to 1) stimulate a certain degree of media coverage and attention from government officials and other community leaders, and 2) have significant impact on the community at large.   Overall, the FCC is quite lenient in regard to license holder's practices and seldom questions routine operations, let alone invokes severe sanctions against
some breach of the doctrine.   The FCC does no monitoring
but depends upon viewer and listener input.   The party seeking to revoke the license of a broadcaster has a typically
heavy burden of proof.   All the broadcaster need demonstrate
is that a good faith and reasonable effort was made to abide
by the doctrine's precepts.

Personal Attack Rules--As the Fairness Doctrine evolved
over the past several decades, a number of court cases
dealt with situations where an individual or group was maligned
publicly. A series of "personal attack" rules emerged. One
of the most important "personal attack" cases was Red Lion
Broadcasting.

Red Lion Broadcasting Company, Inc. v. Federal Communications
Commission
United States v. Radio Television News Directors Association
395 U. S. 367 (1969)

In November, 1964, the Red Lion Broadcasting Company of Red Lion, Pennsylvania, carried a series entitled
The Christian Crusade.   One of the programs included an
attack by Reverend Billy James Hargis against a book entitled
Goldwater--Extremist of the Right.   Hargis attacked the book's
author, Fred Cook, calling attention to the fact that Cook was
fired from the New York Telegram for making a false charge
on television against a New York City public official.   Several
New York publications and Newsweek magazine revealed that
Cook and his friend Eugene Gleason had fabricated the whole
story.   Cook later made a confession to the district attorney
to that effect.   According to Hargis, Cook then took a job
with the "left wing publication, the Nation, " and wrote articles
condemning the FBI and the CIA and an article absolving Al-
ger Hiss of any wrongdoing.   By pointing to Cook's background,
Hargis attempted to discredit Cook's most recent book about
Senator Barry Goldwater.

The personal attack rule--an aspect of the Fairness Doctrine--required that when an individual was personally attacked, the station carrying the attack had to provide an opportunity for reply. A question that was unclear, however, was whether the station had to furnish free broadcast time if the person attacked could not obtain a sponsor and was unable to pay for the time. Cook asked the radio station for an opportunity to reply to Hargis's attacks. The station replied that the personal attack rule only required a licensee to make free time for reply available if no paid sponsorship could be found. The station insisted that Cook had to attest that no sponsor could be located. Cook complained to the FCC. Upon hearing, the FCC held that the station was obligated to furnish reply time, paid or not. It was not necessary for Cook to show that he could not afford or find a sponsor before the station's obligation to make reply time available went into effect. According to the FCC, the public interest required that the public be given an opportunity to hear both sides of an issue, even if the time had to be paid for by the station. The FCC entered a formal order to that effect and the station appealed. The Court of Appeals for the District of Columbia noted that on July 1, 1964, the FCC had issued a Public Notice entitled "Applicability of the Fairness Doctrine in the Handling of Controversial Issues of Public Importance." This document contained a specific explanation of the personal attack principle and the rules implementing it. In its Red Lion decision, the court held that both the Fairness Doctrine and the personal attack rules were constitutional.

In a related case, the Radio Television News Directors Association (RTNDA) decided to institute suit for judicial review of FCC orders regarding personal attack rules and reply time for political editorials. Suit was filed in the United States Court of Appeals for the Seventh Circuit, a court that was thought to be less sympathetic to government agencies than the Washington-based court of appeals. The court ruled that the personal attack rules and the political editorial rules violated the First Amendment.

> In view of the vagueness of the Commission's rules, the burden they impose on licensees, and the possibility they raise of both Commission censorship and licensee self-censorship, we conclude that the personal attack and political editorial rules would contravene the first amendment.

Eventually both the Red Lion and RTNDA cases reached the U.S. Supreme Court. To the amazement of the broadcast industry, the Court affirmed (7-0) the Red Lion decision and reversed the RTNDA decision. In its ruling, the Court strongly supported the principle of fairness and also affirmed a newer doctrine--access. The Court stated that both the personal attack rules and the rules governing political broadcasts were consistent with the First Amendment. In supporting its argument, the Court noted that without such rules, broadcasters would have "unfettered power to make time available only to the highest bidders, to communicate only their views on public issues, people, and candidates, and to permit on the air only those with whom they agreed." In laying the foundation for the strengthened doctrine of access, the Court again noted the inherent problems involved in allocating licenses among competing broadcasters.

> In view of the prevalence of scarcity of broadcast frequencies, the Government's role in allocating those frequencies, and the legitimate access to those frequencies for expression of their views, we hold the regulations and ruling at issue here are both authorized by statute and constitutional. The judgment of the Court of Appeals in Red Lion is affirmed and that in RTNDA reversed and the causes remanded for proceedings consistent with this opinion.

Though the Court by no means broke with the traditional "limitation of the spectrum" approach, its decision contained within it the seeds of a more broadly fashioned "access doctrine." Writing for the Court, Justice Byron White argued,

> ... as far as the First Amendment is concerned those who are licensed stand no better than those to whom licenses are refused.... It is the purpose of the First Amendment to preserve an uninhibited marketplace of ideas in which truth will ultimately prevail rather than to countenance monopolization of that market, whether it be by the Government itself or a private licensee.... It is the right of the public to receive suitable access to social, political, aesthetic, moral, and other ideas and experiences which is crucial here. That right may not constitutionally be abridged either by Congress or by the FCC.

The decision gave much encouragement to those who felt broadcasting should be treated substantially the same as the print medium. However, the scarcity of available wavelengths required the FCC to allocate the fixed number of licenses to those broadcasters who best fulfill the interests of their listeners. Indeed, in the Communications Act itself Congress specifically denied that broadcasting was a common carrier. Scarcity demanded that broadcasters wield some discretion in determining who may have access to the airwaves and for how long. The broad mandate of Red Lion was to allow as much access to airwaves as was consistent with the purposes of the First Amendment. The FCC contended that if broadcasters were meeting the requirements of the Fairness Doctrine they were under no obligation to provide access to all who request air time, either by selling such air time or providing it free of charge.

In Red Lion, the Court affirmed the constitutionality and desirability of the Fairness Doctrine. It further prohibited broadcasters from banning outright any sales of broadcast time for airing of controversial issues. As a general programming policy, such a practice violated the First Amendment. To what extent the Court meant its decision to extend beyond the requirements of the Fairness Doctrine, though, was problematic. A fundamental conflict remained unresolved. Did the First Amendment require that freedom of expression of those desiring access to the airwaves be unabridged, or did it mean that broadcasters were free from governmental censorship and interference? Owing to the scarcity of available frequencies, such conflicts must be resolved on a case-by-case basis in which the legitimate but competing claims of broadcasters and those who would desire access to this unique form of communication are balanced and reconciled. Undoubtedly, the concept of a limited right of access was strengthened in Red Lion. The Court, however, provided only broad guidelines as to its meaning and applicability within a wide range of circumstances. Future cases more specifically delineated the limits of access.

Columbia Broadcasting System, Inc. v. Democratic National Committee Federal Communications Commission v. Business Executives Move for Vietnam Peace Post-Newsweek Stations, Capital Area, Inc. v. Business Executives' Move for Vietnam Peace American Broadcasting Companies, Inc. v. Democratic National Committee 412 U. S. 94 (1973)

In January, 1970, the Business Executives Move for
Vietnam Peace (BEM), a national organization opposed to
U. S. involvement in the Vietnam conflict, filed a complaint
with the FCC charging that radio station WTOP in Washington, D. C. , had refused to sell it time to broadcast a series
of one-minute spot announcements expressing BEM views on
Vietnam. WTOP refused to sell time for spot announcements
to individuals and groups who wished to expound their views
on controversial issues. WTOP contended that since it presented full and fair coverage of important public questions,
including the Vietnam conflict, it was justified in refusing to
accept editorial advertisements. WTOP submitted evidence
indicating that the station had aired the views of critics of
U. S. Vietnam policy on several occasions. BEM challenged
the fairness of WTOP's coverage of criticism of that policy,
but it presented no evidence in support of that claim.

Four months later, the Democratic National Committee
(DNC) filed a request for a declaratory ruling with the FCC
that under the First Amendment and the Communications Act
"a broadcaster may not, as a general policy, refuse to sell
time to responsible entities, such as DNC, for the solicitation of funds and for comment on public issues. " DNC
claimed that it intended to purchase time from radio and
television stations and from the national networks in order
to present the views of the Democratic Party, and to solicit
funds. Unlike BEM, DNC did not object to the policies of
any particular station but claimed that its prior "experiences
in this area make it clear that it will encounter considerable
difficulty--if not total frustration of its efforts--in carrying
out its plan" if the Commission declined to issue a ruling.
DNC cited Red Lion as establishing a limited constitutional
right to access to the airwaves. In dealing with both the
BEM and DNC cases, the FCC ruled that broadcasters who
meet their public obligation to provide full and fair coverage
of public issues were not required to accept editorial advertisements. The court of appeals reversed the FCC, holding
that a broadcaster's fixed policy of refusing all editorial advertisements violated the First Amendment. The court held
that "a flat ban on paid public issue announcements is in violation of the First Amendment, at least when other sorts of
paid announcements are accepted. " However, the court did
not order that either BEM's or DNC's proposed announcements must be accepted by the broadcasters; rather, it remanded the cases to the FCC to develop "reasonable procedures and regulations determining which and how many
'editorial advertisements' will be put on the air. "

The U. S. Supreme Court reversed (7-2) the court of
appeals, arguing:

> More profoundly, it would be anomalous for us to
> hold, in the name of promoting the constitutional
> guarantees of free expression, that the day-to-day
> editorial decisions of broadcast licensees are sub-
> ject to the kind of restraints urged by respondents.
> To do so in the name of the First Amendment would
> be a contradiction. Journalistic discretion would
> in many ways be lost to the rigid limitations that
> the First Amendment imposes on government. Ap-
> plication of such standards to broadcast licensees
> would be antithetical to the very ideal of vigorous,
> challenging debate on issues of public interest.
> Every licensee is already held accountable for the
> totality of its performance of public interest obligations.

The court rejected the argument that the FCC's actions
amounted to governmental intrusion in violation of the First
Amendment. The Court also pointed to historical congressional disapproval of any attempt to mandate individual access.
According to the Court, "in this case, the Commission has
decided that on balance the undesirable effects of the right
of access urged by respondents would outweigh the asserted
benefits."

In agreeing with the FCC's decision, the Court also
reviewed what specifically constitutes the FCC's responsibilities concerning application and enforcement of the Fairness
Doctrine.

> Under the Fairness Doctrine the Commission's re-
> sponsibility is to judge whether a licensee's over-
> all performance indicates a sustained good faith ef-
> fort to meet the public interest in being fully
> and fairly informed. The Commission's responsi-
> bilities under a right-of-access system would tend
> to draw it into a continuing case-by-case determin-
> ation of who should be heard and when. Indeed,
> the likelihood of Government involvement is so
> great that it has been suggested that the accepted
> constitutional principles against control of speech
> content would need to be relaxed with respect to
> editorial advertisements. To sacrifice First Amend-
> ment protections for so speculative a gain is not war-
> ranted, and it was well within the Commission's dis-
> cretion to construe the Act so as to avoid such a result.

The Court ruled that neither the "public interest standard nor the First Amendment required a right of access for editorial advertising time because such a right would mean an end to the editorial function in broadcast journalism. The CBS case thus broke the apparent momentum of the right of access evidenced in Red Lion. The Court weighed the competing claims of licensees and those who would desire access to the airways and concluded that the broadcaster had a legitimate right to deny air time to the DNC and BEM.

Enforcement--How does the FCC enforce the Fairness Doctrine? Clearly, the FCC allows considerable leeway for broadcasters to choose and air programming dealing with controversial issues of public interest. As long as the broadcaster can demonstrate a good faith effort in fairly and adequately covering controversial issues, the FCC does not impose any sanctions. Nonetheless, the FCC has three enforcement options that it may wield when the situation warrants: 1) a letter of reprimand, 2) the cease and desist order, and 3) denial of license renewal. The use of a letter of reprimand takes place when a third party protests some programming decision by a licensee. The Commission sends a letter to the licensee indicating how the matter should be dealt with. This enforcement method generally lacks force because it is difficult to get judicial review of a course of action outlined by the FCC in a letter. A second option is the cease and desist order. Even though such orders have not been issued on a widespread basis, the FCC is willing to use them. The most severe sanction is the FCC's power to deny an application for license renewal. In 1972, a particularly glaring instance of malfeasance under the Fairness Doctrine resulted in denial of a license renewal.

Brandywine-Main Line Radio, Inc. v. Federal
Communications Commission 473 F. 2d 16 (1972)

In 1965, Brandywine-Main Line Radio, Inc., a company completely owned by the Faith Theological Seminary and presided over by right-wing preacher Carl McIntire, applied for transfer of control of radio station WXUR in Media, Pennsylvania, to them from its owners. Community groups fought this application but the FCC approved the transfer after the McIntire group pledged to provide opportunity for the expression of opposing viewpoints on controversial public issues. At renewal time, citizen groups in the community contended that the McIntire group failed to honor their pledge. The renewal hearing determined that Thomas Livezy, moderator of a WXUR call-in program Freedom of Speech had encouraged and approved of the remarks of some of the program's anti-Jewish callers. Persons attacked on WXUR included New Left celebrities Eugene Genovese, Staughton Lynd, Harvard Law Professor Adam Yarmolinsky, the Black Deacons for Defense, and the Flushing Branch of the Women's International League for Peace and Freedom. Under the personal attack rules, WXUR was required to furnish those who were attacked a notice of the attack and an offer of an opportunity to reply. WXUR had established no procedure for providing notice and response. WXUR's critics claimed the station had failed to make a sufficient effort to provide convincing spokespeople to counteract its conservative, right-wing programming.

In July, 1970, station WXUR became the first licensee in the history of broadcast regulation to lose its license at renewal time because of failure to comply with the Fairness Doctrine. The FCC decided:

> We conclude upon an evaluation of all the relevant and material evidence contained in the hearing record, that renewals of the WXUR and WXUR-FM licenses should not be granted. The record demonstrates that Brandywine failed to provide reasonable opportunities for the presentation of contrasting views on controversial issues of public importance, that it ignored the personal attack principle of the Fairness Doctrine, that the applicant's representations as to the manner in which the station would be operated were not adhered to, that no adequate efforts were made to keep the station attuned to the community's or area's needs and interests, and that no showing has been made that it was, in fact, so attuned. Any one of these violations would alone be sufficient to require denying the renewals here, and the violations are rendered even more serious by the fact that we carefully drew the Seminary's attention to a licensee's responsibilities before we approved transfer of the stations to its ownership and control.

In Brandywine, the court, by affirming the FCC ruling, made it clear to broadcasters that the Fairness Doctrine would be enforced.

Bibliography

Books

Friendly, Fred W. The Good Guys, The Bad Guys, and the First Amendment: Free Speech v. Fairness in Broadcasting. New York: Random House, 1976.

Kahn, Frank J. , ed. Documents in American Broadcasting. 3rd ed. Englewood Cliffs, N. J. : Prentice Hall, 1978.

Shapiro, Andrew O. Media Access: Your Right to Express Your Views on Radio and Television. Boston: Little, Brown and Company, 1976.

Toohey, Daniel W. , Richard D. Marks, and Arnold P. Lutzker. Legal Problems in Broadcasting: Identification and Analysis of Selected Issues. Lincoln: University of Nebraska Press, 1974.

Cases

Brandywine-Main Line Radio, Inc. v. Federal Communications Commission 473 F. 2d 16 (1972)

Carroll Broadcasting Company v. Federal Communications Commission 258 F. 2d 440 (1958)

Carter Mountain Transmission Corporation v. Federal Communications Commission 321 F. 2d 359 (1963)

Citizens Committee to Save WEFM v. Federal Communications Commission 506 F. 2d 246 (1974)

Citizens Communications Center v. Federal Communications Commission; Hampton Roads Television Corporation v. Federal Communications Commission; Citizens Communications Center v. Burch 447 F. 2d 1201 (1971)

Columbia Broadcasting System, Inc. v. Democratic National Committee; Federal Communications Commission v. Business Executives Move for Vietnam Peace; Post-Newsweek Stations, Capital Area, Inc. v. Business Executives Move for Vietnam Peace; American Broadcasting Companies, Inc. v. Democratic National Committee 412 U. S. 94 (1973)

Farmers Educational & Cooperative Union of America, North Dakota Division v. WDAY, Inc. 360 U. S. 525 (1959)

Federal Communications Commission v. American Broadcasting Company, Inc.; Federal Communications Commission v. National Broadcasting Company, Inc.; Federal Communications Commission v. Columbia Broadcasting System, Inc. 347 U. S. 294 (1954)

Federal Communications Commission v. National Citizens Committee for Broadcasting; Channel Two Television Company v. National Citizens Committee for Broadcasting; National Association of Broadcasters v. Federal Communications Commission; American Newspaper Publishers Association v. National Citizens Committee for Broadcasting; Illinois Broadcasting Company, Inc. v. National Citizens Committee for Broadcasting; Post Company v. National Citizens Committee for Broadcasting 436 U. S. 775 (1978)

Federal Communications Commission v. Pacifica Foundation 98 S. Ct. 3026 (1978)

Federal Communications Commission v. Sanders Brothers Radio Station 309 U. S. 470 (1940)

Greater Boston Television Corporation v. Federal Communications Commission 444 F. 2d 841 (1970)

Hale v. Federal Communications Commission 425 F. 2d 556 (1970)

Henry v. Federal Communications Commission 302 F. 2d 191 (1962)

Hoover v. Intercity Radio Company, Inc. 286 F. 1003 (1923)

In re Pacifica Foundation 36 FCC 147 (1964)

In re Palmetto Broadcasting Company 33 FCC 250 (1962)

In re Petition of Robert Harold Scott for Revocation of Licenses of Radio Stations KQW, KPO and KFRC 11 FCC 372 (1946)

In re United Broadcasting Company (WHKC) 10 FCC 515 (1945)

In re WUHY-FM, Eastern Educational Radio 24 FCC 2d 408 (1970)

In the Matter of the Mayflower Broadcasting Corporation and the Yankee Network, Inc. (WAAB) 8 FCC 333, 338 (1941)

KFKB Broadcasting Association, Inc. v. Federal Radio Commission 47 F. 2d 670 (1931)

Letter to Nicholas Zapple 23 FCC 2d 707 (1970)

McCarthy v. Federal Communications Commission 390 F. 2d 471 (1968)

Mansfield Journal Company v. Federal Communications Commission; Lorain Journal Company v. Federal Communications Commission 180 F. 2d 28 (1950)

Miller v. California 413 U. S. 15 (1973)

National Broadcasting Company v. United States; Columbia Broadcasting System, Inc. v. United States 319 U. S. 190 (1943)

New York State Broadcasters Association v. United States 414 F. 2d 990 (1969)

Office of Communication of the United Church of Christ v. Federal Communications Commission 359 F. 2d 994 (1966)

Office of Communication of the United Church of Christ v. Federal Communications Commission 425 F. 2d 543 (1969)

Red Lion Broadcasting Company, Inc. v. Federal Communications Commission; United States v. Radio Television News Directors Association 395 U. S. 367 (1969)

Roth v. United States 354 U. S. 476 (1957)

Simmons v. Federal Communications Commission 169 F. 2d 670 (1948)

Sonderling Broadcasting Corporation, WGLD-FM 27 P. & F. Rad. Regs. 2d 285 (1973)

State of Maine v. University of Maine 266 A. 2d 863 (1970)

Stone v. Federal Communications Commission 466 F. 2d 316 (1972)

Trinity Methodist Church, South v. Federal Radio Commission
62 F. 2d 850 (1932)

United States v. Midwest Video Corporation 406 U. S. 649
(1972)

United States v. Southwestern Cable Company; Midwestern
Television Inc. v. Southwestern Cable Company 392 U. S.
157 (1968)

Yale Broadcasting Company v. Federal Communications Commission 478 F. 2d 594 (1973)

CHAPTER VIII

ADVERTISING

The role advertising plays in the U. S. has expanded
significantly during recent decades. The volume of dollars
spent annually on advertisements has increased many-fold.
New technological achievements have produced complex advertising strategies along with a more sophisticated use of
the mass media. The heightened use of advertising on the
part of business and industrial promoters has resulted in increased concern about fairness and honesty in advertising.
This concern, however, is not new. Misrepresentation in
advertising came under heavy attack during the muckraker
movement of the early 1900s. Since that time, legislatures,
consumer groups, and the courts have had varying amounts
of success in policing the claims of advertisers. In this
chapter, several significant court cases will be considered,
each of which had an impact on the practice of advertising.

COMMERCIAL SPEECH

Over the years, the courts have considered the relationship between advertising and the First Amendment. In a
1942 case, the U. S. Supreme Court determined that purely
"commercial speech" enjoyed less constitutional protection
than other forms of communication. Furthermore, the Court
gave greater protection to editorial rather than commercial
forms of advertising.

Valentine v. Chrestensen 316 U. S. 52 (1942)

F. J. Chrestensen, a citizen of Florida, owned a former United States Navy submarine, which he exhibited for
profit. In 1940, he brought it to New York City and moored
it at a pier on the East River. He printed a handbill that
advertised the boat and solicited visitors for an admission fee.

When he attempted to distribute the ad on city streets, he
was advised by Police Commissioner Lewis Valentine that he
was violating Section 318 of the Sanitary Code, which forbade
the distribution of commercial advertising on city streets.
Chrestensen was informed that he could only distribute hand-
bills strictly limited to "information of a public protest."
Chrestensen subsequently prepared a double-faced handbill.
On one side was a revision of the original; the statement regarding the admission fee was removed, but the notice still
consisted solely of commercial advertising. On the other
side was a protest against the action of the City Dock Department for refusing Chrestensen wharfage facilities at a
city pier where he intended to exhibit his submarine. There
was no commercial advertising on this side of the handbill.
The police advised Chrestensen that distribution of the bill
containing only the protest was allowable and would not be
restrained, but that distribution of the double-faced bill was
prohibited. Nevertheless, Chrestensen distributed the handbill. He was restrained by the police. Chrestensen brought
suit to prevent interference with the distribution of his handbill. The case reached the U. S. Supreme Court.

The Court had to decide whether the application of the
ordinance to Chrestensen's activity constituted an unconstitutional abridgement of the freedoms of speech and press. The
Court acknowledged that the streets were proper places for
communicating information and disseminating opinion, and
though states and cities may apppropriately regulate this
privilege in the public interest, they may not unduly restrict
such communication. However, the Court noted that the Constitution imposed no restraint on government with respect to
purely commercial advertising. New York could lawfully prohibit its citizens from distributing commercial advertising on
the streets. The Court recognized that Chrestensen's protest
was attached to the advertising circular for the purpose of
evading the state prohibition. If such an evasion was allowed,
every merchant could advertise through leaflets in the streets
if they would merely append a civic appeal or moral protest
to the leaflet. The law would be rendered ineffective. The
Court concluded (9-0) that "states can prohibit the use of the
streets for the distribution of purely commercial leaflets,
even though such leaflets may have a 'civic appeal, or a
moral platitude' appended." In Valentine, the Court clearly
extended a preferred position to political rather than commercial communication. The preference continued in later Court
decisions.

Pittsburgh Press Company v. Pittsburgh
Commission on Human Relations 413 U. S. 376 (1973)

On October 9, 1969, the National Organization for
Women filed a complaint with the Pittsburgh Commission on
Human Relations alleging that the Pittsburgh Press Company
was violating the Pittsburgh Human Relations Ordinance by
"allowing employers to place advertisements in the male and
female columns, when the jobs advertised obviously do not
have bona fide occupational qualifications or exceptions. "
The Commission held a hearing and on October 23, 1970,
announced its findings. During 1969, Pittsburgh Press carried a total of 248, 000 help wanted advertisements. Before
October, 1969, its practice was to use columns captioned
"Male Help Wanted, " "Female Help Wanted, " and "Male-Female Help Wanted. " Thereafter, it used the captions "Jobs--
Male Interest, " "Jobs--Female Interest, " and "Male-Female. "
The advertisements were placed in the respective columns
according to the advertiser's wishes. The Commission noted
that the Ordinance forbade employers from submitting advertisements for placement in sex designated columns. Pittsburgh Press violated the Ordinance by maintaining a sex designated classification system. The existence of such classifications did, in fact, aid employers to indicate illegal sex
preferences. The Commission ordered Pittsburgh Press to
cease and desist such violations and to utilize a classification
system with no reference to sex. On appeal in the commonwealth court, the scope of the order was narrowed to allow
Pittsburgh Press to carry advertisements in sex designated
columns for jobs exempt from the antidiscrimination provisions of the Ordinance. The Ordinance did not apply to employers of fewer than five persons; to employers outside the
city of Pittsburgh; or to religious, fraternal, charitable, or
sectarian organizations. It also did not apply to employment
in domestic service or in jobs for which the Commission had
certified a bona fide occupational exception. The case reached
the U. S. Supreme Court.

The issue facing the Court was whether the Ordinance
violated the freedoms of speech and press as guaranteed by
the First and Fourteenth Amendments. The Court noted (5-4)
that this regulation was permissible because the advertisement was commercial speech and was less protected by the
Constitution. The Court claimed:

> In the crucial respects, the advertisements in the
> present record resemble the Chrestensen rather

than the Sullivan [New York Times v. Sullivan] advertisements. None expresses a position on whether, as a matter of social policy, certain positions ought to be filled by members of one or the other sex, nor does any of them criticize the Ordinance or the Commission's enforcement practices. Each is no more than a proposal of possible employment. The advertisements are thus classic examples of commercial speech.

The Court emphasized that Pittsburgh Press could publish advertisements commenting on the Ordinance, the enforcement practices of the Commission, or the propriety of sex preferences in employment. The Court strongly reaffirmed the protection afforded the press regarding the expression of views on controversial issues. The Court, however, held that the Commission's order prohibiting placement of ads in sex designated columns did not violate the First and Fourteenth Amendment rights of the Pittsburgh newspaper.

Bigelow v. Virginia 421 U. S. 809 (1975)

In 1975, the Court extended First Amendment protection to commercial speech. Jeffrey Bigelow, the managing editor of the (Charlottesville) Virginia Weekly, published an advertisement by a New York City organization announcing that its services were available on a low-cost, confidential basis to make arrangements for women with unwanted pregnancies to obtain an abortion in an accredited hospital or clinic. Virginia law made it a misdemeanor to circulate any publication that encouraged or prompted the procuring of an abortion. Bigelow was convicted of violating the statute on grounds that the regulation of commercial advertisements was within the police powers of the state. Bigelow appealed, claiming that the Virginia law violated the First Amendment.

The U. S. Supreme Court ruled that because a particular advertisement had commercial aspects or reflected the advertiser's commercial interests did not negate all First Amendment guarantees. Virginia was not free of constitutional restraint merely because the advertisement involved sales or solicitations. The advertisement under consideration did more than simply propose a commercial transaction. It contained factual material of "public interest." Portions of the message, especially the lines "Abortions are now legal in New York," and "There are no residency requirements," involved the exercise of the freedom of communicating information and disseminating opinion. Viewed in its entirety, the advertisement conveyed information of potential interest and value to a diverse public--not only to readers possibly in need of the services offered, but also to those with a genuine interest in the matter of abortion or the development of the law. It was also of interest to readers seeking reform in Virginia. In fact, the mere existence of the Women's Pavilion in New York City and the availability of the services offered was newsworthy. In this case, Bigelow's First Amendment interests coincided with the constitutional interests of the general public.

The Court stressed (7-2) that advertising was not stripped of all First Amendment protection: "The relationship of speech to the marketplace of products or of services does not make it valueless in the marketplace of ideas." The Court went on to note that Virginia was really attempting to regulate what Virginians may hear or read about the New York services. Virginia was, in effect, shielding its citizens from information about activities outside Virginia's borders, activities that Virginia's police powers did not reach. This asserted interest infringed upon First Amendment rights. In Bigelow, the Court concluded that Virginia could not punish the publisher of a newspaper for printing an abortion referral agency's paid advertisement that not only promoted the agency's services but also contained information about the availability of abortions.

In another recent case, the Court further eroded the "commercial speech" exception to the First Amendment. In Virginia State Board of Pharmacy v. Virginia Citizens' Consumer Council, a case that is examined in more detail later in this chapter, the Court found that Virginia's ban on the advertising of prescription drug prices by pharmacists was unconstitutional. The Court held that commercial speech was not "Wholly outside the protection of the First Amendment." Justice Harry Blackmun reasoned that as long as the United States maintained a free enterprise economy, each individual would make many private economic decisions. It was " a matter of public interest that those decisions in the aggregate be intelligent and well informed. To this end, the free flow of commercial information is indispensable." In its decision, the Court upheld the government's power to regulate any false, misleading, or deceptive uses of "commercial speech." In Virginia State Board, as in Bigelow, the Court extended First Amendment protection to "commercial speech."

REGULATION

Up until the beginning of the twentieth century, the matter of promotion and advertising of goods and services was regulated principally by the doctrine of caveat emptor-- let the buyer beware. A more rigid regulatory policy was initiated with the passage of the Pure Food and Drug Act in 1906 and the creation of the Federal Trade Commission in 1914. During the first years of regulation, the courts tended to protect competitors against false and deceptive advertisements; consumer rights were secondary and at times ignored entirely. More recently, consumer interests have received increased attention from the Federal Trade Commission as well as the U. S. Supreme Court.

Deception

The movement to regulate advertising took root with the passage of the Pure Food and Drug Act in 1906 and the creation of the Federal Trade Commission in 1914. The U. S. Supreme Court first acted on behalf of the consumer interest in 1922. The case involved deceptive labeling.

Federal Trade Commission v. Winsted Hosiery Company 258 U. S. 483 (1922)

The Winsted Hosiery Company manufactured underwear, which it sold to retailers throughout the United States. It labeled the cartons in which the underwear was sold as "Natural Merino, " "Gray Wool, " "Natural Wool, " "Natural Worsted, " or "Australian Wool. " None of the underwear was all wool. Much of it contained only a small percentage of wool, some as little as 10 percent. The Federal Trade Commission decided that the labels were false and deceptive. It was in the best interest of the public to stop this practice. The FTC subsequently directed the company to "cease and desist" from using as labels, on goods not composed wholly of wool, the words "Merino, " "Wool, " or "Worsted, " unless the labels also indicated any material other than wool that went into the garments, or unless they contained words clearly indicating that the underwear was not made wholly of wool. The company brought suit against the FTC.

The U. S. Supreme Court examined the meaning of the words used on the Winsted Hosiery labels. According to the

Court, the word "Merino, " as applied to wool, meant a fine long-staple wool that commanded the highest price. The words "Australian Wool" meant a fine grade of wool grown in Australia. The word "wool, " when used as an adjective, meant made of wool. The word "worsted" meant a fabric made wholly of wool. In this instance, a substantial part of the consuming public understood the words "Merino, " "Natural Merino, " "Gray Merino, " "Natural Wool, " "Gray Wool, " "Australian Wool, " and "Natural Worsted" to mean that the underwear was all wool. The public was misled into selling or into buying as all wool, underwear that was in large part cotton. The labels in question were literally false. They were calculated to deceive a substantial portion of the purchasing public. The practice constituted an unfair method of competition against manufacturers of all wool knit underwear and against those manufacturers of mixed wool and cotton underwear who labeled their product truthfully. The Court concluded that puffery--exaggerated use of superlatives to describe goods and services--was permissible only if it stopped at the point of clear deception.

Federal Trade Commission v. Raladam
Company 283 U. S. 643 (1931)

The Federal Trade Commission's power came under attack in 1931. The Raladam Company manufactured a preparation for internal use, designated as an "obesity cure. " The company advertised that the preparation was the result of scientific research, that it was safe and effective, and that it could be used without discomfort or danger to health. However, one of the ingredients, "desiccated thyroid, " did not act with uniformity on all users or without impairing the health of a substantial portion of them, without previous consultation with a competent medical adviser. The FTC recognized that many persons were seeking obesity remedies and the company's advertisements were calculated to deceive the public into believing that the preparation was safe, effective, and without harmful results. The FTC concluded that the practice constituted an unfair method of competition. A cease and desist order was issued. The Commission ordered Raladam to stop claiming that the preparation was a scientific method for treating obesity and from representing the preparation as a remedy for obesity, unless they stated that it could not be taken safely except under medical direction. Raladam brought suit.

When the case reached the Supreme Court, the judges

noted that if protecting the public against misleading advertisements was all that was necessary to give the FTC jurisdiction, the cease and desist order issued against Raladam could not be overturned. But that was not all. The Federal Trade Commission Act that gave the Commission the power to issue an order to desist required that 1) the methods complained of were <u>unfair</u>, 2) they were methods of <u>competition</u> in commerce, and 3) a proceeding by the Commission to prevent the use of the methods appeared to be in the <u>interest of the public.</u> The Court claimed the existence of the first and third requirements, then considered the second. The word "competition" in the act required the existence of present or potential competitors, and the unfair methods must injuriously affect the business of these competitors. It was that condition of affairs that the Commission was given the power to correct, and not some other. Official powers could not be extended beyond the terms of the act. In this case, the Court found no evidence that the advertisements substantially injured the business of any competitor. No competitor was called upon to show what, if any, effect the misleading advertisements had upon his business. The Court ruled (9-0) that the Commission could not, by assuming the existence of competition, give itself jurisdiction to make an order. The FTC order was set aside.

<u>Federal Trade Commission v. Raladam</u>
<u>Company 316 U.S. 149 (1942)</u>

In 1935, the FTC instituted another proceeding against Raladam. This time much evidence was heard that indicated that Raladam's misleading statements had the "tendency and capacity" to induce people to purchase and use the medicine for reducing purposes in preference to and to the exclusion of the products of competitors. The FTC issued a cease and desist order, which Raladam again appealed.

The Court ruled (9-0) that it was not necessary that the evidence show specifically that losses to any particular competitor arose from Raladam's success in capturing part of the market. When the Commission found that deceptive statements were made with reference to the quality of merchandise that was in active competition with other merchandise, it was authorized to infer that trade would be diverted from competitors who do not engage in such "unfair methods." In 1942, the Court overruled the finding in the 1931 <u>Raladam</u> case.

Federal Trade Commission v. Standard
Education Society 302 U. S. 112 (1937)

In 1937, the Court took a strong position against the
rule of caveat emptor. At that time, the Federal Trade Commission became aware that the Standard Education Society was
using deceptive advertising to sell the Standard Reference
Work and New Standard Encyclopedia. As part of its sales
plan, the Society claimed to select specific prospects to give
them a free set of books, and that the only return desired
for the gift was permission to use the name of the prospect
as a reference for advertising purposes. The only cost to
the prospect was $69. 50 for a loose-leaf extension service.
The prospect was told that the regular price of the books and
the extension service was between $150 and $200. These
statements were false, deceptive, and misleading, as $69. 50
was the standard price for both the encyclopedia and the loose-
leaf extension. The FTC issued a cease and desist order.
The case reached the U. S. Supreme Court.

According to the unanimous opinion prepared by Hugo
Black, the Court noted that "the best element of business has
long since decided that honesty should govern competitive enterprises, and that the rule of caveat emptor should not be
relied upon to reward fraud and deception. " Promising free
books and deceiving unwary purchasers about the price of the
books were practices contrary to decent business standards.
If the Court failed to prohibit such practices, deception in
business would be elevated to the standing and dignity of truth.
The Court upheld the FTC order.

In 1938, Congress amended Section 5 of the Federal
Trade Commission Act to add: "Unfair methods of competition in commerce, and unfair or deceptive acts or practices
in commerce are declared unlawful. " Congress also amended Section 12 to include an explicit prohibition of "false advertisements" that were designed "to induce purchase of food,
drugs, devices or cosmetics. " This action, known as the
Wheeler-Lea Amendments, legislated the end of the doctrine
of caveat emptor.

P. Lorillard Company v. Federal Trade
Commission 186 F. 2d 52 (1950)

In 1950, the courts clarified the scope of FTC powers.
The Commission issued a cease and desist order against P.

Lorillard, forbidding the company from advertising that Old
Gold cigarettes contained less nicotine, less tars and resins,
and were less irritating to the throat than the cigarettes of
any of the six other leading brands. The company appealed,
arguing that the order was not supported by substantial evidence and that the order exceeded the power of the Commission.

The United States Court of Appeals for the Fourth Circuit heard the case. The court noted that laboratory tests
introduced in evidence indicated that the difference in the
amount of nicotine, tars, and resins of the different leading
brands of cigarettes was insignificant; testimony of medical
experts claimed there was no difference in the physiological
effect upon the smoker. The evidence amply supported the
Commission's findings. P. Lorillard also challenged the
validity of the order on the ground that the comparison with
the six other leading brands might be true sometime in the
future. The court indicated that the FTC order dealt with
the false advertising that was before the Commission. If,
in the future, advertising of the sort prohibited should become
truthful, application could be made to the Commission for a
revision of the order. Consideration could be given to that
matter when the occasion warranted. The court thus concluded that the possibility that false and misleading advertising might become truthful in the future did not prevent the
FTC from prohibiting such advertising.

Rhodes Pharmacal Company, Inc. v. Federal
Trade Commission 208 F. 2d 382 (1953)

In 1953, the courts further delineated the scope of
FTC powers. The Rhodes Pharmacal Company engaged in
an extensive campaign of newspaper, magazine, and radio
advertising. The first line in the printed ads contained the
statement, printed in large, bold type, "Amazing New Discovery for Rheumatism, Arthritis, " followed by a subhead,
"Hospital Tested. Stops Swelling, Uncorks Joints, Contains
Sensational New Research Discovery. " The ads contained
pictures of men and women with faces or bodies seemingly
contorted with pain, and further down in the ad, under such
headings as "Resume Confident Pain-Free Living with Amazing New Imdrin, " appeared pictures of men and women golf-
ing or bowling, apparently vibrant and healthy. Radio announcements used the following narration: "Persons whose cases
of suffering have been thought almost helpless ... yes, even

people who had suffered and hoped for twenty years, were able to live free of pain ... like happy human beings once again. " The ad also claimed: "No other medicine for rheumatism and arthritis thus far discovered by medical science has such an amazing record. ... " The FTC determined that Imdrin was not an effective or reliable treatment for any arthritic or rheumatic condition. Futhermore, Imdrin had no significant effect upon severe aches or pains accompanying any arthritic or rheumatic condition and would afford temporary and partial relief of only minor aches and pains. The Commission found that Rhodes Pharmacal Company's representations in its advertisements of Imdrin were deceptive and misled a substantial portion of the purchasing public. Rhodes appealed the FTC decision.

The court agreed with the FTC, noting that the company had engaged in unfair and deceptive practice in commerce. In this case, the court acknowledged that the Commission's broad regulatory authority over deceptive and misleading advertising included product naming, product packaging and labeling, product descriptioning, and product claims--especially where claims were made for curative effects. In Rhodes, the cease and desist order was upheld against a drug company's extravagant claims concerning the curative powers of a tablet the company had developed for arthritis and rheumatism sufferers.

Federal Trade Commission v. Sterling Drug, Inc. 317 F. 2d 669 (1963)

Another FTC claim of deceptive advertising was decided by the courts in 1963. The December 29, 1962, issue of the Journal of the American Medical Association carried an article entitled "A Comparative Study of Five Proprietary Analgesic Compounds. " The article analyzed the effects of certain pain-relieving drugs sold in pharmacies and supermarkets. These five were Bayer Aspirin, St. Joseph's Aspirin, Bufferin, Anacin, and Excedrin. Also used in the experiment as a form of control was a placebo, the name given a harmless non-medicinal substance administered in the form of a pill. After investigating the efficacy of the five agents, the study noted that the data failed to demonstrate "any statistically signigicant difference among any of the drugs. ... There are no important differences among the compounds studied in rapidity of onset, degree, or duration of analgesia. " Fifteen minutes after the drugs were administered, so-called "pain-relief scores" were computed. Bayer earned a score of 0. 94, while the next most effective drug at that point in time, Excedrin, earned a score of 0. 90, and the other drugs were rated at 0. 76 and lower. The researchers also concluded that the incidence of upset stomach was significantly greater with Excedrin and Anacin than with Bayer, St. Joseph's, Bufferin, or the placebo. The article also stated that "this study was supported by a grant from the Federal Trade Commission, Washington, D. C. "

This article was received with enthusiasm by the Sterling Drug Company, producer of Bayer Aspirin. Almost immediately, the company initiated an advertising campaign that was conducted throughout the country. The following excerpts are representative of company advertising:

GOVERNMENT-SUPPORTED MEDICAL TEAM COMPARES BAYER ASPIRIN AND FOUR OTHER POPULAR PAIN RELIEVERS.

FINDINGS REPORTED IN THE HIGHLY AUTHORITATIVE JOURNAL OF THE AMERICAN MEDICAL ASSOCIATION REVEAL THAT THE HIGHER PRICED COMBINATION-OF-INGREDIENTS PAIN RELIEVERS UPSET THE STOMACH WITH SIGNIFICANTLY GREATER FREQUENCY THAN ANY OF THE OTHER PRODUCTS TESTED, WHILE BAYER ASPIRIN BRINGS RELIEF THAT IS AS FAST, AS STRONG, AND AS GENTLE TO THE STOMACH AS YOU CAN GET.

UPSET STOMACH
According to this report, the higher priced combination-of-ingredients products upset the stomach with significantly greater frequency than any of the other products tested, while Bayer Aspirin, taken as directed, is as gentle to the stomach as a plain sugar pill.

SPEED AND STRENGTH
The study shows that there is no signigicant difference among the products tested in rapidity of onset, strength, or duration of relief. Nonetheless, it is interesting to note that within just fifteen minutes, Bayer Aspirin had a somewhat higher pain relief score than any of the other products.

PRICE
As unreasonable as it may seem, the products
which are most likely to upset the stomach--that
is, the combination-of-ingredients products--actually
cost substantially more than Bayer Aspirin. The
fact is that these products, as well as the buffered
product, cost up to 75% more than Bayer Aspirin.

The FTC claimed that the advertisements falsely represented
1) that the findings of the research were endorsed and approved by the United States Government, 2) that publication in the
Journal of the American Medical Association was evidence of
endorsement by the medical profession, and 3) that the research team found that Bayer Aspirin, after fifteen minutes
following administration, afforded a higher degree of pain relief than any other product tested.

When the case reached the court of appeals, the FTC
admitted that none of the advertising claims were literally
false, but it contended that half-truths and ambiguities would
mislead a subintelligent, less-than-careful reader. Concerning the FTC claim that the ads falsely represented government backing, the court noted that the expression "Government-Supported" could not be characterized as misleading.

... surely the concise statement of an established
fact, immediately thereafter expanded--"This important new medical study, supported by a grant
from the federal government ... "--cannot fairly
be proscribed by the Commission; the alternatives
are complete omission of the admittedly true statement or long-winded qualification and picayune cir-
cumlocution. ...

The Commission's attack upon the use of the phrase "Findings
reported in the highly authoritative Journal of the American
Medical Association" as misleadingly connoting endorsement
and approval was also unfounded. It seemed unlikely that an
ordinary reader would conclude from the use of the word
"authoritative" that the study was endorsed by the medical
profession. The reader would be likely to think that the
study, because of publication in the Journal, was accurate
and well documented. Such an interpretation seemed warranted. The Commission also objected to the claim that "nonetheless, it is interesting to note that within just fifteen minutes, Bayer Aspirin had a somewhat higher pain relief score
than any of the other products. " The court noted that the

statement was literally true; Bayer's score was 0.94 while its closest competitor was rated 0.90. An examination of the statistical evidence revealed that the difference between the drugs was not "significantly different." But that was precisely what the Bayer ad stated in the sentence preceding its discussion of the specific pain-relief scores. The court could not accept the FTC claim that the language warranted proscription. The court concluded that "Sterling Drug can in no sense be said to have conveyed a misleading impression as to either the spirit or the specifics of the article published in the Journal of the American Medical Association." In Sterling, the court determined that the FTC had to abide by strict standards in cases involving alleged deception by means of half-truths and ambiguities.

Federal Trade Commission v. Colgate-Palmolive Company 380 U.S. 374 (1965)

In 1965, the U.S. Supreme Court heard a case involving deceptive advertising on television. The case regarded the use of a demonstration that purported to prove what in fact it did not prove. Colgate-Palmolive Company presented a 60-second television commercial for Rapid Shave aerosol shave cream. The commercial showed a professional football player, which the voice of an announcer described as having "a beard as tough as sandpaper ... a beard that needs Palmolive Rapid Shave ... supermoisturizer for the fastest, smoothest shave possible." The Rapid Shave lather was then spread on sandpaper and a hand appeared with a razor and shaved a clean path through the gritty surface. "To prove Rapid Shave's supermoisturizing power," the announcer concluded, "we put it right from the can onto this tough dry sandpaper. It was apply--soak--and off in a stroke." Research showed that sandpaper of the type depicted in the commercial could not be shaved immediately following application of Rapid Shave, but required a substantial soaking period of approximately 80 minutes. In fact, the substance resembling sandpaper was really plexiglass to which sand had been applied, and if real sandpaper had been used it would have appeared to viewers to be plain colored paper.

Some viewers, disturbed because they could not shave sandpaper with Rapid Shave the way it was done on television, complained to the FTC. In support of a cease and desist order against Colgate-Palmolive, the FTC acknowledged that the limitations of the television medium may challenge "the creative ingenuity and resourcefulness of copywriters; but surely they could not constitute lawful justification for resort to falsehoods and deception of the public. " If a company did not believe that it could effectively market a product on television within the legal requirements of truthful advertising, it did not follow that the Commission should relax those requirements. Rather, if a company did not "choose to advertise truthfully, they may, and should, discontinue advertising. " The FTC order instructed Colgate-Palmolive to cease and desist from any misrepresentation of any product on pain of a $5, 000 per day fine for each offense. The Commission took preventative as well as punitive action. The case was appealed to the U. S. Supreme Court.

The Court upheld (7-2) the Federal Trade Commission's order. The Court accepted the Commission's determination that the commercials contained three representations to the public: 1) that sandpaper could be shaved by Rapid Shave, 2) that an experiment had been conducted that verified this claim, and 3) that viewers were seeing this experiment for themselves. The Court noted that Section 5 of the Federal Trade Commission Act prohibited the intentional misrepresentation of any fact that would constitute a material factor in a purchaser's decision whether to buy. According to the Court, "the undisclosed use of plexiglass in the present commercials, was a material deceptive practice, independent and separate from the other misrepresentation found. " The Court was not sympathetic to Colgate-Palmolive's claim that it would be impractical to inform the viewing public that it was not seeing an actual experiment or demonstration. If it became impossible or impractical to show simulated demonstrations on television in a truthful manner, then television was not a medium that lent itself to this type of commercial. It was not imperative that the commercial must survive at all costs. In Colgate-Palmolive, the Court said that simulated demonstrations or the use of mock-ups in television advertising must be done in a truthful manner.

United States v. J. B. Williams Company, Inc. 498 F. 2d 414 (1974)

This case illustrates the procedural and enforcement problems the FTC faces in regulating false and deceptive advertising. The Commission initiated an investigation of advertising for Geritol in 1959. The Commission found that Geritol advertisements, which promoted a product for the

relief of iron deficiency anemia, were deceptive. They created a misleading impression on the public by representing
common symptoms as generally reliable indications of iron
deficiency anemia. The Commission issued a complaint in
1962, and a cease and desist order in 1964. The main thrust
of the Commission's order was that the Geritol advertising
had to disclose that a great majority of persons who experienced these symptoms did not experience them because there
was a vitamin or iron deficiency. J. B. Williams, the producer of Geritol, appealed.

In 1967, the court of appeals upheld the FTC order.
The court noted:

> ... the evidence is clear that Geritol is of no bene-
> fit in the treatment of tiredness except in those cases
> where tiredness has been caused by a deficiency of
> the ingredients contained in Geritol. The fact that
> the great majority of people who experience tired-
> ness symptoms do not suffer from any deficiency
> of the ingredients in Geritol is a "material fact"
> under the meaning of that term as used in Section
> 15 of the Federal Trade Commission Act and Pe-
> titioners' failure to reveal this fact in this day when
> the consumer is influenced by mass advertising
> utilizing highly developed arts of persuasion, ren-
> ders it difficult for the typical consumer to know
> whether the product will in fact meet his needs un-
> less he is told what the product will or will not do.

A year later, the Commission reported that Geritol's commercials still did not comply with the order. In 1969, the
FTC turned the case over to the Department of Justice, which
on April 20, 1970, filed a $1-million suit against the com-
pany and its advertising agency. In January, 1973, the company and its agency were fined a total of $812,000. In 1974,
a court of appeals dismissed the fine and sent the case back
to district court for a jury trial. Finally, in 1976, the FTC
won a $280,000 judgment against the company. But during
the intervening seventeen years, millions of dollars were
spent on television advertising for Geritol. The company
thereby was able to solidify its control of the tonic market.
Clearly, enforcement can be a significant problem for the FTC.

The cases considered in this section indicate the scope
of FTC regulation of deceptive advertising. In Winsted, the
Court decided that puffery had to stop at the point of clear

deception. Ultimately, <u>Raladam</u> established that the FTC did
not have to show evidence that specific losses to competitors
resulted from deceptive advertising prior to proscription of
the deceptive practices. <u>P. Lorillard</u> determined that the
FTC could ban false advertising even if the possibility existed
that such advertising might become truthful. In such an event,
the company could apply to the Commission for revision of
the order. <u>Rhodes</u> clearly granted the FTC broad regulatory
authority over deceptive advertising, especially when claims
for curative effects were involved. In <u>Sterling</u>, however,
the court stressed that the FTC had to abide by strict standards in determining deception by half-truths and ambiguities.
In <u>Colgate-Palmolive</u>, the Court decided that simulated demonstrations in television advertising had to be done in a truthful manner. In all of these cases, the courts defined the
broad regulatory powers the FTC may employ to deal with
deceptive advertising. <u>J. B. Williams</u>, however, illustrates
that the FTC can have problems in enforcing those regulations.

Corrective Advertising

Recently, the FTC has used affirmative or corrective
advertising. Sometimes, merely stopping an ad is insufficient.
When a promotional campaign has been effective for a long
period of time, a residue of misleading information remains
in the public's mind even after the deceptive ad is discontinued. In such instances, the FTC may impose corrective disclosures.

<u>Alberty v. Federal Trade Commission 182 F. 2d 36 (1950)</u>

The FTC first attempted to force affirmative advertising in 1950. Ada Alberty owned a company that sold the
drug product Oxorin Tablets. A typical advertisement for
Oxorin claimed:

> Pep up your blood! A principal factor in Red
> Blood Cells ... The disease Fighting Units of the
> Blood.
> When you are weary, tired, run-down, just
> dragging yourself around with no ambition left, when
> every effort you make seems to leave you weak and
> spent then try Oxorin Tablets, a tonic for the blood.

The FTC found that these tablets had no beneficial effect upon the blood except in cases of simple iron deficiency anemia
and that there were several causes of rundown conditions and
lack of energy that would not be beneficially affected by the
tablets. The FTC issued a cease and desist order that forbade the company from claiming that Oxorin had any therapeutic effect upon the blood except in cases of simple iron
deficiency anemia. The FTC also ordered that the advertisement state that the condition was "caused less frequently by
simple iron deficiency anemia than by other causes and that
in such cases this preparation [Oxorin] will not be effective
in relieving or correcting it. " To this extent, the FTC ordered Alberty to provide corrective advertising. Alberty appealed.

The Court of Appeals, District of Columbia, held that
the FTC had exceeded its authority. The Commission had
to find either of two things before it could require a corrective action: 1) that failure to make a statement was misleading because of the consequences from the use of the product, or 2) that failure to make a statement was misleading
because of the things claimed in the advertisement. There
was no such finding in this case. The court was concerned
about the scope of the power sought by the FTC. If particular advertisers, selected by the Commission, could be required not only to state accurately the limited benefits of
their products but also to call attention to what the products
would not do, such power could have a significant control
over marketing. The court concluded:

> We think that neither the purpose nor the terms of
> the act [Federal Trade Commission Act] are so
> broad as the encouragement of the informative func-
> tion. Both purpose and terms are to prevent fal-
> sity and fraud, a negative restriction. When the
> Commission goes beyond that purpose and enters
> upon the affirmative task of encouraging advertis-
> ing which it deems properly informative, it exceeds
> its authority.

Feil v. Federal Trade Commission 285 F. 2d 879 (1960)

Ten years later, the courts reversed the Alberty decision. Maurice Feil and Leo Loeb operated the Enurtone
Company in Beverly Hills, California. They engaged in leas-
ing a device named "Enurtone" for use in cases of enuresis,
or bed-wetting. They claimed, by means of advertisements

inserted in newspapers, "that the use of said device will stop bed-wetting and correct the bed-wetting habit in all cases." The FTC determined that the representations were false in that the use of the device did not stop bed-wetting "except in cases of functional bed-wetting not involving organic defects or diseases." The FTC ordered Feil and Loeb to cease and desist from advertising that the device was of value in stopping bed-wetting "unless expressly limited in a clear and conspicuous manner to cases of bed-wetting not involving organic defects or diseases." Feil and Loeb appealed, contending that the FTC had exceeded its authority.

The Court of Appeals for the Ninth District agreed that the advertisements were false, misleading, and deceptive. However, the court found that the FTC order was couched in language too broad by limiting the advertising to "cases of bed-wetting not involving organic defects or diseases." The word "involving" had many meanings. By contrast, the word "caused" was simple and easily understood. Any advertising so worded would be clearly understood as claiming that the device was not helpful in cases of bed-wetting caused by organic defects or diseases. The court modified the FTC order to substitute the word "causes" for "involving." The court then examined the range of FTC powers. The court concluded that the Commission had the power to compel Feil and Loeb to state, clearly and unequivocally, that Enurtone did not achieve results in cases caused by organic defects or diseases.

> The requirement that future advertisements state positively that the device does not help in enuresis caused by organic defects or disease does not involve the statement or disclosure of an unrelated negative fact. It seeks to avoid the misleading effect of the claim that the device cures "bed-wetting," without qualification, i.e., all bed-wetting.

The court upheld the FTC order as modified by the court "requiring disclosure of 'informative' facts in the interest of truth."

In re ITT Continental Baking Company, Inc. 79 FTC 248 (1971)

In 1971, the FTC issued a corrective advertising order to ITT Continental Baking Company concerning Profile Bread. In an advertising campaign, Profile was promoted as lower in

calories than ordinary bread and of significant value for use
in weight control diets. The ads implied that consuming two
slices of Profile Bread before lunch and dinner would result
in a loss of body weight, without any rigorous adherence to
a reduced calorie diet. These advertising claims were not
true. As a result of the "false" advertising consumers
were led to believe that they could lose weight by eating Profile Bread. The matter came before the FTC.

After an investigation, the FTC ordered that the company cease and desist from disseminating any false advertising claims. In addition, the FTC required that corrective
advertisements constitute 25 percent of the advertising for
Profile Bread during the following year. As a result, one
ad that appeared on television had Julia Meade make the following statement:

> I'm Julia Meade for Profile Bread. And like all
> mothers I'm concerned about nutrition and balanced
> meals. So I'd like to clear up any misunderstanding
> you may have about Profile Bread from its adver-
> tising or even its name. Does Profile have fewer
> calories than other breads? No, Profile has about
> the same per ounce as other breads. To be exact
> Profile has seven fewer calories per slice. But
> that's because it's sliced thinner. But eating bread
> will not cause you to lose weight. A reduction of
> seven calories is insignificant. It's total calories
> and balanced nutrition that counts. And Profile can
> help you achieve a balanced meal. Because it pro-
> vides protein and B vitamins as well as other nu-
> trients.

The ad was so well received by the public that the company
considered spending more than the 25 percent required by the
FTC. In this case, the corrective ad gave the company a
credibility it did not deserve.

In re Ocean Spray Cranberries, Inc. 70 FTC 975 (1972)

One year later, the FTC ordered corrective advertising for Ocean Spray Cranberry Juice. In its advertising,
Ocean Spray claimed that their cranberry juice was more nu-
tritious and had more "food energy" than orange or tomato
juices. The Commission decided that Ocean Spray's claims
were false, misleading, and deceptive.

The FTC ordered the company to cease and desist from disseminating any false advertising. In addition, the Commission ordered that corrective advertising constitute 25 percent of the promotion for Ocean Spray Cranberry Juice Cocktail during the ensuing year. As a result, Ocean Spray presented the following ad:

> If you've wondered what some of our earlier advertising meant when we said Ocean Spray Cranberry Juice Cocktail has more food energy than orange juice or tomato juice, let us make it clear: we didn't mean vitamins and minerals. Food energy means calories. Nothing more.
> Food energy is important at breakfast since many of us may not get enough calories, or food energy, to get off to a good start. Ocean Spray Cranberry Juice Cocktail helps because it contains more food energy than most other breakfast drinks. And Ocean Spray Cranberry Juice Cocktail gives you and your family Vitamin C plus a great wake-up taste. It's ... the other breakfast drink.

In Ocean Spray, as in Feil and Continental, the FTC ordered corrective advertising. It is a tool that the FTC can employ to curb the impact deceptive advertising has on the public consumer.

ACCESS

During the past decade or so, the issue of access has played a substantial role in developing a body of law regarding the regulation of advertising. Three specific questions faced the courts: 1) Can a communication medium deny access to a particular advertiser while at the same time accepting similar ads from other promoters? 2) Under what conditions does the Fairness Doctrine grant a person the right to counter-advertise? 3) To what extent may legislative bodies ban the advertising of various services or products? These questions are considered in the following section.

Rejection by Media

The courts have grappled with the question of whether a particular medium can reject a specific advertisement while at the same time accepting similar ads for publication and/or display. The courts have been quite consistent in their view that a medium is not bound to accept the advertising of all who apply for it.

Approved Personnel, Inc. v. Tribune Company 177 So. 2d 704 (1965)

Approved Personnel, Inc., a private employment agency operating in Hillsborough County, Florida, competed with thirteen other similar business organizations conducting private employment agencies in the area. The company needed to advertise in order to carry on its business. The Tampa Tribune Company published the only two English-speaking daily newspapers in the county--the Tampa Tribune in the morning and the Tampa Times in the evening. For many years, Approved Personnel advertised in the Tribune. In May, 1959, the paper notified the company that no further ads would be carried. No cause for this action was given. The Tribune Company continued to publish ads of Approved Personnel's competitors. Approved Personnel sued, arguing that the paper had a monopoly over the dissemination of advertising and had engaged in illegal practices that restrained the free pursuit of Approved Personnel's business.

The Florida District Court ruled in favor of the newspaper. The court decided that a newspaper publisher was under no obligation to accept advertising from all who apply for it.

> Even though a particular newspaper may enjoy a virtual monopoly in the area of its publication, in absence of statutory regulation, newspaper may publish or reject commercial advertising tendered to it as its judgment best dictates without incurring liability for advertisements rejected by it.

Kissinger v. New York City Transit Authority 274 F. Supp. 438 (1967)

In 1967, the courts decided a case involving a request by a student-activist group to display, on the walls in New York City subway station platforms, two posters opposing United States participation in the war in Vietnam. During 1962, the New York Transit Authority agreed to allow the New York Subways Advertising Company to place advertisements in the subway trains and on the walls in subway stations. Students for a Democratic Society, a left-wing, student-activist group, requested that two posters be displayed at the same rates for advertising space and upon the same terms applicable to all others seeking advertising space.

They were refused access because of the controversial and unpopular nature of the views expressed. The posters carried a picture of a child with what appeared to be a scarred back and arm and on the left side of the posters the following words were printed in large lettering: "WHY ARE WE BURNING, TORTURING, KILLING, THE PEOPLE OF VIETNAM?--TO PREVENT FREE ELECTIONS. " In smaller lettering the posters continued: "PROTEST this anti-democratic war--WRITE President Lyndon B. Johnson, The White House, Washington, D. C. " and "GET THE STRAIGHT FACTS-- WRITE--Students for a Democratic Society, 119 Fifth Avenue, New York, N. Y. , 10003. " In small print the poster stated: "This 10-year old girl was burned by napalm bombs. " SDS brought suit. The group claimed that the refusal denied their rights to freedom of speech under the First Amendment.

The Transit Authority contended that the refusal was consistent with the company's policy of limiting advertising it would accept to 1) commercial advertising for the sale of goods, 2) public service announcements, and 3) political advertising at the time of and in connection with elections. The SDS posters failed to come within any of these categories. The Authority also pointed out that it was responsible for the safe operation of the subways and had a duty to protect subway passengers from the possibility of physical harm. The posters were provocative and inflammatory and would be displayed to a large "captive audience" in the confined areas of the subways. Under these circumstances, the posters could cause serious disturbances, endanger the safety of the subways, and interfere with the transportation of passengers.

The court noted that the posters were an expression of political views. They were not obscene. Consequently, the Transit Authority could not refuse to accept the posters for display unless the posters presented a serious and immediate threat to the safe operation of the subways. According to the court, the posters might actually involve less danger to safety than other forms of expression because no person was physically present to publicize the views expressed on the posters. The court concluded that the Authority's practice of selling ads for some controversial ideas while refusing to sell for others was unconstitutional. Even though the court granted all the preceding points to SDS, it gave the decision to the Transit Authority. The court held that questions of whether the posters could be refused because they presented a "clear and present danger" or posed a "threat to public safety" could be determined only by a jury trial. The court rejected the SDS motion for a summary judgment that would have required the Authority to accept the posters.

Wirta v. Alameda-Contra Costa Transit
District 64 Cal. Rptr. 430 (1967)

During the same year, the courts decided a similar
case.   In September, 1964, a protest group named Women
for Peace sought to place advertising placards in buses owned
by the Alameda-Contra Costa Transit District.   The placards
said:

> "Mankind must put an end to war or war will put
> an end to mankind. "   President John F. Kennedy.
> Write to President Johnson: Negotiate Vietnam,
> Women for Peace, P. O. Box 944, Berkeley.

Metro Transit Advertising, the agency that handled advertising for the Transit District, refused the placards.   The agency declared that it operated under an agreement whereby political advertising and advertising on controversial subjects
was not acceptable unless approved by the District.   The
peace advertising violated the District's policy regarding paid
advertisements.   The District accepted only commercial advertising for the sale of goods and services and political advertising that related to a duly called election.   Women for
Peace claimed that the rejection of the advertising placards
was an "unconstitutional abridgement of their right of free
speech" and that "the exclusion of advertisements not connected with a political campaign constituted a denial of equal
protection of the laws. "

Women for Peace won its case.   The California Supreme Court declared:

> We conclude that defendants, having opened a forum
> for the expression of ideas by providing facilities
> for advertisements on its buses, cannot for reasons
> of administrative convenience decline to accept ad-
> vertising expressing opinions and beliefs within the
> ambit of First Amendment protection.

The court acknowledged that an occasional advertiser might
post controversial messages that would offend some, perhaps
a majority, in the community.   Nonetheless, annoyance and
inconvenience were a small price to pay for preservation of
the right to free speech.   In Wirta, the court decided that a
regulation that permitted those who sold goods and services
and those who campaigned in elections access to transit advertising while denying it to those who desired to express
other ideas violated the First Amendment.   In both 1967 de-

cisions, the court denied a medium the right to refuse advertising.   However, both <u>Kissinger</u> and <u>Wirta</u> dealt with publicly owned transit authorities; these decisions did not apply to privately owned facilities of the mass media.   Both cases involved political rather than strictly commercial messages.   Overall, these decisions represent only a limited inroad into the courts' general tendency to support the right of media to reject advertising.   Cases following <u>Kissinger</u> and <u>Wirta</u> reaffirmed that tendency.

<u>Chicago Joint Board, Amalgamated Clothing Workers of America, AFL-CIO v. Chicago Tribune Company 435 F. 2d 470 (1970)</u>

A 1970 case involved a dispute between a labor union and a large Chicago department store, Marshall Field.   The Union, the Chicago Joint Board, Amalgamated Clothing Workers of America, AFL-CIO, objected to the sale by Marshall Field of imported clothing on the ground that the sale jeopardized the jobs of American clothing workers.   The Union said it would protest such sales until the importing countries agreed to voluntary quotas on the amount of clothing to be sent into the United States.   The Union sought to place an ad explaining its position in each of the four daily newspapers--<u>Chicago Tribune</u>, <u>Chicago Today</u>, <u>Chicago Sun-Times,</u> and <u>Chicago Daily News</u>.   None of the papers would publish the ad.   Refusal was based on the claim that the advertisements failed to meet standards prescribed in the newspapers' Advertising Acceptability Guide, which, along with other standards, provided for the rejection of any advertisement that "reflects unfavorably on competitive organizations, institutions or merchandise. "   The Union sued the papers, asking the court to enjoin them to publish the ads and to fine them compensatory and exemplary damages.   The Union contended that the papers could not arbitrarily refuse to publish advertisements expressing political or social ideas as long as the party submitting the ad was willing to pay the usual rate.

The court decided in favor of the Tribune Company.

We glean nothing from the constitutional guarantees, or from the decisions expository thereof, which suggests that the advertising pages of a privately published newspaper may so be pressed into service against the publisher's will either in the context of a labor dispute to which the publisher is not a party or otherwise.

The court rejected the Union's argument that the First Amendment protection afforded a newspaper carried with it a reciprocal obligation to serve as a public forum, and, therefore, if a newspaper accepted any editorial advertising it had to publish all lawful editorial advertisements submitted to it. According to the court, the Union's right to free speech did not give it the right to make use of Chicago's printing presses and distribution system without the newspapers' consent. The court affirmed the lower court ruling against the Union.

Associates & Aldrich Company, Inc. v. Times Mirror Company 440 F. 2d 133 (1971)

In 1971, the courts heard a case that involved the editing of an ad by a newspaper publisher. A motion picture producer sought to enjoin the publisher of the Los Angeles Times from screening, censoring, or changing his advertising copy. The producer sought especially to restrain the Times from altering ads for the motion picture The Killing of Sister George. When the Times received the ad copy, it used its own "Screening Code" to exercise editorial judgment. The sketch of a female figure was slightly altered and a reference to deviate sexual conduct was omitted. As altered, the ad was printed and paid for.

The U. S. Court of Appeals for the Ninth District noted that "unlike broadcasting, the publication of a newspaper is not a government conferred privilege. " Clearly, the press and the government have had a history of disassociation. The court could find nothing in the Constitution that compelled "a private newspaper to publish advertisements without editorial control of their content merely because such advertisements are not legally obscene or unlawful. " The court noted that the advertisement was printed, except for the deletion of items that were not essential to the producer's message and that did not alter its fundamental nature. Citing Valentine, the court concluded that "this type of commercial exploitation is subject to less protection than other types of speech. "

Lehman v. Shaker Heights 418 U. S. 298 (1974)

In 1974, the access issue reached the U. S. Supreme Court. On July 3, 1970, Harry Lehman, a candidate for the office of State Representative to the Ohio General Assembly, sought to promote his candidacy by purchasing car card space

on the Shaker Heights rapid transit system.   He was informed
that although space was available, political advertising was
not permitted.   In fact, during the twenty-six years of public operation, the Shaker Heights system had never permitted
any political or public issue advertising on its vehicles.   Lehman sued, arguing that the car cards constituted a public
forum protected by the First Amendment and that there was
a gurantee of nondiscriminatory access to such publicly owned
and controlled areas of communication.

In a sharply divided opinion, the U. S. Supreme Court
ruled (5-4) that

> in much the same way that a newspaper or peri-
> odical, or even a radio or television station, need
> not accept every proffer of advertising from the
> general public, a city transit system has discretion
> to develop and make reasonable choices concerning
> the type of advertising that may be displayed in its
> vehicles.

Justice Harry Blackmun's majority opinion found no First
Amendment issue involved.   The city had limited access to
its transit system advertising space in order to minimize
chances of abuse or the appearance of favoritism.   These
legislative objectives advanced by the city were judged to be
reasonable.   Blackmun was joined in the opinion by Chief
Justice Burger and Justices Byron White and William Rehn-
quist.   Justice William Douglas supplied the fifth vote on the
ground that a political candidate had no right to force his
message on a "captive audience" of commuters--customers'
privacy rights should shield them from exposure to all advertising.   Justices William Brennan, Potter Stewart, Thur-
good Marshall, and Lewis Powell dissented on the ground
that the city's actions were unconstitutional; the city had preferred commercial advertising on its buses to the exclusion
of political advertising.   Shaker Heights had opened up its
advertising space on its buses as a "public forum" and having done so the city could not exclude the category of political advertising.   However, in Lehman, as in most other
cases examined in this section, the Court majority upheld
the right of the media to determine the specific types of advertising that it will display.

Fairness

Beginning in the late 1960s and continuing for the next

decade, several groups sought to apply the Fairness Doctrine to advertising. A 1968 court case involved a request to reply to cigarette advertising.

Banzhaf v. Federal Communications Commission
WTRF-TV, Inc. v. Federal Communications Commission
Tobacco Institute, Inc. v. Federal Communications Commission
405 F. 2d 1082 (1968)

In December, 1966, a young lawyer, John Banzhaf, asked WCBS-TV in New York for free reply time for anti-smokers to respond to the pro-smoking views implicit in cigarette commercials. WCBS rejected Banzhaf's request. The station claimed that it had broadcast several news and information programs about the smoking-health controversy. Within recent months, it had aired five American Cancer Society public service announcements free of charge. WCBS was confident that "its coverage of the health ramifications of smoking has been fully consistent with the fairness doctrine. " Banzhaf complained to the FCC. The Commission held that time should be provided for reply to cigarette advertisements because the question of whether or not cigarettes were harmful to health was a controversial issue. The decision was appealed.

The Court of Appeals, District of Columbia, affirmed the Commission's order on three grounds: 1) the Fairness Doctrine, 2) the public interest standard, and 3) the First Amendment. In terms of the Fairness Doctrine, cigarette smoking's affect on health was considered to be a controversial public issue. The Commission's ruling aimed at providing fair and balanced coverage of this issue. In terms of the public interest, reply time could be deemed appropriate in light of extraordinary and unique circumstances, and when consistent with a demonstrably clear federal policy. In this case, a debate between cigarette advertisers, whose ads consisted of a sizeable fraction of all broadcast revenues, and opponents of cigarette smoking with no such financial clout might have been no debate at all. Under the circumstances, providing free television reply time to cigarette ads appeared to be in the public interest. In terms of the First Amendment, the court ruled that government intervention in the form of compulsory reply time was permissible when it served as a "countervailing" force where meaningful broadcast debate would otherwise be impossible.

... where, as here, one party to a debate has a

> financial clout and a compelling economic interest
> in the presentation of one side unmatched by its
> opponent, and where the public stake in the argu-
> ment is no less than life itself--we think the purpose
> of rugged debate is served, not hindered by an at-
> tempt to redress the balance.

The court upheld the ruling of the FCC that required radio
and television stations that carry cigarette advertising to devote a significant amount of broadcast time to presenting the
case against cigarette smoking. A few years later, Congress
passed a law that banned cigarette commercials from the airways completely.

Retail Store Employees Union, Local 880, Retail Clerks International Association, AFL-CIO v. Federal Communications
Commission 436 F. 2d 248 (1970)

The courts heard another Fairness Doctrine case in
1970. The Hill Department Store in Ashtabula, Ohio, advertised on local radio station WREO. The ads extolled in cus-
tomary style the value and the variety of the goods offered
for sale. All was not well at the Hill store, however, where
Retail Store Employees Local 880 was on strike. The Union
organized a boycott of Hill's stores in Ashtabula and other
Ohio cities. The Union wanted to publicize its side of the
dispute with one-minute spot advertisements that announced
the strike against the Ashtabula store and urged the public
to respect the picket line. Between February and April, 1966,
WREO carried more than three hundred such announcements.
Gradually, the Union found it more and more difficult to pur-
chase radio time for the ads. In 1966, no station in the Ashtabula area was willing to carry advertisements for the Union.
A complaint was filed with the FCC, charging violation of the
Fairness Doctrine. The case subsequently reached the U. S.
Court of Appeals, District of Columbia.

Writing for the court, Judge David Bazelon hinted that
the reason WREO may have stopped selling ads to the Union
was because Hill's put economic pressure on the station. In
any event, Bazelon thought the public interest was violated
when a radio station sold time to carry the ads of one side
of a labor dispute while refusing to sell time to the other.
Bazelon suggested that in some circumstances the Fairness
Doctrine and the public interest standard could both serve as
independent bases for a right to purchase reply time to answer
broadcast advertisements. He wrote:

In the present case, it seems clear to us that the
strike and the Union boycott were controversial
issues of substantial public importance within Ashtabula, the locality primarily served by WREO.
The ultimate issue with regard to the boycott was
simple: whether or not the public should patronize Hill's Ashtabula. From April through December, Hill's broadcast over WREO more than a hundred sponsored programs explaining why, in its
opinion, the public should patronize its store.
During that same period, the Union was denied any
opportunity beyond a single roundtable broadcast to
explain why, in its opinion, the public should not
patronize the store. We need not now decide whether, as the Union would have us hold, the facts
make out a per se claim of a violation of the fairness doctrine. We do believe, however, that the
question deserves fuller analysis than the Commission has seen fit to give it.

The judge remanded the case to the Federal Communications
Commission for further proceedings consistent with his opinion.

Green v. Federal Communications Commission
G. I. Association v. Federal Communications
Commission 447 F. 2d 323 (1971)

In 1971, the courts faced other attempts to expand the
Fairness Doctrine's application to advertising. Two peace
organizations, a Quaker and a serviceman's group, asked
stations in Washington, D. C., and San Francisco to donate
time so that they could inform the public of alternatives to
military service. The peace groups contended that the Fairness Doctrine required an allocation of time to them since
both stations had carried recruiting spots advertising military
service. The military recruitment announcements were appeals for voluntary enlistment in the various branches of the
Armed Forces. They did not deal with the Vietnam War;
they presented only the attractive side of military service.
The counter-ads submitted by the peace groups focused on
the Vietnam War, the draft, participation in war in general,
and the undesirability of military service. The FCC rejected
the request. The organizations brought suit. This case, like
WREO, involved an effort to extend the Fairness Doctrine to
broadcast advertising, an area where traditionally it had been

352 / JOURNALISTIC FREEDOM

considered inapplicable. But, unlike WREO, the Green case
involved the question of whether there was a right to counter-
broadcast commercials when the group seeking to counter had
no money.

The court of appeals decided that the Fairness Doctrine
was concerned with informing the public about controversial
issues of public significance, but it was not concerned with
giving particular groups a specific right of reply. The peace
groups had placed too broad an interpretation on the military
recruitment announcements. The advertisements could reasonably be viewed by the broadcast stations as involving only
the issue of military personnel recruitment by voluntary means.
That was not a "controversial issue of public importance."
In addition, the draft issue and the Vietnam War question had
been "ventilated in extenso for years on [probably] every television and radio station in the land." The court concluded
that "no individual member of the public had the right of access to the air." The court rejected the requests of the
peace groups.

Friends of the Earth v. Federal Communications Commission 449 F. 2d 1164 (1971)

On February 6, 1970, Friends of the Earth, a national
organization dedicated to the protection of the environment,
sent a written complaint to WNBC-TV. The group objected
to the spot advertisements for automobile and gasoline companies that bombarded New York area viewers with pitches
for large-engine cars and high-test gasolines, which were
described as "efficient, clean, socially responsible, and auto-
motively necessary." Friends of the Earth asserted that
these products were heavy contributors to air pollution, which
had become especially dangerous in New York City. They
claimed that the station had not met its Fairness Doctrine
responsibility of informing the public of the other side of
the antipollution controversy. WNBC responded. The station
took the position that the FCC's Banzhaf decision was limited
to cigarette advertising and that it did not impose any Fairness Doctrine obligation "with respect to other product advertising." WNBC said there was no controversy about whether automobile transportation should continue and therefore
the advertising of automobiles and fuels was not related to
any controversial issue of public importance. Nonetheless,
WNBC cited several programs it had broadcast that discussed
the problem of air pollution by automobiles. According to

the station, this met any public interest obligation the station had to inform its viewers on this subject. Friends of the Earth lodged a formal complaint with the FCC. The Commission decided that no action was warranted against WNBC. The Commission acknowledged that automobile air pollution contributed to many deaths each year, but that was true of numerous other products. Cigarettes were distinguishable from such products since smoking was a habit that could cease without having a significant impact upon other aspects of life. Also, officials had urged the public to quit smoking. Contrarily, the government did not urge discontinuance of the use of automobiles. The Commission refused to extend the Banzhaf ruling "generally to the field of product advertising. " Such regulation could be imposed by Congress, but in the absence of such action the Commission could not act.

The Court of Appeals, District of Columbia, disagreed with the FCC's insistence that, because cigarettes posed a unique threat to human health, the public interest considerations that caused the FCC to reach the result it did in Banzhaf had no force in this case. That distinction was not apparent to the court. On another issue, the court agreed with the FCC that Fairness Doctrine obligations could be met by public service programs that gave reasonable exposure to views contrary to those reflected in the offending commercials. The FCC, however, had explicitly avoided that issue in Friends of the Earth and instead explicitly restricted the basis of its ruling to the inapplicability of the Fairness Doctrine. The court ruled that this case was indistinguishable from Banzhaf in the reach of the Fairness Doctrine, and since the FCC had not ruled whether WNBC had aired a sufficient number of commercials exposing the dangers of air pollution from automobiles, the case was remanded to the Commission for determination of that specific issue.

Clearly, the Banzhaf case expanded the scope of the Fairness Doctrine. WREO, Green, and Friends of the Earth illustrate the difficulty the FCC and the courts had in keeping the Banzhaf principle from expanding to other areas. However, the counter-advertising movement lost considerable momentum in 1973, when the U. S. Supreme Court ruled that a medium that meets its obligation to provide full and fair coverage of public issues was not required to accept any editorial advertisements.

Columbia Broadcasting System, Inc. v.
Democratic National Committee
Federal Communications Commission v. Business
Executives Move for Vietnam Peace
Post-Newsweek Stations, Capital Area, Inc. v.
Business Executives Move for Vietnam Peace
American Broadcasting Companies, Inc. v. Democratic
National Committee 412 U. S. 94 (1973)

In this case, the specific details of which were presented in the previous chapter, the Court agreed with the
FCC that the public interest in providing access to the marketplace of "ideas and experiences" would not be served "by
a system so heavily weighted in favor of the financially af-
fluent, or those with access to wealth. " If broadcasters were
required to accept editorial advertisements, the ideas of the
wealthy could well prevail over those of others because they
had the financial capability to purchase time more frequently.
As a result, the time a station "allotted for editorial advertising could be monopolized by those of one political persuasion. " The ultimate effect might be the

> erosion of the journalistic discretion of broadcasters
> in the coverage of public issues, and a transfer of
> control over the treatment of public issues from the
> licensees who are accountable for broadcast per-
> formance to private individuals who are not. The
> public interest would no longer be "paramount" but,
> rather, subordinate to private whim, especially
> since ... a broadcaster would be largely precluded
> from rejecting editorial advertisements that dealt
> with matters trivial or insignificant or already fair-
> ly covered by the broadcaster.

The Court concluded (7-2) that if the Fairness Doctrine was
applied to editorial advertising, there would be a "substantial
danger that the effective operation of that doctrine would be
jeopardized. "

Banning

Over the years, federal, state, and local agencies have
banned certain subjects from advertising channels. At times,
the constitutionality of such bans has been decided by the courts.
Some recent cases reached the U. S. Supreme Court.

Capital Broadcasting Company v. Mitchell 333 F. Supp. 582 (1971)
Capital Broadcasting Company v. Kleindienst 405 U. S. 1000 (1972)

In 1965, in an effort to alert the general public to the documented dangers of cigarette smoking, Congress passed legislation requiring a health warning to be placed on all cigarette packages.   In 1969, Congress enacted the Public Health Cigarette Smoking Act.   Section 6 of this act stipulated that after January 1, 1971, it was unlawful to advertise cigarettes on any broadcast medium.   Capital Broadcasting Company sued, alleging that 1) the ban on advertising prohibited the "dissemination of information with respect to a lawfully sold product ... " in violation of the First Amendment, and 2) the cigarette advertising ban law violated due process because print media were not prohibited from publishing cigarette ads.   Only the electronic media were so restricted.   The company claimed that such a distinction was "arbitrary and invidious. "

The district court rejected both of Capital Broadcasting Company's allegations.   First, Section 6 only restricted the airing of commercial messages; it did not prohibit anyone from disseminating information about cigarettes.   Therefore, the act did not conflict with the exercise of First Amendment guarantees.   Second, Congress could regulate one medium at a time if there was a rational reason for such regulation. The Court noted that

> substantial evidence showed that the most presuasive advertising was being conducted on radio and television, and that these broadcasts were particularly effective in reaching a very large audience of young people.

The court decided that the unique characteristics of electronic communication made it especially subject to regulation in the public interest.   The court upheld the ban against advertising cigarettes on any broadcast media.   In 1972, the U. S. Supreme Court affirmed the district court's decision without opinion.

Virginia State Board of Pharmacy v. Virginia
Citizens Consumer Council 425 U. S. 748 (1976)

In 1976, the U. S. Supreme Court heard a challenge to a state's ban against drug price advertising.   Virginia law punished as unprofessional conduct advertising by pharmacists of the prices on prescription drugs. Seeking to promote competition in the hope of lowering prices, the Virginia Citizens Consumer Council brought suit to have the statute declared unconstitutional and to enjoin the Virginia State Board of Pharmacy from enforcing it. The consumer group alleged a violation of the First and Fourteenth Amendments. The group argued that the First Amendment entitled a user of prescription drugs to receive information that pharmacists wished to communicate through advertising, concerning the prices of such drugs. Investigation showed that drug prices in Virginia varied from outlet to outlet even in the same locality. The group asserted an interest in their own health that was "fundamentally deeper than a trade consideration." The Board of Pharmacy contended that the advertisement of prescription drug prices was outside the protection of the First Amendment because it was "commercial speech."

The Court held (8-1) that First Amendment protection extended not only to the right to disseminate information but to receive it as well. Since the consumer had a strong receiver interest in the free flow of commercial information, state law could not suppress the dissemination of truthful information about a lawful activity. A state could not keep "the public in ignorance of the lawful terms that competing pharmacists are offering." The Court rejected the argument that the professional image of the pharmacist would suffer when price advertising lowered the pharmacist's status to that of a mere retailer. Virginia was free to demand whatever professional standards it desired of its pharmacists. But it could not do so by keeping the public in ignorance regarding the drug prices that competing pharmacists offered. The Court also acknowledged that some forms of commercial speech regulation are permissible. In this case, however, any legitimate time-place-and-manner restrictions on commercial speech were exceeded by the Virginia statute, which singled out speech of a particular content--drug price advertising--and sought to prevent its dissemination completely.

Bates v. State Bar of Arizona 433 U. S. 350 (1977)

A year later, the U. S. Supreme Court heard a similar case--this time involving lawyers. John Bates and Van O'Steen, licensed attorneys and members of the Arizona State Bar, placed an advertisement in the February 22, 1976, issue of the Arizona Republic. In the ad, Bates and O'Steen claimed that they were offering "legal services at very reasonable fees" and listed their fees for such services as uncontested divorces, uncontested adoptions, simple personal bankruptcies, and changes of name. The State Bar issued a complaint, indicating that attorneys were prohibited from advertising in newspapers and other media. Upon review of the incident, the Board of Governors of the Arizona State Bar imposed a one-week suspension on both Bates and O'Steen. They appealed, arguing that the State Bar regulations violated the First Amendment. The Arizona Supreme Court upheld the findings of the State Bar.

The issue before the U. S. Supreme Court was whether the State of Arizona could prevent the publication in a newspaper of Bates and O'Steen's truthful advertisement concerning the availability and terms of routine legal services. The Court held (6-3) that the flow of such information could not be restrained and that the State Bar disciplinary action against Bates and O'Steen violated the First Amendment.

Ohralik v. Ohio State Bar Association 436 U. S. 447 (1978)

One year later, the Court heard a related case. Albert Ohralik practiced law in Montville and Cleveland, Ohio. On February 13, 1974, he learned about an automobile accident in which Carol McClintock, a young woman with whom he was casually acquainted, had been injured. Ohralik went to the hospital, where he told Carol he would represent her and asked her to sign an agreement. Carol said she would have to discuss the matter with her parents. In a conversation with the McClintocks, Ohralik learned that the McClintocks' insurance policy would provide benefits of up to $12, 500 each for Carol, and for Wanda Lou Holbert, a passenger in the automobile, under an uninsured motorist clause. The McClintocks told Ohralik that Carol had phoned to say that he could "go ahead" with her representation. Ohralik returned to Carol's hospital room to have her sign a contract, which provided that he would receive one-third of her recovery. Ohralik then visited Wanda Lou at her home, without having been invited. He offered to represent her, also for a contingent fee of one-third of any recovery, and Wanda Lou said "O. K. " Shortly thereafter, Wanda's mother informed Ohralik that she and her daughter did not want to sue anyone or to have Ohralik represent them, and that if they decided to sue they would consult their own lawyer. Ohralik insisted that Wanda had entered into a binding agreement. Wanda also confirmed in writing that she wanted neither to sue nor to be represented by Ohralik. Carol eventually discharged Ohralik. However, although another lawyer represented her in concluding a settlement with the insurance company, Carol paid Ohralik one-third of her recovery in settlement of his lawsuit against her for breach of contract. Carol and Wanda Lou filed complaints against Ohralik with the Ohio Bar Association. After a hearing, the Bar found Ohralik had violated Disciplinary Rules of the Ohio Code of Professional Responsibility. The case reached the U. S. Supreme Court.

The Court noted (8-0) that "the solicitation of business by a lawyer through direct, in-person communication with the prospective client has long been viewed as inconsistent with the profession's ideal(s). " Such behavior posed a significant potential harm to the prospective client. The lawyer's behavior in this case was significantly different from Bates. The Court concluded that the Bar Association "acting with state authorization constitutionally may discipline a lawyer for soliciting clients in person for pecuniary gain under circumstances likely to pose dangers that the State has a right to prevent. " The Court upheld the ruling; Ohralik's transaction was "commercial speech. "

> To require a parity of constitutional protection for commercial and noncommercial speech alike could invite dilution. . . . Rather than subject the First Amendment to such a devitalization, we instead have afforded commercial speech a limited measure of protection, commensurate with its subordinate position in the scale of First Amendment values, while allowing modes of regulation that might be impermissible in the realm of noncommercial expression.

Linmark Associates, Inc. v. Township of Willingboro 431 U. S. 85 (1977)

In 1977, the Court decided a case involving the sale of homes. In an attempt to stop "panic selling" by whites who feared that the community was becoming all black and that property values would decline, Willingboro Township banned the placing of "For Sale" signs on all but model homes. Linmark Associates, owners of real estate in the township, wanted to attract attention to their property by placing a "For Sale" sign on the lawn. They brought action for declaratory

and injunctive relief. The case presented the question of
whether the First Amendment allowed a city to ban the post-
ing of "For Sale" or "Sold" signs when the city acted to stop
what it perceived to be the flight of white homeowners from
a racially integrated community.

The U. S. Supreme Court noted that the Township Council acted to prevent residents from obtaining certain information. That information, which pertained to sales activity,
was of vital interest to Willingboro residents. It affected one
of the most important decisions citizens had a right to make--
where to live and raise their families. The Council restricted the free flow of this data because it feared that otherwise
homeowners would choose to leave town. The Council's concern, then, was not with any commercial aspect of "For Sale"
signs, but with the substance of the information communicated
to the citizens. The Court concluded (8-0) that even though
the ordinance was designed to promote an important governmental objective--integrated housing--it clearly violated the
First Amendment. The Willingboro Township Council had
enacted an ordinance that was based solely on the township's
interest in regulating the content of the communication and
not on any desire to control the form. As in Virginia State
Board of Pharmacy, the Willingboro ordinance exceeded legitimate time-place-manner restrictions on commercial speech.

Carey v. Population Services International 431 U. S. 678 (1977)

Another 1977 case involved the advertising of contraceptives. Population Planning Associates was engaged in the
mail-order retail sale of non-medical contraceptive devices.
PPA regularly advertised its products in periodicals published
in New York. Neither the advertisements nor the order forms
accompanying them limited availability of the products to persons of any particular age. Various New York officials advised PPA that its activities violated state law, which prohibited sales of contraceptives to minors, and outlawed sales
by non-pharmacists. The Company was warned that if it
failed to comply "the matter will be referred to our Attorney
General for legal action. " PPA challenged the statute in
court.

The U. S. Supreme Court first of all examined the
matter on privacy grounds. The Court noted that the decision
whether or not to have a child was a constitutionally protected
choice that held "a particularly important place in the history

of the right of privacy. " Furthermore, the right to privacy regarding decisions affecting procreation extended to minors as well as to adults. The Court also examined the matter of advertising and concluded that New York's prohibition of any "advertisement or display" was unconstitutional. The Court noted that in this case, as in Virginia State Board of Pharmacy, the statute sought "to suppress completely any information about the availability and price of contraceptives. " The information suppressed by the law "related to activity with which, at least in some respects, the State could not interfere. " New York argued that the advertisements were offensive and embarrassing to many who were exposed to them and that allowing them would legitimize sexual activity of young people. The Court concluded (7-2) that the fact that protected speech may be offensive to some did not justify its suppression.

In recent years, in Bigelow and Virginia State Board of Pharmacy, the Court extended First Amendment protection to "commercial speech. " A close examination of those cases, however, as well as an analysis of Capital Broadcasting Company, Bates, Ohralik, Linmark, and Carey reveals that the Court still distinguishes between commercial and informative communication. In these cases, the Court established a clear connection between the concepts of commercial and informative speech--namely, the free flow of commercial information must be protected.

Bibliography

Books

Francois, William E.   Mass Media Law and Regulation.   2nd ed.   Columbus, Ohio: Grid, 1978.

Keeton, Page, and Marshall S. Shapo.   Products and the Consumer: Deceptive Practices.   Mineola, N. Y. :   The Foundation Press, 1972.

Preston, Ivan L.   The Great American Blow-up: Puffery in Advertising and Selling.   Madison: University of Wisconsin Press, 1975.

Articles

Alexander, Lawrence.   "Speech in the Local Marketplace:

Implications of Virginia State Board of Pharmacy vs. Virginia Citizens Consumer Council, Inc. for Local Regulatory Power, " San Diego Law Review 14 (March, 1977), 357-77.

"Commercial Speech Doctrine--A Clarification of the Protection Afforded Advertising Under the First Amendment, " Brigham Young University Law Review (1975), 797-811.

DiPippa, John M. "The Demise of the Commercial Speech Doctrine and the Regulation of Professional's Advertising: The Virginia Pharmacy Case, " Washington and Lee Law Review 34 (Winter, 1977), 245-62.

Merrill, Thomas W. "First Amendment Protection for Commercial Advertising: The New Constitutional Doctrine, " University of Chicago Law Review 44 (Fall, 1976), 205-54.

Rotunda, Ronald D. "Commercial Speech Doctrine in the Supreme Court, " University of Illinois Law Forum (1976), 1080-1101.

Schiro, Richard, "Commercial Speech: The Demise of a Chimera, " Supreme Court Review (1976), 45-98.

Winslow, Helen L. "The First Amendment--Status of Commercial Advertising, " North Carolina Law Review 54 (February, 1976), 468-77.

Cases

Alberty v. Federal Trade Commission 182 F. 2d 36 (1950)

Approved Personnel, Inc. v. Tribune Company 177 So. 2d 704 (1965)

Associates & Aldrich Company, Inc. v. Times Mirror Company 440 F. 2d 133 (1971)

Banzhaf v. Federal Communications Commission; WTRF-TV, Inc. v. Federal Communications Commission; Tobacco Institute, Inc. v. Federal Communications Commission 405 F. 2d 1082 (1968)

Bates v. State Bar of Arizona 433 U. S. 350 (1977)

Bigelow v. Virginia 421 U. S. 809 (1975)

Capital Broadcasting Company v. Kleindienst 405 U. S. 1000 (1972)

Capital Broadcasting Company v. Mitchell 333 F. Supp. 582 (1971)

Carey v. Population Services International 431 U. S. 678 (1977)

Chicago Joint Board, Amalgamated Clothing Workers of America, AFL-CIO v. Chicago Tribune Company 435 F. 2d 470 (1970)

Columbia Broadcasting System, Inc. v. Democratic National Committee; Federal Communications Commission v. Business Executives Move for Vietnam Peace; Post-Newsweek Stations, Capital Area, Inc. v. Business Executives Move for Vietnam Peace; American Broadcasting Companies, Inc. v. Democratic National Committee 412 U. S. 94 (1973)

Federal Trade Commission v. Colgate-Palmolive Company 380 U. S. 374 (1965)

Federal Trade Commission v. Raladam Company 283 U. S. 643 (1931)

Federal Trade Commission v. Raladam Company 316 U. S. 149 (1942)

Federal Trade Commission v. Standard Education Society 302 U. S. 112 (1937)

Federal Trade Commission v. Sterling Drug, Inc. 317 F. 2d 669 (1963)

Federal Trade Commission v. Winsted Hosiery Company 258 U. S. 483 (1922)

Feil v. Federal Trade Commission 285 F. 2d 879 (1960)

Friends of the Earth v. Federal Communications Commission 449 F. 2d 1164 (1971)

Green v. Federal Communications Commission; G. I. Association v. Federal Communications Commission 447 F. 2d 323 (1971)

In re ITT Continental Baking Company, Inc. 79 FTC 248 (1971)

In re Ocean Spray Cranberries, Inc. 70 FTC 975 (1972)

Kissinger v. New York City Transit Authority 274 F. Supp. 438 (1967)

Lehman v. Shaker Heights 418 U. S. 298 (1974)

Linmark Associates, Inc. v. Township of Willingboro 431 U. S. 85 (1977)

Ohralik v. Ohio State Bar Association 436 U. S. 447 (1978)

Pittsburgh Press Company v. Pittsburgh Commission on Human Relations 413 U. S. 376 (1973)

P. Lorillard Company v. Federal Trade Commission 186 F. 2d 52 (1950)

Retail Store Employees Union, Local 880, Retail Clerks International Association, AFL-CIO v. Federal Communications Commission 436 F. 2d 248 (1970)

Rhodes Pharmacal Company, Inc. v. Federal Trade Commission 208 F. 2d 382 (1953)

United States v. J. B. Williams Company, Inc. 498 F. 2d 414 (1974)

Valentine v. Chrestensen 316 U. S. 52 (1942)

Virginia State Board of Pharmacy v. Virginia Citizens Consumer Council 425 U. S. 748 (1976)

Wirta v. Alameda-Contra Costa Transit District 64 Cal. Rptr. 430 (1967)

CHAPTER IX

CONCLUSION

The courts have generally supported the claims of journalists against competing constitutional claims. Especial importance has been ascribed to the free flow of information in our democratic republic. Unhampered publication and dissemination of newsworthy information has been given broad protection under the First Amendment. The public's right to know has frequently been given a preferred position over conflicting rights of individuals or groups. Journalists, in short, may legitimately report upon a broad range of people, places, or events. However, they cannot go beyond specific limits. Even though journalistic activities are generally protected by the courts, the First Amendment does not give reporters license maliciously to libel individuals, infringe upon copyrighted material, intrude upon an individual's privacy, or unduly impede the administration of justice. Congress, legislatures, regulatory commissions, and courts exhibit an overriding concern for the public interest. Consequently, regulation of broadcasting and advertising, and the limited management of information have become legitimate government activities.

Libel

Libel consists of defamatory words that are either written or broadcast. Libelous statements have a crippling effect on an individual's ability to relate to her or his fellows. Appropriate legal relief must thus be made available to anyone so harmed.

There are two kinds of libel. Libel per se is a statement judged defamatory on its face (Hornby). Libel per quod is not immediately apparent--the words themselves are not defamatory, but become so when other relevant facts are associated with them (Karrigan). A successful libel action

364

must demonstrate publication, identification, and defamation. To show publication, plaintiffs need demonstrate only that a third person read or heard the libel and interpreted it in a defamatory sense (Arvey, Di Giorgio). In demonstrating the element of identification, the plaintiffs must prove that the defamatory meaning applies specifically to them (Hope). Defamation must be proven by demonstrating that the words in question belong to one of the classes of libelous statements: 1) words that damage esteem or social standing (Roth), 2) words that expose one to public ridicule, scorn, or derisiveness (Zbysko), 3) words that cause one to be avoided (Sally, Fort, Cowper), and 4) words that damage one in one's trade, occupation, or profession (Blende, Nichols). If these elements are sufficiently demonstrated, compensatory (Dalton), punitive (United Press International), special (MacLeod), and/or nominal (Goldwater) monetary damages may be assessed against the offender. While laws vary from state to state, the following are usually recognized as complete defenses: truth (Empire Printing), absolute privilege (City of Chicago, Langford, Farmers Union, Barr), qualified privilege (Stice), and fair comment (Oswalt). In addition, there are six partial defenses, including retraction and apology (Brush-Moore Newspapers), right of reply (Dickins), settling out of court (November), previous bad reputation (Nichols), usually trustworthy source (Wood, Szalay), and provocation (Farrell).

While the courts most often deal with cases involving libel of individuals, they have recognized that corporations can be damaged by unfair and malicious statements (Neiman-Marcus, Cosgrove). In addition, the courts have acknowledged that groups or classes of people can be the victims of libel (Crane, Spielman, Beauharnais). Criminal libel is a passing phenomenon, and has been considerably weakened by the courts (Ashton).

Within the past two decades, the Supreme Court has formulated several doctrines that make it comparatively difficult for a public official or celebrity to win a libel suit. Information about topics of immediate public interest cannot be suppressed regardless of the effect on the "involuntary newsmaker." According to New York Times, it must be demonstrated that the defendant made the libelous statement with knowledge that it was false or with "reckless disregard" of the truth. Public officials, in particular, must demonstrate that the libel was maliciously motivated (Rosenblatt, Monitor Patriot, Ocala Star-Banner). Generally, the lower the person is in the official hierarchy, the greater is the risk of libel.

Other cases further clarified the doctrine of "actual malice. " In Garrison, the concept of "reasonable belief" was rejected, thus making it more difficult for public officials to win libel suits. The concept of "hot news" was introduced in the Curtis-Walker cases. In St. Amant, the court noted that negligence does not constitute reckless disregard, and in Goldwater, a circuit court indicated that even public officials could expect some degree of protection from maliciously motivated defamation. In Pape, the Court noted that freedom of expression required "breathing space, " and that minor misstatements are protected by the First and Fourteenth Amendments. Another concept, "robust debate, " was introduced in Greenbelt. In all these cases, freedom of expression and the right of the public to be informed usually held a preferred position.

In 1971, the Court attempted to clarify the law of libel as it concerned private citizens (Rosenbloom). If a matter was a subject of public interest, it could not suddenly become less so because a private individual was involved. Thus, even in the case of private citizens, the public's right to know was overriding. Within three years, though, the Court overturned this ruling (Gertz). The Court, in effect, conditioned a libel action by a private individual on a showing of negligence, as opposed to a showing of reckless disregard. This ruling was reinforced in Firestone.

Privacy

Though the framers of the Constitution did not provide for a "right to privacy, " the right has been recently recognized by both courts and legislatures. Privacy torts include: 1) appropriation of some element of an individual's personality for commercial use, 2) intrusion of physical solitude, 3) publication of private matters, and 4) putting an individual in a false position in the public eye.

Appropriation involves taking an individual's name, picture, photograph, or likeness without that person's permission and using it for commercial gain. The use of photographs in newspaper or magazine advertising is, however, comparatively free from restraints provided such use fulfills legitimate journalistic interests (Sarat Lahiri, Booth). Conversely, advertisers must seek permission to use the names of those whom it is hoped will aid in the marketing of a product (Palmer, Uhlaender). Celebrities from the worlds of sports, politics, and entertainment have argued that they are entitled to control their own publicity. In Spahn and Zacchini, the courts acknowledged this "right of publicity." However, when celebrities engage in activities of legitimate public interest, they surrender the right (Paulsen, Man).

Intrusion involves the act of thrusting oneself into the private life of an individual. Generally, when a newspaper reporter received stolen property that was subsequently used in a published article, courts have sided with the press (Pearson, Kunkin). Nonetheless, the First Amendment is not a license to trespass, steal, or intrude by electronic means into another's privacy (Dietemann). Similarly, intrusion resulting in harassment is not within the domain of the First Amendment (Galella).

Publication of private information constitutes an actionable invasion of privacy if such publication causes embarrassment to an ordinary person of reasonable sensitivity and serves no legitimate ends (Daily Times Democrat). This doctrine, however, did not apply to publicity concerning newsworthy events (Javoca, Williams, Virgil). The Supreme Court, moreover, ruled that no State can impose sanctions on the accurate publication of the name of a rape victim obtained from public judicial records that were maintained in connection with a public prosecution and that were open to inspection (Cox). The courts have also rejected privacy suits that involved publication of photographs of children who died as a result of accidents. The photographs illustrated accurate news stories about events of legitimate public interest (Kelley, Costlow).

A final privacy tort involves the publication of false information about an individual, whether it is defamatory or not. This can involve either fictionalization of known facts or presentation of information in a false light. Fictionalization sufficient to result in an actionable invasion of privacy must involve exaggerations of fact (Strickler); minor fictionalization is thus not actionable (Carlisle). If news writers allow their imagination to roam outside the realm of objective reporting, though the facts were by themselves newsworthy, fictionalization can be demonstrated (Aquino). False light concerns the creation of a false impression, even if the impression is not unfavorable. In Time v. Hill, the Supreme Court ruled that the First Amendment shields the press from invasion of privacy suits involving matters of public interest unless there is proof of actual malice. While such malice was not evident in Hill, it was in other cases (Varnish, Cantrell).

368 / JOURNALISTIC FREEDOM

Copyright

There was little need to protect an author's literary property before the advent of the printing press. With the introduction of mass copying, however, instances of unauthorized reproduction and distribution of literary works became increasingly numerous. Copyright law in America ultimately emerged from the English example and has two sources, common and statutory. Common-law copyright provides automatic protection for authors as soon as their work is created and is in effect prior to publication. Common-law copyright has been recognized by the courts (Pushman, Chamberlain, Estate of Hemingway). The common-law copyright belongs to authors until disposed of by them (Chamberlain). Speech may also fall under the protection of common-law copyright (Hemingway). The Constitution provides the basic authority for statutory copyright (Article I, Section 8). The Copyright Acts of 1790, 1909, and 1976 were passed in response to specific problems faced by authors.

Orginality is the fundamental requirement of copyright-ability Bleisten, Jewelers' Circular, Triangle, Amsterdam, Donald, and Lipman). Originality requires that the authors or artists create the work through their own skill and effort. The specific meaning, however, has been largely determined on a case-by-case basis. In securing and maintaining a copyright, authors or artists must abide by certain procedural requirements. The work should bear a copyright notice, and should be properly registered (Holmes, Mifflin v. White, Mifflin v. Dutton). Recently, the Court has been less rigid about the notice requirement (Wrench), and the registration requirement as well (Washingtonian Publishing).

Usually, what constitutes infringement is left for the courts to determine. The Supreme Court has ruled that while the news itself cannot be copyrighted, the style or manner in which it is presented can be (International News Service, Chicago Record-Herald). Fictional characters may also be protected. A character that actually constitutes the story being told falls within the protection of the law (Warner Brothers, Walt Disney). Concerning copyrightability of books, in Holt the court held that the whole or even a large part of a book need not be copied to constitute an infringement. The copying of word lists from another book also constitutes infringement (College Entrance Book Company). In Toksvig, the court found copyright infringement occurred when a writer failed to do independent research. Determination of infringement of musical pieces has been on an ad hoc basis (Herbert, Heim, Berlin). Material from movies may also be protected from infringement, especially by television. The extent of this protection is limited, however (Benny, Columbia Pictures). Speeches also may come under the domain of copyright protection. Public speeches are protected by common-law copyright provided the speaker did not previously make an extensive distribution of copies to the press or to those who desired copies (Rickover, King). Limited photocopying in libraries is usually allowed. The law, however, does not approve of copying for purposes of commercial gain. Neither does the law approve of systematic or multiple photocopying (Williams and Wilkins). Regarding cable television, in Fortnightly the Court decided that Fortnightly's systems did not "perform" copyrighted works and was not liable for infringement. Six years later, the Court affirmed that principle, noting that "importation of signals" does not constitute a performance (Teleprompter).

The primary remedies for copyright infringement include: 1) an injunction to curtail the infringing activity, 2) recovery of actual damages, 3) recovery of the infringer's profits, 4) recovery of statutory damages, and 5) recovery of attorney's fees in the court action. A "fair use" of copyrighted materials is not an infringement, and not subject to any of the above remedies. According to the 1976 Copyright Act, whether a use of copyrighted material is fair involves consideration of 1) the purpose and character of use, 2) the nature of the copyrighted work, 3) the amount used, and 4) the effect of the use upon the value of the copyrighted work (Time v. Geis). Generally, the courts have been lenient when the quotations copied are used in scholarly works, and less lenient toward the use of such materials for commercial purposes (Rosemont).

Fair Trial

The freedom of communication and the right to a fair trial are occasionally in conflict. Instances in which these two conflict usually involve questions of contempt or pretrial publicity.

Contempt was defined in the Federal Contempt Act of 1831 as disobedience to any judicial process or decree and misbehavior in the presence of the court "or so near thereto as to obstruct the administration of justice. " In Toledo,

the Court rendered a causal rather than a geographical interpretation of the phrase "so near thereto. " In <u>Nye</u>, the Court
rejected the causal interpretation. "Near" suggested physical
proximity rather than "relevancy. " In 1941, the Court further
expanded the power of the press to comment on pending court
cases and judges (<u>Bridges</u>, <u>Times-Mirror</u>). The substantive
evil must be extremely serious and the degree of imminence
extremely high before the utterances can be punished. The
<u>Bridges</u> principle was affirmed in other cases (<u>Pennekamp</u>,
<u>Craig</u>, <u>Baltimore Radio Show</u>, <u>Wood</u>). Occasionally, judges
have imposed restrictive orders concerning the acceptable
scope of media coverage. When these orders have been appealed, the courts usually give priority to the competing claim
of free expression (<u>Wood</u>, <u>Miami Herald</u>, <u>Sun Company</u>, <u>Dick-
inson</u>, <u>CBS</u>, <u>Times-Picayune</u>, <u>Nebraska Press Association</u>).
In order for a judge to impose a "gag order, " there must
be imminent, not merely potential, threat to the administra-
tion of justice (<u>Seymour</u>, <u>Schuster</u>). The <u>Dickinson</u> requirement that reporters exhaust all available court remedies be-
fore violating an unconstitutional gag order poses a potential
barrier to thorough news coverage of courtroom proceedings.

The press, in its coverage of courtroom proceedings,
disseminates information about the crime, the victim, the
accused, the jury. Clearly, the courts are willing to reverse a conviction in order to offset "sensational" publicity
(<u>Shepherd</u>, <u>Marshall</u>, <u>Irvin</u>, <u>Rideau</u>, <u>Sheppard</u>). In <u>Murphy</u>,
however, the Court ruled that jurors need not be totally ig-
norant of the relevant facts and issues. It would be sufficient that they could set aside their impressions and render an
impartial verdict. The use of cameras and tape recorders
in the courtroom may also result in an unfair trial. In <u>Estes</u>,
the Court advanced the doctrine of "implied bias"--that is,
prejudice is inherent in a televised trial. The courts have,
nonetheless, emphatically preserved the principle of a public trial in the interests of the accused, the public, the victim, and the press (<u>Valente</u>, <u>Kobli</u>, <u>Oxnard</u>, <u>Oliver</u>).

Management of Information

When legislatures have attempted to manage information, the courts have generally condemned such attempts.
Prior restraint of publication, in particular, carries a heavy
burden of proof. When the Court upheld the power of the
Postmaster General to suspend the mailing privilege for "un-
mailable material" (<u>Milwaukee Social Democrat</u>), Justices

Brandeis and Holmes's dissent became the basis for the Court's decision, which unequivocally gave immunity to the press from prior restraints (Near). In the Pentagon Papers case, a divided Court once again sided with the First Amendment.

Various means of external restraint on the publication and dissemination of information have been proscribed by the courts. A legislature, for example, cannot control newspaper publication and circulation through unfair taxation (Grosjean). While the Court required publishers to file certain information with the Post Office (Lewis Publishing), it subsequently banned the Post Office from restricting the flow of information by revoking mailing privileges (Hannegan). In Lamont, the Court affirmed an individual's right to receive information without Post Office infringement or control.

The courts have also been willing to break up monopolistic combinations in order to protect freedom of the press (Associated Press, Lorain, Times-Mirror). However, in Times-Picayune the Court sided with the newspaper after determining that the company did not enjoy a dominant position as a result of unit advertising. The Court adopted the "failing company" doctrine (Maryland and Virginia Milk Producers), and established prerequisites for the "failing company" defense (Citizen Publishing). The Newspaper Preservation Act provided an exemption from antitrust laws to newspapers in the same city, which had preexisting joint operating agreements (Bay Guardian).

Occasionally, legislation has been directed at controlling the publication of politically oriented information. In Alabama, such a law was declared unconstitutional (Mills). The Federal Campaign Act of 1971, which prohibited particular types of media advertising on behalf of candidates for federal office, was similarly struck down (ACLU v. Jennings). In Tornillo, the Court rejected a right to reply. Operation of such a right could blunt the publication of political campaigns and elections.

Recently, journalists have claimed a privilege to refuse to testify before grand juries, and in courts. A divided Court ruled that requiring reporters to testify before grand juries did not abridge First Amendment guarantees (Branzburg). The issue was not settled, however. Much controversy yet remains. Courts have recognized the privilege (Baker, McCord), while other courts have rejected the concept (Bursey, Liddy, Dow Jones). More than half the states have passed "shield laws" that set forth the specific conditions under which a journalist's privilege applies. When state laws are interpreted by the courts, the interpretation has tended to be narrow (Lightman, Bridge). Shield laws may not even protect a reporter in certain cases (People v. Dan, WBAI-FM, Farr).

In the 1970s, several court actions banned journalists from specific sources of news. The Court upheld the regulation of the Bureau of Prisons that bans them from interviewing individual inmates (Pell, Saxbe). In Borreca and Forcade, the courts specified that a government official could not, without good reasons, ban a reporter from a press conference.

Information gathering has also been impeded by government secrecy. In Reynolds, the Court balanced the public's right to know with the government's right to maintain secrecy in the interest of national security, and upheld the Air Force's claim of privilege--thus protecting the interests of government secrecy. The Freedom of Information Act was designed to facilitate access to information. The Court, however, upheld exemptions specified in the Act (Mink). Decisions in Vaughn and Robertson have slowly shaped a public freedom of information. The power of enforcing the FOIA has been placed largely with the courts. However, the courts may refuse to exercise that power (Knopf).

Executive privilege also may be invoked to prevent the dissemination of certain information (Marbury). Recently, the privilege was invoked by President Richard Nixon. According to the Court, executive privilege is not absolute (Nixon v. Sirica, U. S. v. Nixon). In Nixon v. Administrator of General Services, the Court upheld the constitutionality of the Presidential Recordings and Materials Preservation Act.

Overall, the courts have made certain information accessible to the public, but have refused to grant news reporters the unqualified freedom to gather news.

Broadcasting

From its outset, government regulation of broadcasting has been and will continue to be based ostensibly on the public interest, convenience, and necessity. The authority of government to license radio broadcasting under the Radio Acts of 1912 and 1927 was firmly established in the KFKB and Trinity

Methodist cases. Congress, aware of the increasing complexity of broadcasting, passed the Federal Communications
Act of 1934. The FCC's power to regulate chain broadcasting,
defined as the "simultaneous broadcasting of an identical program by two or more connected stations, " was soon recognized by the Court (NBC-CBS). The Commission's powers,
in short, went beyond merely technical or engineering questions. The FCC's regulatory power, moreover, was recognized to extend to cable television (Carter Mountain, Southwestern Cable, Midwest Video). With the passage of the Public Broadcasting Act of 1967, the FCC became responsible
for regulating non-commercial public television.

In licensing new broadcasting facilities or renewing
the licenses of exisitng ones, the FCC is concerned with certain programming considerations. The courts have consistently
affirmed the desirability of local service programming (Simmons, Henry). The courts have made it clear that broadcasting of lottery information is regulated but not prohibited
(ABC, New York State Broadcasting). In 1971, the United
States Court of Appeals, District of Columbia, introduced
the doctrine of "superior service" (Citizens Communication
Center). In 1973, the court established the license holder's
responsibility for knowledge, evaluation, and control of programming consistent with the public interest (Yale). Another
programming consideration concerns the broadcasting of obscenity. The FCC retained its power to prohibit the broadcasting of obscene material on public interest grounds (Palmetto, Sonderling, WUHY-FM, Pacifica). The effects of
program format changes on the public interest are also taken
into account in the licensing decision (WEFM).

The licensing decision is affected substantially by two
economic considerations: 1) the effect of competition on incumbent license holders, and 2) the extent to which ownership
of broadcasting facilities diversified among different groups
or individuals. In Sanders Brothers, the Supreme Court argued that economic injury to a competitor was not, by itself,
ground for refusal to grant a license. The incumbent did not
possesses a vested property right to continue broadcasting. In
Carroll, the court made it clear that such economic considerations could indeed be relevant if potential competition seemed
to affect the public interest adversely. Secondly, the concentration of the media--both electronic and printed--was looked
upon with great disfavor by the courts. The greater the diversity and scope of information presented, the better the
chance that the public will be served (Mansfield, Greater Boston).

Procedural guarantees constitute another important licensing consideration. In general, legal standing to bring action is not absolute. The courts have granted the FCC "broad discretion" in settling rules for evidentiary hearings. Legal standing of a petitioner, for example, must be judged in relation to other petitioners' claims (United Church of Christ I). In the second United Church case, the court established that the burden of proof rests with the incumbent licensee. In Hale, the court rejected the requirement of an evidentiary hearing except in certain cases, and again reversed the burden of proof.

In addition to its influence on broadcasting through the authority to license, the FCC exercises direct control over programming through the Equal Time and Fairness Doctrines. The Equal Time provision--Section 315 of the Communications Act--required broadcasters to provide equal opportunity to all legally qualified candidates for use of its facilities if the station afforded such opportunity to any one candidate. In Farmers Educational and Cooperative Union, the Supreme Court ruled that any system of station censorship would undermine the purpose for which Section 315 was passed. However, the Court also granted broadcasters immunity from defamation suits based on remarks made by the candidates over the air. In McCarthy, the court attempted to define a "legally qualified candidate. "

The emphasis of the Fairness Doctrine is on the broadcaster's affirmative responsibility to cover fairly and adequately issues of public importance. Mayflower provided the foundation for the emerging doctrine, and subsequent rulings in WHKC and Scott signaled a new approach to the coverage of controversial issues. As the Fairness Doctrine has evolved over the past several decades, a series of "personal attack" rules emerged in response to situations in which individuals or groups were maligned publicly (Red Lion, RTNDA). While a concept of a liberal right of access had emerged, the Court determined that not all proposed announcements need be accepted by broadcasters (CBS-BEM). In 1972, the courts denied license renewal to a station that failed to comply with the requirements of the Fairness Doctrine (Brandywine).

Advertising

Since misrepresentation in advertising came under attack in the early 1900s, legislatures, consumer groups, and the courts have had varying success in policing the claims of advertisers. In general, the Court has given greater protection to editorial rather than commercial forms of advertising. Purely "commercial speech" enjoyed less constitutional protection than other forms of communication (Valentine). The Court continued to extend a preferred position to political as opposed to commercial communication (Pittsburgh Press Company). However, merely because a particular advertisement had commercial aspects, all First Amendment guarantees are not negated (Bigelow). The "commercial speech" distinction has further been eroded (Virginia State Board of Pharmacy).

During the twentieth century, the courts have frequently acted to halt deceptive advertising practices (Winsted Hosiery, Raladam I, Raladam II, Standard Education, P. Lorillard, Rhodes, Sterling Drug, Colgate-Palmolive). In J. B. Williams, the courts had difficulty in enforcing its ruling. Sometimes, merely stopping an ad is insufficient. Recently, corrective advertising has been used by the FTC to eliminate any residue of misleading information that may remain in the public's mind after an ad is discontinued (Ocean Spray, Feil, Continental).

The issue of access has also been dealt with by the courts. In general, a medium is not bound to accept the advertising of all who apply for it (Approved Personnel). However, the First Amendment provides guarantees of free speech. Political, as opposed to strictly commercial messages, must be allowed on publicly owned conveyances, providing they are not obscene or dangerous to the public safety (Kissinger, Wirta). Overall, the courts have upheld the right of the media to determine the specific types of advertising that will be displayed (Lehman, Chicago Joint Board, Aldrich).

Beginning in the late 1960s, groups sought to extend the application of the Fairness Doctrine to advertising. The courts supported the Commission's ruling in Banzhaf, aimed at providing fair and balanced coverage of a controversial issue. Courts have subsequently had some difficulties in keeping the Banzhaf principle from expanding to other areas (WREO, Green, Friends of the Earth).

The courts have decided that the unique characteristics of electronic communication make it especially subject to regulation in the public interest. The court upheld the ban against cigarette advertising (Capital Broadcasting). In some recent cases, the Supreme Court distinguished between commercial and informative communication; while purely commercial advertising can be banned, a free flow of legitimate commercial information must be protected (Bates, Linmark, Ohralik, Carey).

Epilog

As this volume indicates, journalists frequently find their claims in conflict with competing societal interests. In such instances, the courts have had to resolve the conflict. Fortunately, in most instances, the courts have sided with free expression. Clearly, however, the courts have not given journalists free license to investigate, gather, and report the news.

SELECTED BIBLIOGRAPHY

"An Accomodation of Privacy Interests and First Amendment Rights in Public Disclosure Cases, " University of Pennsylvania Law Review 124 (June, 1976), 1385-417.

Aitchison, Bill. "The Right to Receive and the Commercial Speech Doctrine: New Constitutional Considerations, " Georgetown Law Journal 63 (February, 1975), 775-803.

Alberich, H. Glenn. "Nebraska Press Association vs. Stuart: Balancing Freedom of the Press Against the Right to Fair Trial, " New England Law Review 12 (Winter, 1977), 763-88.

Alexander, Lawrence. "Speech in the Local Marketplace: Implications of Virginia State Board of Pharmacy vs. Virginia Citizens Consumer Council, Inc. for Local Regulating Power, " San Diego Law Review 14 (March, 1977), 357-77.

Amoroso, Frank. "The Freedom of Information Act: Shredding the Paper Curtain, " St. John's Law Review 47 (May, 1973), 694-724.

Anderson, Karen Gatsis. "Attorney 'Gag' Rules: Reconciling the First Amendment and the Right to a Fair Trial, " University of Illinois Law Forum (1976), 763-82.

Anderson, Richard E. "Branzburg v. Hayes: A Need for Statutory Protection of News Sources, " Kentucky Law Journal 61 (1973), 551-9.

Antonelli, Carol S. "Fair Trial/Free Press--Nebraska Press Association vs. Stuart: Defining the Limits of Prior Restraint in the Trial by Newspaper Controversy, " Loyola University Law Journal 8 (Winter, 1977), 417-37.

Archer, John F. "Advertising of Professional Fees: Does the Consumer Have a Right to Know?" South Dakota Law Review 21 (Spring, 1976), 310-31.

Ashdown, Gerald G. "Gertz and Firestone: A Study in Constitutional Policy-Making, " Minnesota Law Review 61 (1977), 645-90.

Ashley, Paul P. Say It Safely: Legal Limits in Publishing, Radio, and Television. 5th ed. Seattle: University of Washington Press, 1976.

Atkinson, Elliott W., Jr. "Free Speech v. Fair Trial: Insulation Against Injustice, " Louisiana Law Review 33 (1973), 547-59.

Baer, Robert L. "Right to Report Judicial Records, " Washburn Law Journal 15 (1976), 163-7.

Bagdikian, Ben H. "Governmental Suppression of the Media, " University of Miami Law Review 29 (Spring, 1975), 447-55.

Baker, C. Edwin. "Commercial Speech: A Problem in the Theory of Freedom, " Iowa Law Review 62 (1976), 1-56.

Barron, Jerome A. "Access to the Press--A New First Amendment Right, " Harvard Law Review 80 (June, 1967), 1641-78.

_____. Freedom of the Press For Whom?: The Right of Access to Mass Media. Bloomington: Indiana University Press, 1973.

Barrow, Roscoe L. "The Fairness Doctrine: A Double Standard for Electronic and Print Media, " Hastings Law Journal 26 (January, 1975), 659-708.

Bayus, Elaine. "Constitutional Status of Commercial Expression, " Hastings Constitutional Law Quarterly 3 (Summer, 1976), 761-801.

Bennett, Richard V. "Branzburg v. Hayes--Must Newsmen Reveal Their Confidential Sources to Grand Juries?" Wake Forest Law Review 8 (October, 1972), 567-80.

Bennett, Stephen. "Fair Trial v. Free Press, " Trial 12 (September, 1976), 24-5.

Berner, Richard Olin. Constraints on the Regulatory Process: A Case Study of Regulation of Cable Television. Cambridge, Mass.: Ballinger Publishing, 1976.

Berns, Walter. "Freedom of the Press and the Alien and Sedition Laws: A Reappraisal, " Supreme Court Review (1970), 109-59.

Beytagh, Francis X. "Privacy and a Free Press: A Contemporary Conflict in Values, " New York Law Forum 20 (Winter, 1975), 453-514.

Bittner, John R. "Politics and Information Flow: The Oregon Shield Law, " Western Speech 39 (Winter, 1975), 51-9.

Blackmun, Sally A. "The Press Cannot Be Restrained from Reporting Facts Contained in Official Court Records, " Emory Law Journal 24 (Fall, 1975), 1205-28.

Blake, Jonathan S. "Red Lion Broadcasting Co. v. FCC: Fairness and the Emperor's New Clothes, " Federal Communications Bar Journal 23 (1969), 75-92.

Blanchard, Robert O. Congress and the News Media. New York: Hastings House, 1974.

Block, Bradford E. "Commercial Speech--An End in Sight to Chrestensen?" De Paul Law Review 23 (Spring, 1974), 1258-75.

Boisseau, Merribeth. "Time, Inc. vs. Firestone: The Supreme Court's Restrictive New Libel Ruling, " San Diego Law Review 14 (March, 1977), 435-57.

Bollinger, Lee C. , Jr. "Freedom of the Press and Public Access: Toward a Theory of Partial Regulation of the Mass Media, " Michigan Law Review 75 (November, 1976), 1-42.

Botein, Michael. "The New Copyright Act and Cable Television--A Signal of Change, " Bulletin of the Copyright Society of the U. S. A. 24 (October, 1976), 1-17.

Boyce, David S. "Commercial Speech: First Amendment Protection Clarified, " University of Florida Law Review 28 (Winter, 1976), 610-20.

"Broadcasting: Limited Access to Purchase Public Issue Advertising Time, " Rutgers Law Review 27 (Spring, 1974), 738-62.

Brosnahan, James L. "From Times v. Sullivan to Gertz v. Welch: Ten Years of Balancing Libel Law and the First Amendment, " Hastings Law Journal 26 (January, 1975) 777-96.

Butler, Richard J. "Libel and the First Amendment, " Nebraska Law Review 56 (1977), 366-81.

Caginalp, Aydin S. "Newsman's Privilege, " Tulane Law Review 47 (June, 1973), 1184-91.

Canby, William C. , Jr. "The First Amendment Right to Persuade: Access to Radio and Television, " UCLA Law Review 19 (June, 1972), 723-58.

Chafee, Zechariah, Jr. Government and Mass Communications Hamden, Conn.: Archon Books, 1965.

Chatzky, Michael G. , and William Eric Robinson. "A Constitutional Right of Access to Newspaper: Is There Life After Tornillo?" Santa Clara Law Review 16 (Summer, 1976), 453-94.

Clark, David G. , and Earl R. Hutchison, eds. Mass Media and the Law: Freedom and Restraint. New York: John Wiley & Sons, 1970.

Coase, R. H. "Advertising and Free Speech, " Journal of Legal Studies 6 (January, 1977), 1-34.

Cohen, Mark C. "United States v. Columbia Broadcasting System, Inc.: Courtroom Sketching and the Right to Fair Trial, " New England Law Review 10 (Spring, 1975), 541-9.

Cohn, Marcus. "Who Really Controls Television?" University of Miami Law Review 29 (Spring, 1975), 482-6.

Cole, Barry, and Mal Oettinger. Reluctant Regulators: The FCC and the Broadcasting Audience. Reading, Mass.: Addison-Wesley, 1978.

Cole, Jeffrey, and Michael I. Spak. "Defense Counsel and the First Amendment: A Time to Keep Silence, and a Time to Speak, " St. Mary's Law Journal 6 (Summer, 1974), 347-85.

Collins, E. L. , and J. D. Drushal. "Reaction of the State Courts to Gertz v. Robert Welch, Inc. , " Case Western Law Review 28 (Winter, 1978), 306-43.

Collins, Tom A. "Positing a Right of Access: Evaluations and Subsequent Developments, " William & Mary Law Review 15 (Winter, 1973), 339-52.

"Commercial Speech Doctrine--A Clarification of the Protection Afforded Advertising Under the First Amendment, " Brigham Young University Law Review (1975), 797-811.

Conine, Gary B. "Copyright: Unfair Use in Fair Competition--A Search for a Logical Rationale for the Protection of Investigative News Reporting, " Oklahoma Law Review 30 (Winter, 1977), 214-38.

Coombs, Frederick S. , III. "Access vs. Fairness in Newspapers: The Implications of Tornillo for a Free and Responsible Press, " Ohio State Law Journal 35 (1974), 954-73.

Crawford, Tad. The Writer's Legal Guide. New York: Hawthorn Books, 1977.

Dannay, Richard. "An Overview of Teleprompter v. CBS and Other Recent Developments--Ominous Signals for Copyright Law, " Bulletin of the Copyright Society of the U. S. A. 22 (October, 1974), 10-18.

Davis, Chee. "The Firestone Case: A Judicial Exercise in Press Censorship, " Emory Law Journal 25 (Summer, 1976), 705-36.

Decker, Jack W. "Commercial Speech and the First Amendment: Virginia State Board of Pharmacy vs. Virginia Citizens Consumer Council, " Capital University Law Review 6 (1976), 75-93.

DeSoto, Amey E. "Advertising and the Legal Profession: An Analysis of the Requirements of the Sherman Act and the First Amendment, " UCLA-Alaska Law Review 6 (Fall, 1976), 67-89.

DeVol, Kenneth S. Mass Media and the Supreme Court: The Legacy of the Warren Years. 2nd ed. New York: Hastings House, 1976.

DeVore, P. Cameron, and Marshall J. Nelson. "Commercial
Speech and Paid Access to the Press, " Hastings Law Journal 26 (January, 1975), 745-75.

DiPippa, John M. "The Demise of the Commercial Speech
Doctrine and the Regulation of Professional's Advertising:
The Virginia Pharmacy Case, " Washington and Lee Law
Review 34 (Winter, 1977), 245-62.

"Discrimination in Classified Advertising--Pittsburgh Press
Company v. Pittsburgh Commission on Human Relations, "
Albany Law Review 38 (1974), 847-65.

Dixon, Robert G. , Jr. "The Constitution Is Shield Enough
for Newsmen, " American Bar Association Journal 60 (June,
1974), 707-10.

Douberley, William M. "Resolving the Free Speech--Free
Press Dichotomy: Access to the Press Through Advertising, " University of Florida Law Review 22 (1969), 293-
320.

Edlavitch, Susan T. "The Fairness Doctrine and Access to
Reply to Product Commercials, " Indiana Law Journal
51 (Spring, 1976), 756-82.

Elman, P. "New Constitutional Right to Advertise, " American
Bar Association Journal 64 (February, 1978), 206-10.

Ernst, Morris L. , and Alan U. Schwartz. The Right to Be
Let Alone. New York: Macmillan, 1962.

"Expanding Constitutional Protection for the News Media from
Liability for Defamation: Predictability and the New Syn-
thesis, " Michigan Law Review 70 (August, 1972), 1547-80.

Fahringer, H. P. "Charting a Course from the Free Press
to a Fair Trial, " Suffolk University Law Review 12 (Winter, 1978), 1-15.

"Federal Regulation of Television Broadcasting--Are the Prime
Time Access Rule and the Family Viewing Hour in the Public Interest?" Rutgers Law Review 29 (1976), 902-20.

"First Amendment and Commercial Advertising: Bigelow v.
Commonwealth, " Virginia Law Review 60 (January, 1974),
154-62.

"First Amendment--Commercial Speech: The Public Interest in Preventing Panic Selling Outweighs Any Incidental Infringement of Freedom of Expression or the Right to Travel Caused by a Municipal Ordinance Banning 'For Sale' and 'Sold' Signs on Residential Property, " Georgia Law Review 11 (Fall, 1976), 230-40.

"First Amendment: The Public's Right to Access to the Broadcast Media for the Airing of Editorial Advertisements, " Valparaiso University Law Review 8 (Fall, 1973), 125-39.

Fischer, Madeleine. "Commercial Speech Is Not Protected by the First Amendment, " Tulane Law Review 48 (February, 1974), 426-32.

Fischman, Bruce D. "Miami Herald Publishing Company v. Tornillo; Editorial Discretion v. The Electorate's Right to Know--Freedom of the Press for Whom?" Ohio Northern Law Review 2 (1975), 562-8.

Flynn, Thomas J. "Freedom of the Press--Civil Contempt--Incarceration of Newsperson for Refusal to Disclose Confidential Sources Does Not Abridge First Amendment, " Santa Clara Law Review 16 (Spring, 1976), 379-90.

Francois, William E. Mass Media Law and Regulation. 2nd ed. Columbus, Ohio: Grid, 1978.

Franklin, Marc A. "Freedom and Control of Communication, " in Handbook of Communication. Ithiel de Sola Pool, et al., eds. Chicago: Rand McNally, 1973, 887-908.

_____. The First Amendment and the Fourth Estate: Communications Law for Undergraduates. Mineola, N. Y.: Foundation Press, 1977.

Friendly, Fred W. The Good Guys, The Bad Guys, and the First Amendment: Free Speech v. Fairness in Broadcasting. New York: Random House, 1976.

Geller, Henry. "Does Red Lion Square with Tornillo?" University of Miami Law Review 29 (Spring, 1975), 477-81.

Georgetown Law Journal Association. Media and the First Amendment in a Free Society. Amherst: University of Massachusetts Press, 1973.

Gerald, J. Edward. The Press and the Constitution: 1931-1947. Minneapolis: University of Minnesota Press, 1948.

Gillmor, Donald M., and Jerome A. Barron. Mass Communication Law: Cases and Comment. St. Paul, Minn.: West Publishing, 1974.

Godofsky, Stanley. "Protection of the Press from Prior Restraint and Harassment Under Libel Laws," University of Miami Law Review 29 (Spring, 1975), 462-76.

Goines, M. Douglas. "The Application of the Fairness Doctrine to Editorial Advertising," Wake Forest Law Review 10 (October, 1974) 621-34.

Goldstein, Paul. "Copyright and the First Amendment," Columbia Law Review 70 (June, 1970), 983-1057.

Goodale, James C. "Branzburg and the Protection of Reporter's Sources," University of Miami Law Review 29 (Spring, 1975), 456-8.

_____. "Branzburg v. Hayes and the Developing Qualified Privilege for Newsmen," Hastings Law Journal 26 (January, 1975). 709-43.

Gorski, James M. "Access to Information? Exemptions from Disclosure Under the Freedom of Information Act and the Privacy Act of 1974," Willamette Law Journal 13 (Winter, 1976). 135-71.

Goss, Patricia. "The First Amendment's Weakest Link: Government Regulation of Controversial Advertising," New York Law Forum 20 (Winter, 1975), 617-32.

Grant, Alan. "Pretrial Publicity and Fair Trial--A Tale of Three Doctors," Osgoode Hall Law Journal 14 (October, 1976), 275-85.

Hachten, William A. The Supreme Court on Freedom of the Press: Decisions and Dissents. Ames: Iowa State University Press, 1968.

Hagelin, Theodore M. "The First Amendment Stake in New Technology: the Broadcast-Cable Controversy," University of Cincinnati Law Review 44 (1975), 427-524.

Handler, Michael. "The Expanding Right to Publish," University of Pittsburgh Law Review 32 (Spring, 1971), 450-6.

Hannigan, Michael J., and Francis J. Nealon. "The Freedom of Information Act--the Parameters of the Exemptions," Georgetown Law Journal 62 (October, 1973), 177-207.

Hansen, Emily R. "Lawyers' Advertising: Beyond the Yellow Pages," Idaho Law Review 13 (Spring, 1977), 247-62.

Hill, Alfred. "Defamation and Privacy Under the First Amendment," Columbia Law Review 76 (December, 1976), 1205-313.

Hoak, Jon. "Obscenity: Court Upholds the Activities of the Federal Communications Commission in Curtailing Sex-oriented Talk Show on Radio," Drake Law Review 25 (Fall, 1975), 257-65.

Hoffer, Mark D. "Power of the FCC to Regulate Cable Pay-TV: Jurisdictional and Constitutional Limitations," Denver Law Journal 53 (1976), 477-500.

Hoyt, James L. "Courtroom Coverage: The Effects of Being Televised," Journal of Broadcasting 21 (Fall, 1977), 487-95.

Hunsaker, David M. "Freedom and Responsibility in First Amendment Theory: Defamation Law and Media Credibility," Quarterly Journal of Speech 65 (February, 1979), 25-35.

Hunter, Howard O. "Prescription Drugs and Open Housing: More on Commercial Speech," Emory Law Journal 25 (Fall, 1976), 815-48.

Hurst, Walter E. Copyright: How to Register Your Copyright & Introduction to New & Historical Copyright Law. Hollywood, Calif.: Seven Arts Press, 1977.

Johnson, Mark. "The FCC: The Urge to Censor," Free Speech Yearbook 1978, 73-81.

Johnson, Nicholas, and Tracy A. Weston. "A Twentieth-Century Soapbox: The Right to Purchase Radio and Television Time," Virginia Law Review 57 (May, 1971), 574-634.

Johnston, Donald F. Copyright Handbook. New York: R. R. Bowker, 1978.

Jones, Lawrence. "Time Inc. vs. Firestone: Is Rosenbloom Really Dead?" University of Miami Law Review 31 (Fall, 1976), 216-25.

Kahn, Frank J., ed. Documents of American Broadcasting. 3rd ed. Englewood Cliffs, N. J.: Prentice-Hall, 1978.

_____. "From 'Fairness' to 'Access' and Back Again: Some Dimensions of Free Expression in Broadcasting, " Free Speech Yearbook 1974, 1-10.

Kalven, Harry, Jr. "The New York Times Case: A Note on 'The Central Meaning of the First Amendment, ' " Supreme Court Review (1964), 191-221.

_____. "The Reasonable Man and the First Amendment: Hill, Butts, and Walker, " Supreme Court Review (1967), 267-309.

Kaplan, Benjamin, and Ralph S. Brown. Cases on Copyright; Unfair Competition, and Other Topics Bearing on the Protection of Literary, Musical, and Artistic Works. 2nd ed. Mineola, N. Y.: Foundation Press, 1974.

Kaplan, John. "Free Press/Fair Trial--Rights in Conflict: Freedom of the Press and the Rights of the Individual, " Oklahoma Law Review 29 (Spring, 1976), 361-9.

Kaplan, Nancy Federman. "Beyond Branzburg: The Continuing Quest for Reporters Privilege, " Syracuse Law Review 24 (1973), 731-73.

Katz, Ellen Edge. "Freedom of Speech--Commercial Speech Doctrine--Use of Sex-Designated Classified Advertising Column Headings, " Duquesne Law Review 12 (Summer, 1974), 1000-8.

Keeton, Page, and Marshall S. Shapo. Products and the Consumer: Deceptive Practices. Mineola, N. Y.: Foundation Press, 1972.

Kinsley, Philip. Liberty and the Press: A History of the Chicago Tribune's Fight to Preserve a Free Press for the American People. Chicago: Tribune Company, 1944.

Kohn, William I. "State Tort Actions for Libel After Gertz v. Robert Welch, Inc.: Is the Balance of Intent Leaning in Favor of the News Media?" Ohio State Law Journal 36 (1975), 697-720.

Kops, John Michael. "The First Amendment and Advertising: The Effect of the 'Commercial Activity' Doctrine on the Media Regulation, " North Carolina Law Review 51 (January, 1973), 581-92.

Landau, Jack C. "Free Press Boon: A Stop to Direct Gag Orders?" Trial 12 (September, 1976), 26-29.

Lange, David L. "Role of the Access Doctrine in the Regulation of the Mass Media: A Critical Review and Assessment, " North Carolina Law Review 52 (November, 1973), 1-91.

Larson, Milton R. "Free Press vs. Fair Trial in Nebraska: A Position Paper, " Nebraska Law Review 55 (1976), 543-71.

Lawhorne, Clifton O. Defamation and Public Officials: The Evolving Law of Libel. Carbondale: Southern Illinois University Press, 1971.

Lea, K. M. , ed. John Milton--Areopagitica and On Education Oxford: Clarendon Press, 1973.

LeDuc, Don R. Cable Television and the FCC: A Crisis in Media Control. Philadelphia: Temple University Press, 1973.

_____. " 'Free Speech' Decisions and the Legal Process: The Judicial Opinion in Context, " Quarterly Journal of Speech 62 (October, 1976), 279-87.

Levy, Leonard W. Freedom of Speech and Press in Early American History: Legacy of Suppression. New York: Harper & Row, 1963.

_____. ed. Freedom of the Press from Zenger to Jefferson: Early American Libertarian Theories. Indianapolis: Bobbs-Merrill, 1966.

_____. Legacy of Suppression: Freedom of Speech and Press in Early American History. Cambridge, Mass. : Harvard University Press, 1960.

Light, Jonathan D. "Gertz v. Welch, Inc. : Redefining Defamation for a Private Citizen, " New England Law Review 10 (Spring, 1975), 585-98.

Lindsey, Michael K. "Public Broadcasting: Editorial Restraints and the First Amendment, " Federal Communications Bar Journal 28 (1975), 63-100.

Lipsky, Abbott B. , Jr. "Reconciling Red Lion and Tornillo: A Consistent Theory of Media Regulation, " Stanford Law Review 28 (February, 1976), 563-88.

Lohmann, Paul M. "Protection of Commercial Speech, " Marquette Law Review 60 (Fall, 1976), 138-52.

McKeever, Joyce. "Right of Privacy: Publication of True Information on the Public Record, " Duquesne Law Review 14 (Spring, 1976), 507-20.

McKenna, Donald J. "Time, Inc. v. Firestone: More Than A New Public Figure Standard, " St. Louis University Law Journal 20 (1976), 625-39.

McKey, Arthur Duncan. "Defamation Law After Time, Inc. vs. Firestone, " Idaho Law Review 13 (Winter, 1976), 53-65.

Maeder, Gary William. "Right of Access to the Broadcast Media for Paid Editorial Advertising--A Plea to Congress, " UCLA Law Review 22 (October, 1974), 258-322.

Mann, Frederick. "The Consumer's Right to Know: New First Amendment Weapon in the War on Price-Advertising Bans, " University of Florida Law Review 29 (Winter, 1977), 354-64.

Marnell, William H. The Right to Know: Media and the Common Good. New York: Seabury Press, 1973.

Mason, Roy L. , and Robert E. Ganz. "Columbia Broadcasting: Public Access to the Media Denied, " Catholic University Law Review 23 (Winter, 1973), 339-58.

Meeske, Milan D. "Editorial Advertising: A New Form of Free Speech, " Free Speech Yearbook 1973, 51-9.

Meiklejohn, D. "Commercial Speech and the First Amendment, " California Western Law Review 13 (1977), 439-55.

Merrill, Thomas W. "First Amendment Protection for Commercial Advertising: The New Constitutional Doctrine, " University of Chicago Law Review 44 (Fall, 1976), 205-54.

Miami Herald v. Tornillo: The Trial of the First Amendment. Columbia, Mo.: Freedom of Information Center, 1975.

Mink, Patsy, T. "The Mink Case: Restoring the Freedom of Information Act, " Pepperdine Law Review 2 (1974), 8-27.

Morrison, Brian A. "Newsman's Privilege to Refuse Disclosure of Confidential Sources in Criminal Trial, " Washington Law Review 51 (October, 1976), 1005-24.

Mundy, Larry J., and William J. Paprota. "Price Advertising of Legal Services: The Move Toward a Balancing Test, " Washburn Law Journal 16 (1977), 683-708.

Murasky, Donna M. "The Journalist's Privilege: Branzburg and Its Aftermath, " Texas Law Review 52 (May, 1974), 829-917.

Nasri, Wiliam Z. Crisis in Copyright. New York: Marcel Dekker, 1976.

Naughton, James M., and Eric R. Gilbertson. "Libelous Ridicule by Journalists, " Cleveland State Law Review 18 (September, 1969), 450-5.

Nelson, Harold L., ed. Freedom of the Press from Hamilton to the Warren Court. Indianapolis: Bobbs-Merrill, 1967.

_____, and Dwight L. Teeter, Jr. Law of Mass Communications: Freedom and Control of Print and Broadcast Media. 2nd ed. New York: Foundation Press, 1973.

Neubauer, Mark. "The Newsman's Privilege After Branzburg: The Case for a Federal Shield Law, " UCLA Law Review 24 (October, 1976), 160-92.

"Newspaper Advertisement of Abortion Referral Service Entitled to First Amendment Protection, " University of Richmond Law Review 10 (Winter, 1976), 427-33.

Newton, Sally H. "Commercial Speech Doctrine: Bigelow vs. Virginia, " Urban Law Annual 12 (1976), 221-32.

Nimmer, Melville B. "National Security Secrets v. Free Speech: The Issues Left Undecided in the Ellsburg Case, " Stanford Law Review 26 (January, 1974), 311-33.

Nisely, Robert L. "New York Press Shield Law Applies Only When Confidential Relationship Exists Between a Newsman and His Source, " Buffalo Law Review 23 (Winter, 1974), 529-48.

O'Neil, Robert M. "Shield Laws: Partial Solution to a Pervasive Problem, " New York Law Forum 20 (Winter, 1975), 515-50.

Owen, Bruce M. Economics and Freedom of Expression: Media Structure and the First Amendment. Cambridge, Mass.: Ballinger Publishing, 1975.

Parmelee, Steven G. "Commercial Speech Falls Within the Protections of First Amendment, " Creighton Law Review 10 (1976), 362-77.

Patterson, Lyman Ray. Copyright in Historical Perspective. Nashville, Tenn.: Vanderbilt University Press, 1968.

_____. "Private Copyright and Public Communication: Free Speech Endangered, " Vanderbilt Law Review 28 (November, 1975), 1161-1211.

Paul, Dan. "Why a Shield Law?" University of Miami Law Review 29 (Spring, 1975), 459-61.

Pember, Don R. Mass Media Law. Dubuque, Iowa: Wm. C. Brown Company, 1977.

_____. Privacy and the Press: The Law, the Mass Media, and the First Amendment. Seattle: University of Washington Press, 1972.

Perlman, Harvey S., and Laurens H. Rhinelander. "Williams & Wilkins Co. v. United States: Photocopying, Copyright, and the Judicial Process, " Supreme Court Review (1975), 355-417.

Peters, Robert S. "The FCC's Requirement of Reply to Personal Attack: The Bite in Red Lion, " Tennessee Law Review 37 (Winter, 1970), 383-400.

Pfaff, Ellen O. "Gag Orders on Criminal Defendants, " Hastings Law Journal 27 (July, 1976), 1369-99.

Phelps, Robert H., and E. Douglas Hamilton. Libel: Rights, Risks, Responsibilities. New York: Macmillan, 1966.

Pilpel, Harriet F., and Theodore S. Zavin. Rights and Writers: A Handbook of Literary and Entertainment Law. New York: E. P. Dutton, 1960.

Platt, Neal Robert. "Commercial Speech and the First Amendment: An Emerging Doctrine," Hofstra Law Review 5 (Spring, 1977), 655-71.

Podgor, Ellen S. "United States Supreme Court Held That the First Amendment Protected an Abortion Advertisement," Indiana Law Review 8 (1975), 890-7.

Polking, Kirk, and Leonard S. Meranus, eds. Law and the Writer. Cincinnati: Writer's Digest Books, 1978.

Polsby, Daniel D. "Buckley v. Valeo: The Special Nature of Political Speech," Supreme Court Review (1976), 1-43.

Popper, Mary M. "Commercial Speech--Municipal Ordinance Which Prohibits the Display of 'For Sale' and 'Sold' Signs on Residential Property in Order to Prevent Panic Selling Is Constitutional," Fordham Urban Law Journal 5 (Winter, 1977), 379-89.

Popper, Robert. "Lawyer's Advertising and the First Amendment," Missouri Bar Journal 32 (March, 1976), 81-6.

"Prejudicial Publicity in Trials of Public Officials," Yale Law Journal 85 (November, 1975), 123-35.

Press Freedoms Under Pressure: Report of the Twentieth Century Fund Task Force on the Government and the Press. New York: The Twentieth Century Fund, 1972.

Preston, Ivan L. The Great American Blow-Up: Puffery in Advertising and Selling. Madison: University of Wisconsin Press, 1975.

Preston, Paul. "Purely Commercial Speech and Its Relationship to the First Amendment," Louisiana Law Review 37 (1976), 263-70.

Prettyman, E. Barrett, Jr. "Nebraska Press Association vs. Stuart: Have We Seen the Last of Prior Restraints on the Reporting of Judicial Proceedings?" St. Louis University Law Journal 20 (1976), 654-62.

"Prior Restraint on Media Publication to Protect Criminal Trial Must Meet Strict Requirements, " Kansas Law Review 25 (1977), 258-68.

"Privacy in the First Amendment, " Yale Law Journal 82 (June, 1973), 1462-80.

Prosser, William L. "Privacy, " California Law Review 48 (August, 1960), 383-423.

Raleigh, Harry S. , Jr. "Invasion of Privacy--Unreasonable Intrusions Upon Our Shrinking Right to Privacy, Dietemann v. Time, Inc. , " Notre Dame Lawyer 47 (April, 1972), 1067-77.

Ranney, James T. "Remedies for Prejudicial Publicity: A Brief Review, " Villanova Law Review 21 (October, 1976), 819-38.

"Reaffirming the Freedom of the Press: Another Look at Miami Herald Publishing Co. v. Tornillo, " Michigan Law Review 73 (November, 1974), 186-214.

Redish, Martin H. "The First Amendment in the Marketplace: Commercial Speech and the Values of Free Expression, " George Washington Law Review 39 (1971), 429-73.

Rees, William J. "Invasion of Privacy: Constitutional Privilege--The First Amendment Does Not Protect the Publicizing of Unnewsworthy Private Facts, " Vanderbilt Law Review 29 (April, 1976), 870-80.

"Regulation of Competing First Amendment Rights: A New Fairness Doctrine Balance After CBS?" University of Pennsylvania Law Review 122 (May, 1974), 1283-329.

Relyea, Harold C. "The Freedom of Infomation Act: Its Evolution and Operation Status, " Journalism Quarterly 54 (Autumn, 1977), 538-44.

"Right of the Press to Gather Information After Branzburg and Pell, " University of Pennsylvania Law Review 124 (November, 1975), 166-91.

Robertson, Edward D. , Jr. "Fair Trial--Free Press Debate Continues, " UMKC Law Review 45 (Winter, 1976), 311-20.

Rockwell, Lawrence K. "The Public's Right to Know: Pell v. Procunier and Saxbe v. Washington Post Co., " Hastings Constitutional Law Quarterly 2 (Summer, 1975), 829-58.

Romano, David John. "Libel and Slander--Defamation of Political Candidates, " West Virginia Law Review 78 (February, 1976), 247-58.

Rotunda, Ronald D. "Commercial Speech Doctrine in the Supreme Court, " University of Illinois Law Forum (1976), 1080-101.

Schaplowsky, Richard L. "The First Amendment Does Not Insulate the Press from Liability in a Defamation Action Brought by a Private Person Even Though She Is a Party in the Widely Publicized Divorce Proceeding, " Seton Hall Law Review 7 (Summer, 1976), 861-90.

Schement, Jorge Reina, and Felix Frank Gutierrez. "The Anatomy of License Challenge, " Journal of Communication 27 (Winter, 1977), 89-94.

Scherer, Howard B. "Broadcast Journalism: The Conflict Between the First Amendment and Liability for Defamation, " Brooklyn Law Review 39 (1972), 426-47.

Schiro, Richard. "Commercial Speech: The Demise of a Chimera, " Supreme Court Review (1976), 45-98.

Schmidt, Benno C. , Jr. Freedom of the Press v. Public Access. New York: Praeger, 1976.

Schwartz, Ronnie. "The California Approach to the Yielding of the Newsman's Shield Law, " Pepperdine Law Review 3 (1976), 313-35.

Shapiro, Andrew O. Media Access: Your Right to Express Your Views on Radio and Television. Boston: Little, Brown, 1976.

Shapiro, Martin. "Fair Trial Blow: An End Run Around Miranda?" Trial 12 (September, 1976). 32-9.

_____, ed. The Pentagon Papers and the Courts: A Study in Foreign Policy-Making and Freedom of the Press. San Francisco: Chandler, 1972.

Sheridan, David. "Commercial Speech: The Supreme Court Sends Another Valentine to Advertisers, " Buffalo Law Review 25 (Spring, 1976), 737-51.

Sidlinger, William. "Broadcasting: CATV--The Distant Signal Question, " Washburn Law Journal 14 (1975), 118-21.

Simmons, S. J. "Fairness Doctrine: The Early History, " Federal Communications Bar Journal 29 (1976), 207-300.

_____. "FCC's Personal Attack and Political Editorial Rules Reconsidered, " University of Pennsylvania Law Review 125 (May, 1977), 990-1022.

Simms, Abby Propis. "Sequestration: A Possible Solution to the Free Press-Fair Trial Dilemma, " American University Law Review 23 (Summer, 1974), 923-57.

Simons, Howard, and Joseph A. Califano, Jr. , eds. The Media and the Law. New York: Praeger, 1976.

Singer, Eric, T. "Prohibition of Abortion Referral Service Advertising Held Unconstitutional, " Cornell Law Review 61 (April, 1976), 640-60.

Smith, James M. Freedom's Fetters. Ithaca, N. Y. : Cornell University Press, 1956.

Sobel, Lester A. , ed. War on Privacy. New York: Facts on File, 1976.

Sobel, Lionel S. "Copyright and the First Amendment: A Gathering Storm?" Copyright Law Symposium 19 (1971), 43-80.

Sowell, John H. , III. "Commercial Speech Is Protected by the First Amendment, " Texas Tech Law Review 8 (1976), 419-28.

Special Committee on Radio and Television of the Association of the Bar of the City of New York. Radio, Television, and the Administration of Justice. New York: Columbia University Press, 1965.

Spencer, Dale R. Law for the Newsman. Los Angeles: Lucas Brothers, 1971.

Stern, Carl. "Free Press/Fair Trial: The Role of the News Media in Developing and Advancing Constitutional Processes, " Oklahoma Law Review 29 (Spring, 1976), 349-60.

Stocker, Barbara Larkin. "Analysis of the Distribution Between Public Figures and Private Defamation Plaintiffs Applied to Relatives of Public Persons, " Southern California Law Review 49 (July, 1976), 1131-240.

Studybaker, Deborah, and Steven Studybaker. "Cox Broadcasting vs. Cohn: A Finer Definition of the Publication Privilege, " Capital University Law Review 5 (1976), 267-76.

Summers, David B. "The Commercial Speech Doctrine and the Consumer's Right to Receive, " Washburn Law Journal 16 (Fall, 1976), 197-203.

Taubenhaus, Marsha. "Time, Inc. vs. Firestone: Sowing the Seeds of Gertz, " Brooklyn Law Review 43 (Summer, 1976), 123-46.

Tavormina, John. "Limitation of the Commercial Speech Exception to First Amendment Protection, " Tulane Law Review 51 (December, 1976), 149-56.

Teplitzky, Sanford V. , and Kenneth A. Weiss: "Newsman's Privilege Two Years After Branzburg v. Hayes: The First Amendment in Jeopardy, " Tulsa Law Review 49 (January, 1975), 417-38.

Thayer, Frank. Legal Control of the Press. 3rd ed. Brooklyn, N. Y.: Foundation Press, 1956.

Thompson, John F. "Constitutional Law: Defamation of Private Individuals, " Washburn Law Journal 14 (1975), 645-9.

Toohey, Daniel W. , Richard D. Marks, and Arnold P. Lutzker. Legal Problems in Broadcasting: Identification and Analysis of Selected Issues. Lincoln: University of Nebraska Press, 1974.

Towers, Wayne M. "Empirical Research and Some Major Supreme Court Decisions on Free Press/Fair Trial Conflicts, " Free Speech Yearbook 1978, 60-7.

Towery, James E. "Freedom of the Press, Commercial Speech Applied to Abortion Advertisement, " Emory Law Journal 24 (Fall, 1975), 1165-90.

Trager, Robert, and Harry W. Stonecipher. "Gag Orders: An Unresolved Dilemma, " Journalism Quarterly 55 (Summer, 1978), 231-40+.

Trout, Greg. "Invasion of Privacy: New Guidelines for the Public Disclosure Tort, " Capital University Law Review 6 (1976), 95-110.

Van Valkenburg, E. Walter. "Taskett vs. King: Limitation on Privilege to Defame in Matters of Public Interest, " Willamette Law Journal 13 (Winter, 1976), 183-98.

Vaughn, Robert G. "The Freedom of Information Act and Vaughn v. Rosen: Some Personal Comments, " American University Law Review 23 (Summer, 1974), 865-79.

"Vaughn v. Rosen: Toward True Freedom of Information, " University of Pennsylvania Law Review 122 (January, 1974), 731-44.

Walker, Richard H. "Vaughn v. Rosen: New Meaning for the Freedom of Information Act, " Temple Law Quarterly 47 (Winter, 1974), 390-402.

Weiler, Daniel A. "Gertz v. Robert Welch, Inc.: Constitutional Privilege and the Defamed Private Individual, " John Marshall Journal of Practice and Procedure 8 (Spring, 1975), 531-47.

Werts, John S. "The First Amendment and Consumer Protection: Commercial Advertising as Protected Speech, " Oregon Law Review 50 (Winter, 1971), 177-96.

Weyant, Piers J. "Administrative Law--The FCC's Fairness Doctrine and the First Amendment, " Journal of Public Law 19 (1970), 129-37.

Whalen, Charles W., Jr. Your Right to Know. New York: Vintage Books, 1973.

Wheelwright, Kevin W. "Parody, Copyrights, and the First Amendment, " University of San Francisco Law Review 10 (Winter, 1976), 564-85.

White, Herbert S. , ed. The Copyright Dilemma. Chicago: American Library Association, 1978.

Winslow, Helen L. "The First Amendment--Status of Commercial Advertising, " North Carolina Law Review 54 (February, 1976), 468-77.

Wise, D. Scott. "Communication Law--Growing Deference to the Broadcaster's First Amendment Rights, " Annual Survey of American Law (1976), 399-425.

Wittenberg, Philip. The Protection of Literary Property. Boston: The Writer, 1968.

Yodelis, Mary Ann. "The Rejection of Florida's Right to Reply Statute: A Setback for a 'New Right' of Access to the Press, " New York Law Forum 20 (Winter, 1975), 633-42.

Younger, Eric E. "The Sheppard Mandate Today: A Trial Judge's Perspective, " Nebraska Law Review 56 (1977), 1-22.

Zubras, Joan A. "Gertz v. Welch: Reviving the Libel Action, " Temple Law Quarterly 48 (Winter, 1975), 450-70.

Zuckerman, Harvey L. , and Martin J. Gaynes. Mass Communications Law in a Nutshell. St. Paul, Minn. : West Publishing, 1977.

GENERAL INDEX

INDEX OF CASES